CARIBBEAN
CONNOISSEUR

CARIBBEAN CONNOISSEUR

≈ ≈ ≈

Michele Evans

ST. MARTIN'S PRESS
NEW YORK

Photos by Michele Evans
Map by Vantage Art
Design by Janet Tingey

ISBN 0-312-11251-3

First Revised Edition: May 1995
10 9 8 7 6 5 4 3 2

For Tully

≈ ≈

CONTENTS

≈ ≈

ACKNOWLEDGMENTS

I wish it were possible to list all the people who have generously shared their valuable knowledge, information, experiences, and insights on the Caribbean with me for this book. It is a vast global village network of people throughout the islands, acquaintances and friends, from hotel and restaurant owners and their staffs, island residents, and hotel guests I've spoken to during my travels throughout the Caribbean and visits at resorts and hotels, to those who called to say, "Just got back and here's the latest news"— literally hundreds of scouts and informants, including readers of previous editions who wrote with complaints or praise about places and provided some valuable information and excellent suggestions for additions. I thank you all.

My special thanks go first to the owners and managing directors of this edition's new list of the Caribbean's **Top Ten Super-Luxury Resorts** for graciously taking time from their busy schedules to contribute the quotes that introduce the profiles of their outstanding properties. Alphabetically they are: William K. Anderson, E. David Brewer, Charles Hickox, Howard W. Hulford, Ulrich Krauer, Maruiccia Mandelli, A. Pascal Mahvi, Martin Nicholson, Aldo Pinto, Hazen K. Richardson II, and Leon Roydon.

Among personal friends, I want to thank Amanda Urban and Ken Auletta and Keren and Gene Saks for sharing St. Barts with us every year.

John and Pia Freeman, who spend their winters in St. Thomas, are wonderful traveling companions, always ready to pack their bags to visit other islands. This year they accompanied us on our maiden voyage, a first-rate cruise to seven islands on the sleek, 53-cabin *Renaissance V*. We've also recently traveled to St. Lucia and Anegada together. John and Pia are superb food critics and John is an authority on water-sports facilities, beaches, and amenities, down to the bohio count versus the number of guests.

My good friend and neighbor Margot Bachman, who, as publisher of *St. Thomas This Week* and *St. Croix This Week* and a St. Thomas resident for over thirty years, knows the hotel and restaurant industry well, has accompanied me on many, many island journeys. I'm always grateful for her good company, wit, and expert judgment. We've had great trips together and experienced some hilarious adventures.

Marilyn Mackay, owner of Travel Services in St. Thomas, has given her valuable time and supplied me with important information, particularly about St. John where she lives. Thanks also go to Laurie Lynch McKinney, our travel agent at Travel Services, who has skillfully booked my trips throughout the islands for several years, and has yet to wince over reticketing due to my unpredictable schedule changes.

Sarah Morrisette has provided me with vivid chronicles of her continuing journeys and encounters at hotels thoughout the islands for years. She's had a home on St. John in the U.S. Virgin Islands since the fifties, and always has on-target opinions on Caribbean travel, restaurants, and quality accommodations.

I also want to thank our friends Penn and Cornelia Kavanaugh for their keen observations and reports on Jamaica, the Grenadines, and Anguilla.

Extra thanks to my agent and friend, Esther Newberg, for always being there—for a long time now—as well as my gifted editor, Anne Savarese, who deserves a medal for her guidance, patience, and for translating my hieroglyphics. Thanks also go to editorial assistant Helen Packard.

I could not have written this book without the editorial wisdom and constant encouragement from my husband, Tully, the world's best traveling companion, whose least favorite word in the English language is "deadline."

CARIBBEAN CONNOISSEUR

≈ ≈

INTRODUCTION

In these days of computer databases and other electronic wizardry, I hope readers will find it comforting to learn that *Caribbean Connoisseur* is an old-fashioned, human, hands-on travel guide. In no way is this book a part of the "travel information superhighway." For accuracy, and under deadline pressure, I was forced to gather some hard facts and statistical information by fax, but in evaluating the over 140 listings in this collection, I "punched up" the images, sounds, smells, and tastes of the hotels, resorts, and inns from a memory bank of firsthand experiences.

Caribbean Connoisseur was created completely within the territory it covers. As I write from my office in our home in St. Thomas in the United States Virgin Islands, the view outside through sliding glass doors is of the Tortola ferry cruising by — speeding across a glittering blue sea heading for Charlotte Amalie, right on schedule. The privilege of living in the Caribbean provides me with the distinct advantage of maintaining an intimate relationship with island communities through access. In the spirit of healthy competition, I hope that my insider's status keeps me a few steps ahead of the pack.

Because I live in the Caribbean, I'm fortunate to be able to rely on a personal coconut-vine network of charter-boat crews and captains, grocers, pilots, fishermen, chefs, waiters, bartenders, gardeners, neighbors, resident friends, and their relatives and friends — scattered among the islands of the vast Caribbean village that stretches from St. Thomas to Belize, Mexico, and Venezuela. When a friend calls to tell me that a new hotel just opened in Saba, I can be there within hours or the next day.

This new edition of *Caribbean Connoisseur* would have been impossible to realize without the aid of hundreds of acquaintances, readers, friends, and family, whom I can merely thank in the acknowledgments. From living here and continually traveling in the Caribbean, I also know that I cannot always count on polished reports from hotel representatives, tourist boards, and promotion agencies. They do great work, but their job is to produce numbers. My job is to report what I see.

What you hold in your hands, for better or worse, is a guide to the Caribbean written by an island resident with a passion for the region. *Caribbean Connoisseur* is a thoroughly independent travel guide based on my own opinions and preferences. From the beginning of the more than two decades we've spent here, my husband and I have enthusiastically visited dozens of Caribbean islands, enjoying the unique natural beauty and culture of each. We've stayed in every type of accommodation — from rustic guest houses, intimate inns, and isolated retreats to super-luxury resorts and giant convention hotels. We learned early on that selecting a well-maintained, well-managed hotel that suited our

1

particular tastes and priorities was crucial to a successful, happy holiday. Where you stay in the Caribbean is far more important than where you stay at other travel destinations, because an island holiday means unwinding, relaxing in the sun, romancing, and taking advantage of aquatic and sports activities, usually right on the hotel's grounds. No matter how much island touring, sailing, shopping, or dining out you do, the hotel remains an integral part of your Caribbean vacation; it's normally where you spend most of your day. Temporarily, it's home.

As we traveled, we searched for hotels with special personalities and atmosphere, beautiful surroundings and views, comfortable living quarters, good facilities and food, and an efficient yet sensitive management. Warm greetings, a single hibiscus on a breakfast tray, honest efforts, and good intentions have always carried a lot of weight with us.

Because we live in the Caribbean, friends have continually asked us for hotel recommendations. Some wanted a hotel with a stunning south-facing beach for all-day sun, plus waterskiing and scuba-diving facilities. Others were more interested in an authentic West Indian ambience, but a tennis court was a necessity. More than a few wanted a beautiful Robinson Crusoe retreat with fine cuisine. What began as just a short list of favorite Caribbean hotels for our friends turned into a challenge, and I decided to put together a selective guide. My goal was to provide prospective travelers to the region with a list of the best accommodations available in the Caribbean today, with honest and thorough descriptions. *Caribbean Connoisseur,* the first edition of which was called *Caribbean Choice,* is it. This new third edition has been totally updated, revised, streamlined, and expanded. Over 30 accommodations have been added, plus six new islands, including Anegada and Saba. The book now contains more than 140 hotels, resorts, and inns among over 40 islands.

You'll also find an information chart at the end of each hotel entry that provides data on opening and closing times, reservations, rates, meal plans, extra service charges and government taxes, and policies on children and credit cards. I've also added restaurant and shopping recommendations, suggestions for where to buy the best provisions if you're going to be housekeeping on-island, and some brief, but useful information.

During continued research and travel to well over 50 islands, I have found many outstanding accommodations, lots of conventional, forgettable hotels and resorts, and some lackluster, dilapidated lodgings, but only a few real clinkers. It's easy to detect misrepresentation and experience indifference, shoddy and mediocre lodgings, or all-for-profit managements once you're there. But at home, with only a glossy, splendidly illustrated hotel brochure to peruse and the advice of travel agents (many of whom have never been to all the resorts they recommend and promote), travelers can get stuck spending their precious holiday at a place they'd never have booked "if only they'd known."

The most difficult decision for anyone contemplating a Caribbean vacation is selecting *the* island and lodgings that best suit your individual tastes and requirements. I hope you will find the right destination and hotel among the listings that follow.

Only a few large multiroom convention-type hotels are included here, because in the Caribbean or anywhere else in the world, with rare exception, small hotels are better qualified to give their guests more personalized, special services. In the Caribbean, small hotels ultimately offer more privacy and seclusion and their own distinct atmosphere and surroundings. Often the most reliable key to finding the best hotels in the islands is locating those that are owner-managed.

The hotel entries in this book fall within a wide spectrum ranging from historic, intimate inns, like Rawlins Plantation on St. Kitts, to comfortable, casual West Indian hideaways like Calabash in Grenada, and super-luxury seaside resorts like Jumby Bay Island off Antigua, to entire islands for hire, like Little St. James off St. Thomas. Rates vary from rock-bottom to the super-luxury category. Among the new listings in this new edition are many more reasonably priced, noteworthy options. Cost-conscious travelers, those weary of instant communication, and nature-loving vacationers looking for peaceful, out-of-the-way, casual island living can still find affordable and disarmingly Caribbean lodgings. Some are brand-new. During the last two years, on research trips, I made a special effort to find gems like Blue Waters in Anguilla and Peach and Quiet in Barbados.

Caribbean Connoisseur also reexamines well-known, established resorts such as Petit St. Vincent in the Grenadines and Caneel Bay in the United States Virgin Islands, and explains why they remain so popular, bringing you up-to-date news on what is happening at each, as well as introducing the latest and best, like the Frangipani Beach Club in Anguilla and Habitation Lagrange in Martinique.

I've covered all aspects of each hotel by thoroughly examining the service, management attitudes and skills, decor, ambience, clientele, hotel grounds, scenery and views, sports facilities, and cuisine and restaurant atmospheres. Specific details, from room service and reading lights to environmental concerns such as surf sounds, early-morning rooster crows, noise of construction in progress, or the roar of jet planes, are also revealed.

I've tried to be as accurate as possible in my reporting, but conditions fluctuate tremendously within the hotel industry. This is especially true in the Caribbean, where the vulnerability of island locations means a dependence, for most, on imported foods, furniture, equipment, vehicles, and supplies of all kinds. Management and personnel changes, new ownership, unpredictable weather, or a lost shipment are circumstances that can adversely affect the quality of a hotel's service and your vacation. Having a sense of humor, being understanding, and not demanding the impossible always helps ensure a happier holiday anywhere. A reader wrote to me complaining about a hotel I'd praised that he'd been forced to check out of because there were lizards in the outdoor bathroom. The plain truth is that people looking for a hermetically sealed environment shouldn't travel to the Caribbean.

I can still report, as of this third edition, that I have had no difficulties or unpleasant encounters anywhere during travels alone or accompanied, by air, boat, taxi, or exploring an island in a rental car. Like traveling anywhere in the world, using common sense and taking certain precautions will help you avoid problems. For example, never leave handbags, luggage, cameras, video recording equipment, or packages visible inside even a locked car; never conspicuously reveal large amounts of cash, or wear expensive, eye-catching jewelry. Don't leave valuables unattended on any beach. It's generally inadvisable to travel to remote areas, beaches, or darkened, deserted downtown streets late at night. Unfortunately, crime is on the increase in the Caribbean just as it is everywhere else.

Caribbean Connoisseur is not a comprehensive representation of every island in the Caribbean, but I will continue to discover more of the islands' best as I explore new regions for future editions, and I welcome readers' recommendations (see page 395 for information on where to send comments).

For me, the Caribbean is the world's most seductive destination. Each island has its own history, society and culture, artists, architecture, mix of religions, special dialect or patois, cuisine, vegetation, and geography. The Caribbean islands' extraordinary climate and miraculous flora and fauna truly do compose an archipelago of paradise. Visitors will encounter everything from lush tropical rain forests, waterfalls, volcanoes, and rushing rivers to dry arid plains, salt ponds, picturesque mountainscapes, banana plantations, and coconut groves. Unfortunately, travelers will also experience traffic jams, hordes of cruise-ship passengers, jumbo jetports, and indifferent or rude taxi drivers and hotel staff members, particularly on the larger, more populated, tourist-oriented islands such as Puerto Rico, St. Maarten/St. Martin, and St. Thomas. It's the price we must pay for accessibility, modern conveniences, and overdevelopment.

Still, if you search for it, the Caribbean can be an idyllic world of falling stars and double rainbows; of sun-splashed, soft sand beaches; transparent sparkling seas; romantic sunsets; tingling reggae, zouk, soca, and calypso music; grilled seafood and icy coladas; iguanas dining on hibiscus leaves; and mangoes dripping from towering trees. As Paul Theroux, the arbiter of island sensibilities, has written, "An island is much more than a principate; it is the ultimate refuge—a magic and unsinkable world."

Michele Evans
St. Thomas, U.S. Virgin Islands

On *Caribbean Connoisseur*'s Listings

≈ ≈

This new, expanded edition of *Caribbean Connoisseur* profiles more than 140 of the best inns, hotels, resorts, condominium hotels, and villa accommodations throughout over 40 separate islands. They are my personal choices, based on my own opinions, tastes, firsthand experiences, and inspections, with detailed accounts of truths, facts, and fictions. Evaluations of the best and most expensive hotels and resorts are longer than those of smaller, more modest hotels and inns, so that prospective travelers get a fuller idea of what they're paying for.

Accommodations are listed alphabetically in categories for each island's **Best, Noteworthy Options**, and **Great Expectations**. The **Best** represents the very finest lodgings available on each particular island. **Noteworthy Options** includes some first-class lodgings as well as special retreats, often simpler in terms of services and amenities, with more reasonable rates. There are only a few listings in the **Great Expectations** category: these are promising hotels slated to open within the next year or so. Remember the word *expectations*—until they have opened and I've visited them, they remain just that. Every category does not appear for each island. If your favorite hideaway is missing, please let me hear from you (see page 395).

Among the entries, I've selected the **Top Ten Super-Luxury Resorts**, which are listed on page 18 and identified throughout the book by a crown symbol (▲). These resorts were chosen because they consistently set the highest standards, offer the most outstanding services, and have the most comfortable and stylish accommodations and exceptional surroundings, beaches, and facilities. Although food was important, it wasn't the single determining factor. A beachside location *was* a prerequisite for the Top Ten.

The owners or managing directors of the Top Ten Super-Luxury Resorts have graciously shared some of their personal reflections, philosophies, and goals of their distinct resorts with *Caribbean Connoisseur*. Their individual quotes introduce the profiles of their respective properties.

Also singled out are my **Ten Favorite Special Island Hideaways**. Each hotel was chosen for its unique location, special atmosphere, fine accommodations, and good management; they range from first-class West Indian retreats to super-luxury resorts. These diverse hideaways are listed on page 19 and are indicated throughout the book by a palm tree symbol (❦).

For most islands, the accommodations listings are followed by special sections on **Recommended Restaurants** and **Recommended Shopping, Provisions for Your Is-**

5

land Pantry, and **Useful Information**. These sections are not included for private island resorts because they don't apply.

Recommended Restaurants listings begin with the finest dining that each island has to offer, followed by brief appraisals. Other dependable choices are included as well. On all islands, reservations are required for the best and most popular restaurants, especially during the winter season. Restaurant openings and closings; changes of chefs, key staff members, management, or ownership; and the availability of ingredients and supplies combine to make complete accuracy in this category next to impossible.

Readers will notice that several islands have more extensive listings for restaurants than others. This is simply because certain islands like St. Barts, Anguilla, and St. Maarten/St. Martin have many more high-quality dining options than others.

Price ranges for restaurants are noted as being inexpensive, moderate, expensive, and very expensive. Generally speaking, inexpensive means that a meal for one person will cost less than $10; moderate indicates that a meal for two will be under $50; tariffs over that amount qualify as expensive. If a meal for two is likely to cost more than $100, the restaurant is listed as very expensive. Cocktails and wines are not included in the estimate.

Like restaurants list, **Recommended Shopping** is extremely difficult to keep up to date, with new shops, boutiques, and stores constantly popping up or suddenly disappearing. On islands with large populations or those with duty-free shopping, such as Aruba, Barbados, Curaçao, Puerto Rico, St. Maarten/St. Martin, and St. Thomas, I've included only outstanding or unique shops and boutiques—mostly in categories.

Provisions for Your Island Pantry listings appear only for islands where resorts, condominium hotels, villas (without cooks), or accommodations with equipped kitchens are included. This section lists the individual island's best and most dependable markets and sources for foods, wines, and liquors.

Useful Information is a brief list of helpful hints, such as worthwhile local island publications; valuable, unusual, or new services or facilities; suggestions for nearby excursions, transportation, and ferry schedules; and so on.

≈ ≈

Reservations, Rates, Meal Plans, Telephone Service, and Gratuities

RESERVATIONS

Winter and early spring—roughly from mid-December to mid-April—are high season for human migration to the tropics. Experienced Caribbean travelers book their favorite inns, hotels, and resorts as much as a year in advance for the peak season. My advice is to make your hotel reservations as early as you can, not only to secure accommodations, but to obtain the specific kind that you desire. However, if you can only plan a spur-of-the-moment holiday, there's always a chance you'll find a room at the inn; little pockets often open up on hotels' reservation schedules due to cancellations and unreserved time between other bookings. When reserving late during high season, it's usually easier to find a few days open than a full week or more. Hotels can sometimes accommodate guests willing to switch rooms during their stay. If only a few days at your favorite hotel are available, try booking elsewhere on the island for a new experience.

Reservations can be made directly with the hotel by telephone or fax, although many hotels prefer guests to make reservations through their personal hotel representatives. A growing number of hotels, however, particularly the smaller ones, are eliminating representative services, probably for economical reasons. Of course, a reliable travel agent also can handle reservations for you. In any case, when you make your reservation, be certain to state any special requirements immediately, such as the location of a room (ground-level beachfront; second floor with a seaview—which does not always mean beachfront; or the quietest accommodation possible) or bed needs (twins, king-size, or an extra bed or crib for a child). Once you've arrived and inspected your quarters, if you are not satisfied with the accommodations, inform management immediately and request a change. If another room is available, hotel managements are normally most accommodating.

RATES

Throughout the Caribbean, rates drop dramatically from April to November, ranging anywhere from a 10% to an appealing 50% reduction. Airline fares are reduced significantly, too. May, June, July, and August are excellent times to visit the islands because hotels are less crowded. Temperatures do not soar in the summer throughout the Caribbean, as one might imagine. The thermometer rises only five degrees or so.

7

Special summer packages are offered at many hotels. Be advised that full services and staff are often reduced. In September and October, a few hotels close their doors for renovations, cosmetic and special repairs, or construction of new additions. Managements and key staff members often take their holidays during these months. Also, September and October weather can be unpredictable. The first line of information following each listing indicates the hotel's open and closing schedules.

When figuring out the cost of your accommodations, refer to the information given at the end of the listing for the added service charge and government tax. These extra fees can boost the total cost considerably. A $400-a-day room with a 10% service charge and 8% government tax comes to $3,304 for a seven-night stay—that's $504 beyond the rate for the room. Departure taxes on most islands in the Caribbean today range from $3 per person in the U.S. Virgin Islands, which is automatically added to airline tickets, to $14 per person, charged upon departure from Grenada.

The rates listed for the hotels at the end of each entry are the latest figures obtainable at press time. You can usually count on yearly increases from 5 to 10%. Most hotels rates are subject to change without notice.

MEAL PLANS

Meal plans in *Caribbean Connoisseur* are marked with the following abbreviations: EP (European Plan) includes the room only and no meals; CP (Continental Plan) means that continental breakfast is included with the price of the room; AP (American Plan) includes a full American breakfast; MAP (Modified American Plan) includes breakfast and lunch *or* dinner. FAP (Full American Plan) includes breakfast, lunch, and dinner; sometimes it's all-inclusive, covering bar drinks, wines, afternoon tea, and other special offerings like beverages in room mini-bars.

TELEPHONE SERVICE

The good news is that telephone service throughout the Caribbean has vastly improved. The bad news: International calls made from the Caribbean to the United States are expensive. Note that some hotels will add a surcharge or percentage of the total amount of each call to your bill. If possible, call collect or use an international telephone calling card or credit card; a few hotels will still add a surcharge, however.

GRATUITIES

When a service charge is added to your bill, no further tipping is normally required, and in most cases, hotels discourage guests from extra tipping. However, if a staff member has been especially helpful, he or she should be compensated for time and effort. If no service charge is included in your bill, then gratuities should be given with personal discretion. Fifteen to twenty dollars is an appropriate amount for maids for a week's stay in a luxury or first-class hotel. For other accommodations, one dollar a day is customary. These days, bellmen usually expect one dollar for each suitcase.

≈ ≈

Packing for a Caribbean Holiday

DOCUMENTS, CREDIT CARDS, AND MONEY

Proof of citizenship and confirmed ongoing tickets (proof you will be departing the island for another destination on a specific date) are required on most islands. In the United States Virgin Islands, proof of identity is required upon departure. A valid passport, a birth certificate with a raised notary seal, or a voter's registration card are acceptable. A driver's license or Social Security card are *not* acceptable proof of citizenship or identification. If you are island-hopping from the U.S. Virgin Islands to the British Virgin Islands, a passport is required.

A valid passport is the most acceptable form of identification and best expedites the process of passing through Customs and Immigration on all of the islands.

As a precaution, it's a good idea to have photocopies of your passport, driver's license, and credit cards when traveling. Keep one set of copies in a safe place at home and another with your belongings, separate from the originals.

Like traveling anywhere in the world, it's safer to rely on traveler's checks than to carry large amounts of cash. Keep the identifying numbers listed in a safe place, separate from the actual checks. If you don't want to use traveler's checks and elect to bring cash, take only the amount with you that you need each day and lock the remainder in your room's safe or the hotel's.

The U.S. dollar is accepted throughout the Caribbean, and is the legal currency of the U.S. Virgin Islands, the British Virgin Islands, and Puerto Rico. A number of islands use the Eastern Caribbean dollar (EC$), presently worth about $2.65 to one U.S. dollar.

The French islands use the French franc; Barbados and Jamaica have their own dollars; Aruba uses the Aruban florin; and so on. Exchange rates fluctuate. Currency can be exchanged at official bureaus at airports or in towns or banks on individual islands.

While U.S. dollars are accepted virtually everywhere (I've never had a problem), you will occasionally receive your change from a purchase or a taxi ride in the local currency of the island. If traveling in an island with a currency other than the U.S. dollar, it's helpful to bring along an extra amount of cash in small denominations—one-, five-, and ten-dollar bills so the change that you do receive will be in amounts that can be used up easily on small items or souvenirs.

9

CLOTHING

The art of packing sensibly for any trip is to underpack. When your destination is the informal, twelve-months-of-summer Caribbean, lightweight, light-colored clothing, preferably made of 100% cotton, is best. Evenings in January, February, and March become chilly, especially for sensitive, recently suntanned skin, and air-conditioning in restaurants or hotels can get too cold for comfort, so add a cotton sweater, shawl, or jacket to your suitcase.

Bring at least two bathing suits, so that one is always dry. I always tuck a couple of plastic bags into my suitcase to wrap up damp swimsuits for the trip back home or to another destination. Plastic hotel laundry bags, when available, serve the purpose just as well.

For women, cover-ups or oversized T-shirts are invaluable for seaside lunches, inside hotel lobbies, shopping, or on trips to beaches. Shorts, slacks, skirts, sleeveless or short-sleeved shirts, T-shirts, blouses, sundresses, and pretty resort outfits and separates are all that you'll need.

For men, short-sleeved, cotton-knit polo or cotton shirts, shorts, or Bermudas seem to be the dress of the day. You can wear knit or long-sleeved cotton shirts and slacks for the evening. Several resorts require long pants and shirts with collars during evening hours. A tie, jacket, and a pair of dress slacks are mandatory in only a few resorts. I've indicated which ones in individual entries.

Occasionally it's fun to get dressed up, particularly for a special event or private celebration. It's a personal choice. For the most part, Caribbean couture is casual. Elegantly casual clothing is the fashion of the evening at luxury resorts. For both men and women, thongs, sandals, sneakers, or special walking shoes are the most sensible footwear.

JEWELRY

In the informal atmosphere of the Caribbean, it is unnecessary, and sometimes inappropriate, to wear valuable, ostentatious jewelry or watches. A display of expensive jewelry can be a temptation for thieves anywhere in the world.

Costume jewelry is much more suitable in the islands. Inexpensive, charming, locally made or imported handcrafted jewelry made from colorful beads, shells, or carved wood is sold in many hotel boutiques, island shops, and markets throughout the Caribbean and make delightful mementos.

If you insist on wearing your finest, many hotels now provide wall safes in guest rooms, and almost all hotels will lock up valuables in the office safe.

A note of caution: As any diving instructor will tell you, barracuda and other fish are attracted to sparkling gold and silver objects, so when snorkeling or scuba diving, leave necklaces and bracelets in a safe place until you're out of the water.

DON'T-FORGET LIST

Aside from the obvious—passports, airline tickets, traveler's checks or cash, prescription medicines and sunglasses, protective sun lotions, books, children's necessities, tennis rackets, snorkel masks and fins and other special sports-related gear, cameras, clothing, and jewelry—consider bringing the following items to the Caribbean.

Film and blank video cassettes. It's always practical to bring all the film you'll need from home. Not only is film usually priced higher in the islands, you also might not find the exact brand, type, or speed you want—particularly on remote island outposts. If you do buy film in the islands, be sure to check the expiration dates on each package. Blank video cassettes should be bought back home, too, although they are available on most of the larger islands throughout the Caribbean in downtown specialty shops. They're usually cheaper in the States.

Binoculars. Binoculars are invaluable for birders and for investigating distant vistas and sea activity like whale sightings.

Personal appliances. Most top hotels today have hair dryers. I've noted which ones have them in individual entries. Women who use an electric hair-curling device should bring it along, unless they plan to rely on beauty salons. On islands where the electric current is different from the States, such as the French islands, hotels will generally be able to supply you with a converter or transformer. To be on the safe side, you might want to pack your own.

Beach bags and collapsible shopping bags. A straw or canvas beach or tote bag is indispensable for carrying books and other reading materials, lotions, small purchases, snorkeling equipment, and beach towels. Straw and canvas bags, baskets, and totes are generally available at hotel boutiques and shops on all islands, and many resorts sell their own personalized beach bags. Inveterate shoppers ought to pack an extra collapsible, lightweight bag. Most recently, I used a canvas duffle bag to carry a rolled-up straw rug back home from St. Vincent.

≈ ≈

Safe Sun

As we all know by now, the sun's intense ultraviolet rays are very dangerous and damage the skin. In the Caribbean, the sun can be brutal. The best times to expose yourself to the sun are before 10 A.M. or after 3 P.M., always using blocks, sunscreens, or other protective lotions with at least a 15 to 20 SPF (Sun Protection Factor). Total sunblock is available for extra-sensitive skin and is often used on the nose, which gets burned most frequently. Sun exposure should be limited to 20 to 30 minutes at a time, if possible.

Don't forget that you are exposed to the sun's ultraviolet rays during water activities, so a *waterproof* sunscreen lotion or oil is advisable. Remember to reapply lotions, even so-called waterproof ones, at least every couple of hours, especially on children.

Sand and water reflect the sun on your skin. If snorkeling for extended periods during the day, wear a T-shirt for extra protection.

Although wide-brimmed hats, sun visors, and sunglasses with ultraviolet protective lenses are widely available on most islands, you might want to pack your own favorites from home.

Some Advice About Insects

Unfortunately, mosquitoes and "no-see-ums" are a fact of life in the Caribbean. At certain times of the year they are more abundant, especially after rains or in the early morning, late afternoon, and early evening. No-see-ums are found predominately on or near the beach. Clothing that covers the legs and arms helps protect you from bites.

Almost every hotel listed here supplies its guests with some type of insect repellent (such as OFF! or Cutter) in the rooms, but if you favor a special brand or type, by all means bring it along.

I carry a small repellent stick in my handbag at all times in the Caribbean. It comes in very handy when sightseeing, walking on the beach, or dining by the sea.

In the likely event that you are bitten, my late grandmother's favorite antiseptic remedy, Campho-Phenique, will generally stop the itching. Several other products that promise the same results are on the market. Try not to scratch affected areas. It will only prolong the discomfort.

≈ ≈

Island-Hopping Special Airfare

LIAT (Leeward Islands Air Transport) is the major commuter airline in the Caribbean. Travelers interested in island-hopping will find LIAT's Caribbean Super Explorer ticket an incredible bargain. For a fare of $367 you can have unlimited onward stopovers to 27 destinations, from San Juan to Trinidad, plus Caracas. No stopover airport can be used more than once, except for connecting purposes.

Tickets must be used within 30 days from commencement of travel. They are non-refundable and nonexchangeable. Changes in routing after the individual ticket is issued are subject to a surcharge of $25. LIAT also offers a 21-day Explorer ticket for $199. For exact details, call LIAT's headquarters in Antigua at (809) 462-0700 or fax (809) 462-2682.

Be forewarned that, while LIAT now has many interisland direct flights, some islands can only be reached by numerous stopovers before landing at a particular destination.

Pay attention to packing and purchases made during your travels when flying on LIAT. The airline enforces its luggage weight allowance of 44 pounds per person, and overweight luggage can get expensive. Recently I paid $40 for extra weight, which made me wonder whether I really needed the hot sauces, preserves, pottery, and books I'd purchased.

During the research for each edition of this book, I've traveled on countless LIAT flights, experiencing only a few major delays in all my travels, mostly due to weather conditions. Several flights actually left before their scheduled departure time.

When traveling on LIAT or any other island airline, I suggest arriving at the airport at least one hour ahead of departure time. Lines at the ticket counters can be long and slow-moving. Early arrival also is safer assurance that your luggage will arrive with you. In many years of travel, my luggage has always arrived on the aircraft I traveled on and I've never lost a bag.

Make sure that the baggage tags attached to your luggage have the correct destination printed on them. I caught incorrect tags in a couple of instances, saving myself a lot of time and grief.

The island destinations in the LIAT network include the following:

Anguilla	British Virgin Islands
Antigua and Barbuda	Caracas, Venezuela
Barbados	Carriacou
Bequia	Dominica

Dominican Republic
Grenada
Guadeloupe
Martinique
Mustique
Nevis
St. Eustatius
St. Kitts

St. Lucia
St. Maarten/St. Martin
St. Vincent
San Juan, Puerto Rico
Trinidad and Tobago
Union Island
United States Virgin Islands

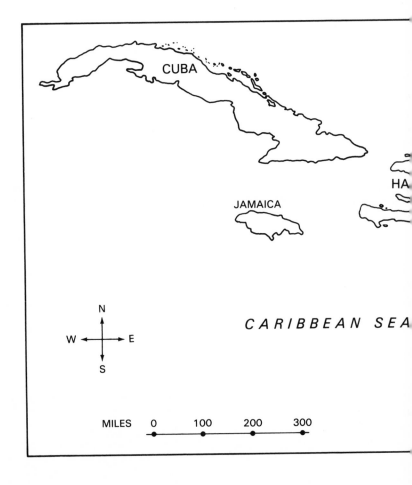

CUBA

HA

JAMAICA

CARIBBEAN SEA

N

W ← → E

S

MILES   0   100   200   300

ISLANDS OF THE CARIBBEAN

ATLANTIC OCEAN

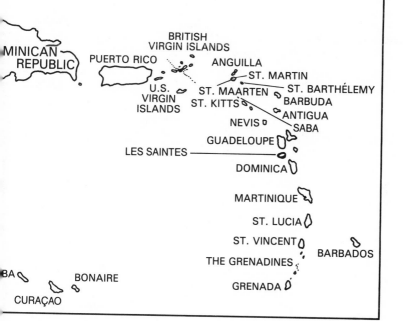

MINICAN
REPUBLIC

PUERTO RICO

BRITISH
VIRGIN ISLANDS

ANGUILLA

ST. MARTIN

U.S.
VIRGIN
ISLANDS

ST. MAARTEN

ST. KITTS

ST. BARTHÉLEMY

BARBUDA

ANTIGUA

NEVIS

SABA

GUADELOUPE

LES SAINTES

DOMINICA

MARTINIQUE

ST. LUCIA

ST. VINCENT

THE GRENADINES

BARBADOS

BA

BONAIRE

GRENADA

CURAÇAO

≈ ≈

◢ *Caribbean Connoisseur's*
Top Ten Super-Luxury
Resorts

(Alphabetical Listing)

Caneel Bay, St. John, United States Virgin Islands
Cap Juluca, Anguilla
Curtain Bluff, Antigua
Jalousie Plantation Resort & Spa, Soufrière, St. Lucia
Jumby Bay Island, Antigua
K Club, Barbuda
La Samanna, St. Martin
Little Dix Bay, Virgin Gorda, British Virgin Islands
Malliouhana Hotel, Anguilla
Petit St. Vincent Resort, Petit St. Vincent, The Grenadines

✳ *Caribbean Connoisseur's*
Ten Favorite Special Island Hideaways

(Alphabetical Listing)

Anse Chastanet, St. Lucia
Coco Point Lodge, Barbuda
Frangipani Beach Club, Anguilla
Galley Bay, Antigua
Guana Island, British Virgin Islands
Habitation Lagrange, Martinique
The Horned Dorset Primavera Hotel, Rincón, Puerto Rico
Le Toiny, St. Barthélemy
Rawlins Plantation, St. Kitts
Saltwhistle Bay Club, Mayreau, The Grenadines

≈ ≈

ANGUILLA

ACCOMMODATIONS

ANGUILLA'S BEST
Cap Juluca 👑
Carimar Beach Club
Casablanca
CoveCastles Villa Resort
Fountain Beach Hotel
Frangipani Beach Club 🌴
Malliouhana Hotel 👑
The Mariners

NOTEWORTHY OPTIONS
Blue Waters Beach Apartments
La Sirena

RECOMMENDED RESTAURANTS

RECOMMENDED SHOPPING

PROVISIONS FOR YOUR ISLAND PANTRY

USEFUL INFORMATION

≈ ≈

≈ ≈

Accommodations

ANGUILLA'S BEST

Cap Juluca ▲▲

In designing the resort, my first four 'musts' were: The resort must have easy worldwide access, cool summers, unequaled beach, and unsurpassed privacy. All hotel accommodations must be beachfront and the design must add beauty, a feeling of uncrowded spaciousness, and set the standard for world-class accommodations. The guest experience must be unique and similar to visiting a very special private home, but with all the services of the finest hotel.

CHARLES C. HICKOX, MANAGING DIRECTOR

Having visited Cap Juluca yearly since its debut in 1988, through all stages of development until completion in 1993, a line from the film *Summertime* starring Katharine Hepburn aptly describes my reaction to the resort. In the movie, two lady tourists with a guide have just reached St. Mark's Square in Venice for their first view of the spectacular piazza. As Katharine Hepburn pauses behind them, one of the women sighs emphatically, "Don't change a thing!" The late David Lean, who directed the movie, could very well have created a spectacular production at Cap Juluca.

A miniature Caribbean Casablanca, Cap Juluca stretches across magnificent 1.2-mile-long Maunday's Bay Beach on Anguilla's southwestern end. Whether you approach from land on the new paved road or by sea, Cap Juluca first appears as a dazzling mirage, then a fantastic village oasis on this dry, flat island.

Cap Juluca's imposing Moorish-style, white masonry buildings, capped by domed turrets, are accented with bougainvillea-draped arches and parapets, all fronted with thick sea grape, palm trees, and a profusion of plantings. Everything at Cap Juluca (*Juluca* is the Arawak name for the rainbow god of Anguilla) pleases the senses.

Brilliantly designed by English architect Oscar Farmer, a genie of symmetry, the twelve two-story, six-room hotel villas—Vermilion, Sienna, Indigo, Emerald, and Persimmon among them—and the six pool villas, named after towns in Morocco like Fez and Marrakesh, are only a few paces from the strikingly clear turquoise sea and white sand beach. The total room count is now 98, including individual rooms in villas.

Pimms and Chattertons restaurants and beach at Cap Juluca, Anguilla.

Each contemporary casbah is a labyrinth of spacious deluxe and luxury rooms, junior suites, and one- and two-bedroom suites of varying sizes and configurations, each with splendid views of French St. Martin, just six miles away. The pool villas are majestically spread out at the western end of the beach. These prime lodgings each have three to five bedrooms with private pools and fully equipped kitchens.

Cap Juluca's minimalist interiors coordinate white tile floors, built-in masonry desktops, and banquettes with thick cushions and pillows in cotton fabrics of earth tones, paisleys, and bright red and blue leafy coral patterns, which are interspersed with good-looking wicker furniture and stone, marble, and wicker tables and antique Moroccan carpets. In the first buildings completed, handsome antique leather saddlebags, wedding belts, and slender carved wooden doors collected from Morroccan souks adorn the walls. About halfway through the project, the decorators were changed. Ceramics, tiles, and appointments for the newer buildings are Portuguese and Mexican rather than Moroccan imports. Vases filled with sprays of bougainvillea add a natural touch.

Dressing room closets have tall wooden louvered and mirrored doors, shelves, and wall safes. Guests can pull out the phone jack if they're not accepting calls. There are no televisions, but TVs, VCRs, and cassettes can be rented, or guests can adjourn to the comfortable TV room in the main building after dinner to watch the scheduled film shown nightly at 9 P.M., selecting their after-dinner drinks at the honor-system bar.

Accommodations have large, sumptuous Italian-marbled, mirrored bathrooms with walk-in showers. In most, you can swing open the outer glass shower door and step into a walled garden patio for private sunbathing. Chaise longues sit in the enclosed gardens and on front verandas. Bathrooms feature Italian white porcelain twin basins whose spigots are artfully off-center.

Cap Juluca has become justifiably famous for its double-size French-molded bathtubs, called *confidences,* that come fitted with white terry-cloth neck rolls on opposite ends and sides. Glass decanters filled with blue bath beads provide bubbly, sybaritic soaking. A pair of terry-cloth robes and an abundance of thick towels are perfectly folded and strategically placed. Natural Molton Brown products imported from London, fold-out hairbrushes, loofahs, and shower caps are provided. Adjacent to the bathroom is a toilet and bidet in a closable niche across from a full-mirrored vanity on which a lighted magnifying mirror and hair dryer rest.

Ceiling fans throughout and air-conditioning in all rooms except the living rooms of the ground-level suites, along with louvered doors and windows, ensure desired temperature control.

Each villa has a ground-level housekeeper's kitchen for the preparation of breakfasts, ceremoniously served by two maids each morning. Along with breakfast is a copy of the day's *TimesFax,* a short version of the *New York Times.* Room service will deliver all meals. Twice-daily maid service keeps rooms in perfect order. When guests return from dinner, beds have been turned down and a tiny oil-burning glass lamp romantically flickers in the room. Dimmer switches on almost every light (most of them conveniently controlled from king-size beds), mini-refrigerators with automatic icemakers, and a stocked bar area complete the list of amenities.

Like any great world-class hotel, check-in and checkout can be tended to in your own quarters if desired. And a well-chilled welcome bottle of champagne from Canadian-born Brian Young, the resort's cordial, top-notch manager, awaits guests. But don't get the wrong impression: Cap Juluca is relaxed, casual Caribbean. The diverse, well-to-do clientele, about 80% American and 20% European, appear to move about in shoeless slow motion. In the evening it's customary for informally but elegantly attired guests to stroll barefoot across the sandy beachfront lawn to one of the resort's three restaurants for dinner, guided by the light of the moon or tiny flashlights (gifts from the hotel).

Shoeshine, a small golden-colored island dog abandoned as a puppy on Maunday's Bay by passengers on a visiting yacht, is the only permanent resident at Cap Juluca. Shiney, as she's affectionately known to management, staff, and repeat guests, was given the name because in her youth she had the habit of filching guests' thongs and sandals left on outside terraces. A quick-thinking, tactful staff member apologized to guests and said that the puppy had taken the footwear off for a shoeshine. Throughout the year, seven-year-old Shiney receives special bowls and collars, and many queries about her well-being. During my last visit I saw guests wearing T-shirts they'd custom-designed featuring Shiney's face on the front. As the resort's information directory states, "Shoeshine is Cap Juluca's self-appointed canine mascot, who you will undoubtedly see strolling along the beach. Do become acquainted with her . . . your vacation will be the better for it." Shortly after our last visit, in February 1994, the Queen of England lunched at Cap Juluca. Liking dogs as she does, I hope she made Shiney's acquaintance.

Pimms, Cap Juluca's attractive 75-seat open-air main restaurant, all decked out in royal blue and white with billowing canopied ceilings and paddle fans, and the adjoining, more informal Chattertons café and bar, are housed in Moorish splendor along Rocky Point's coastline at the far eastern side of Maunday's Bay. Views are breathtaking. Guests and visitors enjoy meals at multilevel Chattertons throughout the day, and dance to live music several evenings a week during season. Chattertons hasn't been clearly defined as a restaurant. It has frequently changed menus and the focus of its cuisine. On our last visit, selections from Pimms menu were being served at Chatterons.

We found the food at Pimm's uneven recently: a bland cucumber soup was followed by sensational fillet of salmon with a couscous crust and beetroot vinaigrette. Desserts were consistently good, but after several meals, we felt the kitchen was in need of renewed inspiration.

Cap Juluca's third restaurant, open only to guests of the hotel, the Pool Terrace is situated at the center of the beach, adjacent to the resort's large freshwater swimming pool in back of the enormous white onion-shaped tented bar, the Beach Pavilion. Currently open for three meals a day, the Pool Terrace is a delightful venue for full breakfasts, light lunches of salads and sandwiches, and simple grilled foods for dinner. After Monday night's manager's cocktail party under the tent at the Beach Pavilion, a delicious West Indian buffet is served on the Pool Terrace accompanied by the live music of local groups. The lobster is always grilled to perfection.

Sports facilities include a new English regulation croquet court, plus three Omni tennis courts, two lighted, under the direction of Peter Burwash International. Windsurfing, waterskiing, and the use of Sunfish, Hobie Holder monohull dinghies, and 14-foot Aquacats are complimentary. Day sails and excursions can be organized by the concierge, who also handles car rentals. As good vehicles on Anguilla are at a premium, be certain to reserve a car when booking your accommodations.

A fitness center located in the lower level of the main building offers LifeCycles, stair-climbers, Trotters, and light weights. Appointments can be made throughout the day for a professional massage from masseuse Monika Struna. Her technique is a blend of Swedish and Shiatsu.

In season on Thursdays, golf enthusiasts can join guests of Malliouhana on a chartered flight from Anguilla to Nevis for a round of golf at Four Seasons Resorts' Robert Trent Jones 18-hole championship course.

Cap Juluca's second beach, Cove Bay, is over 1½ miles long and great for hiking or sunbathing. If you plan to explore it, wear sturdy shoes, because parts are rocky. The hotel will pack a picnic basket of cold lobster and champagne to take along.

The resort's free supervised children's program is available during March school breaks, as well as the spring, summer, and fall seasons.

Shoppers won't be disappointed in Cap Juluca's little souks. The Azemmour Boutique in the main building carries designer sportswear, including Austrilian Helen Kaminski's attractive panama hats and shoulder bags, and costume jewelry. An abundance of Cap Juluca's personalized T-shirts, sweatshirts, visors, bags, island handcrafts, and sundries can be found across the hall in The Gift Shop. A tennis pro shop is located at the west-end courts.

Days on the exquisite beach are languidly spent reading, swimming along with the slow cadence of the sea, or strolling the wide expanse of sand. Icy mineral water is stocked in coolers positioned in front of every villa. If you prefer something stronger, lower the red flag attached to the underside of your beach umbrella and, abracadabra, a beach attendant will appear.

An interesting part of the history of Cap Juluca is that the 179-acre property was once in the hands of the late James Frankel, the industry bellwether of the 1970s. Frankel's La Samanna in St. Martin, still one of the top super-luxury resorts in the Caribbean, was originally to have been located on beautiful Maunday's Bay in Anguilla where Cap Juluca now gloriously stands. At the time, local red tape and frustrating delays led an impatient Frankel to transfer his vision to French St. Martin, where La Samanna opened in 1975 to unanimous raves. A small section of Frankel's foundation still remains under Cap Juluca's library room in the main building. It was meant to be the terrace of La Samanna's restaurant.

Twenty years later, it is ironic that Cap Juluca has now become *the* upscale, premier Caribbean destination to which all other contenders must be compared. By virtue of its originality of design, comfortable, understated luxurious accommodations, and outstanding beachfront location, Cap Juluca is today's best super-luxury Caribbean resort.

CAP JULUCA	**RESERVATIONS**
P.O. Box 240	Cap Juluca
Anguilla, British West Indies	26 Broadway
TEL: (809) 497-6666	New York, NY 10004
FAX: (809) 497-6779	TEL: (800) 323-0139 *or*
	(212) 425-4684
	FAX: (212) 363-8044

Open all year.

Rates: Cap Juluca has numerous separate rate structures for rooms and villas in different seasons. Rates for only three types of accommodations are included here. Rates for other accommodations are available upon request from the hotel. Double occupancy. *December 17 to April 3:* Luxury Room, $525; Junior Suite, $650; One-Bedroom Suite, $925; extra person, $75. *April 5 to May 31* and *November 1 to December 16:* Luxury Room, $355; Junior Suite, $450; One-Bedroom Suite, $560; extra person, $55. *June 1 to October 31:* Luxury Room, $310; Junior Suite, $390; One-Bedroom Suite, $490; extra person, $35.

Meal plan: All quoted rates are CP (includes continental breakfast). MAP (includes breakfast plus lunch or dinner), add $50 per person per day (rates for children under 12 are 40% less than the adult rate, per child). FAP (includes three meals a day), add $65 per person per day (rates for children under 12 are 40% less than the adult price). A 10% gratuity is additional.

Service charge: 10%.

Government tax: 8%.

Children under 6 not permitted during winter season, but welcome all other times.
Credit cards: American Express only.
Note: Spring, summer, and fall special savings plans are available, including A Villa Experience, A Family Getaway, A Romantic Hideaway for Honeymoon/Anniversary, and The Great Escape.

Carimar Beach Club

The Carimar Beach Club, situated on beautiful Meads Bay Beach, is a superb condominium hotel accommodation. The ten-year-old complex of white masonry and red-tile-roofed two-story buildings consists of 22 two-bedroom, two-bath apartments (sometimes available as one-bedroom apartments), and one three-bedroom, three-bath unit.

Each has a balcony or patio with comfortable furniture and soothing arch-framed views. Only seven of the apartments are beachfront; the rest face a spacious, blossoming garden courtyard. The beachfront rooms are prime lodgings for proximity to the beach, lovely views, and privacy. We were fortunate to be booked into 1A, a ground-level, outside corner apartment, only a short sprint across the fine, white sand of Meads Bay Beach to the calm, crystal sea. Chaises are placed under beach umbrellas along the beach in front of the property. Meads Bay is a glorious one mile long. Carimar happens to situated adjacent to the ultra-luxurious Malliouhana Hotel (page 35). The geography of Carimar's location creates the ironic impression that its elegant neighbor shares only a small portion of Carimar's sweep of beach.

Carimar's immaculate, roomy interiors are newly and prettily appointed with tropical trappings of rattan furniture with cheerful colored fabrics and white tile floors throughout. All have ceiling fans. The individual condominium owners add their own furnishings and artwork. Every one I've seen is charming. Upon arrival a complimentary bottle of Mount Gay rum and and few bottles of sodas are waiting for guests on the dining room table next to a cluster of fresh flowers. Daily maid service is included in the rates.

All kitchens, white and black tiled, are fully stocked with dishes, pots and pans, a toaster, and an electric coffeemaker. If you're not of a mind to cook on holiday, Blanchard's new restaurant is open next door, and Le Bistro is only a short walk away. There are plenty of other good dining options in Anguilla (see page 43).

The 2½-acre property has two tennis courts, and snorkeling equipment is available; the staff in the front office will offer suggestions for excursions and other aquatic action. Laundry service is offered, as well as babysitting.

The office sells T-shirts, postcards and stamps, sun lotions, and a few odds and ends. Carimar's only phone for guests is in a nook just outside the office, but the phones in the office can be used, if necessary.

The beach club is professionally looked after by Pamela A. Berry, a welcoming, on-the-job manager. Carimar is a real find—excellent for families, friends, or lovers of all ages.

CARIMAR BEACH CLUB
P.O. Box 327
Anguilla, British West Indies
TEL: (800) 235-8667 *or*
(809) 497-6881
FAX: (809) 497-6071

Open all year.
Rates: *December 16 to March 31:* One-Bedroom Apartment, $300 to $340; Two-Bedroom Apartment, $400 to $440; Three-Bedroom Apartment, $630. *April 1 to December 15:* One-Bedroom Apartment, $225 to $245; Two-Bedroom Apartment, $280 to $300; Three-Bedroom Apartment $450. Rates are for up to 2 people in One-Bedroom Apartments; up to 4 in Two-Bedrooms; up to 6 in Three-Bedrooms. One extra person in any apartment, $50 daily. Daily crib charge, $5.
Meal plan: EP.
Service charge: 10%.
Government tax: 8%.
Children welcome.
Credit cards accepted.

Casablanca

The Moorish architecture of Casablanca's peach-colored main stucco building is crowned with curved green tile, peaked rooftops with crenellated ornamentation, and a muezzin's minaret. Guests enter under a porte cochère adorned with panels of mosaics and white curlicue moldings on scalloped, arched walls. The interlocking redbrick circular driveway is completely enshrouded in exotic palms and tropical flora. Inside is an emir's palace, which is what Saudi owner Kamal Alusltany, former owner of the Mullet Bay Resort in St. Martin, must have had in mind.

A cadre of Morrocan artisans was imported to hand-paint and install motifs, mosaics, and rows of wooden wall and ceiling moldings throughout. Light shines through bright green and red glass in dome-shaped windows high up over the opulent sunken, banquetted lobby. Along the walkway past bubbling sunken fountains, the concierge's desk, and reception is Jenny, a chic boutique, and a shop selling the resort's fabulous custom-designed ceramic bowls, vases, covered pots, tableware, signature bathroom products, and necessities.

Next comes Casablanca's main indoor/outdoor restaurant, where we've had some outstanding dinners with dishes like fresh foie gras salad with roasted crayfish and sautéed loin of rabbit, caramellized fillet of red snapper with green lentils, vegetables, and balsamic vinegar sauce. Since our last visit we haven't tasted any of the offerings of new chef Claude Robert.

At the adjacent Café American, Casablanca's bar, an Anguillian "Sam" plays the piano every night. You're bound to hear "As Time Goes By" several times.

From the terrace restaurant and bar, steps lead out to the resort's large, lovely pool and surrounding terra-cotta and green ceramic-tile veranda. The enormous area is lined with black and white chaises with tables and chairs. The Blue Parrot Grille, in a plain, peaked-roof building at the edge of the beach, is open for drinks and light lunches all day. So startling is this boxy edifice in comparison to the main building, that it looks only temporary.

The Blue Parrot's tables have black-and-white umbrellas, but poolside guests have no place to hide from the blazing sun. On the resort's beautiful three-mile-long Rendezvous Bay West Beach, there is only a handful of crudely constructed wooden bohios, the tops of which have been covered with orangy-red asphalt shingles.

We stayed at Casablanca in February 1993, and have returned several times since for inspections and meals. Our second-floor, beachfront deluxe corner room, number 202, was excellent. From the terrace we overlooked Rendezvous Bay Beach across the sea to St. Martin's undulating hills. Our sizable tile-floored room, with overhead fan and air-conditioning, came fitted with custom-made matching or coordinated peach, aqua, and cream-colored fabrics on chair and sofa cushions, pillows, draperies, and the king-size bedcover. The headboard was actually fabric framed onto the wall. The lamps, the frame on the mirror, end tables, desk, chairs and sofa frames, cable TV cabinet, and bureau were all tinted aqua-green. Walls were painted peach and bordered with gaily designed motifs. My husband said he felt as if he were inside a candy box. I liked it. Also supplied were a basket of fresh fruit, a stocked mini-bar, a telephone, and a safe.

The gray-and-white-streaked marble bathroom contained robes, a hair dryer, signature Casablanca bath products, a makeup mirror, stall shower, and separate tub.

The "Tropical Luxury" rooms set in back of the gardens aren't recommended, simply because the beachfront rooms views are so superior.

Water sports, tennis, and a gym are available for the athletically minded.

Some surprising changes have taken place since Casablanca opened in late 1992, like the switch from the original management to the Jamaica-based FDR Holidays, coupled with an expensive advertising campaign promoting an adults-only package, with all-inclusive daily rates of $1,000 per couple per day. (At press time the rates ranged from $800 to $1,200 per couple per day.) Casablanca also instituted day- and night-admission policies for Anguillians and visitors ranging from $50 to $100, including lunch or dinner, drinks, use of facilities, and service charge.

As much as we liked our room and food and the caring staff, we don't feel the steep price is justified, especially when, several months after these major changes, as of February 1994, pool or extra beach umbrellas had not been added. My crystal ball predicts more changes, so stay tuned.

CASABLANCA
Anguilla, British West Indies
TEL: (809) 497-6999
FAX: (809) 497-6899

RESERVATIONS
FDR Holidays
416 Atlantic Avenue
Freeport, Long Island, NY 11520
TEL: (800) 231-1945 *or*
(516) 223-1786
FAX: (516) 223-4815

Open all year.

Rates: Double occupancy (all-inclusive including rooms, meals, and drinks, transportation to and from airport or ferry, catamaran cruises, rental-car tour of island, shopping trip to St. Maarten/St. Martin, and dining at other restaurants): *December 17 to April 14* Garden Luxury, $800; Junior Suite, $1,000; One-Bedroom Suites, $1,200. *April 15 to December 16:* Garden Luxury, $700; Junior Suite, $800; One-Bedroom Suite, $900.

Meal Plan: FAP. The all-inclusive rate covers meals, afternoon tea, mini-bar beverages, all bar drinks and champagne.

Service charge: Included.

Government tax: Included.

Children: No one under 18 years of age permitted.

Credit cards accepted.

CoveCastles Villa Resort

Ten-year-old CoveCastles Villa Resort's four ultramodern three-bedroom villas on Shoal Bay West's expansive mile-long white sand beach is like an upscale Hampton address in the tropics. The identical beachfront villas are spaced 100 feet apart to ensure privacy. Farther down the beach to the southwest, eight similarly styled connecting beach villas, each with two bedrooms, are optional residences. The small restaurant with a high ceiling is the centerpiece of the beach villas. Lunches like lobster salad with fennel and orange dressing, fresh pasta with a julienne of vegetables, or a marinated red snapper salad niçoise are delivered to guests in their villas. Dinners in the candlelit dining room might be of crayfish salad or grouper fillet with lentils on a mustard sauce.

Architect Myron Goldfinger designed CoveCastles' sleek, geometrically formed white masonry buildings. Their massive molded, half-cylindrical-shaped façades curve up and back from the second-floor bedroom windows, offset by strong, clean, vertical lines used elsewhere. The crests of the buildings appear to have been blown back naturally by the wind. These dramatic abstract sculptures rest on flatland amid wild grass, yucca, aloe, cactus, sea grape, and coconut palms, only steps from the sublime beach and aqua dissolving into deep blue sea. The structures are a stark Mediterranean presence.

CoveCastles' pure white exteriors flow into spectacular, gracious living quarters inside. Nothing adorns the vast white walls. Artwork takes the form of shadows and light moving through skylights or the wide openings of sliding glass doors and wooden louvers playing on the walls. Views from the rooms, or from hammocks on the covered front verandas, are stunningly beautiful Caribbean picturescapes across the sea to the mountains of French St. Martin. The northern kitchen windows frame natural compositions of tangled plains, salt ponds, palm trees, and a cloudless blue sky.

June Goldfinger, the architect's wife and an interior designer, selected handsome rattan furniture with thick, honey-tinted raw-silk-covered cushions. Inside/outside terracotta floors create splashes of earthiness. Living areas are enlivened with potted plants, Anguillian-crafted model sailboats, whimsical pottery pieces from Nevis, vases of fresh flowers, and tiny gaslights. CoveCastles' radios, cable TVs, telephones, and copies of *TimesFax* in season, provide outside communication from this remote end of Anguilla. CoveCastles' bicycles are a great form of exercise and transportation for getting around the west end, but a car is required for mobility. The resort will make rental arrangements with advance notice.

The bilevel living/dining rooms are comfortably large, but the 20-foot ceiling magnifies the space. Off the raised dining area is a sparkling white, fully equipped kitchen that would delight any serious home cook or professional chef. There's a Super-Pro Cuisinart food processor, commercial electric blender for instant piña coladas, and an abundance of quality pots and pans, utensils, flatware, glassware and tableware, including pewter. Upon arrival, the dining room table is fully set with pastel-colored cotton napkins fanning out of green Mexican glass goblets. Guests are welcomed with champagne, mineral water, flowers, and a basket of gourmet foods.

A sweeping curved staircase leads to the airy second-floor bedrooms and baths. Three-bedroom villas have a master bedroom and a two-bedroom wing. A front balcony overlooks the living/dining area and kitchen. The bedrooms' unobstructed views out to sea are splendid. Ceiling fans and prevailing northeasterly winds keep guests comfortable.

Bedcovers on the firm king-size beds are made of gray raw silk. Local artisans have delicately trimmed the white top sheet and pillowcases with hand embroidery.

Bright reading lights from flex-type white metal architect lamps are positioned on wide rattan headboards. CoveCastles cotton robes hang in spacious closets.

Bathrooms have capsule-type bathtub/shower units or single shower stalls. Caswell-Massey toiletries are presented in tiny miniature cases and bouquets of rolled-up plush towels are artfully arranged in baskets.

The villas on the 8½-acre property are privately held, but the complex is run as an exclusive beach resort. There's a lighted Omnicourt tennis court and daily maid service. Beach chairs and umbrellas, snorkeling gear, Sunfish, and fishing lines are complimentary. For an additional fee you can receive tennis instructions or a massage. All water sports can be arranged. CoveCastles has no pool.

The resort operates professionally under the guidance of managing director Andre de Lucinges, who, since 1993, also happens to represent the French Consulary Agency on Anguilla. He and his wife, Josephine, a dedicated team, are sensitive to guests' needs, while skillfully supervising a small, congenial staff. Josephine's boutique, adjacent to reception, carries swim- and resortwear, jewelry, books, handcrafts, and necessities. Also available are exceptionally fine hand-crafted miniature replicas of Anguillian racing boats designed by David Hodge.

I highly recommend CoveCastles as a luxurious hideaway for particular people who can appreciate the unusual harmony of futuristic high style in a casual, comfortable Caribbean environment.

COVECASTLES VILLA RESORT
P.O. Box 248
Anguilla, British West Indies
TEL: (800) 348-4716 *or*
(809) 497-6801
FAX: (809) 497-6051

NY MAILING ADDRESS:
CoveCastles Villa Resort
605 Third Avenue
New York, NY 10158

Open all year.

Rates: *January 5 to March 31:* Villas (2 persons) $790, (3 to 6 persons) $990; Beach Houses (2 persons) $590, (3 to 4 persons) $790. *April 1 to December 20:* Villas (2 persons) $450, (3 to 6 persons) $650; Beach Houses (2 persons) $350, (3 to 4 persons) $450. *December 21 to January 4:* Villas (up to 6 persons) $1,290; Beach Houses (up to 4 persons) $990.

Meal plan: EP; MAP available with a three-day minimum stay for a charge of $55 per person per day.

Service charge: 10%.

Government tax: 8%.

Children welcome.

Credit cards: American Express only.

Note: Summer Dream packages available; rates upon request.

Fountain Beach Hotel

Fountain Beach, open since 1990, is an enchanting five-acre mini-resort situated on the western end of the gorgeous 2½-mile-long Shoal Bay East Beach. At the moment, only ten accommodations are open—two luxury studios and four two-bedroom suites (also available as one-bedroom suites, seaside and poolside)—in a white masonry two-story beachfront building. By winter of 1994–95, six more lodgings should have opened in structures on the west side of the property. The long lap pool with a little arched bridge at its center, added two years ago, is a welcome addition. Ultimately, Fountain Beach hopes to total 24 accommodations, a tennis court, and a fitness room. Phases of development are scheduled during off-season periods to inconvenience in-season guests as little as possible.

Fountain Beach Hotel was the brainchild of the late Carol Amatangel of West Newton, Massachusetts. Mrs. Amantangel's daughter, Coleen Amantangel, and Coleen's fiancé, Andrew Austin, managed the resort during its early years of operation to get things purring along. Derek Coulter now is capably in charge.

The resort is named after the historical Fountain Cavern, just southeast of the hotel, believed to be a religious site of the Arawak Indians. One of the petroglyphs from inside the cavern was selected as the hotel's logo: the "Solar Chieftain," a primitive line-drawn face sprouting four feathers from the head. The Solar Chieftain is hand-painted on rock doorstops at the entrance to each accommodation. The doorstops are just one of the many special decorating touches found at Fountain Beach.

Accommodations are unassuming-island-refined. Caribbean antiques and contemporary pieces, mostly from Haiti, spruce up interiors—mirrors, bamboo bureaus, whimsical cut-steel-drum wall hangings, clusters of clay pots, and rush rugs. Hand-embroidered spreads cover beds, and gauzy white lengths of material hang on the walls as canopies. Rooms are spacious and airy with ceiling fans. Good-sized front balconies, reached through sliding glass doors, provide sitting areas and bird's-eye views. We prefer a second-floor suite for extra-high ceilings and vistas.

The studios and suites have no telephones or TVs, but do feature fully equipped kitchens; refrigerators are stocked with breads, rolls, milk, mineral water, and other items on arrival.

Bathrooms in the luxury studios are spacious with marble floors and wall-to-wall marble tubs and showers, a toilet and bidet, and twin basins. The two-bedroom suites, each with a private bath and entranceway, have whitewashed walls, tile floors, open showers, and one-basin countertops, but no bidets. When booked as one-bedroom suites, the ocean-view quarters have full refrigerators and kitchens; the poolside suites have mini-refrigerators. Everything is immaculately clean.

La Fontana, Anguilla's first trattoria, has been a hit since it opened. The restaurant's charismatic chef, Curaçao-born Shamash "Morris" Brooks, prepares excellent dishes like Anguillian-style fish soup, aracostina alla signora Carol (a combination of chopped lobster, tomatoes, basil, and olive oil), pasta al limone, whole grilled snapper with herbs, and daily veal creations, Shamash's forte.

The two-level al fresco restaurant, open for lunch and dinner, is nestled at the water's edge among sea grape. Italian contemporary music and opera plays softly during meals. Breakfasts and Sunday brunches are served poolside.

The beach in front of Fountain Beach is reefy, but a short stroll away in either direction on vast Shoal Bay East there are plenty of fine swimming opportunities. Several restaurants along the beach provide Fountain Beach guests with agreeable alternative dining.

Fountain Beach Hotel is a charming retreat with caring, personalized service, which is why so many of its guests return every year.

FOUNTAIN BEACH HOTEL
Shoal Bay East
Anguilla, British West Indies
TEL: (800) 342-3491 *or*
　　　(809) 497-3491
FAX: (809) 497-3493

Open all year.

Rates: *December 20 to May 1:* Junior Studio, $245; One-Bedroom Seaside, $280; Two-Bedroom Suite, $365; One-Bedroom Poolside, $150. *May 1 to August 31:* Junior Studio, $150; One-Bedroom Seaside, $175; Two-Bedroom Suite, $225; One-Bedroom Poolside, $100. *September 1 to December 19:* Rates range from $100 to $285.

Meal plan: EP; MAP (includes breakfast and dinner), available at $55 per person per day.

Service charge: 10%.

Government tax: 8%.

Children welcome.

Credit cards accepted.

Frangipani Beach Club 🌴

One of the joys of travel writing is discovering and singing the praises of new small, well-managed hotels. While not exactly Anguilla's best-kept secret since it opened in the summer of 1992, the dazzling Frangipani Beach Club's attributes have yet to be fully recognized. The hotel's reservation lines should be blinking nonstop, the operator responding, "I'm sorry, we're fully, fully booked." Here's why.

Frangipani is a magnificent condominium hotel that at first glance appears to be an immense private Mediterranean villa. It sits beachfront near the center of marvelous

Frangipani Beach Club, Anguilla.

Meads Bay Beach on the northwest coast of the island. Malliouhana Hotel and Coccoloba are at the extreme opposite ends of the mile-long strand. Eight luxury deluxe units—one-, two-, and three-bedroom suites (all are actually spacious apartments and some can be rented as a double room), and a grand two-bedroom penthouse with a whirlpool tub—are housed in a pink stucco, rambling, red-tile-roofed Spanish-style building. French doors, arched windows, and high beamed ceilings are crafted from South American hardwood. Stone balustrades and artfully curled wrought-iron railings embellish second-floor suites and the third-floor penthouse. Views from upstairs are pure tropical magic. Ground-level suites open onto Mexican tiled patios. Voluptuous pink-and-white-striped, thick-cushioned chaise longues and tables and chairs, strategically placed on all verandas, automatically become coveted resting places, second only to shaded chaises under thatched bohios on the beach. Well-groomed tropical gardens with palm trees and thick sea grape encircle the hotel. On my last visit, I spied a large shipment of additional flowering plants and palm trees being delivered.

Inside, the suites have paddle fans and individually controlled air-conditioning. The spacious interiors are luxuriously decorated with high-quality bamboo and rattan furnishings covered in floral pastels or bold striped fabrics. Handsome 10-inch-square Mexican tile floors throughout are accented here and there with charming hand-painted smaller ceramic tiles. Guests have telephones, clock radios, cable TVs concealed in tall standing cabinets, and wonderfully convenient small washers and dryers. In the excellent kitchens nothing has been forgotten. Appliances include an automatic coffeemaker, blender, toaster, and a microwave oven. Oakwood cabinets are stocked with dishes, glasses, and pots and pans. Full refrigerators have automatic icemakers. The round marbletop dining table in our suite was complemented by an ensemble of six upholstered chairs.

French doors in the living room areas, and bedrooms have thick, lined cotton blackout draperies. We slept exceptionally late one morning, unusual for us, due to the absolute darkness inside the room and an extra-firm mattress. The closet space, by the way, was enormous. Maid service is impeccable.

Marble bathrooms come with Kohler plumbing fixtures, shower/tubs, thick monogrammed towels, hair dryers, and Gucci toiletries.

We stayed in Suite A4, a one-bedroom, two-bath, truly beachfront apartment facing north. Our patio was framed by a graceful, columned arched gallery covering overlooking palm trees and sea.

Frangipani's team of warm, proficient overseers—Dorothea Pickering, director of marketing and sales, and Valentin Davis, managing director—are on hand to arrange water sports, tennis, car rentals, sailing, excursions, baby-sitting, or suggest dining options in the immediate area or anywhere on the island. However, as of February 1994, guests at Frangipani could dine right on the premises at Café Albert', a small beach-house bar and restaurant. From the menu, described as cross-cultural, I sampled delicious black bean soup, a tender lobster salad with mangoes, and peach and ginger poundcake parfait. The pretty open-air café overlooks the impossibly clear aqua sea only a few yards from the lapping waterline. It's a spectacular location. A fashionably dressed couple at the next table who happened on the restaurant during a stroll over from Malliouhana, where they were staying, struck up a conversation with me. As they departed, they declared Café Albert' "a delicious serendipity."

Eventually, Frangipani intends to add a pool, tennis court, and two more buildings for a total of 36 suites. In the meantime, I heartily recommend this quiet, enchanting sanctuary. Summer rates are particularly appealing, especially since there is no service charge.

FRANGIPANI BEACH CLUB
P.O. Box 1378
Anguilla, British West Indies
TEL: (800) 892-4564 *or*
(809) 497-6442
FAX: (809) 497-6440

Open all year.

Rates: *December 20 to April 30:* Deluxe Rooms, $325 to $355; One-Bedroom, $450; Two-Bedroom, $765; Three-Bedroom, $1,020; Penthouse, $1,050; additional person, $50. *May 1 to October 31:* Deluxe Rooms, $165 to $195; One-Bedroom, $250; Two-Bedroom, $390; Three-Bedroom: $540; Penthouse $550; additional person in room, $25. *November 1 to December 19:* Deluxe Rooms, $230 to $260; One-Bedroom, $335; Two-Bedroom, $545; Three-Bedroom, $750; Penthouse, $800; additional person in room, $35.

Meal plan: EP.

Service charge: None.

Government tax: 8%.

Children welcome.

Credit cards: American Express only.

Note: Seven Nights Sun, Sea & Land, and Seven Nights Honeymoon special packages are available; information upon request.

Malliouhana Hotel 👑

Malliouhana was built with the belief that new Caribbean resort hotels could provide top luxury and fine cuisine, should be sized around 50 rooms, should be owner-managed, and that continuity of employment throughout the hotel and the subsequent building of relationships between guests and staff are of prime importance.

LEON ROYDON,
OWNER AND MANAGING DIRECTOR

After a recent two-night visit to Malliouhana, I can happily report that sophisticated, elegant Malliouhana has changed very little. Still expertly managed by the Roydon family,

Leon and his son Nigel, the hotel is among the top ten super-luxury resorts in the Caribbean, with a well-deserved reputation for high standards of service, decor, and ambience. Its restaurant is one of the finest in the islands. Undisputedly, Malliouhana has the best dining room and wine cellar on Anguilla. I'll elaborate later.

Malliouhana's main complex, a three-story whitewashed, Mediterranean-style building with red-tile roofs and arched balconies, sprawls on the crest of a promontory at the northeastern end of one-mile-long Meads Bay Beach on Anguilla's northwest coast. Its second beautiful strip of sand, Turtle Cove Beach, lies on the northeastern side of the hotel, accessible only through the hotel's grounds, with chaise longues, umbrellas, and beach-bar service. A third beach, adjacent ½-mile Long Bay, is totally secluded.

The surrounding villas and terrace rooms, exercise hall, garden nursery, four championship Laykold tennis courts (three are lighted for night play, and two were given "plexicushion" surfaces in 1994), water-sports building, two large swimming pools connected by a waterfall, a new Jacuzzi, and the even newer supervised children's play area are judiciously spread throughout the 25-acre property. The play area, a delightful addition, has a paddling pool, swings, sandbox, slides, and a contemporary jungle gym. Children can view videos and enjoy nourishing refreshments in a covered area with child-size picnic tables and benches. The playground also has a lowered basketball net and court, plus a Ping-Pong table for older youngsters.

Malliouhana's 53 accommodations range from doubles in the main building to junior terrace suites perched above Turtle Cove Bay, and one- and two-bedroom suites tucked into gardens, set on the beach or elevated above the sea with wonderful views. The villas are christened with names of trees and flowers: Frangipani, Jasmine, Periwinkle. Allamanda is the prize location for proximity to the pools, Jacuzzi, and lovely sea views. Tamarind and Hibiscus, the only actual beachside accommodations, are directly on Meads Bay. Since they are located adjacent to the children's playground, quarters here are ideal for guests with children. When booking, it is important for guests to request specific room locations.

Director/designer Larry Peabody splendidly orchestrated the hotel's spacious interiors with bamboo and rattan platform or four-poster king-size beds, chaise longues, and other furniture with cushions cloaked in earth tones or cheery repeat-print blue and white fabrics. All accommodations have desks, glass-top tables, straw rugs, glass and brass hurricane lamps, potted palms, and brilliantly colored Haitian paintings, with cream-colored tile floors and Brazilian walnut woodwork used throughout. Rooms include spacious twin louvered-door closets with lots of hanging space, shelves, and multiple drawers, as well as a wall safe. A three-sided mirror and vanity table is situated at the center of these wall-to-wall closet spaces. A separate bar closet reveals a fully stocked mini-refrigerator with an automatic icemaker—a welcome relief, because except for the beachside lodgings, there is climbing involved to all accommodations from all beaches.

Telephones have jacks. No TVs or radios disturb the peace. Air-conditioning in all accommodations except for three villas, along with ceiling fans and doors opening out onto patios or terraces, promise a comfortable temperature.

The large bathrooms have wall-to-wall Italian beige-pink marble, save for an enormous mirrored panel along one side of the oversized tub. There's also a separate stall shower, a bidet, and twin basins. An abundance of thick towels, monogrammed terry-cloth robes, and Floris and Roger & Gallet bath products are always at hand. Hair dryers ought to be added. Uniformed maids are always nearby to help locate a light switch or fulfill any other request. Room service throughout the day and evening is unfailingly delivered on time. A *TimesFax* and local paper, *The Chronicle*, is delivered with breakfast.

Aside from tennis, Malliouhana offers Sunfish, Lasers, catamarans, windsurfers, fishing gear, waterskiing, and mask and fins. Outings on the resort's motor yacht, the 35-foot *KYRA*, are scheduled weekly. Scuba diving can be arranged. And Malliouhana, in conjunction with Cap Juluca and Tyden Air, has organized a weekly full-day excursion on Thursdays to the Four Seasons Resort on Nevis for a round of golf.

The exercise hall, located off a terrace perched above Meads Bay Beach, affords guests splendid views while they march on treadmills or tackle a NordicTrack, two LifeCycle bikes, a StairMaster, a Universal "full gym," and weights. Massages and private aerobic classes are offered.

Also available are a beauty salon, picnic baskets, a TV/video room with a 27-inch screen with a 150-movie video library, a smaller TV for news and sports events in the library, and changing rooms for early arrivals and late departures. I neglected to mention that car rentals with pickup and return at Malliouhana can be organized. Guests receive a personal airport welcome, usually from dedicated Malliouhana ambassador Jasmine Raymond, one of the many longtime members of the 205-person staff.

The hotel's fashionable boutique in the main hall carries exquisite Oro de Sol jewelry, upscale resortwear from La Perla, Manuel Canovas, and Go Silk, plus smart Kaminski straw hats, and Robert LaRoche sunglasses. The exercise hall, a small shop for sundry items, along with the tennis shop, lunch terrace, and beach bar are in a small beachside building.

Under the supervision of Paris-based Michel Rostang, who succeeded his late father, two-star Michelin chef Jo Rostang, Malliouhana's restaurant excels. Head chef Alain Laurent, ably assisted by chef Patrick Mari and pâtissier Olivier Nicod, and a talented cadre of twenty-three, consistently deliver outstanding French/Caribbean-inspired cuisine.

Guests dine on Limoges china, Christofle silver, and white linen tablecloths and napkins on an immense cliffside open-air dining terrace with wide-open sea views.

Chef Laurent, working with local seafood and such imported foods as French Bresse chicken and duck and stateside meats, vegetables, and berries, produces wondrous innovations like foie gras and pumpkin ravioli in a consommé with diced chicken, conch risotto with mushrooms and Parmesan cheese, and perfectly cooked-to-order roast fillet of beef with crunchy cabbage, horseradish sauce, and marrow. The butter-tender roast chicken from Bresse, carved tableside with *pommes mousselines*, is always irresistible. Desserts such as rhubarb crème brûlée served with a light sponge cake or iced pineapple soufflé are all superior.

To match the quality of the food, Malliouhana's 45-page wine list includes selections from the hotel's cellar of more than 20,000 bottles. Leon Roydon and sommelier Albert Hodge annually visit vineyards throughout the world to replenish the cellar.

Service in the restaurant has improved significantly since my last review. It is professional and efficient, although occasionally still rushed. If you enjoy fine food, and are willing to pay the price, do not miss dining at at least once at Malliouhana, even if you aren't staying at the hotel.

Guests at Malliouhana, many of whom are yearly repeaters, range from young couples and families on through the ages, with a large percentage of Americans. The rest are primarily European. Among them all are the discriminating, the wealthy, and the famous.

Malliouhana is a world-class hotel that would fit in and fill up with guests in the south of France or in Singapore. In Anguilla, Malliouhana is haute paradise.

MALLIOUHANA HOTEL
P.O. Box 173
Anguilla, British West Indies
TEL: (809) 497-6111
FAX: (809) 497-6011

RESERVATIONS IN U.S.
TEL: (800) 835-0796

Closed September and October.
Rates: Double occupancy. *December 18 to March 31:* Double Rooms, $480 to $550; Junior Suites, $690; One-Bedroom Suites, $660 to $810; Two-Bedroom Suites, $1,240; extra bed for child, $50. *November 1 to December 17* and *April 1 to May 31:* Double Rooms, $320 to $365; Junior Suites, $460; One-Bedroom Suites, $440 to $575; Two-Bedroom Suites, $825; extra bed for child, $50. Rates for *June 1 to August 31* approximately 50% less than December 18 to March 31 rates.
Meal plan: EP. CMAP (a special Malliouhana plan including continental breakfast and dinner is offered only out-of-season, April 1 to August 31 and November 1 to December 17), available at $75 per person per day plus a service charge.
Service charge: 10%.
Government tax: 8%.
Children welcome, but none under 3 in Main House.
Credit cards not accepted.
Note: Romantic Interlude and Unwinding Together packages available during the summer; rates upon request.

The Mariners

The Mariners is a West Indian–style retreat on 8½ acres, under protective cliffs, just off Sandy Ground's lovely crescent-shaped beach at Road Bay. The resort opened in 1983 with only five cottages. The traditional West Indian cottages, trimmed in gingerbread with bright-colored shutters, corrugated roofs, and full verandas, can be rented as individual homes with two bedrooms, living/dining room, fully equipped kitchen, and three baths. Connecting doors transform these little jewels into flexible lodgings that can be booked as double bedrooms with a refrigerator and a bath each, a twin-bedded studio with full kitchen and bath, or a one-bedroom suite with full kitchen and two baths.

By 1989, the resort blossomed into 17 cottages or 50 rooms. The latest development included two new cottages, two two-story, multiroom buildings consisting of bedrooms or studios, outdoor, side-by-side, small twin Jacuzzis, and a 20 × 40-foot freshwater swimming pool situated next to an open-air gazebo that combines the reception, a lounge, cable TV, café, and pool bar. Mariners' Boutique moved from its nook by the restaurant to a room in a building adjacent to the gazebo. According to general manager/part owner Clive Carty, The Mariners' expansion is now complete. It can be booked all-inclusive or EP.

The Mariners is an island hideaway with a casual, laid-back atmosphere that offers its guests all the amenities of contemporary living. Because of its location, the resort's guests have the rare opportunity to experience true island living, as the hotel property and the nearby village of Sandy Ground converge.

Reclining in chaises under umbrellas at Mariners on the northwest-facing beach, guests view an active harbor, and off to the right, a long jetty. Banana boats and tramp steamers unload their cargoes here. The pier is the beginning of the village of Sandy Ground. Guest houses, restaurants, boutiques, and native homes share the shoreline. Strolling along the sandy lane you'll pass fishermen stringing nets or repairing lobster traps, workers tinkering on dry-docked boats, grazing tethered goats, hens clucking after their chicks, travelers lunching on grilled seafood and chilled wine, passengers from small cruise ships or day sails snapping photos of their friends, and beautiful, spirited children splashing in the sea. It's a barefoot, authentic island ambience.

After checking into The Mariners, guests are driven to their lodgings in a soundless electric van. Inside, under coffered or tray-shaped painted ceilings with fans, are neat interiors dressed up in white and natural bamboo and rattan furniture.

Baths with showers only are small but modern and more than adequate. (Poolside and cliffside bedrooms have showers with tubs.) Bath towels and a supply of beach towels were plentiful.

Rooms have refrigerators and phones, but no TVs or radios. Room service is available for breakfast only.

The Mariners' seaside Terrace Bar & Restaurant offers romantic candlelit dinners. Thursday there's a barbecue and Saturday's special event is a West Indian dinner featuring live entertainment as guests dine and dance. Specialities of the house include Anguilla fish soup, fillet of snapper West Indian–style, and chicken baked with coconut and ginger. Homey desserts include fresh lime cheesecake with coconut and cinnamon crust, and terrine of chocolate.

The wide range of water sports, complimentary to all guests, includes use of snorkeling equipment, Sunfish, and windsurfers, and day and night tennis (there's one court). Special excursions are offered to guests who have chosen inclusive rates.

The Mariners' grounds are shaded by coconut palms and sea grape, with croton, oleander, hibiscus, and much more. Find a hammock and relax near the sea. Wherever you recline you'll enjoy simple, charmed island living.

THE MARINERS	**RESERVATIONS**
P.O. Box 139	TEL: (800) 553-4939
Road Bay, Sandy Ground	
Anguilla, British West Indies	
TEL: (800) 848-7938 *or*	
(809) 497-2671	
FAX: (809) 497-2901	

Open all year.

Rates: The Mariners has all-inclusive *and* EP rates. The all-inclusive rates for *December 21 to March 31* are per person per day with a minimum 3-night stay year-round. There is a separate rate list for Standard Cliffside Accommodations for up to 6 persons. A single ranges from $250 for a Room to $380 for a Cottage. Children up to age 5 are $55 per day per child; children 6 to 12, $105. For Beachfront Air-conditioned Accommodation add: Room, $10; Suite, $20, or Cottage, $30 per day. For Beachfront Special Accommodation add: Room, $20; Suite $40, or Cottage, $60 per day. Full information available upon request. I suggest a faxed copy so you can read the fine print.

Meal plan: FAP (all-inclusive rate covers three meals, afternoon tea, open bar, service charges, and government tax). MAP rate (for EP guests) add $45 per person per day plus 10% service charge.

Service charge: Covered in the all-inclusive rate; 10% on EP rate.

Government tax: Covered in the all-inclusive rate; 8% on EP rate.

Children under 12 welcome upon request (in rooms and suites only).

Credit cards accepted.

Note: Special Villa, "The Admirals Plan," and Summer Saver Package Rates. Be sure to read the fine print.

NOTEWORTHY OPTIONS

Blue Waters Beach Apartments

If you are seeking a reasonably priced apartment in Anguilla on a beach with a view, in a peaceful area with a good restaurant or two nearby so you can alternate eating in and out, Blue Waters Beach Apartments is a treasure. The hotel opened in late 1991 on the eastern end of Shoal Bay West Beach, a 1½-mile-long, beautiful white curved strip. The beach is shared with only three other occupants. At the west end is Cove-

Castles Villa Resort, a group of striking white contemporary structures, with a first-rate restaurant; movie strongman Chuck Norris's private pink villa, and a only few yards from Blue Waters, Paradise Café, a casual open-air restaurant open for lunch and dinner.

Blue Waters has nine apartments—seven one-bedrooms and two two-bedrooms—in five two-story attached buildings, whose veranda front portions are staggered along the beach. Five apartments are beach level and four are upstairs. We stayed in number 2, a one-bedroom second-floor corner apartment adjacent to the owner's two-story home at the eastern end of the property. Carolyn Permuy, who operates Blue Waters with grace and efficiency, lives downstairs. After check-in, you're basically on your own. Carolyn's adorable daughter, Juliet, and various pets give the place a pleasing domestic quality, as if you are part of your very own little beach community.

We loved our second-floor location for privacy and incredible beach views. St. Martin looms dramatically across the water to the south and east. Its lights and the stars twinkle brightly at night and pacifying surf sounds lull you to sleep.

Blue Waters' white masonry buildings are accented with curved arches. Screening the windows are sturdy wooden louvers, and ceiling fans and natural breezes control the temperature. Inside, the all-white rooms, including the tile floors, have built-in masonry desks and L-shaped banquettes with gray cushions. There's a dining area with table and chairs, cable TV, dimmers on wall sconces, and good reading light from gray ceramic-based lamps. No phones or swimming pool.

The large plain, all-white kitchen, in a wide-open area, is fully equipped with unbreakable dishes, plenty of pots and pans, cutlery, utensils, glasses, and an automatic coffeemaker, blender, toaster, and a full refrigerator.

You have the option of dining al fresco at a table and chairs outside on the front balcony or terrace. There are also chaises outside for lounging.

The bedroom's king-size bed has sheets for bed coverings. There's plenty of closet space, plus an iron and mini-ironing board. The spacious bathroom comes with a shower stall. Maids tidy up every day but Sunday.

A few potted palms are placed here and there in the accommodations. The environment is spartan and pristine and thoroughly pleasant.

Lounges and umbrellas line the beach where you'll meet and greet your neighbors each day. Not to worry—during our stay everyone respected each other's privacy. Conversations were mainly "Where are you from?" and "How long are you staying?" and sharing the names of creatures we'd seen while snorkeling during the day.

Rent a car so you can explore Anguilla, and be prepared for the bumpy dirt road that leads to the apartments. The road's north side borders a salt pond where white egrets parade.

Blue Waters, with such reasonable rates and appealing qualities, understandably has become very popular so, if interested, reserve well in advance.

BLUE WATERS BEACH APARTMENTS
P.O. Box 69
Shoal Bay West
Anguilla, British West Indies
TEL: (809) 497-6292
FAX: (809) 497-6982

Open all year.

Rates: *December 16 to April 14:* One-Bedroom Beachfront Apartment, $185; Two-Bedroom Beachfront Apartment, $270; extra person, $30. *April 15 to December 15:* One-Bedroom Beachfront Apartment, $115; Two-Bedroom Beachfront Apartment, $160; extra person, $20.
Meal plan: EP.
Service charge: 10%.
Government tax: 8%.
Children welcome.
Credit cards accepted.

La Sirena

Swiss-run La Sirena (open since 1989) is good value on Anguilla, just a two-minute walk from spectacular Meads Bay. La Sirena has two freshwater pools, decent Caribbean/Italian/International cuisine, well-tended standard accommodations, and an oversized open-air lobby with a small boutique and an inviting bar. Breakfasts and luncheons are brought to guests in a terrace area overlooking the main pool and sea, next to the bar. Up a spiral staircase is a spacious dining room with a high wooden-beamed ceiling. The resort's whitewashed walls and red-tiled roofs give it a Mediterranean look.

Twenty small- to medium-sized rooms wrap around a lawn and tropical gardens to the east and north of the public areas. Rooms have terra-cotta floors, baths with showers, rattan furnishings, mini-bars, ceiling fans, and phones—all at your disposal when you're not out on your balcony stargazing.

The three two-bedroom and two three-bedroom villas have their own freshwater pool and are set below the main part of the property, framed by bougainvillea bracts and blossoms and thick greenery. Villa guests get fully equipped kitchens and barbecues. Dishwashers and cable TV are available for an extra fee.

Every time I've been here the atmosphere has been low-key and quiet. This might be just what you're looking for. Things do liven up on Thursdays, when a West Indian buffet is served and entertainment comes from the Mayoumba Folkloric Theatre.

LA SIRENA
P.O. Box 200, Meads Bay
Anguilla, British West Indies
TEL: (800) 331-9358 or
(809) 497-6827
FAX: (809) 497-6829

RESERVATIONS
International Travel & Resorts
TEL: (800) 223-9815 *or*
(212) 251-1800 in New York
State

Open all year.
Rates: Double occupancy. *November 1 to December 14:* Standard Double, $140; Superior Double, $180. Villas: Two-Bedroom, $190 to 240 (for 1 to 4 persons); Three-Bedroom, $280 (for 1 to 6 persons). *December 15 to March 31:* Standard Double, $195; Superior Double, $255. Villas: Two-Bedroom, $270 to $340 (for 1 to 4 persons); Three-Bedroom, $395 (for 1 to 6 persons). *April 1 to October 31:* Rooms from $95 to $160; Villas, $180 to $270. Special rates for children.
Meal plan: EP. AP (includes full American breakfast), $12 per person; MAP, $44 per person.
Service charge: 10%.
Government tax: 8%.
Children welcome.
Credit cards accepted.

Recommended Restaurants

ANGUILLA'S FINEST*

* **Malliouhana**, 497-6111 (Malliouhana Hotel on Meads Bay). Finest restaurant and wine cellar in Anguilla. Elegantly served French/Caribbean meals in expansive open-air dining room pavilion with lovely views. (See resort listing, page 35.) Expensive for lunch. Very expensive for dinner.

* **Pimms** and **Chattertons**, 497-6666 (Cap Juluca on Maunday's Bay). Two beautiful adjoining restaurants: Pimms is more formal in the evenings. Lunches at either are always casual. Spectacular, romantic seaside location. Good lobster sandwich and salads, and seafood dishes. Excellent wines. (See resort listing, page 21.) Expensive.

* **Mango's Seaside Grill**, 497-6479 (Barnes Bay, just west of the Coccoloba Resort). Enchanting, open-air beachside café featuring great soups, blackened lobster and grouper, barbecued pork loin with rosemary, and lots more. Consistently first-rate. Two seatings nightly. Reservations are a must. Expensive.

* **Blanchard's**, 497-6100 (Meads Bay, next to Carimar Beach Club). Although this restaurant was not open at press time, Melinda and Bob Blanchard, Mango's creators, have returned to Anguilla and taken the location of a previous restaurant called Capers.

The redesigned, totally redecorated and extended, terraced indoor/outdoor dining room with an expanded wine cellar, will feature Melinda's innovations, from macadamia-crusted mahi-mahi with coconut lime sauce to a thin eight-layer tropical trifle with fresh fruits and berries. Reservations are required. Expensive.

* **Casablanca**, 497-6999 (Rendezvous Bay West). Commendable French-inspired cuisine when last sampled. Splendid Moorish setting. New chef. (See resort entry, page 27.) Very expensive.

* **CoveCastles' Cafe**, 497-6801 (Shoal Bay West at CoveCastles Villa Resort). Seafood, pastas, and other well-prepared fare served in an attractive, air-conditioned restaurant (see resort listing page 29). Expensive to very expensive.

* **KoalKeel**, 497-2930 (Warden's Place in Old Valley). A renovated and reopened KoalKeel still dishes up superior food like Anguillian pea soup and snapper fillet on couscous, in a historic, attractive inland setting. New here, *Le Petit Pâtissier*, across a courtyard upstairs in an antique-filled parlor room, serves sublime pastries and imported teas and coffees from 7:30 A.M. until KoalKeel closes. Take-out available. (See "Provisions for Your Island Pantry.") KoalKeel, moderate to expensive; Le Petit Pâtissier, moderate.

* **The Palm Court**, 497-2783 (Cinnamon Reef Resort, Little Harbour). Award-winning chefs Zeff Bonsey and Vernon Hughes offer delicious, imaginative versions of today's classics with local accents. We always go for lunch to have thick black bean soup and a lobster sandwich, but the cuisine gets much more complex at dinner. Ocean view. Moderate to expensive.

* **Hibernia**, 497-4290 (Island Harbour). Very quiet, terraced dining room with a sea view. Chef Raoul Rodriguez consistently prepares interesting fare of mixed cuisines. His wife, Mary Pat O'Hanlon, is a gracious hostess. Calorie counts are given for dishes on menu. Moderate to expensive.

* **La Fontana**, 497-3492 (Fountain Beach at Shoal Bay East). Shamash Brooks combines Italian dishes with local ingredients in this charming seaside location. (See Fountain Beach entry, page 31.) Moderate to expensive.

* **Tropical Penguin**, 497-2253 (Sandy Ground). Chef Erwin Pascher and his wife, Jackie, have opened a small gem right on the beach. Great location for family dining. Formerly head chef at Cap Juluca, Erwin turns out airy lobster puffs, sensational lobster sandwiches on baguettes, burgers, pastas, superior meat entrées, and desserts. Moderate.

* **Gorgeous Scilly Cay**, 497-5123 (Tiny private island a few hundred yards from pier at Island Harbour; wave from the pier and a motor launch will transport you to and from the island—you step off into the sea.) Sandra and Eudoxie Wallace serve excellent grilled lobster, crayfish (my favorite), or half a chicken in a fun-filled, laid-back island atmosphere. Covered areas for dining and chaises in sand. Live music Wednesdays, Fridays, and Sundays. In season, Sundays are crowded, so opt for any other day. Open 11 A.M. to 6 P.M. Potent rum punches are deliciously spiked with Amaretto. Scilly Cay sells great, multicolored polo shirts and soleless foot coverings. Highly recommended for all ages. Moderate to expensive.

OTHER DEPENDABLE CHOICES

Cyril's Fish House, 497-4488 (Island Harbour). Formerly Le Fish Trap. Indoor open-air dining or on expanded cheerful outdoor terrace under palms and umbrellas behind a picket fence. Try the fried calamari, mesquite-grilled kingfish, or Anguillian mako Dijon. Moderate to expensive.

Le Bistro, 497-6700 (on road near entrance to Malliouhana off Meads Bay). Suzanne Westrich and Bruno Couchard's small new French/Caribbean restaurant serves up accras, fresh fish carpaccio with coconut sauce, and veal with lime and caper sauce. Try chocolate fondant for dessert. Moderate.

Paradise Café, 497-6010 (Shoal Bay West). Casual beachside dining on conch fritters, great beach pizza, lobster club sandwiches, West Indian bouillabaisse, and Asian-accented dishes. Moderate to expensive.

Café Albert', 497-6440 (Meads Bay at Frangipani Beach Club). New 10-table beachfront, breezy bistro. Very good salads and seafood. (See resort listing, page 33.) Moderate to expensive.

Smitty's Bay & Restaurant, 497-4300 (Island Harbour). Convivial owner Smitty welcomes guests with his winning smile in this casual, low-key seafront saloon. Delicious grilled crayfish, ribs, chicken, and lobsters (none priced higher than $20) are served with curried rice and salads. Burgers, too. Inexpensive to moderate.

Roy's Place, 497-2470 (Crocus Bay). Good choice for families. Elevated seaside dining room and English pub. Cold draft beer on tap. Good fish and chips, conch chowder, local crayfish, and offerings from an extensive menu. Sunday brunch always features roast beef and Yorkshire pudding. Moderate to expensive.

La Terrasse, 497-6501 (South Hill Plaza). Courtyard café serving croissants, sandwiches, pâtés, pastries, ice creams, and coffees. Take-out, too.

Among the dining options on Anguilla, here are a few more to consider: **Riviera** and **Barrel Stay** in Sandy Ground for reliable meals; **Lucy's Harbour View** for good West Indian fare; **Johnno's** serves barbecued ribs, and chicken, or fresh fish—go for the weekly Sunday "jump-up," with live music. **Arlo's Place**, a favorite with locals, dishing up Italian meals. Restaurants in the following hotels offer good choices, too: **Coccoloba, La Sirena, Pineapple Beach Club, Ferry Boat Inn**, and **Rendezvous Bay Hotel**. There are now two pizza possibilities—**J&J's Pizza** in South Hill and **Chick-King & Pizza Palace** in The Valley.

Recommended Shopping

Boutiques at Cap Juluca (Azemmour), Malliouhana, Casablanca, and CoveCastles Villa Resort provide some of the best shopping on Anguilla. (See individual resort listings.) Also check the boutiques at the Coccoloba resort.

Neitiv Antiques, 497-3222 (George Hill Road, next to Studio Hair). This tiny, recently opened shop has a small, interesting collection, from china pieces and silver salvers to furniture.

Caribbean Style, 497-6717 (Pineapple Beach Club Anguilla). Suzanne Seitz has collected unique West Indian objects, jewelry, handcrafts, sandals, fabrics, antiques, furniture, and clothing in an overflowing, welcoming shop.

New World Gallery, 497-5950 (Old Factory Plaza in The Valley). Paintings, antiques, pottery, one-of-a-kind jewelry pieces. Changing art exhibits, always including works by artist/owner Penny Slinger.

Devonish Cotton Gin Art Gallery, 497-2949 (Old Factory Plaza in The Valley). Courtney Devonish's pottery and sculpture creations can be viewed daily. Paintings and arts and crafts by other gifted artists are also on display.

L'Atelier Art Studio, 497-5668 (North Hill). Michele Lavalette's showroom in a West Indian house features her works in oils and watercolors, plus prints and special T-shirts.

Lydia Séméria Art Studio, 497-3318 (Sandy Ground). Ms. Séméria paints enchanting West Indian scenery and portraits in oils, acrylics, and watercolors. Prices range from inexpensive to a few thousand dollars. I especially liked her artwork painted inside embroidered golden frames on T-shirts. She also works in dried coconuts and wood.

Cheddie's Carving Studio, 497-6027 (The Cove, near Casablanca turnoff). Cheddie Richards's original mahogany and driftwood birds, fish, and animal carvings are inspired by nature. The shop is located in a charming two-story West Indian house.

Jessica, Cerise, and **Gallery D'Art**, 497-6501/2/3/4 (Lower South Hill in new South Hill Plaza). New boutiques and art gallery next to a new wine cellar—a retail shop selling wines, liquors, and accessories.

Caribbean Silk Screen Co. Ltd. and **Petit Boutique**, 497-2272 (North Hill). There is a computerized embroidery and silk-screening studio on the premises. The boutique carries a small but special selection of T-shirts, polo shirts, coverings, totes, and visors. The company makes custom-designed resortwear for many luxury resorts on Anguilla and throughout the Caribbean.

Java Wraps, 497-5497 (George Hill Road). Indonesian batik, multicolored designs in clothing for men, women, and children are sold here.

The Sunshine Shop and **Butterflies**, 497-6964 (on I-95 at the Blowing Point Expressway just beyond the traffic light). Here are two small gift shops that carry batiks, resortwear, costume jewelry, artwork, and handcrafts.

Beach Stuff, 497-6814 (Back Street, South Hill overlooking Sandy Ground). This pretty little West Indian–style house is stocked with beachwear, lots of attractive, bold-colored separates and T-shirts, plus snorkeling equipment, sunglasses, and beach necessities.

The Arts & Crafts Centre, 497-2200 (The Valley). Local crafts, paintings, books, ceramics, and prints.

Provisions for Your Island Pantry

Vista Food Market & Liquor Store, 497-2804 (at the South Hill Round-About). Best all-round supermarket on Anguilla. It's no Grand Union, but has good selections of staples, canned goods, cheeses, crackers, frozen meats and prepackaged foods, plus limited produce, beverages, wines, and liquors. Hydroponically grown lettuce is usually available, as are Cuban and other quality cigars.

Housekeeping gourmets might want to take the ferry to French St. Martin to find gastronomical heaven at the huge supermarket, Match, at Howells Center in Marigot. Beyond general food items, look for imports and excellent meats and pâtés. A wonderful little bakery adjacent to Match sells crusty baguettes and confections. (For other fine food shopping in St. Martin, see page 309, and take note of Marigot's outdoor market.)

A & C Fleming Mini Mart, 497-6309 (on road about ½ mile before reaching Malliouhana at Meads Bay). Modest selection, but convenient for self-caterers in Meads Bay area. Open 6 A.M. to 11 P.M. daily.

Galaxy Supermarket, 497-2232 (The Valley). General foods, meat, and poultry. Also trucking and backhoe rental.

The People's Market, no phone (The Valley). Good local and imported (from other islands) seasonal fresh fruits and vegetables. Giant-size tubers and other special Caribbean produce.

Fat Cat Gourmet To Go, 497-2307 (George Hill). Very good catering establishment. Try daily specials like roasted chicken halves, beef curry, and pasta primavera, or place an order from the enticing menu 24 hours in advance. Desserts include scrumptious lime bars, coconut cream or guava cream pies, and bread pudding with rum sauce.

Le Petit Pâtissier, 497-2930 (Old Valley at KoalKeel). Excellent baguettes, croissants, chocolate brioches, lime tarts, and lots more. You can buy imported teas and coffees, too.

Amy's Bakery & Dining Room, 497-6775 (Blowing Point). Call ahead to order rich brownies, a banana cream pie, or Amy's tasty lobster pie—actually a large quiche. Stop in any time for good breads and other sweets or a quick lunch.

The Valley Bakery (The Valley). Super coconut tarts, breads, and other delicious offerings.

LeGout du Vin, 497-6501 (Lower Low Hill, South Hill Plaza). New retail outlet for fine wines. Tastings. **La Terrasse**, 497-6501 (at same plaza). Also sells pâtés, cheeses, sandwiches, salads, and pastries to take out.

Pizza takeout: **J&J's Pizza**, 497-3215 (South Hill), or **Chick-King & Pizza Palace**, 497-5410 (The Valley). The latter also cooks up Jamaican patties and chicken-and-chips to take home or pack for a picnic.

Ice Cream Café on George Hill Road has a drive-through window for Häagen-Dazs and Colombo cones.

Useful Information

Pick up free copies of **Anguilla Life Magazine** (a quarterly) and **What We Do in Anguilla** (small yearly tourism magazine) immediately for good information. **The Light,** a weekly TV guide with local information and news, costs one East Caribbean dollar (E.C.$, 37¢ U.S.).

Studio Hair, 497-3222 (George Hill). This is a full-service hair salon also offering reflexology, massages, and facials.

Highway Gym, 497-5893/2839 (George Hill). Fully equipped gym with free and stack weights. Aerobics classes daily.

Rogers Photo Studio, 297-2832/3832 (Stony Ground). Film and one-hour photo processing available here.

Nell's Executive Limousine & Taxi Service. Call 497-6409 or fax (809) 497-6401, if in need of a white stretch limousine.

Tyden Air, 497-3079 (the airport). Scheduled round-trips direct to St. Barts Monday, Wednesday, and Friday in season. Available for charter flights to other islands in the region as well.

Sandy Island day trips, 497-5643/6395 (Sandy Ground). Tiny, 650 × 160-foot isolated oasis where you can lunch on barbecued chicken, fish, or lobster, and drink rum punch, or swim, snorkel, windsurf, or just relax on the snow-white beach. **Sandy Island Enterprises** also arranges special trips to Prickly Pear, Dog Island, or anywhere in the area. Ask for Neville Connor.

Ferries to St. Martin (trip lasts 20 to 25 minutes) depart daily from Anguilla every half hour from 7:30 A.M. until 5 P.M. There are evening ferries at 6:15 P.M. and 10:15 P.M. Ferries depart Marigot in French St. Martin to Anguilla daily beginning at 8 A.M., every half hour until 5:30 P.M. The evening ferries are at 7 P.M. and 10:30 P.M. Day-ferry fares are $10 per person one way; evening ferries, $11 per person one way. Children's fare, half price. A $2 departure tax per person is also collected in Anguilla and in St. Martin. A passport or driver's license with photograph is required.

There are several rental car companies on Anguilla, and most hotels will organize a vehicle for you. We always rent from Maurice Connor at **Connor's Car Rental,** 497-6433/6541, fax (809) 497-6410. Book ahead for a Isuzu 11-Mark, Honda Civic, or Isuzu Amigo jeep, all with air-conditioning. Other vehicles are also available.

ANTIGUA

ACCOMMODATIONS

ANTIGUA'S BEST
Curtain Bluff
Galley Bay
Jumby Bay Island

A NOTEWORTHY OPTION
Long Bay Hotel

GREAT EXPECTATIONS
Carlisle Bay Club

RECOMMENDED RESTAURANTS

RECOMMENDED SHOPPING

PROVISIONS FOR YOUR ISLAND PANTRY

USEFUL INFORMATION

≈ ≈

Accommodations

ANTIGUA'S BEST

Curtain Bluff ♛

Our thirty-three years of operation owe much to the loyalty of our guests and our staff. In a beautiful setting we provide the best in accommodations, food, wines, and sports facilities—but it's they who've made possible our success. Our guests say it's the welcome and the warmth that captivate.

HOWARD W. HULFORD,
OWNER/CHAIRMAN, BOARD OF DIRECTORS

Curtain Bluff, the venerable Antiguan resort, opened in 1961 on the southern coast of the island on a bluffed peninsula flanked by two beautiful stretches of golden sand. One is windward at Grace Bay, with a varying quiet to rough surf, where the accommodations are located. The other beach is leeward, on calm, inviting Morris Bay, where most of the action is.

What prompts hundred and hundreds of guests to return each year to this exclusive retreat is the 20-acre-plus manicured tropical environment (there are 38 different species of palm trees alone), quality seaside accommodations, expansive sports facilities, dependable and friendly service, fine food and excellent wines, but, most of all, *consistency*. Howard Hulford, Curtain Bluff's creator, is an on-the-scene proprietor who passionately oversees every aspect of the resort's operation. An island Renaissance man of sorts, his passions extend from tennis and horticulture to vintage wines, which he has skillfully incorporated into amenities at Curtain Bluff. His wife, Chelle, is a warm, caring hostess.

Curtain Bluff's rates include all meals, beverages and bar drinks, tea, and cocktail hors d'oeuvres. Free water-sports facilities outshine most other resorts: Sunfish, windsurfers, waterskiing, and scuba-diving gear and complete equipment for certified divers; there are also guided trips to Cades Reef, a glorious underwater world. Charters for day sailing on the resort's 47-foot Wellington ketch, *Tamarin*, and deep-sea fishing can be arranged for a fee. But a whole lot more comes with the price of the room—an impressive, fully equipped exercise room (with several aerobics classes each week), a squash court, a putting green, and a croquet lawn, plus four tennis courts (two lighted for night play).

50

(Curtain Bluff hosts an Antigua Tennis Week in May and a European Tennis Week in October.) Another plus is the full-service hair salon on the premises.

Every night of the week guests can enjoy live entertainment and dancing. The well-to-do, mostly conservative set doesn't mind the five-night-a-week jacket-and-tie rule for men after 7 P.M. in season from December 19 to April 14. Wednesdays and Sundays are casual, with Beach Party buffet luncheons and dinners.

Curtain Bluff's 63 accommodations are made up of appealing deluxe rooms on the windward beach in two-story buildings that have new full baths and decor as of fall 1994. Six pairs of these rooms have connecting doors. The more luxurious one- and two-bedroom suites that ascend on up the bluff have striking views from windswept balconies. Single bedrooms available here are called "Executive Deluxe Rooms" and feature balconies, baths, and private entrances on the ground level. These rooms are actually the second bedrooms of suites.

We've stayed in several accommodations, but we liked the one-bedroom suites the best. From the entrance you climb steps to a spacious white-tiled living room with a balcony. On the opposite side of the room is a raised terra-cotta-tiled courtyard fitted with a hammock and potted plants. Up a few steps more is a charming open-air dining room. Room service is available for all meals. Dinners here are highly recommended.

The two-room bath features an oversized bathtub, twin vanity basins, ceiling fan, lots of toiletries arranged in a rattan shell, and a tray with a filled ice bucket and complimentary Antiguan rum samples. The second room in the bath houses a big walk-in shower, bidet, toilet, and plenty of fluffy towels. Terry-cloth robes are supplied as well.

The cheery, balconied bedroom has twin closet spaces, a safe, a chest of drawers, a king-size bed, and a chaise longue with piles of pillows. Rattan and cane furnishings are cushioned in bright blues and greens or soft pastel cottons. The reading lights are first rate. You're only seconds from a telephone—there's even one in the bathroom—but no TVs, radios, or air-conditioning. Paddle fans and breezes through louvers and sliding glass doors control the temperature. Room don't have keys, but they can, of course, be locked from the inside.

Curtain Bluff's small boutique, in a cozy shop opposite reception, carries swimwear, souvenirs, and sundries. At Morris Bay Beach, next to the water-sports building, is a local market selling floral-printed clothing and handcrafts.

The resort's culinary pleasures are many. We had our first welcome cocktail and meal, an enormous lobster salad, in the main dining room due to our late arrival. For lunch, guests normally enjoy a splendid seaside terrace dining room and bar.

Before-dinner hors d'oeuvres are served in the round stone Sugar Mill Bar and terrace. Dinners are formal, multicourse affairs. The staff, dressed impeccably in uniforms, serve meals with choreographed efficiency. Swiss chef Ruedi Portmann, who has run Curtain Bluff's kitchen for about 30 years, and his pastry chef conduct their work in an immaculate, multiroomed kitchen. Dishes range from steaming callaloo soup to casserole of rabbit Forestière to charcoal-broiled veal steak and beef fillets to side servings of asparagus hollandaise, château potatoes, ending with a variety of tempting desserts like white chocolate mousse framboise. The food is consistently good, sometimes perfection. Curtain Bluff's 25,000-bottle wine cellar, is one of the very best in the Caribbean.

Howard Hulford is always delighted to conduct guests on a tour.

The Hulfords look after clientele as they would guests in their own home, with the able assistance of managing director Rob Sherman, general manager Cal Roberts, and a staff of 163 loyal employees. Refurbishing takes place during the five-month period when the resort is closed, so that everything is fresh for the fall and winter season.

Wise, sophisticated travelers will find charming Curtain Bluff a reliable, deluxe address in paradise.

CURTAIN BLUFF	RESERVATIONS
P.O. Box 288	Ms. Ruth Herd
Antigua, West Indies	Curtain Bluff
TEL: (809) 462-8400	68 East 93rd Street
FAX: (809) 462-8409	New York, NY 10128
	TEL: (212) 289-8888

Closed May 14 to October 10.

Rates: Double occupancy. *October 10 to December 18* and *April 15 to May 14:* Rooms, $495 to $675; Executive One-Bedroom Suite, $775; Executive Two-Bedroom Suite, $1,350; extra person $130. *December 19 to April 14:* Rooms, $595 to $775; Executive One-Bedroom Suite, $855; Executive Two-Bedroom Suite, $1,550; extra person, $140; children under 5, $65 per child per day when permitted.

Meal plan: FAP. All-inclusive rate covers all meals, beverages and bar drinks, afternoon tea, cocktail hors d'oeuvres, mail service/postage, and free scuba diving for certified guests.

Service charge: 10%.

Government tax: 8½%.

Children under 12 not permitted from January 10 to March 10; welcome all other times.

Credit cards: American Express only.

Galley Bay 🌴

On my first visit to Antigua many years ago, I asked a taxi driver what he thought was the best, most distinctive, small beachfront resort on the island. He answered without hesitation, "Galley Bay. Always has been." Off we went on a 30-minute trip from the airport. En route we passed through the outskirts of St. John's, the island's capital, and through a small community named Five Islands Village, located on the northwestern side of Antigua. The road leading off to Galley Bay was potholed and rutted, but the cab driver had been right. What I discovered was a deliciously isolated resort situated on one of Antigua's most sensational beaches: a curving half mile of sand, bordered by tall arched palm trees and sea grape. The accommodations, however, were showing signs of age. Edie Holbert, who opened Galley Bay in the sixties, was going to sell the place, her social hostessing days spent.

James Lane, who bought the resort in 1987, has made it his business not only to restore Galley Bay's former glory but also to systematically, substantially upgrade it. The hotel was scheduled to close for six weeks during the summer of 1994 for restaurant renovations. It's being redesigned and expanded with a seating area for 100 in addition to the open-air terrace. As of 1995 all accommodations will have attractive new bathroom plumbing fixtures, as well as new walkways throughout the property.

Swiss-born Peter Hoehm came to Galley Bay as manager in February 1989 to organize the resort. Under his direction, the hotel has blossomed. Unfortunately, in May 1994 he left, seeking new challenges. Meantime, the excellent news is that Galley Bay's new manager is Daniel Reid, formerly at Necker Island in the British Virgin Islands.

Galley Bay sits on 40 tranquil tropical acres between a large lagoon (excellent bird-watching here) and the ocean. The resort's 30 units consist of two very different kinds of accommodations. Private beachfront rooms with patios are located in single-story buildings (each has two double rooms) under palms, a few yards from the sea. These medium-sized rooms with terra-cotta-tile floors, attractive new tropical furnishings, and king-size or double beds, all covered with bright pastel fabrics, offer simple luxury. The accommodations have private patios, louvered windows, ceiling fans, coffeemakers, safes, and mini-refrigerators. The small, newly spruced-up baths with showers come with hair dryers and robes. Galley Bay has no TVs, radios, or pool.

For more exotic tastes there are picture-postcard huts called Gauguin Cottages, 50 yards from the ocean, on a lawn alongside a lagoon. Each charming hut consists of twin palm-thatched peaked-roof cottages connected by a thatch-covered breezeway. The exterior walls of the huts are half whitewashed and half classic African "wattle and daub" — thin woven tree branches. Interior walls are whitewashed; ceiling fans hang overhead.

The bedroom section of each has a king-size bed, bureau, sitting area, and adequate closet space. The breezeways lead to the bathroom side of the cottages. Bathrooms have brand-new fixtures. The huts remind me of luxury-class permanent-campsite safari living quarters.

The focal point of the hotel is a towering, wattle-roofed pyramid roof structure sitting over the bar and lounge. The spacious open-air lounge and entertainment area sweeps around one side of the pyramid to a terrace facing the beach. The terrace is lined with old-island-style planter's chair/lounges. Snacks, hors d'oeuvres, and cocktails are served here in the evening. In season, live entertainment might include a steel drum and guitar trio, piano music with a singer, or a steel band for the West Indian barbecue buffet on Saturday. The food for this special event is cooked on old-time coal pots and features loins of pork, ribs, and chicken accompanied by a variety of sauces, rice, and vegetables. Our dinner on a regular weeknight in March 1994 was good, but average. Service at dinner and throughout the hotel is always agreeable.

I can't comment on the newly designed restaurant, since I haven't seen it yet, but lunches served seaside are magical.

Galley Bay's rates are all-inclusive, and include meals, drinks, house wines and champagne, tennis, water sports (windsurfers, Sunfish, kayaks, catamarans, and snorkeling equipment), taxes, and service charges.

Typical dress at Galley Bay is very casual during the day, and guests prefer informal sportswear in the evenings, although they are asked not to wear jeans, shorts, or T-shirts after 7 P.M. in the bar and restaurant areas. The clientele is about 40% American, 30% British; the rest is a European mix.

At Galley Bay, you're ensconced in a remote, romantic hideaway, yet only minutes by car (and you'll need one) from several other hotels and downtown St. John's for shopping.

Galley Bay is for young-at-heart travelers of all ages seeking an unusual resort with a superior beach, comfortable lodgings, and a totally relaxed atmosphere. We hope the new restaurant and chef provide excellent food here, too.

GALLEY BAY
P.O. Box 305
Five Islands, St. John's
Antigua, West Indies
TEL: (809) 462-0302
FAX: (809) 462-4551

RESERVATIONS
Robert Reid Associates
TEL: (800) 223-6510

Open all year.
Rates: Double occupancy. *December 16 to January 10* and *January 22 to April 15:* From $440 to $560; extra person, $175. *January 11 to January 21* and *April 16 to May 15* and *November 1 to December 15:* From $385 to $495; extra person, $155. *May 16 to October 31:* From $335 to 445; extra person, $135.
Meal plan: FAP (all-inclusive rate covers meals, drinks, house wines, and champagne).
Service charge: Included.
Government tax: Included.
Children welcome except for month of February, when children under 8 are not permitted.
Credit cards accepted.

Jumby Bay Island ◣◢

In selecting a resort, discriminating guests consider four important criteria: environment, accommodations, cuisine, and service. For Jumby Bay Island, nature has provided the first, lavishly: surrealistically turquoise waters, white sandy beaches that seemingly stretch for miles, and a landscape lush with some 400 species of rare tropical flowers and foliage. The resort itself assures the other three: rooms and villas of understated elegance, a cuisine that's literally the talk of the Caribbean, and gracious, unobtrusive service.

WILLIAM K. ANDERSON,
VICE PRESIDENT — OPERATIONS

The ten-minute boat ride to Jumby Bay Island, off the northern coast of Antigua, acts as a decompression chamber from the harsh realities of life to the ultimate luxury of this 300-acre private island resort. The tone of your welcome to Jumby Bay is set aboard a catamaran launch where a mate, dressed in crisp whites, serves guests icy rum punches before registration. The welcome continues upon arrival at the dock, where ladies are handed dainty orchid bouquets. Guests are then escorted to their quarters in a white minibus, which follows winding pathways on a brief tour of the resort's principal facilities.

The best luxury resort seemingly functions effortlessly, but actually requires tremendous organization, a competent, hardworking staff, and, like any premier hotel in the world, the ability to anticipate every requirement of its guests. Jumby Bay Island has mastered the delicate formula. The resort is all-inclusive: Everything from transportation from and to the airport, boat launch service (to and from Antigua), all meals, drinks, house wines and champage with meals, to the use of three tennis courts (two lighted), Sunfish, floats, sailboards, waterskiing and snorkeling gear, bicycles, croquet, a putting green, and even guided tours, is covered in the rates. An exercise facility is coming soon.

Meantime, there's always work to be done. Jumby Bay continually strives to offer imaginative, top-quality amenities. New in 1994 were yards and yards of artfully framed diaphanous mosquito netting hanging over the beds. What enchanting gossamer incubators they are. At turn-down each night, orchid blossoms are placed on bed pillows. Another fragrant amenity is the introduction of Hermès toiletries.

Upon arrival in their accommodations, guests find an iced bottle of champagne, a pitcher of lemonade or tea, mineral waters, a variety of sodas, and a platter of dried fruits—mango, pear, papaya, and apricots—as well as cookies and biscuits. An ice bucket is replenished twice daily; there's no need for a refrigerator.

On our latest visit, we were booked into one of the dozen rondavels, the first accommodations built at Jumby Bay Island—small cottages dotting the manicured lawns from the dock and central activities area (that includes the breakfast and lunch dining pavilion, expansive bar and banquetted lounge terraces, boutique, reception, and tennis courts) to the southern-positioned Estate House. The 26 other deluxe rooms at Jumby Bay are found in newer accommodations in the two-story seaside Spanish-style villa, Pond Bay House, or in an adjacent sprinkling of separate two-room villas—all near the northern end of Jumby Bay Beach.

Having stayed in all types of rooms (eight two-bedroom villas and some fabulous private villas also are available as rentals), we prefer the Pond Bay House second-floor accommodations for privacy and views. These lovely spaces, actually mini-suites, are decorated with cheery pastel stripe and print fabrics on rattan sofas and chairs, and king-size beds. Ceiling fans, numerous louvered windows and doors, and quarry-tile floors act as cooling devices. There are no telephones, TVs, radios, or telephones to disturb the tranquility. For wake-up calls, a courier gently taps on the door.

The white-and-aqua-tiled bathrooms are extra-spacious with twin basins that seem miles apart. (Hair dryers, wall-to-wall mirrors, and assorted Hermès toiletries await all guests.) In a separate area are large open-air showers, a toilet and bidet, plus piles of plush towels and a pair of terry-cloth robes. On the first floor, louvered doors adjacent to the shower open onto a lushly planted, walled garden. Closets are walk-in size with wall safes. All rooms have private patio or balcony lounging areas.

Ronvadels are smaller in size, but totally comfortable. We enjoyed room 11 because of its expansive view over the grounds to the sea and a nearby private speck of beach with bohios and chaises, as well as the proximity to the Estate House restaurant—a two-minute walk away.

The library and bar, are situated on the second floor of the handsome 200-year-old great house. Outside are breezy verandas, sitting areas, and twinkling views of Antigua.

Jumby Bay's attractive guests, from young women and men through affluent older generations (the majority Americans, followed by British and other Europeans), gather at the bar each evening for drinks and hors d'oeuvres in a lively cocktail-party atmosphere. Eventually, in pairs and groups, they repair downstairs to the open-air terrace dining room.

Executive chef Rex Hale composes excellent dishes from tender chilled Barbuda lobster with tomato and ginger vinaigrette and peppered tuna with roasted potato salad to conch and herb risotto, and sesame-crusted salmon with wild mushrooms and leek ragout. Meals conclude with fruit and cheese, and superb confections from pastries to frozen fruit delicacies. Lunches at the Beach Pavilion combine buffets of seafood salads, pastas, delicious pizzas, and quiches with such daily grilled specials as tuna or halibut. Mountains of tropical fruits and a first-rate cheese tray are always present. Chef Hale's cuisine focuses on light foods with Caribbean touches. Lighter doesn't always describe the specials at breakfast: After perusing the daily *TimesFax*, we chose from a menu that included coconut-crusted french toast with local fruit and banana-and-cinnamon pancakes with Antiguan rum syrup.

The resort's two main beaches are vast white-powder sand crescents. Facing west for all-day sun, Jumby Bay Beach is lined with sea grape and palm trees, hammocks, thatched-roof wooden umbrellas, and lounge chairs.

Pasture Bay Beach, a popular nesting area for the endangered Hawksbill sea turtle, is deliciously isolated, facing windward. From June to November, biologists document the turtles' mating habits. Guests hoping to observe the phenomenon may leave instructions for a wake-up call when sightings occur—from 8 P.M. to 4:30 A.M.

Quayside Beach, fronting the new Harbor Beach Villas, is small but fine for guests booked nearby. Beach-bar service is offered at all beaches. The only swimming pools are in the villas.

Jumby Bay's accommodations, public areas, and many walkways are engulfed in blooming tropical gardens. We especially like the beautiful orchids and magenta bougainvilleas planted in wide-mouthed shallow pots like immense technicolor bonsai. Throughout, artist Fran Deardon has transformed broad white wall spaces into colorful floral canvases.

Jumby Bay hasn't ignored entertainment. A local steel band plays for beach barbecues and Caribbean buffets. Jazz is featured in the Pond Bay House on Saturday nights. Mixed round robins, welcome receptions, garden tours, and champagne sunset cruises keep guests more than happily occupied.

I should mention that several times a day jets roar by Jumby Bay Island from Antigua's

V.C. Bird Airport, only a short distance across the sea. The sound passes quickly, and I've never actually heard guests here complain, as if it's a given, like a spot of rain. Don't let a spot of sound prevent you from discovering ravishing, sunny Jumby Bay Island.

JUMBY BAY ISLAND
P.O. Box 243
St. John's, Antigua, West Indies
TEL: (809) 462-6000
FAX: (809) 462-6020

RESERVATIONS
TEL: (800) 421-9016

Open all year.

Rates: Double occupancy. Rates include transportation from and to the airport, private launch service, U.S. newspapers, a weekly sunset cruise, and postage. *Mid-December to mid-April:* Deluxe Rooms, $975; Two- and Three-Bedroom Luxury Villas, $1,525. *Mid-April through October:* Deluxe Rooms, $645; Two- and Three-Bedroom Luxury Villas, $1,195. *November to mid-December:* Deluxe Rooms, $745; Two- and Three-Bedroom Luxury Villas, $1,325. Extra person in Deluxe Rooms, $175. Extra person in Villas, $300 to $500. Several other privately owned, exclusive villas and guest cottages are available as rentals. Contact Jumby Bay Island for information and rates. All villa rates based on resort's all-inclusive plan.

Meal plan: FAP. (All-inclusive rate covers all meals, unlimited cocktails, house wine with meals, hors d'oeuvres, welcome bottle of champagne, and Jumby Bay Rum departure gift.)

Service charge: 10%.

Government tax: 8½%.

Children over 8 welcome.

Credit cards accepted.

A NOTEWORTHY OPTION

Long Bay Hotel

In 1996, the Long Bay Hotel will celebrate its thirtieth birthday. It's a small, old-fashioned Caribbean resort that has an easygoing atmosphere with personalized services. Located on the northeastern coast of Antigua, it rests on a point of land straddling a calm lagoon and a quarter-mile-long wonderful white sand beach with a good reef. Checking in here is like returning for yearly family reunions to a never-changing, quiet aunt and uncle's unpretentious, orderly place—the reason, I think, that so many American and European families return each year. Although I like it very much, it's not for everyone, especially those seeking up-to-the-minute decor or amenities like TVs and daily copies of *TimesFax.* However, the rooms have recently been redecorated.

Jackie and Jacques Lafaurie have owned the hotel since 1961, but turned the management over to their son, Chris, and David Woodcock a few years ago. Guests can sense the reassuring heritage here. Travelers also come because this hotel lacks the frenzy of the more conventional "try too hard" hotels, such as the Pineapple Beach Club at the opposite, western end of Long Bay Beach. On my last visit to this nicely looked-after, all-inclusive 140-room retreat, heaps of suitcases were piled in the entranceway, and the youngish to middle-aged lodgers lined up in lounges at the pool all appeared to be holding a full colada or rum punch in their hands, as if it were an organized game activity. Still, Pineapple Beach offers entertaining diversions when things get too quiet back at Long Bay, especially for younger folks.

Long Bay features 20 rooms in a two-story building on the lagoon facing a dock, and six cottages spread on or near the water's edge around the activity in the main building's lobby and bar lounge, game room and library, and dining room. The newest addition, a bayview villa complex that can house up to eight people, is really a one-bedroom cottage house adjacent to a main house with a living room, kitchen and dining area, and lots of beds, and a separate annex studio. The most coveted address at Long Bay is The View House, which looks out over both the ocean and the lagoon. It has one bedroom with a queen-size bed, two baths, a living room with twin sofa beds, and a kitchen. The hotel accommodations have no air-conditioning, and only the villa complex rooms have ceiling fans.

Long Bay's water-sports center offers scuba diving, waterskiing, windsurfing, snorkeling, and sailing. There is one tennis court.

Dinners are set menus of pleasant continental and island fare (nothing exotic), graciously served in the arched, stone-walled dining room with a lagoon view, under ceiling fans. My favorite dining spot is at the Beach House terrace restaurant, a short walk from the accommodations and main facilities, where lunches and a weekly beach barbecue are served right next to the sea. Guests plop down on old-style planter's chairs on the lovely beach. It brings back nostalgic memories of "the way the Caribbean used to be." Warmly recommended for unfussy people seeking an out-of-the-way refuge in Antigua.

LONG BAY HOTEL
P.O. Box 442
Antigua, West Indies
TEL: (809) 463-2005
FAX: (809) 463-2439

RESERVATIONS
Resorts Management, Inc.
The Carriage House
201½ East 29th Street
New York, NY 10016
TEL: (800) 225-4255 *or*
(212) 696-4566
FAX: (212) 689-1598

Closed June 1 to mid-October.
Rates: Double occupancy. *Mid-October to December 15* and *April 1 to May 15:* Rooms, $250; Cottages and Villa, $165 to $395. Extra person in Cottages or Villa, $75. *December 16 to March 31:* Rooms, $320 to $365; Cottages and Villa, $220 to $420. Extra person in Cottages or Villa, $100.

Meal plan: MAP (includes breakfast and dinner) for Room guests only, available at $55 per person per day. EP (no meals) for Cottage or Villa guests.
Service charge: 10%.
Government tax: 8½%.
Children welcome.
Credit cards accepted.

GREAT EXPECTATIONS

Carlisle Bay Club

On the next bay over to the south from Curtain Bluff at Old Road Village is Carlisle Bay Club, a luxurious condominium resort hotel. All apartments (32 at the moment, with 56 more units planned in future phases), in two two-story buildings, are situated on a prime Antiguan location, set back only a few yards from its own exquisite palm-lined west-facing beach.

British-born Deborah Green, the hotel's guest services manager and sales director, took me on a full tour of the nicely landscaped premises in spring 1993. What I saw were quality-furnished, air-conditioned, spacious, superior one- and three-bedroom apartments with white tile floors throughout; attractive, roomy, fully equipped kitchens; and 10 × 16½-foot seafront patios. Chairs and lounges on the patios had thick, comfortable cushions—no standard strap outdoor furnishings here. The ground-level units open directly onto the beach, a few steps down.

Back then, Carlisle Bay Club already had 10 all-weather, hard tennis courts ready for play. At the center of the courts rests a large, handsome two-story observation pavilion with a pro shop, first-floor bar, and veranda. A resident professional will be engaged to supervise the courts.

The hotel has failed to open as this book was getting ready to go to press, due to a continuing string of unanticipated delays, but Ms. Green assured me the hotel will be in operation by winter season 1994–95.

I revisited Carlisle Bay only a few weeks before my deadline and here's what I can report had been completed: an outside beach bar and grill, a freeform freshwater pool on a big terrace adjacent to the club house's main restaurant, and a bar and lounge with a baby grand piano, ready to be played. The restaurant opening had been further postponed because of some needed work in the kitchen.

Furnishings in the breezy lobby were attractive, featuring comfortable chairs and sofas. I especially liked interesting odd pieces like the imported carved-wooden-elephant chairs. The ground's plantings were thriving and, quite frankly, everything looked neat and orderly.

Plans for the winter season include a fully equipped fitness center and a full range of expected water sports. Scuba diving, deep-sea fishing, and yacht charters and car rentals can be arranged. A boutique for resortwear and necessities is also being designed. Ms. Green and manager Gordon Gowers will be looking after things.

Carlisle Bay Club has the potential to become one of Antigua's outstanding resorts, especially for tennis lovers. Ten tennis courts! We'll just have to wait and see.

CARLISLE BAY CLUB
P.O. Box 1515
St. John's, Antigua, West Indies
TEL: (809) 462-1377
FAX: (809) 462-1365

Open all year.
Rates: Double occupancy. *December 15 to May 14:* One-Bedroom Apartment, $295; third person, $125. *May 15 to December 14:* One-Bedroom Apartment, $195; third person, $83. Three-Bedroom Apartments, child rate reductions, and other information available upon request.
Meal plan: EP. MAP (breakfast and dinner), available at $50 per person per day.
Service charge: 10%.
Government tax: 8½%.
Children welcome.
Credit cards accepted.

Recommended Restaurants

ANTIGUA'S FINEST*

* **Curtain Bluff**, 462-8400 (Curtain Bluff Hotel on Old Road). Elegant dining room and fine food impeccably served. Jackets and ties required for men most nights in winter. Nightly entertainment and dancing. First-rate wine cellar. Reservations required. (See resort listing, page 50.) Expensive.

* **Jumby Bay Island**, 462-6000 (10-minute boat ride from pier beyond Beachcomber Hotel near airport). Reservations necessary for wonderful lunches or dinners at this splendid resort. Fine wines. (See resort listing, page 54.) Expensive to very expensive.

* **La Perruche**, 460-3040 (English Harbour). The current "in" dining spot on the island. Imaginative French West Indian dishes from duck to lobster in candlelit indoor/outdoor restaurant. Good wines. Moderate to expensive.

* **Alberto's**, 460-3007 (Willoughby Bay). Receives high marks from Howard Hulford, Curtain Bluff's owner. Excellent Italian dishes and seafood served in a breezy gazebo. Fine wines. Expensive.

* **Le Bistro**, 462-3881 (Country Club Drive in Hodges Bay). Consistently excellent French cuisine in attractive inland country restaurant. Food, service, and wines stand up to its good reputation. Expensive.

* **Chez Pascal**, 462-3232 (Cross and Tanner streets, St. John's). Chef Pascal Milliat from Lyon dishes up commendable French cuisine in a 150-year-old town house and art gallery. Garden or inside dining room. Moderate to expensive.
* **L'Auberge de Paris**, 462-1223 (Trade Winds Hill overlooking Dickenson Bay). Romantic dining experience in terrace restaurant. Chef combines French and West Indian food successfully. Moderate to expensive.
* **Shirley Heights Lookout**, 460-1785 (All Saints, overlooking Nelson's Dockyard and English Harbour). The star is for good food, fabulous views, and fun, especially on Sunday afternoons—a barbecue of lobster and steak is served, usually to a gregarious crowd who've come with a big appetite to party. Feast from 3 to 6 P.M. accompanied by a steel band. Reggae takes over from 6 P.M. on. There's also a bar and gift shop. Moderate to expensive.

OTHER DEPENDABLE CHOICES

Le Cap Horn, 460-1194 (English Harbour). Everyone's jamming into this new eatery for Argentinian steak, grilled lobster, and great wood-oven-cooked pizzas. Moderate to expensive.

Calypso Restaurant and Bar, 462-1965 (Upper Redcliffe Street, St. John's). Charming, colorful dining room serving fish and seafood and West Indian specialties, satisfying salads, and sandwiches for lunch. Nice spot in town to rest and have a drink. Open from 10 A.M. to five P.M. only. Inexpensive to moderate.

Coconut Grove, 462-1538 (Dickenson Bay). Beachfront all-day dining in funky thatch-roofed bar and restaurant. Seafood is excellent. Nightly live entertainment. Moderate.

Lemon Tree, 462-1969 (Long Street, St. John's). Pretty little air-conditioned restaurant in town. Well-prepared American/Continental selections. Live entertainment most of the time. Moderate.

Hemingway's, 462-2763 (St. Mary's Street, St. John's). Everyone still seems to show up on the second-floor veranda of this West Indian restaurant to meet over lunches of fresh grilled fish or seafood. Terrific noisy place. Moderate to expensive.

There are many other good dining possibilities on Antigua, particularly at hotels like **Hawksbill Beach Resort, The Inn at English Harbour, Blue Waters, Galley Bay**, and **Half Moon Resort**—all with sea views.

Informal places worth a visit are **Harmony Hall Restaurant** and **The Lobster Pot** at Runaway Beach Club. For West Indian and Créole food in St. John's, try **Brother B's** on Long Street, **Commissioner Grill** on Commissioner Alley, **Kaieteur Créole Corner** on Lower Nevis Street, and the **Curry House** at Redcliffe Quay.

The **Crazy Cactus Cantina** on All Saints Road is the island's first Mexican restaurant. Go to **Pizza's on the Quay** at Redcliffe Quay or **Al Porto** at Jolly Harbour for a slice fix.

Recommended Shopping

Shoppers in downtown St. John's will find a mix of modern shopping complexes and old-island perusing. Midday bumper-to-bumper traffic, narrow sidewalks, and potholes make maneuvering about an unpleasant obstacle course. Still, a lot is going on and I always make it my business to head for two shops first: **The Coco Shop**, 462-0825 (St. Mary's Street, plus a branch at the airport). Open since 1948, this unpretentious but delightful store sells a bit of everything, most of it locally made—fragrances, baskets and other handcrafts, clothing, pottery, jewelry, and books. Favorites are small, pretty shell-bordered circles of netting used to cover pitchers, bowls, and bottles, to keep critters out.

The Map Shop, 462-3993 (St. Mary's Street). Good selection of old and new maps, books of local interest, postcards, and stationery supplies.

Island Newstand, in Camacho's Arcade on High Street, carries international newspapers, magazines, and books.

The two prime duty-free shopping areas are Redcliffe Quay and Heritage Quay.

Redcliffe Quay, an area at Lower Redcliffe Street and a former slave compound until 1834, is now a window-shopper's and buyer's bazaar. Over 30 shops, restaurants, and stores are located here. New and most appealing here is **Debra Moises's** designer boutique. It features original gauzy natural fabrics and silk clothing and enchanting hair combs, barrettes, and accessories. Also **Base** for casual clothes. Among the best of the other shops are **Bona**, for imported china and glassware, ceramics, antiques, and household accessories; **Jacaranda**, a Caribbean collection of clothing, handcrafts and artwork, herbs and spices, and more; **A Thousand Flowers** boutique, which carries island resortwear; **Toucan Crafts & Gifts** sells pottery, baskets, and wood carvings; and **The Goldsmitty** jewelry store, featuring designs by Hans Smit, is worth investigating. Also here is **Iris**, a shop carrying imported Egyptian handcrafts and things, and cotton clothing. **Seahorse Studios** carries original art, pottery, and other nice choices.

At **Heritage Quay**, a newer shopping center with a casino, you'll mingle with cruise-ship passengers, as it's situated at the dock for their convenience. There are such well-known shops as **Little Switzerland, Gucci, La Parfumerie, The "Land" Shop,** and **Colombian Emeralds**, plus others such as **Beach Stuff, Base Island Arts, Naf-Naf, Sunseekers,** and **World of Leather**. **The Cigar Shop** sells Cuban and other quality cigars.

There's also shopping at **Jolly Harbour Marina & Shopping Centre**. Several boutiques already mentioned have branches there—**Beach Stuff, Jacaranda, Seahorse Studios,** and **La Parfumerie**. **The Magazine Rack**, for international newspapers and magazines, and books, is also located there.

At **The New Pottery** at The Bucket in Coolidge, 2 miles north of the airport, you never know what'll be in stock—leftover ashtrays made for the islands' hotels or gaily hand-painted hangable fish platters, ceramic-fruit lamp bases, vases, and so on.

Cockleshell Pottery, 462-0471 (Fort Road, underneath Cockleshell Restaurant). Here you'll find a wide variety of Kim Warman's fetching ceramic creations. Especially nice are her personalized house plaques. A week's notice is required to have your own created. She does not ship orders.

Harmony Hall in Freetown near Nonsuch Bay is a lovely art gallery, craft shop, and restaurant; it's fashioned after Ocho Rios' Harmony Hill in Jamaica. It's a bit of a trek to get there, but after shopping, there's a pool to cool off in and a pleasant terrace open-air dining room. The bar's in a historic sugar mill. At the inland **Sea View Farm,** with a lovely view of Parham Sound, several families continue to pass on a tradition of pottery making. Watch artists at work and buy a figurine or vase.

Antigua's many hotels and resorts all have boutiques.

Provisions for Your Island Pantry

The Epicurean on Old Parham Road carries gourmet items plus fresh meat and produce.

Bryson's Supermarket and **Dew's Supermarket**, both on Long Street, are fine for regular groceries, as is **Bailey's Supermarket** in Falmouth Harbour. **Island Provision Ltd.** on the Airport Road sells mostly wholesale meats, poultry, fish, produce, and wines, but is also open to the public. Visit **the market** for fresh produce on Friday and Saturday mornings. Be certain to try Antigua's "black pineapples": they aren't black at all, but they *are* small, sweet, juicy, and delicious.

Susie's Hot Sauce on Upper North Street sells fiery condiments to splash on grilled fish or take home as gifts. The **West Indian Coffee and Tea Shop**, which sells island specialties, is located in Jolly Harbour Marina & Shopping Centre.

Quin Farara's Liquor Stores are located at Heritage Quay; Jolly Harbour Marina; Nugent Avenue, and on Long Street. Other liquor stores are **Manual Dias Liquor Store** on the corner of Long and Market streets, **Buyright** on Lower All Saints Road, and **Wadadli Smoke & Booze** in Heritage Quay.

Beer drinkers ought to try Antigua's own **Wadadli** brand produced in the island's new brewery.

Useful Information

V. C. Bird International Airport has been remodeled, expanded, and painted a blazing tangerine color. A taxi driver confided to me that the color was selected so the pilots could see it glowing in the dark. In any case, it's now a much more comfortable place, especially the baggage-claim area and waiting lounge.

Antigua & Barbuda Adventure Tourist Guide and *The Antiguan Guide to Antigua and Barbuda* are very helpful giveaway publications.

Apart from the island's glorious beaches, purported to number 365—one for every day of the year—water sports and sailing are major delights. Our favorite is **Darkwood**, a western expanse of sand that's never crowded. Fishermen bring their catches from small boats right up from the shore.

Antigua Sailing Week, held each year in the spring, is one of the most popular events in the Caribbean. It brings hordes of young visitors, sailors, salty-dog types, and spectators, so consider the pros and cons of the festivities in terms of crowded hotels, restaurants, and so on, particularly in the English Harbour area.

Drives around the island are worthwhile, but the roads are poor and rarely marked, so keep a good map in the front seat. **Hertz, Avis, Budget, Dollar**, and **National** all have offices in Antigua.

English Harbour and **Shirley Heights** are fascinating, both historically and visually. Be sure to drive through the **Fig Tree Hills** ("fig trees" are what West Indians call banana trees) en route to Curtain Bluff. The road winds through a dense rain forest of giant silk-cotton, breadfruit, mango, avocado, coconut, and soursop trees. Stop at the **Fig Tree Drive Culture Shoppe**, a tiny roadside store, for some fresh figs (bananas) or papayas and a cold drink. Owner Elaine Duberry will greet you with a smile and provide local information. She also sells beautiful shells.

A day trip to **Barbuda**, Antigua's sister island, blessed with stunning white and pink sand beaches, is a worthwhile experience. (For information about Barbuda and flights to the island, see page 102.)

For a marvelous day of snorkeling, a West Indian lunch, and sunbathing, consider a day trip to **Prickly Pear Island**, just off Antigua's northeast coast. **Miguel's Holiday Adventures** will take you there. For information call 461-0361.

The **Cedar Valley Golf Club** has an 18-hole championship course. Call 462-2101 to make arrangements.

ARUBA

ACCOMMODATIONS

ARUBA'S BEST
Hyatt Regency Aruba Resort & Casino

RECOMMENDED RESTAURANTS

RECOMMENDED SHOPPING

USEFUL INFORMATION

≈ ≈

Accommodations

ARUBA'S BEST

Hyatt Regency Aruba Resort & Casino

The best luxury resort on Aruba is the 12-acre Hyatt Regency Aruba Resort & Casino, which opened October 1, 1990. Located on the island's southwestern coast on magnificent Palm Beach, it's eight miles from Queen Beatrix Airport and five miles from Aruba's capital, Oranjestad. Granted, it's large. The hotel has 360 rooms, the majority of which are in a nine-story building; the rest in four- and five-story wings. And, of course, groups and conventions book into the hotel. But in Aruba, the best happens to be big. What makes the difference between the Hyatt and most of the island's other hotels is that, large as it is, it offers its guests outstanding services, amenities, and stylishness throughout, including the beautifully appointed deluxe rooms and we-go-out-of-our-way features. To me, little things always count, such as the room numbers on pretty ceramic tiles on walls by each door, and receiving butter at lunch piped through a pastry tube into a tiny black ceramic boat, instead of a pat wrapped in foil. Several people here must be employed as full-time cloth-napkin folders, so intricate are the designs.

At the Hyatt I never felt crushed, whether I was in the spacious, palm-lined lobby, accented with a high wooden-beamed ceiling that supports huge chandeliers; on the vast pearly white beach; or in the handsome 8,000-square-foot, three-level freshwater pool, a Hyatt trademark. True, two tennis courts aren't enough for the number of guests, and I did have to wait in line a few moments to get my turn in the two-story twisting water slide—an exhilarating experience for grown-ups and children alike.

Everything during my visit was smoothly orchestrated by a well-trained staff and management, headed by Cuban-born manager Carlos Cabrera, who has been with Hyatt for nearly twenty years.

However, the hotel isn't for everyone, just as Aruba isn't for everyone. First I'll tell you a little about the island itself.

Aruba is a sunseeker's fantasyland, situated 18 miles north of Venezuela, 12 degrees north of the equator, and outside the hurricane zone. The sun shines an average of eight hours a day, with only about 20 inches of rain annually. (Water is supplied by a desalination plant, the world's second largest.) Temperatures, normally in the 80s, are bearable because the steady, and often strong, northeasterly tradewinds provide a natural coolant. The desertlike, low-lying island lacks lush tropical greenery, except at the hotels. The northern, windward coast, with ferocious seas, is a no-man's-land. Vegetation that you will see on a tour around the island includes aloe plants, cactus fields, incredible cactus fences, and haunting divi-divi trees. These skinny-trunked specimens have small green leaves on thin, wispy, thickly woven branches that look like Elsa Lanchester's hairdo in *The Bride of Frankenstein.* The verdant coifs are permanently bent the way the wind blows them. As the tour guides and brochures promote, the divi-divis point toward the west-coast beaches and Oranjestad, where the action is.

Action on Aruba means duty-free shopping, gambling, wonderful water-sports facilities, good food, and lots of hotels, many of them high-rises. Building continues along Eagle and Palm beaches. Towering cranes loom like giant tinkertoys swinging and swaying. Some sit dormant, halted by developers' financial problems.

Arubans are genuinely friendly people. Their musical native tongue, Papiamento, is derived from Arawak, Spanish, Dutch, and African dialects. Dutch, Spanish, and English also are spoken. The other language in Aruba is resort-island-speak—low-rise and high-rise time-shares. Salespeople in kiosks, in shopping malls, in booths at hotels, and on the street offer incentives to prospective time-share buyers in exchange for a little time to see for yourself and hear a pitch. These well-advertised incentives are "free gifts"—anything from a photograph of your arrival at the airport or a cocktail, to dinner or casino chips. This traveler found the whole process a complete turn-off. Still, I like Aruba a lot, and the good far outweighed the bad at the Hyatt.

The Hyatt Regency's pink buildings are vaguely Spanish in style with red-tiled roofs and arched doorways at the ground level. Gardens flourish. Room balconies are, for the most part, lean-out types with no space for chairs or chaises.

Decor, executed splendidly by Hirsch Bedner & Associates of Atlanta, Georgia, is a funky Caribbean/Spanish kind of modern art deco. Draperies are speckled prints. Wildly colorful cottons cover beds, skirted with green/blue dust ruffles. Amenities in the rooms include phones, remote-control cable TV, air-conditioning, ceiling fans, clock radios, minibars, and safes. Suites have wet bars.

For ablutions, bathrooms are the kind you'd be happy with at home, with tubs and showers. Full mirrors over the basin are met on each side with wallpapered walls of pale peach printed with white feathers and black confetti. Floor tiles are black-and-white-checkerboard squares. Wall-mounted hair dryers and all the toiletries you could possibly need are supplied. I found myself asking, What, no lipstick?

Sumptuous breakfast buffets and dinners are served in Las Ruinas Del Mar, an indoor/outdoor modern-day Aruban gold mine, straddling a 5,000-square-foot lagoon. Rotating dinner menus might begin with cioppino salad or pasta paella and continue with Caribbean crab cakes or tender lamb shish kebabs served with couscous. Try the fresh lemon tart with raspberries, or the chocolate walnut terrine for dessert.

At the seaside Palm Grill, also indoor/outdoor, I savored a huge, tasty Cobb salad. Others sampled calamari fritters, grilled swordfish, and a variety of hefty sandwiches, plates piled high with crisp, curly french fries. The Grill is adjacent to its thatch-roofed bar. Both are open 24 hours a day. *Tapas* are available at Olé Restaurant. For pasta there's Café Piccolo, an Italian trattoria. Drinks can be also be had in the Hyatt's two other bars, Al Fresco, off the lobby, or The Balashi, which has a swim-up bar. Room service is available 24 hours a day.

Hyatt's own diving and water-sports facility, Red Sail Sports, is a full-service operation. Sailing crafts and beach toys include Hobie Cats, Sunfish, paddle boats, Yamaha Wave Runners and more. *Balia,* a 50-foot catamaran, sails daily for snorkeling and sunset and dinner cruises. PADI certification programs and deep-sea fishing expeditions are available.

If you're not exhausted after all that, the Hyatt has two lighted tennis courts and a complete health and fitness center.

Camp Hyatt's daily program for children between the ages of 3 and 15 years of age is led by professional camp counselors. Water sports, games, arts and crafts, lunch and sea excursions, and movies are just part of the itinerary. Kids get special rates, menus, room service, and check-in packets. Book in advance.

There are several upscale shops and a beauty salon.

Last but not least is the 10,000-square-foot "Carnival in Rio"–theme casino. Several steps down just off the lobby, it boasts a small, raised platform stage above the bar for nightly entertainment. If one can call a casino attractive, this is. And it's lively and can be fun, too, just like Aruba.

HYATT REGENCY ARUBA RESORT & CASINO
85 L. G. Smith Boulevard
Palm Beach, Aruba
TEL: (011-297-8) 3-1234
FAX: (011-297-8) 3-5478

RESERVATIONS
Hyatt Resorts Corporation
TEL: (800) 233-1234

Open all year.
Rates: Double occupancy. *December 20 to April 6:* $340 to $430; One-Bedroom Suite, $600 to $1,000; Two-Bedroom Suite, $825 to $1,265. *April 7 to June 1:* $155 to $250; One-Bedroom Suite, $420 to $700; Two-Bedroom Suite, $635 to $950. *June 2 to September 30:* $125 to $240; One-Bedroom Suite $225 to $600; Two-Bedroom Suite $420 to $800. *October 1 to December 19:* Rates upon request.
Meal plan: EP. MAP (includes breakfast and dinner): $50 per person per day; children 15 and under, $30 each per day. Gourmet MAP: $70 per person per day; children 15 or under, $40 each per day.
Service charge: 11%.
Government tax: 5%.
Children welcome.
Credit cards accepted.

Recommended Restaurants

ARUBA'S FINEST*

* **Papiamento**, 2-4544 or 3-2135 (Washington 61, Noord, a few minutes' drive from Palm Beach). Best intimate dining experience in Aruba. Quality meals served in Lenie and Eduardo Ellis' own home (she's hostess, he's chef). Dine in charming indoor room or outside (preferable) on the expansive garden terrace under palms and other trees around the swimming pool. Select from small menu offering such dishes as seafood pasta with saffron and spinach sauce, chicken breast with fresh fruit and Grand Marnier, or dishes "on the stone"—delicious seafood, chicken, or beef served sizzling on Italian marble stone. Fresh herbs from the Ellises' garden enhance the cuisine. A favorite with locals. A quiet, romantic spot for individual couples; no tour groups. Good wines. Expensive.

* **Chez Mathilde**, 3-4968 (Havenstraat 23, Oranjestad). Fine French food served in 19th-century Aruban house. Must dress for dinner. Good wines. Expensive.

* **Las Ruinas Del Mar** and **Palms**, 3-1234 (Hyatt Regency Aruba, 85 L. G. Smith Boulevard, Palm Beach). Both first rate. (See resort listing, page 67.) Moderate to expensive.

* **Brisas Del Mar**, 4-7718 (Savaneta 222, southeast end of the island, a 20-minute drive from Palm Beach). A long-standing favorite casual seaside restaurant producing fresh seafood dishes like conch fritters, turtle or fisherman's soup, lobster salad, baby shark, and coco shrimp. Peach Melba or quesillo are the best desserts. Moderate to expensive.

OTHER DEPENDABLE CHOICES

There are more than 100 restaurants in Aruba including those in hotels, and many are very good. These are at the top of my list:

Le Petit Café Restaurant, 2-6577 (Downtown Main Street on corner Square). Pretty pink and white façade outside, cozy café downstairs, more formal dining room and bar upstairs, evenings. Friendly service. Variety of local and Continental dishes, although famous for "on the stone" meat, chicken, and shrimp dishes. Nothing fussy, but good. There's also a branch at the Americana Hotel. Moderate.

Boonoonoonoos, 3-1888 (Wilhelminastraat 18, Oranjestad). Funky, small, air-conditioned restaurant with party decorations. Good place to take children; special dishes for the "Little Ones" include Steak Piggy Wiggly and Chicken Tok Tok. Try Aruban and Caribbean dishes like keshi yena, an Aruban chicken casserole baked in cheese, mountain chicken Montserrat (frog legs), Jamaican jerk ribs, and curried chicken Trinidad. Reasonably priced wines. Moderate to expensive.

Driftwood, 3-2515 (Klipstraat 12, Oranjestad). Aruban fresh seafood. Moderate.

Charlie's Bar, 4-5086 (Zeppenveldstraat 56, San Nicolas, half an hour's drive from Palm Beach). Famous island institution and pit stop created by the late Charlie Brouns,

Sr. His son Charlie Jr. has taken over. The establishment celebrated its 50th anniversary in September 1991. Rather close streetside bar and restaurant has everything imaginable hanging from the ceiling and attached to the walls. Lots of character, and Jumbo Dumbo Shrimp is great. San Nicolas is a bit of a ghost town since Exxon's Lago Refinery shut down. Charlie's can be great fun, but it's not for everyone. Moderate.

For local Aruban atmosphere and food, try **Mi Cushina Restaurant** in Savaneta, **Mama & Papa's** in Dakata Shopping Center, **Gasparito** (also an art gallery) and **Buccaneer**, both in Gasparito, and **Old Cunucu House** near Palm Beach. For marvelous steaks go to **The Cattle Baron**, L. G. Smith Boulevard 228, **El Gaucho** in Oranjestad, **The Flame** in Noord near L. G. Smith Boulevard, **Twinklebones** at the Turibana Plaza, or **The Rib Room** at the Golden Tulip Hotel at L. G. Smith Boulevard 81. The famous **Bali Floating Restaurant** at the pier in Oranjestad, once a delightful hokey Indonesian place to dine on 20-plus-dish rijsttafel, has sadly lost its sparkle with the current owners. Find good Italian food at **Ristorante Valentino** in the Caribbean Palm Village, and **La Paloma Restaurant** in Oranjestad. **Javanese** and **Chinese** restaurants also are plentiful in Aruba.

Recommended Shopping

Shopping in Aruba is, as the local officials claim, paradise. With new malls and shopping centers, shops on Main Street, stores and boutiques in the hotels and at the airport, inveterate shoppers will find merchandise from touristy souvenirs to good buys and items of excellent quality. Travelers are allowed $600 per person, including children, from free-zone areas as duty-free purchases. A full morning or afternoon in Oranjestad will cover Aruba's main shopping districts at the various complexes, including **Harbour Town**, **On the Square**, **Seaport Village Mall** and **Sonesta Hotel Arcade**, **Holland Aruba Mall**, **Main Street**, and the **Alhambra Shopping Bazaar**. Here are some suggestions, but there's lots more.

Art galleries and handcrafts: Artishock Gallery, Artesenia Aruba, Creative Hands, Gasparito Art Gallery, Artistic Boutique, and Shema Art Gallery.

Cameras and electronic equipment: Boolchand's and Photokiva.

China and crystal: Little Switzerland, Penha, and DeWit's.

Eyeglasses: Oduber & Kan, Optic Boutique, and Optica Moderne.

Fashions: Two very special designer shops are Les Accessoires and Studio Italia in the Sonesta Arcade. Also: Gucci, Maggy's Boutique, Wulfsen & Wulfsen, Aquarius, Impressions, La Pomme, Aruba Trading Company, Javaruba, Scuba Aruba, and Eva Boutique.

Jewelry and watches: Lucor Jewelers, Gandelman, Spritzer & Fuhrmann, Kenro Jewelers, Colombian Emeralds, Little Switzerland, Classique de l'Isle, Penha, and New Amsterdam Jewelry Center.

Handbags and leather items: Studio Italia, Les Accessoires, Gucci, Leather & Leather, Maggy's, and Confetti Boutique.

Linens and tablecloths: Boolchand's, New Amsterdam Store, and Artistic Boutique.

Useful Information

There are more free island guides in Aruba than I've seen elsewhere in the Caribbean, except for St. Maarten/St. Martin. Most helpful are *Aruba Holiday!*, *Aruba Events*, *The Aruba Experience*, and *Aruba Nights*. Also informative and fun to read is *Where to Go for What*, a 16-page giveaway newspaper. I've very much enjoyed using my copy of *This Is the Way We Cook!*, a paperback cookbook with recipes from outstanding cooks of the Netherlands Antilles. For the best book selection in English, visit **Captain's Log Bookstore** in HarbourTown's shopping center.

All water sports are easily organized in Aruba, but **Red Sail Sports**, based at the Hyatt Regency and Americana Beach Resort, is very reliable. **Divi Winds Center** is the place for the latest windsurfing boards. **De Palm Tours** offers all sorts of tours and water-sports activities at De Palm Island, for morning or afternoon excursions.

Aruba offers visitors everything from a **drive-in movie, golf,** or **bowling** at the new Eagle Bowling Palace (12 lanes), to a **miniature golf course**, all kinds of nightly entertainment, and the island's famous casinos. The **Alhambra Casino** should at least be seen. A **tour** around the island is another must. Highlights are the **Natural Bridge** (Aruba's leading photo opportunity), **Ayo** and **Casibari Rock Formation, Chapel of Alto Vista, St. Anna Church**, plus the island's villages and astounding desertlike countryside.

The 18-hole par 71 Robert Trent Jones championship golf course, **Tierra del Sol**, is scheduled to open in December 1994 on the northwest side of Aruba.

≈ ≈

BARBADOS

ACCOMMODATIONS

BARBADOS' BEST

Cobblers Cove
The Royal Pavilion
Sandy Lane

NOTEWORTHY OPTIONS

Glitter Bay
Mango Bay Club
Ocean View Hotel
Peach and Quiet

RECOMMENDED RESTAURANTS

RECOMMENDED SHOPPING

PROVISIONS FOR YOUR ISLAND PANTRY

USEFUL INFORMATION

≈ ≈

≈ ≈

Accommodations

BARBADOS' BEST

Cobblers Cove

After a recent visit to Cobblers Cove, it remains a sentimental favorite of ours, because, apart from constant refurbishing, nothing's really changed. Our first holiday here was in 1979. The small hotel, a member of the Relais et Châteaux since 1989, is on the northwest coast of Barbados, 18 miles from the airport. Its relaxed, casual atmosphere and many endearing qualities immediately reassure guests, particularly repeaters, with a sense of well-being. A genuinely warm, welcoming staff and dependable, high-quality service turns a simple stay at another hotel into vacationing with old friends. Maureen Holder, the housekeeper of the hotel for 24 years, never forgets a guest's face, even if a few years have lapsed between bookings.

Cobblers Cove's 38 simple, first-rate suites, in several two-story buildings, fan around a green lawn and cheerful gardens in back and to the sides of the main pink and white masonry main building on a couple of acres of choice beachfront property.

All accommodations have their own living room, patio or balcony, telephone, bathroom, and air-conditioned bedroom with a ceiling fan. Each suite claims a fully stocked mini-bar. Rooms are nicely turned out, and floors are tiled throughout. Oceanfront rooms numbers 31 through 36 are favorites for sunset views and lulling surf sounds. Any of the second-floor rooms offer more privacy. Radios and TVs are available upon request.

Cobblers Cove has a luxurious, special Caribbean "room with a view" called the Camelot Suite, on the second and third floors of the main building. Those fortunate enough to stay in Camelot will be indulged in the supreme comfort of a 23 × 16-foot living room/bedroom with a king-size four-poster bed, writing desk, chaise longue, sofa, and armchairs, with a fully stocked mini-refrigerator and wet bar. They'll soak in an oversized whirlpool bath, or shower in a separate stall with English soap. The marble bath with twin basins also has a bidet, twin sinks, terry-cloth robes, and dhurrie rugs. Floors everywhere in Camelot's living quarters are veined gray marble topped with elegant throws. The suite, tastefully decorated in white and varying shades of blue, has a small library of its own, and a marvelous balcony with a comfortably furnished sitting area overlooking the pool and sparkling sea.

Camelot's crowning glory rests above. At the top of a private coral-stone spiral

Terrace view from Camelot Suite at Cobblers Cove in Barbados.

staircase is a 26 × 18-foot rooftop veranda with a small 4-foot-deep plunge pool. The penthouse terrace is bordered by a waist-high, white-latticed wall enlivened with greenery and blooming flowers in potted plants. In the seaview-front covered section of the terrace, a wet bar, a mini-fridge, and a second telephone are hidden away in a louvered door closet.

The flower-filled drawing room lounge at Cobblers Cove is decorated in traditional English style with sofas and chairs in several sitting areas, and possesses all the comforts of home. Guests gather either here or at the open-air bar outside on a terrace in the evenings for cocktails.

Adjacent to the outdoor bar is Cobbler Cove's seaside restaurant. Award-winning French-trained English chef Leslie Alexander is well respected on Barbados for his consistently fine cuisine. A few dishes from recent menus include ravioli of polenta and crab with lime butter sauce; terrine of duck, chicken, and quail wrapped in Parma ham with a fruit topping; and rosettes of lamb seasoned with natural juices and mint. Desserts are ambrosial specials of the day, sorbets and ice creams, and cheese and biscuits. Room service is available for any meal at Cobblers Cove.

General Hamish Watson hosts a weekly manager's party to cordially introduce guests, primarily English and American. Live entertainment is provided several evenings a week in season, as well as at a Tuesday barbecue buffet and Sunday brunch, when a steel band sets the pace.

Water-sports facilities, free to guests, include waterskiing, windsurfing, a lit Omni tennis court, Sunfish sailing, snorkeling gear, and glass-bottom-boat rides. For an additional fee, scuba diving, parasailing, golf, cocktail cruises, and private yacht charters can be had. Rates include daily shopping trips to Bridgetown, the capital.

The freshwater swimming pool and sea are only steps away. Guests can always be found basking in the sun on the lawn or beach in chaises with satisfied expressions on their faces that say they're glad to be back at unchanging, simply delightful Cobblers Cove.

COBBLERS COVE
St. Peter
Barbados, West Indies
TEL: (809) 422-2291
FAX: (809) 422-1460

Closed August 28 to October 17.

Rates: Double occupancy. *December 19 to January 2:* Suites, $580 to $790; Camelot Suite, $1,300. Extra person, $140. *January 3 to April 10:* Suites, $420 to $680; Camelot Suite, $620 to $680. Extra person, $130. *April 11 to December 18:* Suites EP, $170 to $300; MAP, $280 to $410. Camelot Suite EP, $520; MAP, $630. Extra person EP, $50; MAP, $105.

Meal plan: MAP (includes breakfast and lunch *or* dinner), mandatory in winter and included in rates listed above for summer. EP available in summer and fall.

Service charge: 10%.

Government tax: 5%.

Children under 12 not permitted between mid-January and mid-March.

Credit cards accepted.

Note: There are Honeymooners and Lovers and The Gourmet Experience packages available.

The Royal Pavilion

Just after entering the small road leading to The Royal Pavilion, you pass through a regal arbor of gigantic royal palms and turn onto a circular driveway that leads to a sprawling, Mediterranean pink palazzo. Greeted by uniformed attendants, guests are quickly checked in and escorted to junior suites with balconies that all look over a glistening sea.

The Royal Pavilion bears no resemblance to its southern sister resort, Glitter Bay (see resort listing, page 80), except that it's a luxurious hotel with essentially the identical complimentary sports facilities, including two shared floodlit tennis courts, and a concierge to assist in organizing tours, cruises, and outside entertainment.

Through extensive reconstruction and refurbishment, architect Ian Morrison transformed the former aging Miramar Beach Hotel into a youthful princess. The eight-acre Royal Pavilion includes 1,200 feet of golden sand beach. All the hotel's 72 rooms (referred to as junior suites) are beachfront guest quarters. A lovely three-bedroom villa, set well back and apart from the large freshwater pool, can also be booked.

Owners Michael and Lynn Pemberton's horticultural magician, Fernando Tabora, has outdone himself. Saga palms, lacy ferns, and firecracker burst out of custom-made clay pots along walkways, around clay lion-head fountains and lily ponds. Gardeners must care for perpetually blooming ixora, hibiscus, bougainvillea, and ginger, which are only a few of the floral confections Tabora has selected to enhance the landscape.

Rooms are air-conditioned and carpeted. Dust-ruffled king-size beds, padded headboards, loveseats, and draperies are covered in matching blue and pale coral floral and striped cotton fabrics. Bedside round end tables are covered with two tiers of tablecloths topped with glass protectors, ceramic-based lamps, telephones, and AM/FM radios. There are no TVs here, but fully stocked mini-bars hide inside pickled wood cabinets, and closets with shelves provide ample room for two vacationers. Rooms could use a chest of drawers.

The dressing areas and baths are comfortable enough, with Molton Brown toiletries and robes, but monochromatic tones of pale pink and gray marble floors with coordinated marbled half-moon-shaped vanities (one basin each) make one yearn for a bold splash of color. Amenities are also pink and white.

Ground-level rooms have private verandas, plus broad open terraces raised up a few feet from the beach lined with chaise longues for sunning, sunsets, and stargazing. Second- and third-floor junior suites have terraces with built-in cushioned banquettes providing sweeping views of the beach and sea. Breakfasts are always a delight served here.

The resort's main public building includes a central Spanish-style courtyard arcade of shops surrounding a lily pond, the reception area, lounge, bar, and the Palm Terrace restaurant. Duty-free shopping includes Cartier and other upscale boutiques, a gift and sundries shop, and beauty salon.

Afternoon tea is served in the beautiful large, airy, polished-marble lounge, where tall palms reach up to the high ceiling like magnificent feather dusters. Here a pianist plays a combination of jazz, light classical, and Latin rhythms on a grand piano during early evening cocktail and dinner hours. In the connecting elegant Palm Terrace restaurant, one of the most beautiful dining rooms in the Caribbean, English chef Guy Beasley, formerly with top-rated Le Gavroche in London, produces some commendable dinners. At a recent meal we sampled a delicious *petit* lobster pot—creamy brandy-laced soup topped with a crisp dome of puff pastry. A first course of tortellini filled with goat cheese in a pesto and tomato sauce sprinkled with walnuts was a giant portion lacking fresh flavors. We fared better with a tender fillet of duck breast, but its thick layer of fat should have been removed. Side-dish fresh vegetables were excellent. We were sorry not to have picked the night's carvery selection served ceremoniously from a trolley, a different choice each evening ranging from prime rib of beef with Yorkshire pudding, butter-roasted turkey with cranberry sauce, and whole roast suckling pig with mustard sauce, to roast leg of lamb with mint sauce. A dessert of mango crème brûlée was extra creamy with a perfect burnt-sugar crust.

Oceanfront Tabora's, a much more casual, breezy café, is situated in the center of the accommodations buildings, adjacent to the pool, large open terrace, dance floor, and an entertainment shell. Pastas, seafood, and grilled specials are featured and recommended. Live entertainment is provided most evenings.

The Royal Pavilion draws the same mix of English and Americans as Glitter Bay although the The Royal Pavilion attracts a younger crowd that likes the contemporary, romantic atmosphere and lovely surroundings.

THE ROYAL PAVILION
Pemberton Hotels
St. James
Barbados, West Indies
TEL: (809) 422-5555
FAX: (809) 422-3940

RESERVATIONS
Travel Resources Management Group
TEL: (800) 283-8666 *or*
(214) 556-2151
FAX: (214) 556-1538

Open all year.
Rates: Double occupancy. *December 17 to January 1* and *February 4 to February 24:* Junior Suites, $520. *April 23 to December 15:* Junior Suites, $230. Rates upon request for shoulder periods and Three-Bedroom Villa.
Meal plan: EP; MAP (minimum 3 days, includes breakfast and dinner), $55 per person per day.
Service charge: 10%.
Government tax: 5%.
Children under 12 not permitted.
Credit cards accepted.
Note: Wedding, Honeymoon, and Golf packages available.

Sandy Lane

After a $10-million transformation, Sandy Lane securely ranks as Barbados' premier hotel. Reopened on November 11, 1992, officially unveiled by Lord Forte of Ripley, Sandy Lane is the first-class section of a dazzlingly refurbished *QEII* run aground on a lovely stretch of beach on Barbados' exclusive west coast—a 30-minute drive from Grantley Adams International Airport, and 15 minutes by car to Bridgetown. The resort's grounds add up to some 380 acres, but the majestic coral-stone main building complex's reception hall, lounge, terraces, restaurants, unisex hair salon, two upscale shops, drugstore, two- and three-story accommodations, and beach all fit rather snugly together, not unlike the neat decks of a stately ship. The 3,000-square-foot freeform freshwater swimming pool, Oasis Bar, five all-weather tennis courts (four are lit—three Laykold, two with artificial grass), a first-rate fitness center, and an enchanting new children's facility with its own little "Chattel" playhouse are located close by on an adjacent hill on well-kept, flourishing garden grounds spanning several acres. Across the West Coast Road rests the balance of the hotel's property, where the fabulous rambling 18-hole golf course, golf pro shop, and plantation-style clubhouse bar and restaurant are found. Sandy Lane is contemplating adding nine more holes.

Built in 1961, Sandy Lane was an immediate success. It's the kind of chic luxury resort where the wealthy Euro/American upper classes and clubby corporate crowd have always been comfortable vacationing. The words "Sandy Lane" uttered anywhere on the island commands instant respect. After all, Queen Elizabeth II dines at the hotel when she's on the island. Today, anyone who can afford it is welcome here. Seasoned, Barbados-born manager Richard Williams has even relaxed the dress code to two nights a year. Now, only on Christmas evening and New Year's Eve are gentlemen required to wear jackets and ties, but no jeans, T-shirts, or shorts are allowed in public areas after 7 P.M.

Hobnobbing with the international rich and famous can be a great show, but the real star attraction at Sandy Lane is and always has been the handsome resort itself, designed by the late Robertson "Happy" Ward.

Sandy Lane's marbled reception area leads out onto a vast crescent-shaped Starlight terrace overlooking the lower-level dancing terrace, the beach and sea. Afternoon tea and cocktails are served on the upper terrace. Tuesday nights in season a Caribbean floor show is produced after a barbecue on the beach, and some type of live entertainment is offered each evening.

A stay at Sandy Lane begins with a private luxury car transfer from the airport to the hotel, where guests are checked in in their rooms and welcomed with a bouquet of fresh fruit and chilled French champagne. For a price, you can be collected in one of the hotel's two white Rolls-Royces.

All of Sandy Lane's 90 rooms and 30 suites have balconies or terraces with chaise longues and chairs, with garden or sea views. The new luxury accommodations come with plush sofas and chairs. The successful facelift included expansion of 18 rooms and a wide variety of quality furnishings, designer fabrics, and other pleasing decorations. Bathrooms have undergone a total transformation, each enlarged with bathtub and separate shower finished with Zandobbio marble, plus hair dryers, Floris bath and hair products, and bathrobes.

Rooms are air-conditioned with ceiling fans, and contain international clock radios, TVs, telephones, safes, refrigerators, and toasters. The hotel provides 24-hour room service.

Sustenance is taken at two restaurants. The first, the casual Sea Shell ground-floor restaurant, is where full breakfasts and luncheon buffets are served in season. Evenings feature Italian cuisine and seafood. The best meal we had on Barbados during a recent visit was at Sandy Bay, the hotel's pretty open-air pink and white terrace main restaurant. I'm not enamored of buffets in general, but this one rated top honors—Sandy Lane's renowned Sunday lunch. Under a sparkling chandelier, in a flower-bedecked private serving room, a friend and I selected from a groaning board of crayfish split in half, invitingly displayed on a gigantic round tray resting on ice, accompanied by a variety of olive oils and vinegars, including balsamic and raspberry wine; as well as large platters of artfully arranged smoked salmon, stuffed herring rolls, marinated shrimp, cold cuts, pâtés, and various salads and vegetable dishes. The hot dishes included sautéed plantains with coconut, Bajan chicken, blackened flying fish, lamb curry with rice and condiments, and pasta in a tomato sauce—and a chef was at hand to carve delicious roast beef (served with Yorkshire pudding and oven-roasted potatoes) and truly succulent roast suckling pig, both served with their own juices. The dessert table groaned, too, with an enormous mirror plate of fresh blueberries, strawberries, pineapple, papaya, coconut strips, and much more: strudels, puddings, cakes, crêpes with ice cream—every dish was first-rate. Head chef Mel Rumbles left Sandy Lane in 1994 after many years. With luck, his successor will be one of the skilled chefs who have trained closely with him.

Sandy Lane's services would satisfy the most demanding guest, and the fact that many staff members are longtime employees no doubt adds to the consistency of fine service. However, during our visit there were a lot of young faces here, including dedicated, gracious Michael Ford of guest services. Concierges are on hand to arrange a multitude of tours, make dinner reservations, or anything you require.

Taking long walks or slumbering on the beach seems the goal of many guests. Chaise longues are stationed in a long line under royal blue umbrellas, and beach-bar service is provided. (Vendors here now have their own kiosks from which to sell their wares.) Indulge in complimentary windsurfing, snorkeling, Hobie Cats, and Sunfish sailing, as well as great tennis and golf.

While Sandy Lane's "all-inclusive value rates" include airport transfers, breakfast and dinners, and all that is listed below in the information box, they may make you gasp. In high season, a luxury oceanview room for two is $1,300 a night (not a suite with an ocean view—they're $1,600), plus 10% service charge and 5% tax. That comes to $1,495, and we haven't had lunch, cocktails, or wines with dinner yet. When you add the extra reasonable daily expenditures, it looks as if beautiful, royal Sandy Lane can claim the title as one of the most expensive resorts in the Caribbean.

80 | BARBADOS

SANDY LANE
St. James
Barbados, West Indies
TEL: (809) 432-1311
FAX: (809) 432-2954

RESERVATIONS
TEL: (800) 225-5843 *or*
(800) 223-6800

Open all year.
Rates: (Inclusive of airport transfer in luxury private car, breakfast and dinner, unlimited complimentary green fees, tennis, water sports, fitness room, and exchange dining.) Double occupancy. *December 19 to January 6:* Garden View, Ocean View, and Luxury Ocean View Rooms, $820 to $1,300; Garden View and Ocean View Suites, $1,200 to $1,600; Penthouse $2,200. *January 7 to April 21:* Garden View, Ocean View, and Luxury Ocean View Rooms, $720 to $1,100; Garden View and Ocean View Suites, $1,000 to $1,400; Penthouse, $2,000. *April 22 to December 18:* Garden View, Ocean View, and Luxury Ocean View Rooms, $495 to $645; Garden View and Ocean View Suites, $595 to $750; Penthouse $950.
Meal plan: MAP (includes breakfast and dinner). Between April 22 and December 15 rates for rooms with breakfast only are available upon request.
Service charge: 10%.
Government tax: 5%.
Children welcome.
Credit cards: accepted.
Note: Special Classic Wedding, Honeymoon, Golf, and Gold Experience holidays are available; information upon request.

NOTEWORTHY OPTIONS

Glitter Bay

Michael Pemberton opened luxurious Glitter Bay on December 15, 1981, followed by its beautiful sister hotel, The Royal Pavilion (see page 76), on northern adjoining beachfront property six years later. For his third venture, he created the magnificent Grand Palazzo Hotel on the eastern coast of St. Thomas in the United States Virgin Islands, which debuted in October of 1992 (see page 362). No longer affiliated with that hotel, he is concentrating on another spectacular project at his Caribbean home base in Barbados; it is called The Royal Westmoreland, a 480-acre resident and membership resort with luxury residences and homesites, and a 27-hole championship golf course. The target date set for a partial opening is by April 1995.

During our last stay at Glitter Bay in March 1994, Mike Pemberton and his wife, Lynn, were in London, where the young Englishman is a successful entrepreneur in the leisure business. On this visit to Glitter Bay we found ups and downs.

Glitter Bay is a condominium hotel built on a lovely 10-acre-plus piece of beachfront property on Barbados' west coast (30 minutes from the airport) that was formerly the Sir Edward Cunard estate.

One of Pemberton's greatest coups was enlisting respected landscape architect Fernando Tabora, a delightful Venezuelan, to preserve the legacy of nature left from previous owners (sky-high palms, flamboyant trees, and other splendid specimens) and create gardens of his own design.

Architect Ian Morrison designed the resort's attractive three-story, red-tile-roofed Mediterranean-style white masonry buildings, which contain 83 accommodations— deluxe rooms, one- or two-bedroom suites, and a three-bedroom penthouse. All lodgings have private balconies with cushioned banquettes overlooking tropical gardens, but only a few actually face the sea.

A couple of years ago several million dollars was spent renovating the bathrooms and adding new furnishings. Interiors reflect quiet elegance—built-in banquette sofas, rattan and bamboo furniture combined with throw rugs on terra-cotta-tiled floors. The suites have fully equipped kitchens. Air-conditioned bedrooms have king-size beds, desk/ vanities, and lots of closet space, plus ceiling fans as an alternative coolant. Rooms have telephones, stocked mini-bars, and clock radios, but no TVs.

The small but charming bathrooms come with tub/showers, toilet, and a bidet. Twin basins are set into countertops with three sides of mirrors from the backsplash to the ceiling. An array of Molton Brown toiletries, hair dryers, and striped seersucker robes are on hand.

We were booked into Glitter Bay's crown jewel, The Beach House. The refurbished replica of the Cunards' palazzo in Venice has five special suites on two floors set apart from the rest of the hotel, right on the beach on its own expansive raised terrace, with gardens, lily pond, and a pergola under which dead plants in broken pots were found. The Pembertons' own coral-stone mansion, Bachelor Hall, sits only a few yards away.

We were in Sir Edward Suite 502, a ground-floor one-bedroom suite that provided us comfortable, modern hotel living space, except for the undersized but fully stocked kitchen—a plain small room with yesteryear fixtures. The most desirable accommodation in The Beach House is the second-floor Marquis Suite, with high ceilings and an elegant veranda overlooking the terrace and sea.

Glitter Bay's clientele ranges in age from toddlers to ancient dowagers, predominantly British and American. The resort's long beige sand beach is a perfect place to read, sun, and people-watch. In season, the beach gets crowded, so for more tranquil surroundings, guests can relocate to the freeform freshwater pool and expansive lawn. A second pool for children is separated from the grown-ups' lagoon by a drawbridge over a waterfall.

The renovations a few years ago included the creation of a vast marbled reception area with spaces for an upscale boutique, art gallery, and a sundries shop that carries, among other things, Pemberton Hotel Group signature perfumes, beachwear, jewelry, and Lynn Pemberton's novel *Platinum Coast*, about a woman whose husband builds a hotel in the Caribbean.

The huge air-conditioned Residents' Lounge off reception is where the manager's weekly reception and afternoon teas are served. Low-backed sofas and chairs, all in the same muted pink colors, were unimaginatively grouped around the walls of the room like an airline-terminal waiting room. The oversized TV screen there on my last visit had been replaced by a very small one. The large round table in the center of the room that used to hold newspapers and stacks of brochures covering everything you needed to know about Barbados was bare, save for a lonely flower arrangement. Even the little bar area here looked temporary. It's a soulless place.

Upstairs in the building is a fitness and massage center. Aerobics classes are regularly scheduled. There are two lit tennis courts and a pro shop. Waterskiing, Sunfish, Hobie Cats, windsurfing, and snorkeling are complimentary. All other water sports, as well as golf, parasailing, and horseback riding can be arranged for a fee. Glitter Bay's concierge will book a variety of tours, cruises, and dinner shows.

Adjacent to Glitter Bay's pretty, hand-painted white-and-pink-tiled bar is the seaside al fresco two-level restaurant Piperade, with pretty table settings and tiny bouquets of flowers on pink cloths. I'm sorry to report, aside from breakfast, the food we were served rated ordinary to poor. A dry Caesar salad lacked any flavor of lemon or Worcestershire sauce whatsoever. A plain grilled fillet of beef ordered medium-rare came to the table well-done. Another order was brought properly cooked. Happily, at least this trip, guests at Glitter Bay can dine at The Royal Pavilion's two restaurants, a short stroll next door. Both Royal Pavilion restaurants are oceanfront and served better food during our recent stay. Casual Tabora's offers good pasta, pizza, and grilled foods. The romantic, formal Palm Terrace's menus feature nouvelle Caribbean and some traditional English food. (See the Royal Pavilion listing, page 76.) Live entertainment varies throughout the week at both hotels.

Stephen J. Grant, Pemberton Hotels' engaging, proficient managing director who kept a keen eye on all aspects of both hotels for many years, left at the end of 1993, pursuing new opportunities. It appears he hadn't yet been replaced with anyone in authority with comparable abilities and standards. The Pembertons, with a reputation for seeking perfection, will surely take things in hand and return this physically stunning resort to the top-ranking status it deserves.

GLITTER BAY
Pemberton Hotels
St. James
Barbados, West Indies
TEL: (809) 422-5555
FAX: (809) 422-3940

RESERVATIONS
Travel Resources Management Group
TEL: (800) 283-8666 *or*
(214) 556-2151
FAX: (214) 556-1538

Open all year.

Rates: Double occupancy: *December 17 to January 1* and *February 4 to February 24:* Double Room, $395; One-Bedroom Suite, $515; extra person, $95. *April 23 to December 15:* Double Room, $195; One-Bedroom Suite, $220; extra person, $30. Rates available upon request for shoulder periods and other accommodations.

Meal plan: EP; MAP (minimum 3 days, includes breakfast and dinner), $55 per person per day.
Service charge: 10%.
Government tax: 5%.
Children welcome.
Credit cards accepted.
Note: Wedding, Honeymoon, and Golf packages available; inquire about details.

Mango Bay Club

Brand-new, seaside Mango Bay Club, bordering the little Caribbean Soho-like village of Holetown, is a thoroughly enchanting, reasonably priced, all-inclusive resort. Its 65 rooms, divided among two white stucco two- and three-story buildings (one is new; the other the completely renovated former Palm Beach Hotel), face each other. Most rooms look out over a large undulating freeform swimming pool dressed up with a tiny arch-backed bridge, small gardens, and a lovely open-air, beachside restaurant and bar. Only a few of the rooms actually face the creamy sand strip of beach. (Mango Bay is located on Barbado's western coast, a short distance north of Sandy Lane.) Although a bit of a climb, and the most expensive, the second- and third-floor corner seaside rooms in the new wing are the real charmers.

To begin with, the hotel is pleasing on the eyes, especially the new wing with peach-colored fretwork that trims the shingled rooflines. Second- and third-floor rooms have matching peach latticed railings on private balconies; first-floor rooms have verandas with stucco arches leading directly onto the grounds. All terraces are furnished with a pair of white Adirondack chairs and a table.

Interiors have tile floors, modern tub/shower bathrooms, pickled wood furniture, and draperies in bright patterned fabrics, plus air-conditioning, hair dryers, and safes. Rooms have no phones, TVs, or mini-bars.

The extensive list of offerings and activities in the all-inclusive rate includes a TV and baby grand piano in the lounge, and all meals, afternoon tea, drinks, and house wines with dinner. A bulletin board in reception posts daily scheduled activities that range from a weekly cocktail party, nightly entertainment, a round-trip to Bridgetown for shopping, to waterskiing, sailing, windsurfing, snorkeling, a free scuba lesson in the pool, and a romantic cruise on the hotel's catamaran.

Owner/manager Peter Odle has gathered together a friendly staff to operate cheery, youthful-rhythmed Mango Bay Club.

MANGO BAY CLUB
Holetown, St. James
Barbados, West Indies
TEL: (800) 79-MANGO *or*
    (809) 432-1384
FAX: (809) 432-5297

RESERVATIONS
International Travel & Resorts Inc.
4 Park Avenue
New York, NY 10016
TEL: (800) 223-9815 *or*
    (212) 545-8469
FAX: (212) 545-8467

Open all year.
Rates: Double occupancy. *December 15 to April 15:* Standard Room, $280; Pool View, $300; Beachfront, $340. *April 16 to December 14:* Standard Room, $210; Pool View, $240; Beachfront, $260. Extra person, $65. Children under 3 years old, free.
Meal plan: FAP. All-inclusive rate covers meals, afternoon tea, beverages, cocktails, and house wines with meals, plus the option of two meals at other selected restaurants.
Service charge: Included.
Government tax: Included.
Children welcome.
Credit cards accepted.

The Ocean View Hotel

The 34 rooms and suites in the meandering corridors of Barbados' oldest operating hotel are one-of-a-kind, idiosyncratic designer showrooms of varying sizes from small to quite grand. Designated an historic landmark in 1987, 94-year-old Ocean View Hotel is alive and whimsically well. John Chander, the hotel's dashing young owner/manager, an avid antique collector, has an exuberance for life and great flair as a decorator. The majority of rooms and suites are tasteful, traditional Colonial plantation-style lodgings with Victorian sofas and chairs upholstered in designer fabrics, canopied four-poster beds, and so on. Others are—well, let's say exotic.

Because I had reserved a suite with air-conditioning (only a few rooms and suites have individual wall units), my bags were taken to the second-floor room 46, the bizarre red and gold Indian suite. The floor-to-ceiling draperies (over a huge window only a few yards up from the ocean and the hotel's snip of beach), the dressing table skirt and bench cushion, cornices, and wall canopy over the king-size bed, all matched in a satiny, fire-engine red paisley-print material. The room's complementing color was yellow-gold; the bed's headboard a high, curved wrought-iron gate. Two ceramic elephants stood guard at the doorway while I hung my clothes in a large, handsome antique armoire. In the small living room, an Indian wedding tent hung from the ceiling over a writing table with an old Spanish leather chair, Oriental rugs, a sitting area, a thermos of ice water, and a telephone. My first impression was, Should I put on sunglasses, or close the draperies and hold a séance? I could have moved to a prettier, less noisy environment, but decided to *experience* the Indian suite, which turned out remarkably pleasant, even though halfway through the balmy night the air-conditioning failed. I simply opened the large window for cooling breezes and fresh ocean-scented air. Note that while the bathrooms at Ocean View work, they're antiquated, with tiny sinks and high-sided tubs with showers.

Ocean View's heirloom-furnished lobby, bar, and dining room, interspersed with gigantic bouquets of tropical fronds and flowers and chandeliers, are charming places. The vast peach-colored dining room, embellished with wall sconces, white draperies, and hanging antique china plates, paintings, and old photographs, rests under a white latticed ceiling. Most guests take evening cocktails in the long, cozy oceanfront terrace lounge where large louvered window shutters open over the beach and sea. We expected modern-day Auntie Mames and Noël Cowards, but instead we joined several reserved young British couples, a smartly dressed young woman waiting for guests to arrive from London, a dowager of a certain age—intently knitting, and a few comely pairs from outside hotels. I suspect things liven up considerably on three evenings a week in season when Ocean View presents a cabaret in the Xanadu Room. Last year's production was called "Boo." On cabaret nights dinners are served downstairs in an oceanfront dining room.

The menus at Ocean View are as eclectic a mix as the accommodations, but just as satisfying. Prepared by longtime Ocean View cooks Esmay Forde and Germaine Bynve, selections one evening were stuffed plantain delights, filet mignon with sautéed onions, old-fashioned seafood crêpes, and flying fish (a Bajan specialty). In an East Indian mode, I opted for vegetable samosas and chicken curry with condiments and rice, and was now seriously considering buying a sari. Desserts listed were Belgian chocolate torte and a Pineapple Ice Box, neither of which were available. We had the only dessert offered, a slice of spice cake and, for an after, Bajan coffee with rum.

Ocean View's famous pink building sits right on the southern coastal road: a marvelous venue for shopping and dining out in the many restaurants in Hastings, Christ Church. The hotel is roughly 20 minutes from the Grantley Adams International Airport. A car is recommended, and there's a private parking lot at the hotel.

The small strip of beach at Ocean View provides limited swimming and lounging. The beach side of the hotel, with wonderful arched balcony openings, was in need of a coat of paint when we were there. Never mind. Donya Benjamin at reception informed me that Mr. Chandler never ever stops painting, renovating, remodeling, and decorating. We certainly hope he never ever changes the singular character of this reasonably priced southern Barbadian treasure.

OCEAN VIEW HOTEL
Hastings, Christ Church
Barbados, West Indies
TEL: (809) 427-7821
FAX: (809) 427-7826

Open all year.
Rates: Double occupancy. *December 15 to April 15:* Roadside Rooms, $75; Central Rooms, $95; Oceanside Rooms, $120; Suites, $150. *April 16 to December 14:* Roadside, $65; Oceanside, $75; Suites, $120. (Central rooms not suggested.) Extra person, $40. Children under 12 years old, $25 each; children 2 years old or under, free.
Meal plan: EP; MAP (includes breakfast and dinner), $40 per person per day.
Service charge: 10%.
Government tax: 5%.
Children welcome, however not recommended until independent age.
Credit cards accepted.

Peach and Quiet

Travelers in search of small, secluded, inexpensive, well-run owner/managed island retreats will want to put a check mark next to Peach and Quiet, a four-acre, 22 mini-suite resort concealed beyond a local residential neighborhood on the southern tip of the Barbados coast in Inch Marlow, Christ Church. The nightly rate of $79 in season for a couple is hard to beat anywhere in the Caribbean.

The resort is rustic with modest, spare furnishings, a crack here, a smudge on the wall there, but dedicated remodeling and repair work is in progress, and the buildings do have a pedigree. Formerly the Arawak Inn, built in 1975, Peach and Quiet has the distinction of being the first resort designed by architect Ian Morrison, who later achieved fame masterminding luxurious hotels throughout the Caribbean, including Glitter Bay and The Royal Pavilion, also in Barbados. Recognizable here are his signature Mediterranean/Andalusian red-tile-roofed white stucco buildings with quarry-tile floors and curved walls gracing the grounds.

Proprietors Margaret Shaw and Adrian Loveridge opened Peach and Quiet in 1989. They share managerial duties equally and amicably. She is the cook; he's the plumber. She minds the books; he tends the gardens.

Called suites, the small quarters have a tiny baths with showers and basins. The bedroom and living room areas are separated by draperies. The sitting area of the living room has a corner cushioned banquette, stool, and table. No artwork adorns the walls, and the only amenity is an electric kettle for making coffee or tea. Louvered windows provide air circulation. No ceiling fans, phones, or TVs.

What Peach and Quiet does have are tropical grounds, beautiful views (especially from the oceanside building's second-story rooms), and a lovely freshwater pool surrounded by a few new shingled bohios, chaises, and chairs on a sun terrace set right at the sea. The shoreline here is rocky with a surfy sea, but ocean swimming is available in a sizable rock pool. Guests who don snorkel masks can become human inhabitants of an open ocean aquarium. The pool is invariably filled with a variety of small fish representing all colors of the rainbow.

Co-owner Margaret Shaw, as resident chef, serves $8 buffet breakfasts, light lunch offerings starting at $5, and $20 three-course dinners with menus like pumpkin soup, kingfish in lime sauce, and, for dessert, "exotic ice cream creations"—18-ounce stemmed glasses filled to the brim with ice cream, toppings, and fruit. Nice wines are available. A barbecue buffet night with a steel band is held every Wednesday. Friday night is lobster and salads, and a Sunday barbecue is served poolside. Guests dine on an open-air terrace under the stars or a covered dining area. Peach and Quiet's small beach-bar pavilion serves up special rum-and-fruit drinks.

Clientele is predominantly English. Few Americans have discovered the place. Young in-the-know Bajans frequent Peach and Quiet for the reasonably priced good food and convivial atmosphere.

A car is necessary for exploring Barbados, although regularly scheduled bus service connects the resort to Bridgetown for Bds$1.50 (Barbados dollars)—75¢ U.S.—each way, and within walking distance is beautiful, white-sand Long Bay Beach. All water sports can be arranged.

From a second-floor window overlooking the garden, pool, and sparkling blue sea— no sound but the surf, two snorkelers in the rock pool, a handful of people reading or asleep on the sun terrace—I found Peach and Quiet an unpretentious, delightful sanctuary conducive to total relaxation and, I must say, peace and quiet.

PEACH AND QUIET
Inch Marlow, Christ Church
Barbados, West Indies
TEL: (809) 428-5682
FAX: (809) 428-2467

Open all year.
Rates: Double occupancy. *December 15 to April 15:* Rooms, $69 to $79. *April 16 to December 14:* Rooms, $59 to $69.
Meal plan: EP.
Service charge: None.
Government tax: 5%.
Children discouraged.
Credit cards: American Express only.

Recommended Restaurants

BARBADOS' FINEST*

* **Carambola**, 432-0832 (Derricks, St. James). Still in first place for splendid, open-air cliffside dining by the sea. Chef Paul Owens's superior cuisine, especially his seafood creations, just get better and better. Good wine list. Expensive.

* **The Mews**, 432-1122 (Holetown, St. James). Owner/chef Josef Schwaiger's new restaurant is a gem. Meals served in garden courtyard or throughout rooms and balconies of renovated home. Barbados's current "in" dining spot. Casual atmosphere. A sample menu: chilled cucumber soup, fillet of snapper Cajun style, and tiramisu. Moderate to expensive.

* **La Maison Restaurant**, 432-1156 (Holetown, St. James). Enchanting venues for dining in this coral-stone old Bajan home are indoors, in the courtyard, or on the seafront terrace. Innovative fish and seafood dishes are best bets. Fine wines. Expensive.

* **Sandy Bay**, 432-1311 (Sandy Lane, St. James). Elegant terrace dining room near the sea serving one of *the* best Sunday brunches anywhere. Evenings, select from such dishes as glazed terrine of duck, pork, and chicken or char-grilled tenderloin of lamb with ratatouille. (See resort listing, page 77). Expensive to very expensive.

* **Cobblers Cove**, 422-2291 (Cobblers Cove Hotel, St. Peter). Delightful beachside dining terrace and first-rate fare. (See resort listing, page 73). Expensive.

* **Bagatelle Great House**, 421-6767 (Highway 2A, St. Thomas). This restaurant is still serving formal, superior French Créole meals in a lovely 17th-century great house. Excellent wines. There's an art gallery upstairs. A favorite with tourists, but worth a visit. Expensive.

Barbados has many other top-rated restaurants. **Finest*** choices are ***Ile de France, *Josef's, *Fathoms, *La Cage aux Folles, *The Legend Restaurant, *39 Steps Wine Bar, *Raffles, *The Palm Terrace at the Royal Pavilion**, and ***Sandpiper Inn**. From moderate to expensive.

OTHER DEPENDABLE CHOICES

Ragamuffins, 432-1295 (First Street, Holetown, St. James). This is a spirited favorite with young Bajans for reasonably priced pasta, vegetable, seafood, and chicken dishes. It's located in a bright green chattel house. Inexpensive to moderate.

Koko's, 424-4557 (Prospect, St. James). Pleasant seaside dining featuring such Caribbean dishes as coconut shrimp and chicken stuffed with bananas. Inexpensive to moderate.

Ocean View Restaurant, 427-7821 (Ocean View Hotel, Hastings, Christ Church). You'll find a charming atmosphere in this old-fashioned seaside hotel with a distinct personality, as well as good Continental and Bajan food, graciously served. (See hotel listing, page 84.) Moderate to expensive.

The Big Bamboo, 432-0910 (Paynes Bay, St. James). A fun-filled, great choice for families or anyone young at heart. Children can order "monkey fist" spaghetti (Bolognese), while grown-ups savor smoked-flying-fish mousse or baked crab back. Very good food. House wines are available "by the giraffe." Open from 11 A.M. until late. Live entertainment daily. Inexpensive to moderate.

Other good choices include **Tapps Tavern and Grill** for all grilled foods, at St. Lawrence Gap; oceanside **Southern Accents**, featuring good Caribbean food; **Pisces**, for excellent seafood right at the water's edge; and **Peach and Quiet** (see resort listing, page 86) in Christ Church. In Holetown, a miniature, Soho-like village of boutiques and restaurants, aside from those already mentioned are several charming options—**Mango Bay Club, The Garden Grill and Gourmet Shop, Nico's Champagne & Wine Bar, Crocodile's Den, St. Elmos Restaurant,** and **Min's Chinese Restaurant**. A favorite seaside location is **Mullins Beach Bar & Restaurant** in St. Peter. Stop at second-floor **Fisherman's Wharf** for a drink or lunch break after shopping and view Bridgetown's action in Trafalgar Square. If cruise ships are in, the place gets mobbed, so retreat and return another day. The **Atlantis Hotel** and **Edgewater Inn** in Bathsheba, St. Joseph, and **Kingsley Club** in Cattlewash-on-Sea, near Bathsheba, St. Joseph, all serve good authentic Bajan food. Go to either Atlantis or Edgewater for a multi-dish Sunday brunch. Melinda Blanchard, chef/owner of Blanchard's in Anguilla, recommended Kingsley Club's flying-fish cutters (Bajan sandwiches). They are the best!

Recommended Shopping

Barbados has a population of over a quarter of a million, so apart from the increasing numbers of fine tourist-oriented stores (**Colombian Emeralds** has three shops on the island now), there are many department stores and shops catering to local trade as well. All this adds up to a great Barbadian shopper's world.

Major shopping areas in **Bridgetown** are in large stores and in several new shop-filled malls like **Da Costas Mall** or **Mall 34** (located on Broad Street) and the new **Passenger Cruise Terminal** at the harbor. The terminal houses a multitude of duty-free shops fashioned after colorful fretwork-trimmed West Indian houses. Other shopping options are in the many boutiques and shopping centers in **Holetown**, St. James (check out **Sopadilla Island, Gaye,** and **Cuckoo's Nest** boutiques here), **Hastings** in Christ Church, like the **Chattel House Shopping Village**. Historic **Speightstown** in St. Peter is coming into its own with new shops and a branch of **Cave Shepherd**. The **Grantley Adams Airport** shops includes outlets from **Cave Shepherd, Colombian Emeralds, Harrison's,** and **Louis Baley**. First a few standouts followed by suggestions in categories.

Best of Barbados shops. The many shops and outlets that feature local artist Jill Walker's colorful designs on everything from glasses, placemats, and plastic trays to stationery and coasters, also carry an excellent selection of island-related books, and other artists' works in ceramics or pottery—all made or designed in Barbados, are located throughout the island in about ten shops and outlets; be on the lookout because items are reasonably priced and make wonderful gifts from Barbados.

Carol Cadogan's Cotton Days Designs, 427-7191 (Lower Bay Street, Bridgetown, and also at Colours of D'Caribbean at the Waterfront in Bridgetown). Have a look at the designer's outstanding collection of hand-painted tropical fantasyland fashions in 100% cotton. Often adorned with sequins, beads, and appliqué, her outfits of separates, handbags, hats, and more, are all one-of-a-kind, expensive treasures.

Wild Feathers, 423-7758 (near Sam Lord's Castle). Jeff and Joanie Skeete's delicate wood carvings and paintings of birds in accurate, minute detail are displayed in their studio/home. Also "Bird Art" on shirts, note cards, and prints.

Daphne's Sea Shell Studio, 423-6180 (Congo Road Plantation, off Highway 5 in St. Philip). Daphne Hunte and her family welcome visitors to their studio showroom packed with shell designs on mirrors, soap dishes, painted on clothing, and practically everything else. Tiny pastel chattel houses are adorable. Individual shells also are available. Some items overly precious, but for shell lovers, the studio is worth a visit. Also seek out **The Shell Gallery** in the Chattel House Shopping Village and at Carlton House in St. James. Maureen Edgill's shell art pieces are fabulous creations.

Antiques: Visit Antiquaria, Greenwich House Antiques, La Galerie Antique, Antiques and Collectibles, and sometimes there are real finds at the Women's Self-Help Shop.

Art and handcrafts: Apart from those mentioned above, The Studio Art Gallery, Bagatelle Caribbean Art Gallery, Coffee & Cream Gallery, The Barbados Museum, Finecrafts Roslyn of Barbados, Mango Jam Gallery, The Verandah Art Gallery, Earthworks and The Potter's House Gallery, Southern Arts & Crafts, Pelican Village, Castle Pottery, and Chalky Mount Pottery, are places to visit and browse.

Cameras: Cave Shepherd and Louis Baley.

Cigars: Grand Cigars of Barbados and The Connoisseur.

Crystal and china: Louis Baley, Harrison's, and Cave Shepherd.

Fashions and resortwear: Apart from those mentioned above, try Ela Boutiques, Colours of the Caribbean, Simon, Abeds, Harrison's, Cave Shepherd, Sherigo, Swinki, Gailies, Upbeat.

Jewelry and watches: Visit Colombian Emeralds, The Royal Shop, India Shop, and Louis Baley.

Handbags and leather items: Seek out Harrison's, Cave Shepherd, and Mademoiselle.

Linen and tablecloths: Cave Shepherd, Harrison's, and the Women's Self-Help Shop.

Liquor and wines: The Connoisseur, Bernie's Discount Wines & Spirits, St. Elmo's Variety & Liquor Den, and Wells Grog & Spirits Ltd. are the places to go.

Perfumes and cosmetics: Parfum de Paris, Signatures, Louis Baley, Cave Shepherd, and Harrison's.

Shoes: Try the Mademoiselle Shoe Shop, The Shoe Locker, and Glitzy.

There are also excellent boutiques in many Barbados hotels—**Sandy Lane, Glitter Bay, The Royal Pavilion, The Sandpiper Inn, Sam Lord's Castle,** and the **Barbados Hilton** hotel.

The newsstand in the departure lounge at the airport has an excellent selection of Caribbean-related books.

To take home Barbados' flying fish, other seafoods, seasonings, spices, and flowers, see the **Fly Fish Inc**. entry on page 91. Also visit **The Connoisseur** for gourmet foods and cigars, and **The Gourmet Shop**, where I couldn't resist buying delicious sesame cheese morsels to bring home.

Provisions for Your Island Pantry

The Gourmet Shop, 432-7711 (First Street, Holetown, St. James). Do not miss my favorite take-out catering store in Barbados, owned for nearly two years by Ruth Lambie and her daughter, Sarah Hamilton. Great fixings here for picnics: fine pâtés, specialty meats, and incredible cheeselets, crunchy breadsticks, and other nibbles. The small shop carries other prepared foods like samosas and mini-quiches, plus special oils, Barbados' honey, jams, and sauces, and a host of delectable desserts, such as orange rum cake and passion fruit délice. Order specials a day or two in advance. Sarah's husband, Leo, is chef at the adjoining restaurant called **The Garden Grill**.

The Connoisseur, 432-5737 (Les Palms, Paynes Bay, St. James). Travelers and Bajans are customers of this impressive new gourmet, liquor, and wine shop, which also sells Cuban cigars. Select from prepared foods like crabbacks, whole cooked lobster, and salads, plus an array of pâtés, caviar, deli meats, fresh baked bread, and desserts. Coffees, teas, and excellent wine selections are also available. Catherine Rothwell and John Austin are the in-the-shop owners.

Good supermarkets include **Plantations** in Worthings, Christ Church, **Super-Center** in Holetown, and **Eddie's, Jordon's** and **Elmer's**, plus **Golden Press Bakery** and the **fish market**, at Speightstown in St. Peter.

Wonderful produce is available at the **public markets** and **Vegetables Unlimited**, Lands End and Baxter Road.

For wines and spirits, aside from The Connoisseur, mentioned above, see the liquor listings under "Recommended Shopping."

Fly Fish Inc., 428-1645 (Grantley Adams Airport). If you've fallen in love with flavorful flying fish, buy vacuum-packed boxes of 10 or 20 filleted and frozen flying fish to take home. A package of Bajan seasonings is included. (The fish are airline and Customs approved.) Fly Fish also sells other seafood, Lotties Pepper sauce, Barbados sugar, and bouquets of tropical flowers.

The best selection of fish and seafood for use on the island is found at **Oistins** in St. Lawrence Gap.

Useful Information

Barbados' best complimentary guides are the annual *Ins and Outs of Barbados* and the weekly *Visitor*.

Barbados will keep you on the go if you're a sightseer. Go on your own or take **tours** to one or more of the island's 16 beautifully restored, historic **Plantation Houses.** For information, call the Barbados National Trust, 426-2421. A special Passport or Mini-Passport with a 50% discounted admission to all homes is available. The trust also conducts Sunday-morning walks and tours of private mansions in season. Consult your hotel and the well-organized *Ins and Outs of Barbados* listing for the many historical and interesting sights, as well as all sports, including water sports and day sails and cruises— everything you want to know.

Ms. Margaret Leacock, 425-0099, provides custom, cultural tours of the island for $25 an hour—a minimum of four hours.

Two full-service beauty and hair salons are **The Palms** therapy and unisex salon, 428-8712 (Southern Palms Beach Club, St. Lawrence Gap, Christ Church), and **Profile Health & Beauty Club**, 432-1393, offering everything from massages and yoga to body mud and peel treatments.

Two one-hour photo-processing shops are at Cave Sheperd on Broad Street and **Graphic Photo Lab** in Hastings, Christ Church.

Barbados has numerous car rental companies. Among them are **National Car Rentals**, (809) 426-0603; **Courtesy Rent-A-Car**, (809) 431-4160; and **P & S Car Rentals**, (809) 424-7591.

BARBUDA

ACCOMMODATIONS

BARBUDA'S BEST
Coco Point Lodge 🌴
K Club 👑

A NOTEWORTHY OPTION
Palmetto Beach Hotel and Villas

USEFUL INFORMATION

≈ ≈

Accommodations

BARBUDA'S BEST

Coco Point Lodge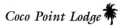

Coco Point Lodge's owner, William Cody Kelly, first sighted Coco Point from the air on February 14, 1960. "On Valentine's Day! It was the most breathtaking stretch of white sand beach I had ever seen, and there wasn't one coconut tree," he told me during a recent conversation at the exclusive resort. A pioneer in the industry, Bill Kelly engaged the late Robertson "Happy" Ward, architect for premier Sandy Lane in Barbados, among others, to design Coco Point Lodge. Open since 1963, the first and only luxury resort on Barbuda for over two decades, Coco Point is in excellent shape. Now there are hundreds of palm trees as well as yearly additions of other tropicana like bougainvillea bushes in round natural stone planters dotting the grounds. The generator has been moved a good distance away, no longer disturbing the peace. But not much else has really changed. Coco Point's 72% repeat clientele (90% North American, the balance European), most of whom are affluent conservatives of all ages, prefer it remaining the same. What I found this time was a jolly collection of guests, repeaters and new, invigorated by the climate, tranquil surroundings, and the breathtaking beach and sea views. What an incredibly romantic, isolated oasis it is, especially because Barbuda is not a lush tropical island. It's dry and mostly plain. The highest point is about 200 feet, with scrub brush, mangroves, and a large lagoon. Apart from the amenities of the resort, the chief draw is the miraculous beach, and the total privacy of the place. Only guests and staff are allowed on the resort's property, and no outsiders for meals, except guests' friends, some of whom arrive by sea on yachts.

The only neighbor is the young, glamorous K Club to the north (see the following resort listing). While the two resorts endure each other's existence, they don't exchange-dine. It's really too bad, because they are two one-of-a-kind, very different resorts that happen to border each other on a spectacular white-platinum coastline.

Since Coco Point is closed from May to the first week in November, and there are a mere 34 rooms, booking is done on an advance yearly basis by peak-season repeaters. One retired CEO was contentedly celebrating his twentieth holiday at the resort with a monthlong stay. Don't let the number of repeat guests deter you from trying for reservations, however, especially in the early and late winter.

Kelly's energetic, business-minded son, Patrick, now runs the operation from New York, visiting Coco Point many times during season. Here's why my husband and I like it so much.

After passing through customs at Antigua's V. C. Bird International Airport, Coco Point's pilot transfers you to one of the resort's two private planes for a 15-minute 27-mile flight to the low-lying, unspoiled island of Barbuda. The resort is situated on a 164-acre peninsula on the southern tip of the island. At Kelly Field, Coco Point's recently expanded, private grass airstrip, you are met by Martin Price, the comanager/host, and whisked off to the main lodge to meet the other half of the efficient, congenial English team, Caroline Price. After registering, collecting the drinks of your choice and tiny pencil flashlights, you are deposited in your beachfront room.

From here on, the pace diminishes significantly to the slow rhythm of the leeward sea, and calm prevails. You're a few seconds from pillow to sea on one of the Caribbean's truly most beautiful superfine white sand beaches, stretching 2½ miles along the resort's property, and miles beyond. As of last year, there are two new accommodations called Hill House Rooms, formerly management housing, on the windward side of the narrow peninsula, a short walk away. Guests who stay in these refurbished, spacious quarters (a one-room and a two-room suite) have their own seaview terraces and designated spaces with bohios and chaises on the beautiful beach.

Coco Point Lodge is a casual, all-inclusive resort, providing all meals and beverages (except champagne), two tennis courts—one Omni surface, the other hard court—Sunfish, kayaks, windsurfing, waterskiing, superb snorkeling and scuba diving, deep-sea fishing on the 43-foot motor sail *Barbuda Belle*, reef and bone fishing from Whalers, and informal trap shooting. All the gear for these sports, plus laundry service every other day, is included.

Guests congregate in the airy lounge and bar to socialize before and after dinner. Coco Point is decidedly clubby, although one is usually welcome to either join in the repartee or remain private.

Caroline and Martin Price, Barbudan residents and fifteen-year Coco Point veterans, are two of the best, most conscientious resort managers in the Caribbean, anticipating and responding to the needs of all guests while commanding a small, friendly Barbudan staff, many of whom have been at the hotel for years. The Prices are natural hosts who share the multitude of responsibilities. Mrs. Price's boutique, called Caroline's, is a miniature variety shop/bazaar for immediate needs, Caribbean handcrafts, costume jewelry, and attractive resortwear.

The resort's one-story keyless rooms are judiciously spaced in a string along the beach, with the exception of the two new lodgings mentioned above. Guests in 32 accommodations face west to endless open sea for guaranteed sensual sunsets.

The ten connecting small lodge rooms just off the main lodge house have been totally upgraded, retiled, painted aqua and white, and redecorated. They're quite comfortable and appealing now, and they command the lowest price. Other, more spacious rooms are found at Highland House farther along to the north of the beach. The five remaining large cottages, Gravenor Bay, Palaster Reef, Martello Tower, Spanish Point, and Sea Crescent, to the north with two to four bedrooms, share living room and bar areas, except for corner outside rooms of Gravenor Bay. The cottages are particularly appropriate for friends or families—they're the roomiest and most expensive. The buildings themselves are plain, reflecting old-fashioned, sensible seaside living. The beach furniture still doesn't all match, but if nothing's wrong with it why make a change? While accommodations are not super-luxurious, they are certainly first-rate and welcoming. Interiors vary in size and configuration, but all have been redecorated or refurbished with cheery fabrics on white or natural rattan. Bouquets of fresh flowers are everywhere. All rooms have ceiling fans and louvered windows and doors, private patios, excellent reading light, room safes, thermoses of fresh water, chests of ice, Vidal Sassoon bath and hair products, and stall showers (some with adjoining rock and leafy gardens). Toasters come with every room so the morning toast and muffins are melt-the-butter hot. There are no TVs, radios, or swimming pool, but a cellular phone is available for emergencies.

Meals at Coco Point are wonderful. Full breakfasts are served on guests' private patios. The open-air dining room has a cozy, homey atmosphere, with nautical and tropical appointments, plants, and flowers. A new beach pavilion features light, healthy grilled lunches like shrimp kebabs, wahoo, marinated chicken breasts, filet mignon, or burgers, with a buffet of salads and vegetables. From the à la carte menu I sampled an exquisite creamy, light lemon yogurt soup spiced up with few drops of sherry-based hot-pepper sauce (a recipe the Prices brought from Bequia). Always available is highly prized Barbudan lobster salad, plus a daily choice of five other entrées such as West Indian curry with chutney and poppadums. Chef Norman Beazer's dinners might consist of Barbuda fish broth with saffron and farfalle, French rack of lamb Dijonnaise, eggplant Provençale, and, for dessert, a choice of bananas Caroline with rum or hot fudge sundaes.

The only programmed entertainment at Coco Point is a steel band on Saturday nights at a buffet barbecue on the beach.

At Coco Point you spend your days blissfully engaged in aquatic pleasures, promenading the sandy boulevard, reading, contemplating nature, and stargazing below the heavens in a rare place in paradise that the Kellys and Prices are carefully preserving.

COCO POINT LODGE
P.O. Box 90, St. John's, Antigua,
West Indies
TEL: (809) 462-3816 in Antigua
FAX: (809) 462-5340

RESERVATIONS
Coco Point Lodge
275 Madison Avenue, Suite 1901
New York, NY 10016
TEL: (212) 986-1416
FAX: (212) 986-0901

Open from first week in November to April 30.
Rates: Double occupancy. *From first week in November to December 17* and *all of April:* Lodge Rooms, $550; Hill House Rooms, $550 to $730; Highland House Rooms, $670 to $730; five Houses, most with shared living rooms and bar areas, from $670 to $880. Extra person, $175. *From December 18 through March 31:* Lodge Rooms, $625; Hill House Rooms, $625 to $835; Highland House Rooms, $780 to $835;

five Houses, most with shared living rooms and bar areas, $780 to $1,000. Extra person, $200. Plus $150 per person mandatory associate membership good for one season to be paid at time of booking and $100 per person round-trip airfare.
Meal plan: FAP (all-inclusive rate covers all meals, wines, and drinks, except champagne).
Service charge: 10%.
Government tax: 8½%.
Children accepted at discretion of management.
Credit cards not accepted.

K Club ◣◥

A dream of an island, a pink powdery spread of sand, an incredible turquoise, limpid, calm sea, a very gentle climate, absolute peace, large spaces, maximum comfort, splendid Mediterranean food. It sounds like a dream, but it is reality: It is the K Club in Barbuda, the jewel of the Leeward Islands.

MARUICCIA MANDELLI AND ALDO PINTO, OWNERS

The exquisite K Club, open since December 1990, is one of the most stunning ultra-luxurious resorts in the Caribbean. Against all odds, Krizia fashion designer Maruiccia Mandelli and her husband and business partner, Aldo Pinto, transformed a bleak, sandy savanna into a beautiful modern-day Cinderella retreat with superb taste and colossal effort at a haute price tag of over $35 million. The reason for the enormous feat was that the southwestern property lies on one of the Caribbean's most spectacular long strips of white sand, which just happened to be Ms. Mandelli and Mr. Pinto's favorite island beach. They knew it intimately from years spent as guests at Coco Point Lodge (see previous listing). After a dispute of some kind, Mandelli and Pinto checked out and proceeded to buy (a 99-year lease) 200 or so adjoining acres to build their own sanctuary. Designed by Gianni Gamondi, a friend of the owners who designed many beautiful hotels on Sardinia's Costa Smeralda, K Club's 25 one-story cottages and 40 accommodations are made up of single and double cottages, suites, and villas, all oceanfront (with the exception of an inland garden bungalow with five rooms, called Lodge Rooms, the least expensive to be had). The appealingly simple white masonry bungalows have pinnacled, shingled roofs that fit comfortably into the natural environment. Inside they are refined and dramatically striking in their simplicity.

Bedrooms, 20 × 20 square feet, feature king-size beds, enormous walk-in closets, and white tiled bathrooms, replete with Krizia's own line of toiletries and perfumes, twin basins, wall-mounted hair dryers, and soft Krizia robes. Large square shower stalls have top-louvered windows, affording bathers full seaviews. Fixtures are rust-resistant white. Each cottage has an all-white outdoor kitchen and mini-refrigerator fully stocked with beverages and ice. When we arrived after lunch, a bottle of champagne, a platter of panini (little sandwiches), and a basket of fruit were chilling inside the refrigerator. The roomy sea-facing verandas are grand spaces with roll-up bamboo shades, tables and chairs, and oversized bamboo chairs and chaises for siestas and watching marvelous sunsets. Ceiling fans, and air-conditioning or breezes through the louvered windows and doors, keep the temperature just as you like it.

Floors throughout are tiled in white with occasional strips of aqua, and the white ceilings are accented with aqua-painted beams. Ms. Mandelli's special aqua color is to aqua what baby is to blue. Her aqua covers headboards, dressers, desks, and end tables and is the color of the resort's logo, stitched into towels, printed onto white T-shirts, and set in tiles at the bottom of the spacious, tiled saltwater pool. Two Jacuzzis are at the pool—one has regular jet streams, the other has a much more powerful force. There's also a TV and video room.

Custom-made poolside chaise longues and chairs, and sofas in the airy string of sitting rooms, have cushions and pillows covered in wide or thin aqua-and-white-striped cotton fabrics. Ms. Mandelli has broken up the repeat colors with artwork like gaily colored Haitian paintings and fanciful, hand-carved wooden banana trees. Cane-seated black desk chairs throughout have carved, brilliant blue pineapple backs. Vases filled with white or magenta impatiens (Mrs. Mandelli's favorite flower) and bougainvillea are strategically placed throughout. Interiors possess a gentle liquidity complementing sand, sky, and sea.

At the center of the resort, the public areas consist of an expansive passageway of open-air lounges, supported by 146 columns, a second-floor library reading room, and a Krizia boutique. Windows in the lounge have screen-louvered shutters that prop open to desired light and breeze angles. At one end is a bar with a tented, lower-beach-level lounge adjacent to the pool, with small white tables and chairs and an inviting L-shaped, white-cushioned banquette.

After a third visit to K Club since it opened, I found the rooms impeccable, the service and food excellent, and a pleasant, carefree atmosphere. British-born Sean Armstrong, the manager this year, hadn't arrived during my stay, nor had the current chefs from Roger Vergé and Cipriani. Still, we had absolutely no complaints. Even our 15-minute flight from Antigua on the resort's private white-and-aqua *Britton Norman* to Codrington's airport was on schedule. K Club's van and driver were waiting to take us on the 20-minute bumpy ride down a wide dirt road that eventually narrows through a new, softer topped lane. Upon arrival, guests get a partial view of the new 9-hole, links-style golf course: At 3,570 yards long, it's laid over 60 acres, with 27 sand traps and two lakes.

K Club's delicious meals are presented on one of three different elegant sets of specially designed dinnerware, crystal, and cutlery, served on tables of green-and-white-dappled ceramic. My dinner of asparagus risotto and medallions of Barbudan lobster with caviar butter was excellent. For lunches we had delicious soups, pasta dishes, or lobster and other well-composed salads. Dessert featured flawless, rich ice creams and fruit sorbets and delicious pastry inventions. The fine selection of wines ranged from fairly reasonable to pricey vintages.

The all-inclusive rate includes airport transfers, all meals (including picnics), tennis—there are two lighted courts—snorkeling, windsurfing, and Sunfish.

The guests during our stay were equally divided between Americans and Europeans, among them supermodel Claudia Schiffer, with a doting agent and crew who were photographing her calendar. Another celebrity guest, Ken Follett, traveling with his wife, said he had no plans to leave the hotel's beautiful grounds during a two-week holiday. While guests chatted amiably on the beach and offered pleasant greetings in the bar and restaurant in the evenings, most remained private in pairs or cliques. We simply tried to absorb every beguiling moment of our stay at dazzling, expensive K Club.

K CLUB
Barbuda, West Indies
TEL: (809) 460-0300
FAX: (809) 460-0305

Open November 15 through April.
Rates: Double occupancy. Lodge Room, $700; Cottage, $1,100; Suite, $1,600; Garden Villa, $2,100; Beach Villa, $2,700. Additional $125 per person round-trip airfare from Antigua.
Meal plan: FAP (includes all meals and picnic service and transportation round-trip from Codrington Airport).
Service charge: 10%.
Government tax: 8½%.
Children over 12 welcome.
Credit cards accepted.

A NOTEWORTHY OPTION

Palmetto Beach Hotel and Villas

We thought it would never happen, but finally there is a reasonably priced, first-class option to upscale Coco Point Lodge and K Club on Barbuda. Open since November 1992, the Palmetto Beach Hotel and Villas is one of the best-kept secrets in the Caribbean. That overused phrase truly applies here, because the Italian owner, the Impressa Guffanti Company, also owns the Marie Danielle Linea Hotel in Milan, does hardly any marketing or advertising.

On the approach into Codrington Airport in Barbuda, the plane flies along the immense strand of beach that rims the western side of the island from Coco Point on the southeastern tip to Cedar Tree Point at the northwest corner, a distance of about 17 miles. Roughly halfway between the two points, Palmetto Point, a huge, sandy triangle-shaped peninsula, juts into the sea. Palmetto Beach Hotel and Villas is set back several hundred yards from the beach on several flat acres at the point's center.

Although lots of tropical flora and hundreds of young palm trees have been planted, the site remains a sandy, barren wilderness. The stark white clubhouse building, the adjacent barracks-like, long curve of 22 cottage rooms, the nearby four-bedroom villa, and three double-room bungalows topped with orange-red pointed roofs, appear an exaggerated, ungainly architectural complex. They are. Palmetto Point clearly is not for everyone, but once ensconced, we came to like it.

First of all, we were pleasantly surprised to find excellent, if spare, accommodations inside our immaculate, spacious cottage room; the wood-beamed ceiling soared over cool tile floors. There was a large closet, bureau, two queen-size beds, a writing table and chair, and two peach-and-gray-striped upholstered love seats that made up a cozy sitting area. The mini-refrigerator was stocked with water and beverages. Bathrooms were superb, all tiled in white with a tub and shower, and extra-thick white terry-cloth towels embroidered with the hotel's logo in cheery peach. The villas and bungalows are spacious and similarly inviting.

Each accommodation has a small private terrace with a table and chairs. The sun is so fierce and relentless here that the air-conditioning is a blessing.

The clubhouse's modest, homey lounge, bar, and spacious restaurant opens out onto a terrace connected to an enormous tiled deck surrounding a 25 × 12-meter saltwater swimming pool. Chaises and chairs are placed in the sun or under a shaded area. A covered gallery has been erected off the restaurant for cocktails and occasional meals.

Palmetto has one lighted tennis court, and any water-sports activity can be arranged — bone or deep-sea fishing, diving, or snorkeling — but bring your own gear. Tours to the frigate bird sanctuary and horseback riding are other leisure options. A jeep can be rented locally for about $50 a day.

After unpacking, we immediately strolled the meandering concrete walkway through a tropical desert to the glorious west-facing beach to get a close-up look at the famous pink sand. Lounge chairs and a couple of bohios were placed at the end of the walkway on the beach, but next time we'll bring along a small packable, portable beach umbrella so we can relax in the shade anywhere we please along the expanse of beach. You might also consider bringing along a small cooler to keep iced beverages at hand, as well as any snacks or other nonperishable foods you might enjoy; the grocery selection in Codrington is minimal. Sunblock and a wide-brimmed hat are vital.

The southern side of the beach at Palmetto Point had a strong undertow during our visit, which is not uncommon. Swim with caution, as there's usually no one in sight if you get into trouble.

Barbuda's truly outstanding feature is its extraordinary stretch of beach. The rest of the island is a flat never-never land. For beach lovers and seekers of solitude, it's heaven.

Only Anegada in the British Virgin Islands comes close to comparison. Like Anegada, the treacherous reefs surrounding Barbuda discourage visitors, while supplying countless havens for lobsters, conchs, and an abundance of fish — delicacies that provide superlative meals for the local population as well as travelers.

Italian chef Lara Prestini, assisted by Barbudan Ranna'e Hamlet, prepares exceptionally good meals, a blend of Italian and American dishes. We dined on an inspiring carpaccio of uncooked thin zucchini slices topped with shavings of Parmesan cheese, drizzled with dark green virgin olive oil and vinegar, and a marvelous spaghetti dish tossed with generous hunks of lobster in a light tomato sauce, served with a good '91 Placido Chianti. Dessert was a sweet coconut layer cake, followed by espresso. Other offerings were homemade tagliolini with conch sauce and roasted ribs of beef with sweet pepper sauce. Lunch menus offer a variety of salads, always Barbuda lobster, a pasta of the day, sandwiches, burgers, and omelets. The iced cappuccino was super.

Palmetto Point's staff couldn't have been more accommodating. Barbudan Randolph Beezer, the deputy manager, and Armondo Mason, the general manager, are warm overseers. Only two other couples were in residence during our visit, one French, one German, who'd booked at Palmetto for two weeks. That would be too long a stay for us, but we're looking forward to returning for a four-day weekend of quiet time together, swimming and long walks on the beach, sleeping whenever we feel like it, and devouring books as well as Ms. Prestini's satisfying dinners.

PALMETTO BEACH HOTEL AND VILLAS
Barbuda, Antigua, West Indies
TEL: (809) 460-0440 (Ask for fax.)

Closed from September to mid-November.
Rates: Double occupancy. *Mid-December to mid-April:* Standard Cottage Rooms, $252; Superior Rooms in Villa and Hotel, $300; Deluxe Suite in Villa, $348. *Mid-April through August:* Accommodations $202 to $278. *Mid-November to mid-December:* Accommodations $176 to $244. Singles, deduct $75. Extra person, add $75. Children under 12 free (1 child maximum) when sharing room with parents. (Substantially lower EP, room-only rates also available.)
Meal plan: MAP (includes continental breakfast and dinner). FAP rates offered in winter ranging from $312 to $408 for accommodations and three meals a day, double occupancy. Children 6 to 12 MAP, $25 per child per day; FAP, $35 per child per day.
Service charge: 10%.
Government tax: 8½%.
Children welcome.
Credit cards accepted.

Useful Information

In 1993 I was on Barbuda for the grand opening of its first public gas station. A sign on the tiny gingerbread-trimmed office building read "Welcome to the Washington Gas Station. No Credit."

If you want to rent a car on Barbuda for exploring the island, try **Thomas and William Car Rental** on River Road. Several locals rent Jeeps, so inquire upon arrival.

Non-guests are not allowed at either Coco Point Lodge or K Club for meals, but **Palmetto Beach Hotel and Villas** accepts reservations (see page 99); call 460-0440. You might also find sustenance at the restaurant at **Sunset View Hotel**, adjacent to the airport, if it's open; 460-0266. The only real bar in town is called **The Pavilion**. Locals here might be able to tell you who and where someone's grilling lobster.

Philatelists should stop at the post office in the village for rare Barbudan stamps. The supply is very limited.

Apart from the island's extraordinary beaches, the main attraction is the **frigate bird rookery**, reached only by a small boat with a driver/guide that can carry a maximum of three or four passengers. Ask about it once you land at the airport; visits are normally easily arranged.

I wholeheartedly recommend a full-day excursion to Barbuda from Antigua if you're not planning on an island stay. Independent souls should carry along a cooler with lunch and beverages, sunblock, wide-brimmed hats or visors, and a portable beach umbrella. If you don't rent a vehicle, almost anyone who has one will be happy to transport you to a secluded beach for a fee. Agree on the amount in advance and be certain to organize a pickup time. Particularly beautiful is a pink beach that locals call Palm.

LIAT schedules daily flights from Antigua, (809) 462-0700, or **Carib Air** will book a charter for you, (809) 462-3147. **Caribeep** arranges Barbuda day tours departing from Antigua at around 8:30 A.M., returning at 4:30 P.M. Tours include a trip to the frigate bird sanctuary by boat, Codrington Estates, the Highlands plateau, the Martello Tower, and Spanish Well Point.

≈ ≈

BONAIRE

ACCOMMODATIONS

BONAIRE'S BEST
Harbour Village Beach Resort

A NOTEWORTHY OPTION
Captain Don's Habitat

RECOMMENDED RESTAURANTS

RECOMMENDED SHOPPING

PROVISIONS FOR YOUR ISLAND PANTRY

USEFUL INFORMATION

≈ ≈

≈ ≈

Accommodations

BONAIRE'S BEST

Harbour Village Beach Resort

Bonaire's most luxurious hotel is Harbour Village Beach Resort. Formerly managed by Sonesta and known as Sonesta Beach Resort, Harbour Beach hugs a quarter-mile-long curve of powdery, calm, leeward beach. It's located on a four-acre peninsula a few miles north of Kralendijk, Bonaire's capital, 10 to 15 minutes from the airport. Only a portion of the resort's 72 accommodations, made up of deluxe rooms and one- and two-bedroom suites, are beachfront. Others are spread around facing courtyards or, to the east, rest at the foot of spiffy marina dock. Under the direction of Mauricio Iza, president of Tecnoconsult, Venezuela's largest engineering and construction company, plans are in the works for condominiums, a small convention and health spa, a casino, tennis courts, and a golf course. The resort has many other acres of adjacent land on which to build; there's a total of 100 acres.

Expansion is likely to alter the ambience, but it's so quiet and peaceful that the added excitement probably will be a welcome attraction instead of an unwanted distraction. And, if guests book into beachfront accommodations, the new facilities are set a good distance away on the other side of the western road, Kaya Lechi.

Harbour Village possesses a cozy layout and an immensely attractive architecture. The two-story ochre-colored stucco buildings are capped with roofs of red tile. Façades are elegantly accented with graceful arched balconies, French doors, and windows trimmed in a contrasting but complementing bright greenish turquoise.

On this arid, almost always sun-drenched island, Harbour Village's luxuriant foliage is extravagantly refreshing, with gardens of imported oleander, bougainvillea, coconut, and saga palms.

Ducking into my room from the scorching heat, I was grateful for the air-conditioning. Ceiling fans stir the breeze for those who want natural cooling. Amenities include cable TV with a movie channel, private patios or balconies, and telephones. White-tiled floors support quality rattan furniture with colorful leaf prints on matching cushions, draperies, and bed covers. Closet space is ample. Standard small bathrooms have vanity and basin areas with hair dryers and an assortment of toiletries. The toilet, tub, and shower are in an attached nook with terry-cloth robes hanging on the back of the door.

Full room service, delightfully presented, is available from 7:30 A.M. until 11 P.M. Great Adventure Bonaire is guests' on-site sports facility, offering a full range of water sports, including scuba diving, windsurfing, sailing, deep-sea fishing, and powerboat rides. Don't miss a day trip to the offshore island of Klein Bonaire, directly across the sea from the hotel, for an underwater wonderland adventure.

Just beyond the entrance's circular courtyard a driveway leads to reception, a small boutique, and offices. Around the corner and up a few stairs, guests indulge themselves sunning and reading on a terrace that surrounds a beautiful freshwater swimming pool. The Kasa Coral, the resort's attractive three-level restaurant adjacent to the pool, also connects to a bar and lounge area. Dishes sampled were all excellent—crunchy conch fritters, Caesar salad, and keshi yena, a Dutch speciality composed of chicken, green peas, raisins, peppers, tomatoes, and spices baked in creamy rich Dutch cheese. Accompaniments were fried plantains and a sizable serving of delicious sautéed potatoes and mixed vegetables. The menu, although not extensive, offers an interesting variety, such as pasta putanesca or broiled breast of chicken with pineapple sauce. Creamy ice creams and Linzer torte were satisfying desserts.

Waiters were attentive, serving diners at tables covered with coral-colored cloths and carefully set with colorful dinnerware.

Informal lunches of grilled seafood, chicken, and burgers are served in the shade of La Balandra Bar and Grill, an elevated airy pavilion with a circular bar situated at the southern end of the beach. Attached to La Balandra is a wide and long, spacious wooden-planked pier furnished with wooden deck chairs, which provide a sunny, wide-open spot for watching the boating action during the day. At dusk, the pier turns into a romantic outdoor drawing room, where guests and visitors gather with cocktails to watch Bonaire's huge orange sun quickly plunge into the sea. Night comes quickly, but guests linger on. Linger is just what you'll want to do at delightful Harbour Village.

HARBOUR VILLAGE BEACH RESORT
P.O. Box 312, Kralendijk
Bonaire, Netherlands Antilles
TEL: 011-599-7-7500
FAX: 011-599-7-7507

RESERVATIONS
First Class Resorts
1 Alhambra Plaza, Suite 1150
Coral Gables, FL 33146
TEL: (800) 424-0004 or
(305) 567-9509
FAX: (305) 567-9659

Open all year.
Rates: Double occupancy. *Mid-April to mid-December:* Courtyard, Marina Front, and Oceanfront rooms, $215 to $270; One-Bedroom Suite, $430; Two-Bedroom Suite, $620. *Mid-December to mid-April:* Rooms, $260 to $395; One-Bedroom Suite, $435; Two-Bedroom Suite, $695.
Meal plan: EP; CP (continental breakfast), $10; MAP (includes breakfast and dinner), $50; FAP (three meals), $65.

Service charge: 10%.
Government tax: $4.50 per person per night.
Children welcome.
Credit cards accepted.

A NOTEWORTHY OPTION

Captain Don's Habitat

Captain Don's Habitat, located on Bonaire's coastline about three miles north of its small capital, Kralendijk, has been around since the mid-seventies as a no-frills retreat for serious divers. It's been expanded and upgraded a few notches, and that's good news.

Owner Captain Don Stewart, an engaging island character and transplanted Californian, has been on Bonaire for more than 30 years. He's responsible not only for the resort's enhancement, but more importantly, is known for his dedication to protecting and preserving Bonaire's delicate marine life. Regulations that ban spear fishing, lobster trapping, and anchoring or stepping on coral are strictly enforced. If fragile coral is damaged, the dive site is immediately closed for its slow repair process. These are but a few of the rules and restrictions you'll discover during orientation. There is, of course, plenty of spectacular marine life open to exploration in Bonaire's glass-clear waters.

Captain Don's Habitat would be my choice of reasonably priced lodging for travelers concentrating on diving during a holiday in Bonaire. The resort offers diving instruction, from beginning to PADI specialty courses, and has all the latest diving and camera equipment. The dive packages are real bargains here.

Some of the resort's 63 accommodations, all in slim, two-storied white masonry buildings with orange-tiled, peaked Dutch-style roofs, are clustered around a spacious freshwater pool area, the Rum Runners Restaurant and Kunuku Terrace Bar, and reception. The rest of the lodgings are refurbished cottages, new deluxe rooms, and waterfront villas. The resort's small but inviting beach is located near the villas.

Front and back yards have a stark gravel base, although individual villas, spaced a good distance apart, are surrounded by palm trees and plantings.

Inside villas, dark, ocean-blue tiles cover floors, kitchens, and bathrooms throughout. Standard rattan furniture is covered in a variety of blue prints and stripes. Villas have fully equipped kitchens and patios or balconies. A ceiling fan and air-conditioning cools each lodging. Interiors are tropical standard. Still, they provide comfortable living.

I prefer second-floor rooms in the poolside buildings, with enticing views over the pool and out to sea.

Captain Don's Habitat is one of the jolliest places to be on the island because of Don Stewart's outgoing personality and the excitement generated by enthusiastic diver guests, although non-divers can enjoy the merriment as well.

The food here is average—decent burgers, sandwiches, and salads at lunch and seafood at dinner. Everyone looks forward to Thursday's Tex/Mex night for tastier and spicier fare. The place is packed with locals and travelers who gather to listen to live music, nibble good grub, and socialize with Captain Don, who puts on a Stetson and western attire. Don and divers swap stories at the bar well into the night.

CAPTAIN DON'S HABITAT
P.O. Box 88
Bonaire, Netherlands Antilles
TEL: 011-599-7-8290
FAX: 011-599-7-8240

RESERVATIONS
Habitat North America Office
903 South American Way
Miami, FL 33132
TEL: (800) 327-6709
FAX: (305) 371-2337

Open all year.
Rates: Double occupancy. *Year-round rates:* Studio, Suite, Villa Superior Double, Two-Bedroom Cottage, Entire Villas (4 to 6 persons), $165 to $440. Most guests book special dive packages.
Meal plan: EP. Set rates for separate meals, MAP, and FAP available upon request.
Service charge: 10%.
Government tax: $4.50 per person per night.
Children welcome.
Credit cards accepted.
Note: Special dive packages are available upon request.

Recommended Restaurants

BONAIRE'S FINEST*

* **Kasa Coral**, 7500 (Harbour Village Beach Resort). Excellent food, gracious service, and lovely open-air setting. Also **La Balandra Bar and Grill** for beachside lunches and drinks. (See resort listing, page 104.) Moderate to expensive.
* **The Oceanfront Restaurant & Bar**, 5644 (Coral Regency Resort). Beautiful terrace dining room serving steaks, fresh fish like wahoo and red snapper, or seafood dishes from conch to shrimp. In a romantic setting right at the shoreline, diners are encouraged to feed fish in water below for an instant colorful show. Moderate to expensive.
* **Jardin Tropical**, 5716 (third floor, La Terraza Mall). Dine on satisfying French cuisine overlooking Kralendijk. Moderate to expensive.
* **Bistro des Amis**, 8003 (Kaya L. D. Gerharts 4). Commendable French cuisine in a Bonairean house. A Chaines des Rôtisseurs member. Expensive.
* **Richard's Waterfront Dining**, 5263 (J. A. Abraham Boulevard 60). Check the chalkboard for daily specials—good pasta dishes, lobster and other grilled seafood, steaks, and more in a friendly restaurant. Moderate.

OTHER DEPENDABLE CHOICES

Rendez Vouz Restaurant, 8454 (Kaya L. D. Gerharts 3). Unpretentious but delightful streetside restaurant. Leisurely dining on special ragouts or other good, homey foods of the day. Freshly baked French bread with garlic butter is a highlight. Inexpensive to moderate.

Raffles, 8617 (near Flamingo Beach Hotel). Local cuisine with West Indian overtones in a house across from the sea. Inexpensive to moderate.

Playa Lechi Restaurant and Pelican Bar, 5300 (Sunset Beach Hotel). For beachside breakfast buffets, lunches, sunset cocktails, or dinner, this oceanside thatched dining terrace or beach bar is always a diversion. Food is average to good. Wednesday's Italian; Thursday's barbecue; Saturday's a Bonairean Night with band and folkloric show. Bring your bathing suit during the day. Inexpensive to moderate.

Chibi Chibi, 8285 (Divi Flamingo Beach Resort & Casino). There are splendid water views from this candlelit dining room terrace. Continental and seafood specialties comprise the menu. The seaside Calabas Terrace serves full breakfasts and lunches. Dinners here are "all-you-can-eat" buffets. Very popular. Inexpensive to moderate.

Other possibilities in Kralendijk are **Mona Lisa** and **Karel's Beach Bar**, where you can dive off the pier for a swim. New and untried are **Twins Chicken & Salad Bar** in town and **'t Ankertje** at the customs dock, which serves Dutch and seafood specialties, both at reasonable prices. For Chinese, options include the **China Garden** in Kralendijk or **China Nobo**, just outside of Kralendijk in Nikiboko. Find pizza and heros at **Pizza Pizza** in Harborside Mall.

Toys Grand Cafe, 6666 (Airport Road). New and untried, featuring Indonesian, barbecue, and French cuisines. Moderate. Also untried is **De Roode Pelikaan** at Lac Bay Resort on the east coast, 5686.

Recommended Shopping

Although Bonaire has two malls, **The Harborside Shopping Mall** and the newer **La Terraza Mall**, shoppers will find their favorite pastime a limited experience. Following are the best of a sprinkling of boutiques and stores in Kralendijk or in such hotels as **Harbour Village, Divi Flamingo**, and **Sand Dollar Beach Club**, which all carry resortwear, T-shirts, gift items, and sundries:

Littman Jewelers (Kaya Grandi 33, Harborside Mall, and Divi Flamingo Resort). Features jewelry and watches, crystal, figurines, and other quality items.

Benetton (Kaya Grandi 49). Carries well-known apparel collection, the "United Colors of Benetton."

Try **Little Holland** in The Harborside Mall for Blue Delft and quality cigars. **Bamali**, 5628 (The Harborside Mall), has lovely Indonesian imports from clothing and jewelry to unusual baskets and other handcrafts. **Buddy Dive Shop** has an extensive selection of T-shirts, snorkeling and diving equipment, books, and postcards.

Provisions for Your Island Pantry

The best market in Bonaire is **Cultimara** in Kralendijk. **Uncle Buddy's Sand Dollar Grocery** in the Sand Dollar Shopping Center is a useful mini-market stocking staples, some baked goods, cheeses, meats, beverages, and sundries.

For bakery goods go to **Exito** and **Bonaire Bakery** in town.

Keep **China Nobo**, 8981, on Emerencianastraat 4, just outside of Kralenkijk, in mind for Chinese takeout and deliveries. Italian takeout available at **Pizza Pizza** in The Harborside Mall in town.

Useful Information

Bonaire's official pink guide, *Bonaire Holiday!*, published three times a year, is an indispensable companion to keep at your side.

Most visitors to Bonaire come for diving or other water sports. There are about a dozen qualified dive operations now as well as companies that schedule tours of the island. It takes only a day to tour the island's main sights and features. You can also hire a taxi or rent a car. Three car rental agencies are: **Avis**, 011-599-7-5791; **Budget**, 011-599-7-8300, and **Dollar**, 011-599-7-8888.

Don't miss the **flamingo sanctuary**, the **solar salt works**, and the 19th-century stone **slave huts** near **Pink Beach**, a great place for snorkeling, diving, or sunbathing—plan a picnic. Other must-sees are **Willemstoren**, Lighthouse, and **Boca Cai**, where thousands of conch shells are piled up beachside—all south or southwest of Kralenkijk. There's more to see in the north, especially the **Slagbaai National Park**.

Bonaire has a **casino** at Divi Flamingo Beach Resort.

≈ ≈

BRITISH VIRGIN ISLANDS

(ANEGADA, GUANA ISLAND, JOST VAN DYCK, MOSQUITO ISLAND, NECKER ISLAND, PETER ISLAND, TORTOLA, VIRGIN GORDA)

ACCOMMODATIONS

BRITISH VIRGIN ISLANDS' BEST

Biras Creek Resort, Virgin Gorda
Drake's Anchorage Resort Inn, Mosquito
Guana Island 🌴
Little Dix Bay, Virgin Gorda ♛
Long Bay Beach Resort, Tortola
Necker Island
Peter Island Resort and Yacht Harbour
The Sugar Mill, Tortola

NOTEWORTHY OPTIONS

Anegada Reef Hotel, Anegada
The Pink Houses, Jost Van Dyck
Sandcastle, Jost Van Dyck

RECOMMENDED RESTAURANTS

RECOMMENDED SHOPPING

PROVISIONS FOR YOUR ISLAND PANTRY

USEFUL INFORMATION

≈ ≈

≈ ≈

Accommodations

BRITISH VIRGIN ISLANDS' BEST

Biras Creek, Virgin Gorda

Biras Creek is a splendid escapist's hideaway set on a 140-acre nature preserve. From an overhead view, the resort's property looks like a headless woman dancing, arms stretched up inside billowing sleeves. At the waist is an isthmus touched by two seas; the marina dock and entrance to the hotel on the west, and to the east the long stretch of Berchers Bay, where the accommodations and large freshwater platform swimming pool are tucked away. The white sand beach at Deep Bay to the northeast is where the missing head would be. The lady's flowing skirt and left sleeve are lined with a series of nature trails.

At Biras Creek you can languish in the creature comforts of a quiet luxurious seaside resort and pursue virtually every water sport and boating and sailing activity. You can visit several other resorts in the area as well. All sorts of interesting excursions to neighboring islands are further options. Just getting to the resort is a little adventure in itself.

After a flight into Virgin Gorda's tiny airport, Roman, a cheerful young man from Dominica, drove me across Gorda Peak to Gun Creek dock on the northeast end of the island in one of Speedy's taxi vans. The 20-minute ride is quite a treat. Dazzling seaviews of undulating shorelines and glimpses of distant and nearby islands such as Tortola, Mosquito, Prickly Pear, and Eustatia meet you at every twist and turn of the road. Biras Creek is accessible only by boat. I had just enough time for a cold soda at The Last Stop Bar before the resort's motor launch picked me up for the ten-minute cruise to Biras Creek's private pier on the east end of the North Sound.

The North Sound is an enormous jewel box, loaded with moored sailboats and yachts of all sizes, particularly in season. As you approach the resort, off to the left is the Bitter End Yacht Club, Biras Creek's spirited neighbor.

Upon arrival, all you can actually see of the resort is a large, circular, natural-stone, castlelike complex at the top of a hill, covered with cone-shaped, wooden-shingled roofs skirted with scalloped green canopies. At the pinnacle is the romantic open-air restaurant and breezy bar. Several wide natural-stone terraces on various levels and stairways lead to the lounge/library/game room, the offices, and reception.

111

You don't check into the resort immediately. Instead you are warmly greeted and driven by Mini-Moke to your accommodations, one of 32 terraced suites housed in 16 yellow masonry cottages, most of which are oceanfront. Keys are not used unless you request one. Berchers Bay is not a swimming beach, but it has lovely views and is good for shell hunting.

Before formalities are taken care of, you're urged to relax, unpack, and get acclimated. This is easily accomplished by perusing the resort's excellent information sheet and a map of the layout of Biras Creek that is marked with several nature walks, which take from 12 to 90 minutes. The winding trails are carved out of the arid hills. Virgin Gorda's east end is dry, with scrub brush. You'll see turkhead and pipe-organ cactus, tamarind, white cedar, wild nutmeg, and frangipani trees. Elect to stroll or bicycle (two are waiting at your door) a few minutes past Alvin Harrigan's nursery (Mondays at 10 A.M. he conducts a garden walk), two lighted tennis courts (there's a round-robin tournament every Sunday), and the bird sanctuary at Salt Water Lake en route to the white sand beach at Deep Bay, surrounded by palms, sea grape, and tamarisk.

Water-sports facilities include snorkeling, sailing on Holder 12s or 14s, and windsurfing at Deep Bay. Waterskiing, scuba diving, and day sails are easily organized. You can also indulge in other water sports offered at the Bitter End. To get there, either walk over a hill path, which takes about 20 minutes, or hail a motorboat.

Biras Creek's rooms are tiled and furnished and decorated with attractive rattan. Throw rugs here and there, framed pictures of seashells and flowers, louvered windows, and ceiling fans over firm queen- or king-size beds add up to first-class comfort.

No radios, TVs, or telephones in the rooms, but two pay-phone booths are attached to the charming and well-stocked boutique building. Telex and fax machines are located in the office.

Bathrooms are standard modern with open and walled shower stalls and a few gift toiletries. The two super-deluxe cottages have oversized sunken oval tubs, along with bidets and extra dressing and closet space. Each suite has a refrigerator. Rum and mixers, a filled ice bucket, electric water heater, tea bags, instant coffee, powdered milk, and sugar are provided, as Biras Creek has no room service. Early-morning coffee, orange juice, and Danish pastries are set out by the pool from 7 to 8 A.M., and afternoon tea with sandwiches and cakes is offered in the game room.

Since it opened in 1974, Biras Creek's restaurant and extensive wine list have been highly praised. New York trained, Chef Earl Williams from Nevis changes his elegant menus daily. Lunch lightly on chilled chicken and lemon soup and a platter of smoked Scottish salmon and avocado served with a tossed salad. At dinner, dine more heartily on one of three choices of a first course and entrée. Such a meal might include grilled tenderloin of beef with a green peppercorn sauce, fabulous fresh grilled Anegada lobster, or veal with mushroom and caper sauce. Port and Stilton are always offered. Service is friendly and nicely paced.

General Manager J. Ludwig Mowinckels Rederi from Norway is in charge. Clientele is predominantly American and English of all ages, but in general it's a mature, quiet set with nautical inclinations.

Pelican Point Villa, formerly Biras Creek's manager's home, is rentable. This lovely two-bedroom home, perched high on a hill, overlooks the creek and North Sound. Sensational views from the spacious terrace make this a very special retreat.

BIRAS CREEK
P.O. Box 54
North Sound
Virgin Gorda, British Virgin Islands
TEL: (809) 494-3555
FAX: (809) 494-3557

RESERVATIONS
Ralph Locke Islands
TEL: (800) 223-1108
FAX: (914) 763-5362

Open all year.
Rates: Double occupancy. *December 18 to April 1:* Garden View Suites, $465; Ocean View Suites, $515; Grand Suites, $685. Pelican Point Villa: $840 for two; $998 for four. *April 2 to December 16:* Garden View Suites, $340; Ocean View Suites, $425; Grand Suites, $550. Pelican Point Villa: $575 for two; $710 for four. Extra person, $60 per day.
Meal plan: MAP (breakfast and dinner). Lunch is an additional $12.50 per person per day.
Service charge: 10%.
Government tax. 7%.
Children under 6 not accepted.
Credit cards accepted.
Note: Special Week of Enchantment, Just the Two of Us, Summer Family Vacation, and Sailaway packages available upon request.

Drake's Anchorage Resort Inn, Mosquito Island

When you check into Drake's Anchorage, the 125-acre island of Mosquito on Virgin Gorda's North Sound is yours to share with the occupants of only 11 other accommodations. Visitors from yachts and sailboats come ashore to dine but remain in the small public areas. You are free to wander Mosquito's bosky hiking trails, luxuriate on four separate white-sand beaches, explore offshore caves and coral reefs, or simply eavesdrop on nature from a hammock. All the lodgings are oceanfront and balconied; the views, a nautical Caribbean tableau.

The resort is accessible only by boat. Guests can fly into Virgin Gorda Airport from Beef Island, Tortola, in the British Virgin Islands; St. Thomas, U.S. Virgin Islands; or San Juan, Puerto Rico. After about a 30-minute Speedy's Taxi ride to Leverick Bay dock on the northeast end of Virgin Gorda, guests are picked up for a 10-minute launch cruise to Drake's Anchorage.

Drake's Anchorage is an easygoing escapists' retreat with the extra bonus of having three other resorts within a few minutes' complimentary shuttle: The Bitter End, Biras Creek, and Leverick Bay. These hotels have restaurants, shops, and entertainment. Tours of Virgin Gorda can be organized as well. But Drake's Anchorage enthusiasts are generally seeking precisely what this resort has to offer, namely tranquil tropical surroundings and privacy. The repeat American clientele, young and old, who book here have a proprietary "Don't tell anyone about it" reverence for the hotel.

The white-trimmed brown wooden cottages rest on stilts along the shoreline. There are 12 totally renovated suites named after flora on the island. The small tidy suites are decorated with rattan furniture. Small bathrooms, also refurbished, have showers, a little basket of toiletries, and a pair of robes. Ceiling fans and the tradewinds provide natural air-conditioning.

The two villas, the prize accommodations here, overlook Lime Tree Beach on the southern end of the island. Each has a master bedroom with an extra loft bedroom and bath in one of them. Made of native stone, copper, and hardwood, with floors of Italian, oversized, square white tiles, the villas have pitched ceilings, paddle fans, fully equipped kitchens, and roomy living/dining room areas. The bathrooms have large walk-in showers, oversized tubs, and bidets. Nothing is lavish; it's appealing simplicity, Caribbean style.

Activities include free windsurfers, 19-foot Squibb sailboats, snorkeling equipment, and transfer to nearby islands and coves. No pool, TVs, or radios are available, although there is a TV/video in the game room and an outdoor amphitheater with a projection screen.

Drake's Anchorage's boutique is filled with attractive casual resortwear, necessities, and handcrafts.

Considering the remoteness of the location, the culinary pleasures at Drake's Anchorage have always been substantial, but we haven't tried new chef Shelford Tucker's food yet. The room rate includes three meals a day. No room service is offered.

The oceanside bar and dining room are spruced up with shells, driftwood, and flowers. Wooden tables covered with tablecloths twinkle with candlelight in the evening.

Drake's Anchorage Resort Inn is an informal, tiny hidden treasure for those who succumb to the charms of true island living, where there is a calm atmosphere, sea-scented breezes, blossoming nature, and a hospitable staff to coddle you. Managers are Albert and Gloria Wheatley.

DRAKE'S ANCHORAGE RESORT INN
P.O. Box 2510
North Sound Virgin Gorda,
British Virgin Islands
TEL: (809) 494-2254 (ask for fax)

RESERVATIONS
Drake's Anchorage Resort
Inn
1340 Centre St., Suite 203
Newton Centre, MA
02159
TEL: (800) 624-6651 *or*
     (617) 969-9913
FAX: (617) 969-5147

Open: year-round except for the month of August
Rates: Double occupancy. *December 18 to April 17:* Rooms and Suites, $412 to $485;
     Deluxe Villa, $595. *April 18 to December 17:* Rooms and Suites, $327 to $373;
     Deluxe Villa, $515. Single year-round, $218.
Meal plan: FAP (includes breakfast, lunch, and dinner).
Service charge: 15%.
Government tax: 7%.
Children welcome.
Credit cards accepted.

Guana Island 🌴

Guana Island is all about location, location, location, and nature. If you are looking for comfortable lodgings, a casual, romantic atmosphere in an isolated natural habitat, there are 850 acres of this private island resort to explore. Never more than 32 human guests at a time, the thousands of other denizens occupying this hilly island are rare species of amphibians, and birds, including eight roseate flamingos and Newton's barefoot screech owl. Early in March 1994, a humpback whale was sighted. Guests are completely in touch with nature. Serious research conducted on the premises in July and October attracts scientists and students from as far away as Harvard University and the Guangdong Institute of the Chinese Academy of Sciences. Guana Island now has a small natural-history museum containing unearthed artifacts, shells, marine life, insects, and other species displayed in cases, as well as photographs and a collection of reference books for interested guests' inspection.

Guana Island, located just off the almost uninhabited northeast coast of Tortola, opened its doors in 1934. It was the first hotel in the British Virgin Islands, built on the ruins of a century-old Quaker estate and sugarcane plantation by Beth and Louis K. Bigalow. It's now owned by Gloria and Henry Jarecki.

After a flight into Beef Island Airport, guests are met by a taxi driver representing Guana, and driven to Guana's dock a short distance away. From there they're whisked off for a 15-minute cruise to Guana's private dock in one of the resort's powerboats.

Guana Island pool and seaview from Grenada Villa on Guana
Island in the British Virgin Islands.

Rounding the promontory of Monkey Point gives you the first glimpse of the cluster of
whitewashed, blue-shuttered hotel buildings resting atop the ridge of a hill, which
overlook the magnificent half-mile White Bay Beach. Up close, the buildings resemble
a little Greek village.

After a steep, winding drive up to the hotel, Jonathan and Catherine Morley, the
resort's young managers, greet guests with a cocktail. It's the last drink that will be served
to you, because Guana's bars—one in the clubhouse just off the dining terrace, and one
on the beach—are honor-system self-service. You are not so much pampered at Guana
Island as cared for.

Accommodations here are neither rustic or luxurious, but reach a pleasing balance
somewhere in between. Guana's 18 rooms are named after islands, like Anegada, Barbados, and Dominica. Grenada is a three-bedroom villa with a pool. The entire house
can be rented or rooms here can be rented separately. The newest addition, totally

isolated, is the North Beach Cottage. Completed in summer 1993, the beach cottage sits on the Atlantic coastline on its own one-third mile of coral beach, not really swimmable except for a small pool formed by a clearing within the coral. Enveloped in sea grape and perched above the ground on pilings, the one-bedroom house with a living room, full kitchen, and bath is surrounded by open and protected decks. Meals can be served in the cottage, if desired. Guests in this remote sanctuary are provided with a battery-operated golf cart to drive on a winding trail along an old Quaker stone wall to White Bay Beach. Transportation up to the clubhouse is available from there.

All other rooms, in single cottages or two- to three-room buildings, have been remodeled so that each has its own private lounging veranda. Views from every one are breathtaking. New rattan furniture, bureaus, desks, lamps, and other furnishings have enhanced the lodgings. Floors are cool, painted concrete with area rugs. Bathrooms were recently upgraded with new basin countertops, and the showers are little grottoes enclosed in freeform sculptural whitewashed masonry. Amenities include umbrellas, drying racks, oil lamps, and flashlights. Guana's rooms need no air-conditioning or ceiling fans, so constant are the cooling breezes.

Grenada, the three-bedroom villa with attractive fossil-stone floors (all rooms have private entrances), is the prime location at the top of a hill, adjacent to the Jareckis' new home. It's difficult to leave the inviting 20-foot round pool and fabulous 360-degree, bird's-eye views.

At Guana Island, you'll do your share of climbing up and down paths to and from your room, to the dining and club rooms and bar area, and there are miles of natural trails; a map is supplied. Be sure to bring a good pair of walking shoes, and binoculars for birdwatching.

Transportation to and from White Bay Beach, in Guana's Land Rover, is available at regular intervals.

All meals are served on dining terraces or at a couple of indoor tables. For both breakfast and lunch you select a seat at any table. At dinner, however, compatible seating is arranged by the Morleys unless you request to dine privately.

Breakfasts are plentiful, and lunches are buffets that might be West Indian, featuring chicken roti and a curried ragout served in a bready crêpe; or another day it may be American, with hamburgers topped with sautéed onions and bacon, fresh tuna salad, coleslaw, and mozzarella and tomatoes. For dessert at a recent lunch, we had watermelon sorbet laced with chocolate bits.

During the cocktail hour from 7 to 8 P.M. guests gather to sample some of chef Immanuel "Manny" Thompson's hors d'oeuvres, like tiny beignets or spicy Caribbean baked cheese tidbits. Delicious, crunchy cassava or coconut bread, served with a variety of dips, is made by a Tortola native. Selections for evening entrées include veal picatta, lobster florentine, shrimp with herb sauce, or the fresh fish of the day. Guana's home-made breads and confections are winners, but on the whole, the food is average.

With the Morleys acting as hosts throughout your stay, it takes only a short time to meet all other guests, and no one, including singles, ever feels left out. New arrivals are always cause for great curiosity.

In season, about 80% of the guests are on repeat visits; this drops to 50% the rest of the year. Guana's guests are primarily over-forty Americans, but young couples interested in nature and an exclusive, romantic hideaway are finally discovering Guana Island. Nonguests are not permitted, unless they are friends of in-resident guests who arrive by boat for a visit.

Aside from hiking, birdwatching (Wilson's plover, rare roseate tern, and bridled quail dove, to name only a few), sunbathing, and swimming, there are two tennis courts (one clay, one Astroturf), a croquet court, a small golf meadow, volleyball, and seven beaches, several accessible only by boat—the hotel will provide transportation.

Boat trips to other islands can also be arranged, as can deep-sea fishing, scuba diving, a cocktail cruise, waterskiing, or sailing. Rates for special activities are posted at the bar and beach hut.

The small library, just off the clubhouse living room, brims with hundreds of books and stacks of board games. The only guest phone in the hotel is in the library, and it's available on the honor system.

In keeping with the overall atmosphere of peace and tranquility, there are no radios or TVs, although I'm told that to avert a mutiny, a television is provided each year for the Super Bowl and for important news events. Quiet recorded music is occasionally played in the clubhouse living room.

All of Guana Island can be rented. It's especially appropriate for weddings, special birthdays, family reunions, and small business meetings.

GUANA ISLAND	U.S. RESERVATIONS
Box 32	Guana Island Office
Road Town, Tortola	10 Timber Trail
British Virgin Islands	Rye, NY 10580
TEL: (809) 494-2354	TEL: (800) 544-8262 *or*
FAX: (809) 495-2900	(914) 967-6050
	FAX: (914) 967-8048

Closed September and October.

Rates: Double occupancy. *November 1 to December 15* and *April 1 to August 31:* Room, $435; North Beach Cottage, $660; Rent-the-Island, $5,975. *December 16 to March 31:* Room, $595; North Beach Cottage, $890; Rent-the-Island $8,325. Round-trip taxi and boat transfers, $25 per person.

Meal plan: FAP (includes three meals daily, afternoon tea, and house wines with lunch and dinner, and cocktail hors d'oeuvres).

Service charge: 12%.

Government taxes: 7%.

Children over 13 welcome; younger children upon request.

Credit cards not accepted.

Little Dix Bay, Virgin Gorda ◤◢

Little Dix Bay has the perfect blend of sophistication and island simplicity that creates a unique Caribbean resort that has stood the test of time. We offer genuine service from a staff who has been serving our guests for the past thirty years. Our guest can unwind in a truly relaxing atmosphere, with plenty to do if you want to do it . . . or nothing to do at all.

E. DAVID BREWER, MANAGING DIRECTOR

Little Dix Bay, a Laurance S. Rockefeller original and the sister resort of Caneel Bay in St. John in the U.S. Virgin Islands (see listing page 348), opened in 1964 with 50 rooms situated along a magnificent heart-shaped beach. As of winter 1993, Little Dix had 98 rooms and eight suites. During that summer resort closed for three months for cosmetic remodeling—eight rooms were transformed into four elegant one-bedroom suites; air-conditioning was added to 44 rooms, and telephones were installed in all accommodations. For those guests preferring natural breezes for temperature control and no ringing phones, there are still plenty of louvers and ceiling fans, and telephones can easily be disconnected.

Rosewood Hotels of Dallas assumed management of Little Dix and Caneel Bay on June 1, 1993, with plans to refurbish and upgrate both resorts. As overseers of La Samanna in St. Martin (see listing page 302), and responsible for that resort's successful rejuvenation, it's not surprising that the changes at Little Dix have worked out just fine. The new furnishings in the suites and restaurants, created by Vision Design of Dallas, are cheerful tropical fabrics on island-style quality pieces that enhance the lodgings and public areas considerably. More refurbishing is scheduled in the future for all accommodations.

Rooms at Little Dix Bay are spread from one end of the more than a quarter mile, north-facing beach to the other, and up a little ridge on the western side. Layouts are rectangular or hexagonal shaped; a blend of wood and natural stone walls. Some sit on stilts with hammocks and resting areas underneath—luxurious treehouses.

All rooms have amenities like mini-refrigerators with welcome-beverage setup, safes, umbrellas, toiletries, and tiny squeeze flashlights. Baths are comfortably large with stall showers. There are no TVs, radios, or swimming pool.

The four soaring roofs of Little Dix's redecorated Pavilion dining room rise up like shingled pyramids from behind palm trees and plantings. Manicured tropical lawns and grounds camouflage the majority of beachfront rooms as well as the sea grape–enshrouded seven tennis courts (unlighted) and adjoining tennis shop. Tennis remains under the supervision of Peter Burwash International.

Spread out over 142 acres—more than 350 more acres are untouched except for nature trails—the focal point of the resort is and always has been the splendid strip of beach. All water sports and equipment—floats, Sunfish, windsurfers, kayaks, snorkeling gear, and waterskiing are included in the rates.

The weekly activities schedule at Little Dix lists water taxis to nearby beaches, scuba lessions, aerobics, garden walks, kitchen tours, feature movie presentations in the Activities Pavilion, the managing director's weekly cocktail reception, and more. Live entertainment in the evenings is provided as well. Dancing under the stars or a full moon on the Pavilion's wide terrace is intoxicating.

The public areas at Little Dix consist of the attractive, open-air Activities Pavilion, set apart in gardens adjacent to the Pavilion and Sugar Mill restaurants and bars. The beachside Sugar Mill dining room terrace and bar features grilled seafood with Mediterranean menus that include pizzas, pastas, and salads for lunch and fine entrées for dinner. The Pavilion dining terrace offers wonderful groaning-board daily buffet luncheons, afternoon tea, and dinner by candlelight. The food at the resort is excellent, whether you're sampling roast chicken, fresh asparagus, and a salad for lunch, or filet mignon for a candlelit dinner. Pastries are first-rate. Gentlemen are requested to wear button-down shirts with collars, trousers (no jeans permitted), and closed shoes after sunset. Not surprisingly, the guests at Little Dix Bay are a conservative crowd, overwhelmingly American.

Little Dix is a blissfully peaceful, romantic, restful hideaway on a spectacular piece of property with a stunning beach.

LITTLE DIX BAY
P.O. Box 70
Virgin Gorda, British Virgin Islands
TEL: (809) 495-5555
FAX: (809) 495-5661

RESERVATIONS
Rosewood Hotels
TEL: (800) 928-3000
FAX: (214) 871-5444

Open all year.

Rates: Double occupancy. *December 20 to March 31:* Garden, Ocean, and Deluxe Rooms, $450 to $590; Deluxe and Superior Air-Conditioned, $690 to $790; One-Bedroom Suites, $1,200. *Month of April* and *November 7 to December 19:* Rooms, $320 to $560; One-Bedroom Suite, $930. *May 1 to November 6:* Rooms, $225 to $490; One-Bedroom Suite, $750. Third person in room, $65.

Meal plan: AP (includes full breakfasts). FAP (including breakfast, lunch, and dinner), $70 per person per day. FAP for children ages 5 to 16, $50 per child per day.

Service charge: 15% optional meal plan and beverage selections. 15% service charge added to all meal and beverage checks for guests on EP plan.

Government tax: 7%.

Children welcome.

Credit cards accepted.

Note: Special plans include Honeymoon, Island Hopper, Tennis, Dive, and Land/Sea. Information upon request.

Long Bay Beach Resort, Tortola

Ever since 50-acre Long Bay opened in 1964, its outstanding feature has been an incredibly beautiful, north-facing, mile-long, powdery white sand beach. The sea can be surfy in winter. The resort is about a 45-minute drive from Beef Island Airport or 10 minutes from the West End ferry dock, which has direct service from downtown Charlotte Amalie or Red Hook on St. Thomas' east end. Cars and Jeeps are available for rental at the hotel.

A little over eight years ago, the owners of the Stratton Mountain Resort in Vermont purchased Long Bay. The good news was that the new proprietors had spent a considerable amount of money upgrading the resort and making new additions: There are 32 new beachfront deluxe rooms at the western end of the resort. They're pastel multi-unit buildings with patios overlooking the sea. Second-floor rooms are superior for pitched-ceiling roominess and views. Hurricane Hugo appeared and practically wiped out the hillside accommodations, formerly modest quarters. Twenty new oceanview hillside cottage (rooms and studios) have replaced them. These and the beachfront deluxe rooms are in tiptop shape, with cheery, tropical, upscale furnishings and decor. All rooms have air-conditioning (except the cabanas), direct-dial phones, refrigerators, wet bars, toaster ovens, coffee-makers, and alarm clock radios. The deluxe rooms have cable TVs, separate shower rooms, and a vanity and dressing area. Ten modest beachfront cabanas are built on stilts right at the beach. Bedrooms have queen-size beds, and the small kitchenette fits in between the bedroom and the tiny but adequate bath. Open sliding glass and screen doors and a ceiling fan cool the rooms. These accommodations are still peanut-gallery quality with box-seat prices. If you want crashing surf sounds a few feet away and like to swing from the hammock hung beneath each of these perches, they might suit you. Long Bay also has several two- to five-bedroom villas as rentals.

As you drive into the resort, the first thing you see on the right are ruins around which the breakfast and lunch restaurant and a bar are set. You dine inside the ruins at tables or banquettes or on the adjacent terrace or at tables set right in the sand next to the small elevated freshwater swimming pool. A hard-surfaced, unlighted tennis court is next door, as is Baskin' in the Sea, Long Bay's scuba-diving operation.

The main public complex is located at the center of the resort, across from the hotel's 600-yard-long par-3 pitch-and-putt course. A very attractive small lounge and reception were added by the new proprietors, plus The Pelican's Pouch boutique, carrying essentials, handcrafts, and Caribbean jams, spices, herbs, beverages, and snacks. The lower-level bar just beyond the shop has an al fresco deck. Next comes the two-level Garden Restaurant, pleasingly decorated and elegantly dressed up in the evenings. Food is good in both restaurants. Dinners include a choice of three entrées—like snapper fillets stuffed with crabmeat, mahi-mahi in a champagne saffron sauce, or a vegetarian dish. Peach cobbler or cherry cheesecake for dessert are always served with Caribbean flair and a smile.

Long Bay is a perfect holiday resort for independent couples who enjoy each other's

company, natural beauty, and are addicted to long stretches of "It's almost our own" beaches.
Clientele is mixed British and American—families, friends, and couples of all ages.

LONG BAY BEACH RESORT
P.O. 433, Road Toron
Tortola, British Virgin Islands
TEL: (809) 495-4252
FAX: (809) 495-4677

RESERVATIONS
Island Destinations
Long Bay Beach Resort
P.O. Box 284
Larchmont, NY 10538
TEL: (800) 729-9599 *or*
     (914) 833-3300
FAX: (914) 833-3318

Open all year.
Rates: Double occupancy. *December 19 to April 4:* Hillside Oceanview Rooms, $240; Hillside Oceanview Studios, $280; Beachfront Cabanas, $310; Beachfront Deluxe, $340. *April 5 to December 18:* Rates for accommodations range from $155 to $350. For Villa rates contact resort reservations' 800 number (see page 121).
Meal plan: EP. MAP (includes breakfast and dinner), add $37.50 per person per day; for children under 12, add $20 per child per day.
Service charge: 10%.
Government tax: 7%.
Children welcome.
Credit cards accepted.
Note: Special Honeymoon, Family Escape, Adventure, and Dive packages available upon request.

Necker Island

Sipping a rum-and-tonic on the vast master-suite terrace at the very top of Necker Island's Devil's Hill, clad in a Balinese cotton kimono, I watched a golden sunset and a rising full moon on opposite horizons, as the *Sea Goddess* slowly made her way around the island.

I wondered if Robert De Niro and Steven Spielberg, who have occupied these quarters, had ever told Katharine Hepburn about Necker Island. Recalling a bit of her philosophy from her book *The Making of The African Queen,* she said, "I'll pay anything anyone wants for a house if I like it. I have a passion for locations. I like to be king of the mountain. Don't like things in back of me."

At Necker Island, you are king of the mountain, and of the entire island, because all of Necker is for hire, totally inclusive, from $9,000 to $14,900 a day in season, depending on the number of guests and whether you rent the two newly reassembled, imported authentic Balinese Houses, Bali Ha'i and Bali Lo. Princess Diana has spent several holidays at Necker with members of her family.

In 1974, twenty-four-old Richard Branson, the English entrepreneur (Virgin Records and Virgin Airways), dreamed of having his own island in the Caribbean and turning it into a utopian Balinese paradise with a recording studio. He learned that 74-acre uninhabited Necker Island was for sale. About a year and a half later, he purchased the island. Architect John Osman was engaged, and the herculean task of building Necker's villa took three years.

Plans for the recording studio became impractical and were scrapped. Since Branson and his family would only spend a few weeks a year at Necker, he decided that during his absence the island would become an exclusive resort.

I was a guest at Necker Island for a night and two days between reservations. Preparations were under way for the next booking, a wedding. (Booking Necker for special birthdays and anniversaries is popular, too.) On the day of the event, 40 guests would be conveyed to the island for the ceremony, which was to be performed under an arbor of woven palm fronds and flowers. An elegant reception was scheduled, to be followed by a beach party barbecue. Maids were cleaning, workmen checking on repairs, gardeners pruning and raking sandy roads, and a West Indian cook was at work in the kitchen. The staff totals 20.

I was left on my own to explore the island, which lies a mile northeast of Virgin Gorda, and is accessible by boat transfer from Beef Island, Tortola (a 40-minute trip), or Gun Creek dock in Virgin Gorda (a 10-minute run). If you stay for five or more nights you get free helicopter transfer from St. Thomas, Virgin Gorda, or Beef Island, Tortola, plus a one-day yacht charter, *and* a local calypso band is featured at a party evening.

The immense Balinese-style villa, nine bedrooms and one suite, crowns Devil's Hill. The architect's ingenious concept was so sympathetic to nature that the house's towering shingled roof and natural stone ramparts dissolve right into the landscape peaking the hill.

Since Necker is an arid island, succulents and scrub dominate its Elysian Fields, but an extensive irrigation system keeps the villa cradled in brilliant bougainvillea, allemanda, hibiscus, oleander, and greenery. Necker's gardens are producing tomatoes, peppers, bananas, papayas, and mangoes.

The villa's enormous living room, with exposed beams of Brazilian ipé and floors of Yorkshire granite, is fitted with elephant-sized bamboo chairs and oversized cushions on permanent natural stone banquettes. There's an English snooker table, piano, TV/video cabinet with dozens of movie cassettes stored in banana-leaf chests, and a raised gallery library, well-stocked with tapes, CDs, and a small collection of books. The retractable part of the roof showers sun onto a central garden during the day and is a canopy of stars at night.

The spacious roof-covered gallery that surrounds the villa and a recessed lookout post have breathtaking views. A self-service bar sits cozily under the gallery library next to the dining room. The giant oak refectory table seats up to 24 people, who are summoned to dinner by the sound of a gong. There are two other outside dining areas, where it's easy to envision leisurely hedonistic lunches. Due to the villa's elevation and open exposure, it can get very windy in paradise.

Each terraced bedroom has a ceiling fan and is decorated in large bamboo furniture in individual color schemes with Balinese fabrics that are continually being replaced. Exquisite, silky cotton kimonos hang in armoires. The rooms form a U-shape around central hallways, and each has a different splendid view. Whales are often sighted from the villa in February and March.

Necker's main house has seven very comfortable bathrooms among the nine bedrooms. Showers are round, natural-stone grottoes. Rooms are named after Indonesian islands: Nila, Surabaya, Timor, among others. The upstairs roomy master suite, where I stayed, is Branson's Bali, with a bubbling Jacuzzi out on the vast terrace.

Fat, cushioned chaises line the large freshwater hip-level pool terrace, which also has a waterfall and Jacuzzi.

Devil's Beach on the west side of the island is reached after a few minutes' meander down a pathway. An excellent coral reef is a short snorkel away.

Necker's network of pathways leads to several shingled-umbrella lookout posts, northern Consuelo Beach, and to an incredible 300-year-old Bali *gede,* perched on a hill. Its fanciful curved roof sits on carved wooden support beams with two double beds as part of the structure. From this tiny nirvana there is absolute privacy, reverberating stillness, and a provocative panorama.

The two Balinese Houses located at discreet distances from the main house, and suitable for two, are three-story fantasy lodgings for ultimate privacy and pampering. Each has a small pool.

I found my first sand dollar on Well Beach, a long, curved, southeastern beach. A raised Balinese pavilion here, chock-full of more elephant bamboo chairs and ottomans, overlooks the floodlit, all-weather tennis court.

A sample dinner menu includes tuna teriyaki and pickled ginger, a salad of baby spinach and Barbary duck, grilled mahi-mahi with coriander and lightly curried baby vegetables, and for the finale, a pistachio and chocolate soufflé. British chef Gary Jones came to Necker from Le Manoir aux Quat' Saisons in England.

Peter Wynne, with Necker since August 1993, skillfully manages the island.

Of course, the cost of Necker is prohibitive for most of us, but for those potentates or anyone else who can afford it, Necker's worth it.

For all its grandeur, Necker Island is a low-key, casual oasis where you can dress down-to-the-ones. Natural luxury here means being able to appreciate a gecko darting across a wall while sipping champagne.

Go sailing on a laser dinghy, waterski, windsurf, try out the battery-operated Seasprints, or visit nearby islands in Necker's new 35-foot Marlin speedboat—everything is included—but why anyone would want to leave this intoxicating island fairyland I can't imagine.

NECKER ISLAND
Box 315, Road Town
Tortola, British Virgin Islands
TEL: (809) 494-2757

RESERVATIONS
Resorts Management, Inc.
The Carriage House
201½ East 29th Street
New York, NY 10016
TEL: (800) 225-4255 *or*
    (212) 696-4566
FAX: (212) 689-1598

Open all year.
Rates: *November 15 to May 15:* up to 10 guests, $9,000 per day; 11 to 20 guests, $10,900 per day. *May 16 to November 14:* 1 to 6 guests, $6,000 per day; 7 to 12 guests, $8,000; 13 to 20 guests $10,000. Balinese Houses—Bali Ha'i and Bali Lo—cost $2,000 each per day any season.
Meal plan: FAP (all-inclusive rate covers all meals and beverages, including champagne).
Service charge: 2.5%.
Government taxes: included in rates.
Children welcome.
Credit cards not accepted.

Peter Island Resort and Yacht Harbour, Peter Island

Peter Island's 20 secluded Beach House rooms at the southwestern end of Deadman's Bay's long, beautiful white-sand beach are so outstanding that the resort's 30 older patioed or balconied rooms in two-story A-frame chalets pale by comparison. However, there's nothing wrong with these rooms, called Oceanview Rooms, with ceiling fans and air-conditioning, telephones, clock radios, hair dryers, robes, coffeemaker and mini-bars, and rattan furniture. They are arranged in a curved row on a small point of land between Sprat Bay and breezy Sir Francis Drake Channel. Every room has open exposures and sitting areas on both the north and south sides, featuring two distinct views. From the north, you look out over a lawn across the channel to Tortola. The south faces the active marina and docks and the hills of the almost 1,800-acre private island. The Amway Corporation of Michigan owns the resort, which was originally built by a Norwegian ship owner. You reach Peter Island by the resort's launch transfer from Tortola. Some guests, mainly those checking into the Crow's Nest Villa (a beautiful 4-bedroom hilltop hideaway with its own pool and expansive terrace) fly in by helicopter. There are two other villas with two bedrooms each—the Hawk's Nest Villas.

The oceanview rooms are adjacent to a spacious, freeform freshwater pool, game room (featuring Ping-Pong, Foosball, and exercise equipment), the main restaurant, an entertainment shell, bar, gift shop, and library/lounge rooms with TVs for viewing movies or cable TV, plus a new fitness center. These rooms are the least expensive. If staying here,

I'd reserve a second-floor room near the harbor entrance, as far away as possible from the public areas, for pitched ceilings, better views, and privacy.

Trouble is, I've been forever spoiled by the singularly charming beach accommodations. These cozy rooms are much more like private living quarters than hotel rooms. Imaginatively designed, the four rooms of each of the five buildings are blends of natural stone and cedar with tile floors throughout, extending to roomy patios or balconies. A set of wide, wooden, louvered double doors fold open from one side of the wall to the other. The views before you are glistening Deadman's Bay and outer islands, with resonant surf sounds as background music.

The decorator put together green, peach, and cream tropical trappings of rattan furniture enhanced with pastel fabrics, a living area, a desk, and a bar area with a fully stocked refrigerator.

Bathrooms are treasures, each featuring a built-in hair dryer, robes, and a tray of toiletries. Peter Island gets the award for the most winsome soap dishes in the Caribbean—flat pieces of native stone jut right out of the stone wall on both sides of the twin-sink vanity.

A large walk-in closet includes a nest of drawers, plenty of storage and hanging space, and a full-length mirror.

Rooms have air-conditioning and two ceiling fans. There are no TVs, but rooms do have clock radios, coffeemakers, and phones with direct-dialing. *TimesFax* is delivered daily.

While the immediate resort area is embellished with palm trees, flowering plants, and manicured gardens and grounds, the sprawling island itself is covered in thick scrub brush. It offers miles of pathways to jog, walk, hike, and bicycle (21-speed tandem mountain bikes and beach cruisers are available), and several beaches to explore. Deadman's Bay Beach is a canyon of lofty palm trees. Thatched bohios and chaises rest at the shoreline. You can take an escorted island tour, snorkel above splendid reefs, or sail on Sunfish, Zuma, Hobie Cats, kayaks, windsurfers, or 19-foot Squibbs. Day sails and deep-sea fishing are easily arranged at an extra cost, as are trips to numerous islands in the area and shopping on Tortola or St. Thomas. Peter Island has four Tru-flex tennis courts, two of which are lit for night play. Dive B.V.I., Ltd., the resort's dive operation, is considered first-rate.

Lunches at the open-air inside/outside beach restaurant, Deadman's Beach Bar and Grill, are grand buffets, and are especially good on Sundays, when they feature 20 salads and five entrées.

Dinner in the main restaurant, Tradewinds, a trio of cheerful rooms, serves fine island seafood ravioli, good cream of cauliflower soup, a marvelous citrus-roasted lobster, and delicious sweets. Reservations by guests for dinner are required, since non-guests, mostly from docked or anchored boats at Peter Island, are welcome. Men are required to wear shirts with collars after 6 P.M.

I've rarely been able to visit the Peter Island gift shop without finding something I wanted. Besides the usual sundries and paperback books, the buyer can select very attractive beachwear.

The splendid beachfront accommodations, the spaciousness, and the beauty of the island always remain foremost in my memory.

PETER ISLAND RESORT AND
YACHT HARBOUR
Mailing address:
P.O. Box 211, Road Town
Tortola, British Virgin Islands
TEL: (809) 494-2561
FAX: (809) 494-2313

RESERVATIONS
(800) 346-4451 *or*
(800) 323-7500

Open all year.

Rates: Double occupancy: *December 18 to April 3:* Oceanview Room, $350; Beachfront Room, $475; Hawk's Nest Villas, $575 to $700; Crow's Nest Villa (up to 8 persons), $3,700. *April 4 to December 22:* Oceanview Room, $195; Beachfront Room, $295; Hawk's Nest Villas, $475 to $575; Crow's Nest Villa, $1,400. Round-trip taxi and boat service to and from Beef Island Airport, $20 per person.

Meal plan: EP. MAP (includes breakfast and dinner), $65 per person per day. FAP (all meals), add $85 per person per day. Additional 15% service charge is added for food and beverages.

Service charge: 10%

Government tax: 7%.

Children welcome.

Credit cards accepted.

Note: Summer Island Dreams, Island Romance, Aqua Adventures, Ashore –Afloat, and other special rates or off-season packages are available upon request.

The Sugar Mill, Tortola

One would expect two seasoned food and travel writers, who turn out a monthly column in *Bon Appétit* and have published several cookbooks, to run a very special inn in the Caribbean, if they had one. Jinx and Jeff Morgan, who originally hail from California, do just that. It's a charmer called The Sugar Mill, located on Tortola's quiet northwest coast about 45 minutes from Beef Island Airport and 10 minutes from the West End ferry dock, with direct service to St. Thomas. The Sugar Mill can arrange a car for you to rent. You'll need one.

The Sugar Mill is Tortola's most delightful intimate inn, where you can always count on receiving personal service and attention. The hotel's property is split into two sections by a small road. On the smaller beachfront side at Apple Bay is The Sugar Mill's luncheon restaurant, Islands, adjoining a small shelf of beach with chaises. Open for lunch and dinner, the all-Caribbean menu is made up of delicious choices such as Jamaican jerk ribs, Puerto Rican fried chicken, Trinidadian curried roti, and vegetable "jump-up." Puffy salt cod fritters sampled recently were simply great.

The hotel's main restaurant with a beautiful, Caribbean-style hip roof, lined in cedar, public gathering places, and accommodations rest on the opposite side of the road on a handful of acres which gently climb up a hillside, flourishing with blossoming flowers, plants, and a garden with herbs, vegetables, and fruit trees. The Sugar Mill is only moments by car from two of Tortola's most splendid beaches, Long Bay and Cane Garden Bay.

Entering the hotel, you'll first encounter the West Indian–style multilevel outdoor atrium lounge. Off to the right are the bar and reception, boutique, a few shelves of library books, and a lower breakfast dining area. The attached, stone-walled dining room, one of the hotel's most outstanding features, is part of the ruins of a 300-year-old sugar mill. It's a cozy yet spacious room, with an inviting atmosphere, decorated with greenery and Haitian art (you'll also see some of Mrs. Morgan's pretty watercolors hanging elsewhere on the premises). The tables are dressed up in pink tablecloths, flickering candlelight, and a scattering of fresh red hibiscus under revolving paddle fans. Wooden plate holders are set with white china.

The Sugar Mill's cuisine is what the Morgans themselves describe as "the sort [guests] might have if they were dining in our own home. We try to make it interesting and imaginative"—like flying fish with lime and caper aioli, fresh fish in banana leaves, or roast pork Havana. The recipes can be found in the Morgans' latest book, *The Sugar Mill Hotel Cookbook II*, which I hope includes that marvelous chilled, layered banana bread pudding. Four-course dinners are $38 per person, and wine selections from a thoughtfully prepared list are available.

The Sugar Mill's 18 tropical deluxe rooms are balconied, with kitchen facilities and adequate bathrooms—nothing fancy. Two other rooms are standard twins. Sugar Mill's two-bedroom private villa with a living room and fully equipped kitchen, is the Morgans' former home, prettily refurbished with a front balcony and lovely water views.

Rooms are situated around a small, round, terraced freshwater pool in a flowering garden, where guests unwind and get acquainted. Clientele is mostly American, English, and Canadian, many of whom are repeaters the Morgans consider extended family.

THE SUGAR MILL
P.O. Box 425, Road Town
Tortola, British Virgin Islands
TEL: (800) 462-8834 *or*
　　(809) 495-4355
FAX: (809) 496-4696

RESERVATIONS
Caribbean Inns, Ltd.
TEL: (800) 633-7411
FAX: (803) 686-7411
or Caribbean Information Office
TEL: (800) 621-1270
FAX: (708) 699-7583

Closed August and September.
Rates: Double occupancy. *December 21 to April 14:* Standard Room, $185; Deluxe Rooms, $250; Deluxe Villa, $575. *April 15 to May 31* and *November 1 to December 20:* Standard Room, $155; Deluxe Room, $190; Deluxe Villa, $450. *June 1 to October 31:* Standard Room, $145; Deluxe Room, $175; Deluxe Villa, $390.

ANEGADA | 129

Meal plan: EP. MAP (includes breakfast and dinner), add $50 per person per day plus 10% service charge.
Service charge: 10%.
Government tax: 7%.
Children under 10 not accepted from December 21 to April 14; they are welcome at all other times and are free from April 15 to December 20.
Credit cards accepted.
Note: Special Honeymoon and Adventure packages are available upon request.

NOTEWORTHY OPTIONS

Anegada Reef Hotel, Anegada

Wonderfully isolated Anegada is the second-largest island in the British Virgin Islands, an 11 × 3-mile coral-and-limestone atoll with an elevation no higher than 28 feet. The island's approximately 160 inhabitants earn their livelihood as fishermen, government workers (there are two policemen), shopkeepers, a few artists, employees of nine restaurants, three grocery stores, a tiny airport, and only one actual hotel. (There are a couple of very basic campgrounds, and a few cottages available as rentals; see page 140.) Anegada, about 14 miles north of Virgin Gorda, has only three miles of paved road; the rest are dirt-and-sand rocky byways through the island frontier's interior of desert savannas and salt ponds.

What laid-back Anegada does have to offer, beyond seclusion, are several long, glorious white-sand beaches, great snorkeling and diving among the scores of sunken ships and coral caves, sportfishing, some very good food, wonderfully friendly residents, predictably sunny days, and 16 flamingos that were released into their own natural habitat on March 7, 1992, donated by the Bermuda Zoo. The island's only TV channel is the PBS station from St. Thomas.

Guests reach Anegada either by flying in from Beef Island, Tortola, or Virgin Gorda, about a 15-minute flight (also limited service from St. Thomas), or by boat. Regularly scheduled air service leaves from Tortola on Gorda Aero Service or you can charter Fly BVI, which will try to accommodate your schedule (809) 495-1747. Planes do not land in Anegada after dark.

Many people come to the Anegada Reef Hotel by sea for a day trip or to anchor, sample one of the hotel's famous dinners, and stay overnight, usually aboard their own vessels. Reaching Anegada by sea is considered a serious challenge for sailors who must skillfully maneuver their way through the coral minefields that ring the island and have sunk more than 400 boats. Locals call the reefs "the wicked witch of Anegada."

Most guests who check into Anegada Reef Hotel come to relax and hibernate. Located on the island's southern coast, the simple hotel is a very pleasant place to spend a few days. It's owned by Lowell Wheatley and managed by his efficient, cheerful companion, Sue Robinson. The hotel is modest but nicely furnished; 16 connecting rooms sit on a wide lawn in a motel-like building. Ten rooms face the beach and sea and have air-conditioning, sitting areas, mini-refrigerators, and private patios. (One room has a king-size water bed.) The remaining six rooms are not recommended, unless you're really budgeting: they're on the back side with ceiling fans instead of air-conditioning, have no patios, and face a scraggly garden. There are no phones or TVs, but the hotel has a pay phone, a fax machine, a small library lounge, and bicycles and Jeeps to rent. The dive shop rents tanks and can supply air fills, but offers no instruction or dive tours. Sue's boutique is remarkably well stocked for so desolate a location, carrying casual resortwear, T-shirts, handcrafts, and sundries.

Breakfasts and lunches are basic fare, but dinners, for which guests must place an order by 4 P.M., are quite excellent—grilled lobster, fish, ribs, or chicken cooked over the leaping flames of wood-burning fires in specially constructed metal drums. Guests at the hotel and those who came by sea mingle convivially, sometimes hilariously, over cocktails at the open-air bar pavilion until dinner. Anegada Reef's special Rum Smoothie is as delicious as it is powerful. The bar is open 24 hours a day. If no bar attendant is around, guests sign chits. At 7:30 P.M. guests find their Anegada Reef postcard place cards at tables on the terrace or in the indoor dining room. Side dishes can be anything from stewed cabbage with mushrooms or rice and beans to ratatouille or roast potatoes. Desserts are normally pies like cherry or pecan—all tasty. Guests pour their own coffee.

Two friends joined me for a splendid three-day holiday at Anegada Reef. Exploring the island, we walked on beautiful, vast Pomato Beach, where our footprints were the only ones to be seen. We also lunched at Big Bamboo at Loblolly Bay on the island's north side—highly recommended (see Recommended Restaurants in Anegada, page 133), viewed the flamingos from a distance, watched a pair of dolphins playing, and visited the sleepy village of The Settlement. In the afternoon we collapsed into chaises overlooking the sea, where we read, napped, and observed the parade of boats gingerly making their way to Anegada Reef. After anchoring, one by one, dinghies inevitably filled with passengers who came ashore to stabilize sea legs and reward themselves with Anegada T-shirt trophies and a drink. Sunsets at Anegada Reef were magnificent. I'm looking forward to returning soon with my husband for a full-moon holiday and one more of Lowell's secret-formula after-dinner libations—a creamy zinger called Milk of Amnesia.

ANEGADA REEF HOTEL
Setting Point
Anegada, British Virgin Islands
TEL: (809) 495-8002
FAX: (809) 495-9362

Closed September and October.
Rates: Double occupancy. *December 16 to April 15:* Ocean Rooms, $225; Garden

Rooms, $175. *April 16 to December 15:* Ocean Rooms, $215; Garden Rooms, $160.

Meal plan: FAP (includes breakfast, lunch, and dinner; additional $12 supplement for lobster at dinner if guest in hotel).

Service charge: 12%.

Government tax: 7%.

Children welcome.

Credit cards not accepted.

The Pink Houses, Jost Van Dyck

At the eastern end of the marvelous stretch of White Bay Beach on Jost Van Dyck, which can be reached by taxi on a very bumpy road from Great Harbour or by a small motorboat, are two lovely, reasonably priced bright pink stucco rental homes. They are brand-new with corrugated roofs, white tile floors, and white wooden-beamed ceilings. Interiors are immaculate and nicely decorated.

The beachside villa that sits right above and off the beach has two bedrooms, two baths; a room below the house could act as a third bedroom. A comfy living room, fully equipped kitchen and dining area, plus outdoor terrace areas with lounges make this a very special getaway for independent travelers—a couple, family, or friends—who like the idea of being on the beach in total touch with nature, isolated from the world. There are telephones in both houses. Views are sensational.

The second beautiful pink villa, high up on the hillside, has an even more spectacular panorama with an attached viewing tower to boot. Its great room, large, fully equipped kitchen, three bedrooms and three baths, and expansive terraces look out over White Bay to distant St. Thomas. Guests who book here should be prepared for hiking down to the beach and the steep climb back up. Dining options include Sandcastle (see below), snacks at The Local Flavour Bar & Restaurant at White Bay Campground on White Bay Beach (both reached by a healthy hike along the beach and over a rocky shoreline, or a 20-minute walk over the hill) to Great Harbour (see Recommended Restaurants in Jost Van Dyck, page 134). Lifts from taxis can be organized. There are no car rentals on Jost.

The houses have ceiling fans and linens are provided. Maid service and a cook can be arranged for an extra fee. Tropical plants, flowers, and banana trees enhance the houses. Either villa is a terrific hideaway for self-sufficient recluses.

THE PINK HOUSES
White Bay
Jost Van Dyck, British Virgin Islands
For reservations:
Mary Beth Medley (809) 495-9268

Open all year.

Rates: *Throughout the year:* Two-Bedroom House, $1,500 for a week's rental; Three-Bedroom House, $2,500 for a week's rental.

Meal plan: EP.

Children welcome.

For all other information, contact Ms. Medley. (See phone number above).

Sandcastle, Jost Van Dyck

Life at Sandcastle is elegant bivouacking on about a mile of magnificent powdery white-sand beach facing south on the remote island of Jost Van Dyck. Jost, as locals call it, lies northwest of Tortola, and has a population of about 200.

Shelters at Sandcastle are four modest cottages with two rooms each, set back from the beach off a small restaurant and bar. The hotel has no electricity, therefore no air-conditioning or fans, but a breeze usually blows for comfort. Light is provided by propane lamps, and since the water is heated by the sun, bathing gets chilly a few hours after sunset. Interiors have been refurbished and now have king-size beds. No phones or other frills, except for a small nook boutique selling T-shirts, hats, totes, and the like.

The hotel sits on a one-acre site on a glorious beach. Although a few hundred yards to the east there's a new campground with a small restaurant and bar, and to the left, a tiny shed boutique and bar. It's still peacefully situated—except for Fridays in season, that is, when the 100-plus passengers and crew of the luxurious *Sea Goddess* take over the west end of White Bay for a lobster-and-champagne picnic. They pretty much keep to themselves, and observing the action is quite a spectacle. Normally only a few locals and visiting yachtspeople stop by for a drink and good meal.

The food at Sandcastle has always been a highlight. The three meals, included in the room rates, are served in a pleasant, open-air pavilion next to the Soggy Dollar Bar.

Darrell and Kay Sanderson of St. Petersburg, Florida, the resort's owners, have enlisted Kay's son, Bill Corey, as manager. He's also in charge of the kitchen. With a local staff, he continues the hotel's tradition of serving good food. Our favorite lunch is flash-fried Barbados flying-fish sandwiches. Dinners feature seasonal vegetables, seafood, and fish. Evenings are romantically quiet or lively, depending on the number of guests and personalities. English, Canadian, and American do-it-yourselfers stay here.

A favorite preoccupation is relaxing in hammocks strung at the shoreline under palm trees and thick sea grape. Views from the beach are of distant St. John and St. Thomas beyond the glistening aqua-green to dark-blue sea. It's a fantasy island atmosphere.

To get to Sandcastle, visitors fly into Beef Island, Tortola, and taxi to the West End Ferry Dock, about 45 minutes. By prearrangement with the hotel, you are picked up for a half-hour boat ride to the hotel. There's no dock at Sandcastle, so a small skiff collects you and your luggage for a few yards' row or motorboat transfer to shore. You step into water and from here on it's barefoot living.

A 30-minute hike along the beach and over a hill or a short boat ride brings you to Great Harbour and the island's tiny settlement. There are now several restaurants and bars, including famous Foxy's. (For dining and recreation options see "Recommended Restaurants" for Jost Van Dyck and "Useful Information.")

Most of Sandcastle's guests are serious *limers*, which according to Lito Valls' marvelous book, *What a Pistarkle!*, a dictionary of Virgin Island English Creole, means to "hang around idly." At Sandcastle, lime with a "Painkiller"—a potent rum, coconut cream, and fruit juice libation topped with fresh grated nutmeg.

A word of caution: Sand flies, no-see-ums, and mosquitoes can be pesky at Sandcastle. Bring extra insect repellent, and Campho-Phenique (or similar product) to stop the itching, just in case.

SANDCASTLE
Mailing address:
6501 Red Hook Plaza, Suite 237
St. Thomas, U.S. Virgin Islands 00802
TEL: (809) 771-1611
FAX: (809) 775-3590
Marine VHF Channel 16 is monitored.

Open all year.
Rates: Double occupancy. *December 15 to April 15:* Room, $295. *April 16 to December 14:* Room, $235. Extra person, $75 all year. Boat transportation from West End, Tortola, is free if staying six nights or more; otherwise the charge is $100.
Meal plan: FAP (includes breakfast, lunch, and dinner).
Service charge: 15%.
Government tax: 7%.
Children: No one under 18 permitted.
Credit cards accepted with 5% surcharge. Cash or traveler's checks preferred.

Recommended Restaurants

ANEGADA'S FINEST*

The restaurants on Anegada are all casual. Most serve Anegada's version of good West Indian home-style cooking. Starred listings designate wonderful island atmosphere in unique, remote settings. No fancy places. The only glitter here is from the sun, stars, and sea—bring hats and sunglasses.

* **Anegada Reef**, 495-8002 (Anegada Reef Hotel, Setting Point). Very casual, but the best and liveliest restaurant for dinner on the island. (See hotel listing, page 128.) Moderate to expensive.

* **The Big Bamboo Beach Bar & Restaurant**, VHF Channel 16 (Loblolly Bay). Go

for lunch to meet gregarious Aubrey and Dianne Levons (he fishes, she cooks) and sample super seafood or chicken served at tables and benches at the gorgeous beach. Be sure to make a reservation—if nobody's comin', they may not open. Have at least one of Brother B's potent Bamboo Teasers. Inexpensive to moderate.

* **Flash of Beauty**, 495-8014 or VHF Channel 16 (Loblolly Bay East). Egbert "Cap" Wheatley's new beachside, open-air pavilion bar and restaurant sits at the eastern end of a long Loblolly beach, at the opposite end from The Big Bamboo. The road to get here is pretty bumpy, but gentle Mr. Wheatley never stops improving the place, like decorating the grounds with hundreds of conch shells. The isolated beach is splendid, with little thatch lean-tos. Seafood, burgers, hot dogs, chips, and Flash House Specials make up the menu. Inexpensive to moderate.

* **Pomato Point Restaurant**, 495-9466 (Pomato Point). Indoor dining room in small homelike building (with a little museum and gift shop) on Pomato Point's fabulous mile-long-plus beach. Come for champagne breakfasts or lunches, and candlelit dinners featuring barbecued steak, chicken, fish and lobster. Inexpensive to moderate.

OTHER DEPENDABLE CHOICES

Neptune's Treasure, VHF Channel 16 or Radio 43111 (down the road a piece northwest of Anegada Reef Hotel). The Soares family serve breakfasts and Continental/American-style lunches and dinners. Daughter Pam prepares delicious chutneys, jams, and preserves, cookies, and breads that she sells. Inexpensive to moderate.

In town, try **Del's Restaurant and Bar**, in a little cottage in The Settlement for West Indian food graciously served. The **Banana Well Bar and Restaurant**, also in the village, dishes out sandwiches and West Indian fare.

JOST VAN DYCK'S FINEST*

* **Sandcastle**, VHF Channel 16 (White Bay). Well-prepared food in an island setting by a beautiful beach. (See resort listing, page 131.) Inexpensive to moderate.

The remaining dining spots on Jost are all casual watering holes serving simple but good local fare.

* **Foxy's Tamarind** (Great Harbour) is the most famous bar in the B.V.I., especially for Old Year's Eve night (New Year's Eve) when hundreds of boats raft up for the jump-up at Foxy's welcoming in the New Year all night. Go any day or evening to rap with Foxy Callwood; he'll write a song about you and sing it right on the spot. The garbage can reads "No Garbage" and the ashtrays say "Stolen from a hotel." The food is standard local fixings and barbecue. Inexpensive to moderate.

OTHER DEPENDABLE CHOICES

At Great Harbour are several choices—**Club Paradise** (good eats and great place to crash on the beach all day—hammocks, floats, and beach lounges—pig roast Wednesday nights), **Happy Laury, Ali Baba's** (good johnnycakes and pig roast Mondays and Wednesdays), and **Rudy's Mariners**. Each serves West Indian barbecues, burgers, and the like. All are inexpensive to moderate.

At Little Harbour (the new road from Great Harbour should be completed by now) we prefer **Harris' Place** for fresh fresh lobster and Mrs. Harris' wonderful bread and desserts. **Sidney's Peace and Love** and **Abe's Little Harbour** are other laid-back options. Most of the restaurants serve local lobster and have pig roasts a night or two a week.

Ivan Chinnery's **The Local Flavour Bar & Restaurant** at White Bay Campground, just down the beach to the east of Sandcastle, serves drinks or snacks in the shade at tables in the sand overlooking splendid White Bay.

TORTOLA'S FINEST*

* **The Sugar Mill** and **Islands**, 495-4355 (Apple Bay). Both charmers for well-executed meals, attentively served in a beautiful, historic sugar mill dining room or at seaside terrace tables. Nice wine selection at Sugar Mill. (See resort listing, page 127.) Inexpensive to moderate.

* **Brandywine Bay Restaurant**, 494-2301 (three miles east of Road Town). The cobblestone terrace has a wonderful view of Drake's Channel. For a relaxing dinner try some of the Puglieses' Florentine-accented Italian offerings like carpaccio, bistecca alla fiorentina, tiramisù, and cappuccino or espresso. Expensive.

* **Peter Island**, 494-2561 (at Peter Island Resort and Yacht Harbour; reservations a must with ferry service from Tortola). Expansive buffet lunches at **Deadman's Beach Bar and Grill** are taken in a prime Caribbean location. Bring swimsuits. Dinners are elegant affairs. Fine wines. (See resort listing, page 125.) Moderate to expensive.

* **Garden Restaurant** and **The Beach Restaurant**, 495-4252 (Long Bay Beach Resort). Both serve dependable, commendable food on a pleasant dining terrace or at the beach. (See resort listing, page 125.) Inexpensive to expensive.

* **The Captain's Table & The Hungry Sailor Garden Cafe**, 494-3885 (Wickham Cay 1). At Captain's Table sample linguine pesto, rack of lamb, or shrimp with Pernod in the evenings. Have lunch or dinner at Hungry Sailor for excellent crunchy fish-and-chips, chicken, and Caesar salad, among other offerings. Inexpensive to moderate.

* **Mrs. Scatliffe's Bar & Restaurant**, 495-4556 (Carrot Bay). A delightful Mrs. Scatliffe deserves a star for her good home-cooked meals served on the second floor of her island home. Spicy papaya soup and homemade coconut bread, coconut chicken, local fish—whatever's on the menu is served by family members, who break into song whenever, usually toward the end of dinners, which are more fun than lunch. Mrs. Scatliffe shakes a gourd; Egbert, her son-in-law, strums a ukelele; even the grandchildren contribute. Moderate.

OTHER DEPENDABLE CHOICES

Pusser's Outpost, 494-4199 (Main Street). Upstairs from **Pusser's Pub** (which serves excellent shepherd's and chicken pot pies, pita-pocket sandwiches, pizzas, burgers, and so on) is an attractive harborview dining room turning out admirable rack of lamb, grilled mahi-mahi, jerk chicken, and pies like mud and key lime for dessert. Moderate to expensive. There's also a super **Pusser's Landing**, 495-4554 at Soper's Hole in the West End. Try black bean soup, grilled chicken and artichoke hearts, fried plantains, and a vanilla ice cream creation.

Skyworld, 494-3567 (Ridge Road). The 360-degree views from this mountaintop restaurant are unsurpassed—on a clear day you can see as far as St. Croix. Unfortunately, the service and food aren't up to snuff anymore. Recently we tried for lunch and couldn't get a drink after waiting 30 minutes. We left. I understand it's on the market. Hope new owners arrive soon and return this marvelously located restaurant to its excellence of the past. Moderate.

There are plenty of other good dining options on Tortola, especially for West Indian food—all unpretentious. In Road Town we like **Maria's By the Sea, Oliver's Restaurant, Marlene's, Paradise Pub**, and **Roti Palace**. Around the island, **C&F Bar and Restaurant** in Estate Purcell, **Struggling Man's Place** at Sea Cows Bay, **The Apple** at Apple Bay, and at Cane Garden Bay and beachside, **Quito's Gazebo** and **Rhymer's**. New and untried at Cane Garden Bay is **Myett's**.

For Italian food, other than Brandywine Bay, try **Capriccio di Mare**, modest **Spaghetti Junction**, and two **Paradise Pizzas**—one at Port Purcell and at the road below Fort Burt. **Jolly Roger**, at the West End beyond the ferry dock, is an unpretentious place for pizzas and fast food with the kids to watch the boat traffic parade. **Sebastian's on the Beach** at Apple Bay is inexpensive and very popular locally. Satisfy your urge for Mexican food at **Tamarind Club and Restaurant** at beautiful, surfy Josiah's Bay.

If you feel like a real West Indian party, don't miss the fun to be had every Wednesday night, Full Moon night, and Sunday afternoon at **Bomba's Surfside Shack's** barbecues. The Shack rocks roadside on a spit of beach between Long Bay and The Sugar Mill. The place is a colorful junk collage where everyone lets down their hair and dances in the sand.

At **Beef Island** go to **The Last Resort**, on tiny Bellamy Cay (a boat transports diners), serving English food and buffets. Entertainer Tony Snell is still keeping diners, most of whom are boaties, laughing with his wild nautical humor. Also at Beef Island, **Conch Shell Point** is a pleasant location for steak or seafood dinners, and try **De Loose Mongoose** (Beef Island Guest House) for great breakfasts (banana pancakes), decent burgers, and standard fare.

Other remote island suggestions are Norman Island's floating *William Thorton,* an anchored, converted Baltic Trader where it can be a hoot or a bore. If two dozen day-trippers off a charter or cruise ship are onboard, sail away; otherwise, it's a treat. Food is average burgers, etc. Launch service. For information call VHF 16. And at **Cooper Island Beach Club** at Manchioneel Bay on Cooper Island, there is a special little al fresco restaurant serving commendable conch fritters, grilled seafood dishes, and barbecues. Reservations for a meal a must. VHF Channel 16. A few lodgings here, too.

VIRGIN GORDA'S FINEST*

* **Little Dix Bay**, 495-5555 (Little Dix Bay). Beautiful seaside setting with two restaurant options for seaside lunches and romantic dinners. (See resort listing, page 118.) Moderate to expensive.

* **Biras Creek**, 494-3555 (on North Sound reached only by boat). Fine service, good food and views. (See resort listing, page 111.) Moderate to expensive.

* **Drake's Anchorage**, 494-2254 (just off Virgin Gorda on Mosquito Island, reached only by boat). New chef Tucker is untried by me, but the restaurant has always served quality food like mahi-mahi in curry sauce with bananas and filet mignon au poivre. Romantic setting. (See resort listing, page 113.) Moderate to expensive.

* **Chez Michelle Restaurant**, 495-5510 (Spanish Town). Don't let the unpretentious building fool you, Michelle's an excellent cook. Her grilled ginger-lime shrimp, cashew chicken with three chutneys, rack of lamb with a rosemary Burgundy sauce, are all wonderful. Moderate to expensive.

OTHER DEPENDABLE CHOICES

Pusser's, 495-7369 (Leverick Bay). This is a good place for families in an open-air dining room with a youthful atmosphere, offering lots of choices from spicy chicken wings, nachos, and beef Wellington to penne with broccoli and Pusser's Ice Cream Sundae. Inexpensive to moderate.

The Bath and Turtle, in a courtyard at Virgin Gorda Yacht Harbour, under new management for a couple of years, still has sloooow service, especially when crowded. Lunch features salads and sandwiches; dinner options range from coconut shrimp and filet mignon to pizzas. **Olde Yard Inn** in Spanish Town serves a good Caesar salad, grilled lamb chops, and Continental selections while classical music plays in the background. **Thelma's**, on the north side of The Valley, is a tiny eatery serving first-rate West Indian food at very low prices. Other West Indian restaurants are **Anything Goes on Virgin Gorda**, **The Wheelhouse**, and **Teacher Ilma's**, all a short walk from the Yacht Harbour.

Recommended Shopping

ANEGADA

Pat's Pottery & Art, 495-8031/8043 (East-West Road). Potter Pat Faulkner and her students sell their pottery pieces (like pretty sea grape plates in various sizes and enchanting ceramic Christmas tree angel ornaments) in her new cottage studio, along with watercolors, souvenirs, T-shirts, and other items.

Anegada Reef Boutique, 495-8002 (Anegada Reef Hotel). Sue Robinson's well-stocked shop carries gift items, casual clothing, hats, handcrafts, and sundries. **Neptune's Treasure** sells ceramics, shells, and odds and ends. Pam Soares's preserves, chutneys, jams, cookies, and breads are also on sale. **Pomato Point Restaurant** has a tiny selection of handcrafts and **The Big Bamboo Bar and Restaurant** T-shirts are prized by sailors.

JOST VAN DYCK

Foxy's now has a boutique that even takes credit cards. It stocks an impressive selection of casual resortwear, jewelry, ceramics, flip-flops, hats, totes, and curios. The only other gift options, aside from T-shirts, which everyone seems to sell, are at White Bay at **Sandcastle's**, where there's a tiny collection of beachwear, and **Gertrude's Beach Bar**, a nice little pavilion with a limited selection of jewelry and coverups. Gertrude also offers beverages—promoting "Painkillers"—and does cornrow hair braiding.

TORTOLA

Sunny Caribbee Spice Co., 494-2178 (Main Street). Bob and Susan Gunters and their son Greg from Kennebunk Beach, Maine, have created a thriving island-inspired gift business with outlets in the British Virgin Islands and boutiques in other shops on many other Caribbean islands. Beautifully packaged herbs, spices, teas, chutneys, sauces, lotions, and perfumes, painted decorative pottery, baskets, little West Indian house-shaped hot pads, and other charming handcrafts make special gifts.

Foxy's Boutique at Great Harbour in Jost Van Dyck in the British Virgin Islands.

The Pusser's Company Store, 494-2467 (Main Street). Fine-quality nautical resort-wear for men, women, and children, plus antiques, reproductions, and Pusser's personal-ized aprons, bags, and more are sold here. There's another Pusser's outlet at Sopers Hole at the West End.

Caribbean Handprints, 494-3717 (Main Street). This shop features fabrics hand-printed in Tortola and sold by the yard or transformed into coverups, shirts, dresses, and children's clothing. **Caribbean Fine Arts'** two galleries—**Things Remembered** on Waterfront and **Tropical Gallery** on Upper Main Street—carry island art and pottery. There are numerous small boutiques and shops all along Main Street, at **Wickhams Cay I & II** in Road Town, and at **Sopers Hole Marina** in the pretty, pastel West Indian shopping complex. **Zenaida's** at Sopers Hole is worth a special visit—it's a great bazaar of exotic imported clothing, baskets, jewelry, and handcrafts.

Resort boutiques worth looking into are those at **The Sugar Mill, Long Bay, Prospect Reef**, and **Peter Island**.

VIRGIN GORDA

Little Dix Pavilion Gift Shop is a large, well-stocked boutique carrying a wide selection of better resortwear for men and women, plus jewelry, shoes, hats, cosmetics, handcrafts, periodicals and books, plus sundries. There is also good shopping at the boutiques at other resorts and hotels, especially at **Biras Creek, Drake's Anchorage, The Bitter End Yacht Club, Leverick Bay**, and **Olde Yard Inn**. In Spanish Town look for **Pelican Pouch Boutique, Scoops, BVI Apparel Outlet Store**, and **Dive B.V.I., Ltd.**

Provisions for Your Island Pantry

ANEGADA

Food supplies on Anegada are extremely limited, but **Del's** in The Settlement has the best. Pam Soares at **Neptune's Treasure** sells homemade cookies, breads, preserves, and chutneys.

JOST VAN DYCK

In Great Harbour, **Christine Bakery** produces fresh pastries, bread, pâtés, and sand-wiches, and **Nature's Basket** stocks a limited supply of local fruits and vegetables. If you're housekeeping here and finicky about food supplies, a trip to Tortola to the **Ample Hamper** (see next listing) will probably be required. Consider a day trip to St. Thomas, where shopping could also include picking up excellent provisions. There, you can pick up quality foods like fresh arugula, fresh herbs, boneless duck breasts, thick veal chops, and other gourmet items. (See page 384.)

TORTOLA

The **Ample Hamper** at Village Cay Marina and Sopers Hole is the best all-around specialty food shop on Tortola, carrying meat, produce, cheese and pâtés, and prepared foods, as well as breads, pastries wines, and spirits.

Other choices are **Rite Way Food Market** (at three locations—Main Street, Fort Burt Marina, and Pasea Estate), and **K-Marks Supermarket** (near Port Purcell).

Marlene's Delicious Designs, 494-4634 (Wickhams Cay 1), sells homemade treats such as fried pates, rotis, salads, sandwiches, cakes, and pastries.

For wines and liquor go to **Fort Wines & Spirits**, 494-2388 (at Port Purcell) for good selections selling retail and wholesale. **TICO** is another option at Wickham's Cay II or on Fleming Street near the Road Town roundabout.

VIRGIN GORDA

The **Commissary** and **Buck's Food Market** at Yacht Harbour sell groceries, produce, wines, liquors, and beverages. At the Bitter End resort, the **Emporium and Deli** has a good bakery and excellent provisions and staples as well as take-out prepared foods (pizzas, salads, ribs, West Indian roti), plus dairy products and beverages.

Useful Information

ANEGADA

Just in! On stunning Pomato Point Beach, a few hundred yards away from the Pomato Point Restaurant & Bar, we saw a lone, deliciously isolated one-bedroom **Beach House**, which is available as a rental for $250 a weekend or $550 a week. It has a front porch, ceiling fan, full kitchen with a microwave oven, a one-channel TV, and a full bath with a shower and hot water. Although I haven't inspected it inside, friends who did say it's modest but comfortable and clean. The appeal is the location—nothing around but the restaurant and a long, white strand of beach. Those looking for an inexpensive, secret hideaway might want to check with MacKenzie Vanderpool at (916) 684-7349 or (809) 495-9466. Everad Faulkner (809) 495-8030 rents a couple of two-bedroom **cottages** with living rooms and dining rooms in The Settlement.

Fly BVI (495-1747). Travelers can book air charters on a Cessna 172 or Piper Aztec to and from Anegada. Rates for two with normal baggage or three with light baggage are $125 one way. In a Piper Aztec, the one-way fare for one to five people with normal baggage is $200. For information on **Gorda Aero Service**'s regularly scheduled flights to Anegada call (809) 495-2271 or 495-2261.

Trail bikes and **Jeeps** can be rented at **Anegada Reef Hotel**, 495-8002.

Marilyn's Water Aerobics sessions are held on Tuesdays, Thursdays, and Saturdays at 1 P.M. at the House with Seawall near Anegada Reef Hotel.

Lowell Wheatley, Anegada Reef Hotel's owner, provides **deep-sea** and **bonefishing** trips.

JOST VAN DYCK, TORTOLA, AND VIRGIN GORDA

The complimentary *British Virgin Islands Welcome Tourist Guide* is an excellent bimonthly magazine filled with up-to-date information.

Ferry service between Tortola and Virgin Gorda and to St. Thomas, St. John, and a few other islands is available from either the West End or Road Town, Tortola. **The North Sound Express** (809) 494-2746, at Trellis Bay on Beef Island on the North Shore offers a 30-minute fast boat ride to Bitter End on Virgin Gorda. Stops can be requested at Leverick Bay. Several scheduled trips run back and forth each day. Peter Island also has a scheduled boat service departing from the CSY dock in Road Town. **Captain Arthur Smith**, (809) 495-9296, makes special excursions to Jost Van Dyck, Sandy Cay, or other stops in the area on his motor vessel *When*. There are also regularly scheduled weekend day trips to Jost Van Dyck from Red Hook in St. Thomas and Cruz Bay, St. John.

≈ ≈

CURAÇAO

ACCOMMODATIONS

CURAÇAO'S BEST
Avila Beach Hotel
Sonesta Beach Hotel & Casino Curaçao

RECOMMENDED RESTAURANTS

RECOMMENDED SHOPPING

USEFUL INFORMATION

≈ ≈

Accommodations

CURAÇAO'S BEST

Avila Beach Hotel

The Avila Beach Hotel occupies several acres on Curaçao's southern shoreline road at the eastern edge of Willemstad, a 15-minute walk or short drive to the Punda (shopping district) through a residential area. The hotel is so enveloped in dense trees and plantings that upon arrival Avila's three-story main building's red-tile roof, ocher façade, and circular driveway are barely visible.

The Avila Beach Hotel has always had a relaxed, European inn atmosphere. Built in 1780, the hotel's main building once served as Curaçao's governor's mansion. It was converted into a hotel in the forties. Avila's current Danish owner, Finn Nic Møller, bought the property in 1978. Over the years he refurbished the hotel and grounds, transforming the Avila into Curaçao's most charming and best small hotel. It still is, especially since new life has been pumped into it. In 1991 Møller and his daughter, Tone, the general manager, opened a brand-new deluxe 40-room six-suite oceanfront wing with a small conference center, and a lit tennis court, called La Belle Alliance, on an adjacent lovely, man-made beach. The hotel's other beach, connected by an passageway beneath a pier, is a smaller but inviting cove in front of the old wing.

The rooms in the original mansion part of the hotel, as throughout, are kept immaculately clean by an amiable housekeeping staff, have cable TV, air-conditioning, ceiling fans, telephones, twin, double, or king-size beds, and baths with showers. The two things that this section does not have are ocean views (rooms face the garden courtyard or the road) or 24-hour hot water, because it's solar heated. Guests in rooms here must bathe during the day or early evening or expect teeth to chatter. (The new wing has 24-hour hot water.) Decor ranges from modest modern Danish to pleasing island standard. Sizes of the lodgings range from quite small to comfortably large in categories of moderate, superior, or preferred. Preferred rooms have stocked mini-bars. If you have a look at the rates, you'll see why rooms are still hard to come by here.

The new wing's deluxe rooms and suites are housed in a series of handsome buildings of varying heights designed in the classical style of Curaçao's plantation homes with red-tile roofs and ocher walls. Rooms, furnished in tropical rattan, have white tiled bathrooms with bath/showers and private patios or balconies; some rooms have kitchenettes. All rooms are air-conditioned, have ceiling fans, cable TV, telephones, and the same amenities of the other wing. The six new suites, one or two bedrooms each, have fully equipped kitchens and direct access to the beach.

The Møllers are trumpeting an even newer addition: a terrific jazz restaurant called Blues, perched on the end of the elevated pier that separates the two beaches and wings. Guests convening here can watch beautiful sunsets and enjoy cocktails while listening to live jazz from 6 to 8 P.M., and dine later on renditions of salmon carpaccio from the cold north, veal, chicken, and beef ragout, and warm pear pie with sour cream or other "jam session desserts."

Other dining options include the covered-terrace Avila Café for breakfast buffets and snacks, or the wonderful Belle Terrace, where the roof is formed by intertwined branches of an enormous old flamboyant tree. Lunch dishes here vary from Greek salad and herring plate to breast of chicken with basil sauce. A sample dinner menu might begin with ravioli with tomato confit and pesto sauce, proceed with grilled salmon with poppyseeds and cranberries, or keshi yena, a Curaçaoan specialty of Edam cheese stuffed with a savory chicken and raisin stew, and end with a gratin of fresh fruit with almond cream. The wine list is small, but selections are good and reasonably priced.

The Schooner Bay, a partial replica of a seagoing vessel with a white sail awning, sits at one corner of the beach near a sea terrace and is open from 10 A.M. until midnight for drinks.

Europeans, mostly Dutch and German, make up about 80% of Avila's guests. The balance is Swiss, French, Italian, and American—a combination of business men and women and families of every age. Travelers staying at Avila have a double dividend of the peaceful distinctiveness of the old hotel as well as the new, cheerier wing, which gives everything a livelier rhythm.

Well-run, delightful Avila confirms my belief that the best hotels in the Caribbean are those in which the owner/managers are at the helm.

AVILA BEACH HOTEL
Penstraat 130 (P.O. Box 791)
Willemstad, Curaçao, Netherlands Antilles

RESERVATIONS
TEL: (011-599-9) 614377
FAX: (011-599-9) 611493

Open all year.
Rates: Double occupancy. *May 1 to December 15:* Original Wing—Moderate, Superior, or Preferred Rooms, $90 to $115. New La Belle Alliance Wing—Deluxe Rooms, $145; Suite, $205; Two-Bedroom Suite, $340. *December 16 to April 30:* Original Wing—Moderate, Superior, or Preferred Rooms, $100 to $145. New La Belle Alliance Wing—Deluxe Rooms, $185; Suite, $240; Two-Bedroom Suite, $415.
Meal plan: EP. MAP (includes breakfast and dinner), add $45 per person per day plus 12% meal service charge.
Service charge: 12%.
Government tax: 7%.

Children welcome.
Credit cards accepted.

Sonesta Beach Hotel & Casino Curaçao

At long last, Curaçao has a luxury hotel—the multimillion-dollar Sonesta Beach Hotel & Casino Curaçao, located on a beautiful expanse of beach on the island's southern shoreline at Piscadera Bay, three miles from the airport and the capital city of Willemstad. The handsome 248-room hotel, open since 1992, stretches over the property in a series of three-story structures designed in classic Dutch style. Walls are painted ocher with white trim; red-tiled roofs have gables; doors are standouts in bright turquoise. Fountains bubble and gardens flourish throughout the resort.

Next to the beach, at the center of the hotel, the large angular-shaped freeform swimming pool sports a swim-up bar, wading pool, and two whirlpools on a terrace lined with chaises and umbrellas. Guests who prefer settling down in the sand will find shade under thatched bohios.

It's a lovely, sunny setting, and cooling off periodically in the pool or sea provides welcome relief from the heat. Water sports offered include windsurfing, waterskiing, scuba diving, and snorkeling. Parents can have some free time to themselves here by enrolling their youngsters in the resort's complimentary "Just Us Kids" program for children from five to twelve years of age; open Wednesdays through Sundays from 10 A.M. to 4:30 P.M. Sports facilities include two lit tennis courts and a complete fitness room. Golfers can take advantage of the Curaçao Golf and Squash Club's nine-hole course, about a 15-minute drive from the hotel. For the sport of gambling, the lavish chandeliered 5,000-square-foot Emerald Casino offers roulette, mini-baccarat, craps, blackjack, slot machines, and something called Caribbean polka. Winnings can be spent in the hotel's arcade shops, at Gandelman Jewelers, or on perfumes from Casa Amarilla. There are also several resortwear and accessory shops, as well as Van Dorp, which sells newspapers, books, periodicals, and necessities. A full-service salon is also at your disposal.

Sonesta Beach's rooms are luxurious, contemporary havens all dressed up in coordinated pale pastels. Every room has a patio or balcony with broad or at least partial sea views. I'd opt for the deluxe oceanfront studio or terrace suites on the second or third floors for full beach views and privacy. The air-conditioned rooms come with cable TVs, telephones, stocked mini-fridges, two queen-size or one king-size bed, and bathrooms with hair dryers, toiletries, and tub/showers.

Sustenance at Sonesta Beach is agreeably found in three venues. For breakfasts and informal lunches or dinners, the Palm Café's open-air terrace, by the beach and pool, serves reasonably priced, tasty American and Caribbean selections. Portofino is a most attractive, glass-enclosed restaurant focusing on Northern Italian and Mediterranean dishes from pasta and veal to pizza. The Emerald Bar & Grill, in a totally different environment with tapestry-covered, eclectic furnishings, offers Continental fare such as grilled filet mignon plus other meats and seafood with unusual sauces, fresh vegetables, and delicious desserts. Soft piano melodies are played during dinner. On the adjacent Emerald Terrace, a trio plays livelier tunes from 10 P.M. to midnight.

Clientele at Sonesta is mostly Venezuelans (the coast of Venezuela is only 35 miles away), Dutch, German, and English. Americans curious about the island can now confidently book into first-rate accommodations in lovely surroundings and discover fascinating Curaçao. There are National and Budget car-rental office branches at the hotel.

SONESTA BEACH HOTEL	**RESERVATIONS**
& CASINO CURAÇAO	TEL: (800) SONESTA
P.O. Box 6003	
Piscadera Bay, Curaçao, Netherlands Antilles	
TEL: (011-599-9) 368800	
FAX: (011-599-9) 627502	

Open all year.
Rates: Double occupancy. *December 20 to April 6:* Superior and Deluxe Rooms, $215 to $250; Deluxe Oceanfront, Studio, and Terrace Suites, $280 to $350; Presidential Suite, $770. *April 7 to December 18:* Superior and Deluxe Rooms, $150 to $170; Deluxe Oceanfront, Studio, and Terrace Suites, $200 to $260; Presidential Suite, $550. Children under 12 free (maximum of 2). Extra person, $25.
Meal plan: EP. MAP (includes breakfast and dinner), add $45 per person per day, children (5 to 12 years), add $24 per child per day.
Service charge: 12%.
Government tax: 7%.
Children welcome.
Credit cards accepted.
Note: Ultimate Indulgence, Passion in Paradise, Sensational All-Inclusive, and Family Fun packages are available.

Recommended Restaurants

CURAÇAO'S FINEST*

* **De Taveerne**, 370669 (Landhuis Groot Davelaar, Silena). Elegant dining in a renovated *landhuis* (country home). The changing menu offers rich but inspired seafood and meat dishes. Expensive.

* **Belle Terrace** and **Blues**, 614377 (Avila Beach Hotel). Delightful Belle Terrace is a seaside, romantic spot serving commendable food. Blues, set out on the hotel's pier,

is the hotel's newer restaurant featuring jazz as well as good food. (See hotel listing, page 143.) Moderate to expensive.

* **The Emerald Bar & Grill** and **Portofino**, 368800 (Sonesta Beach Hotel & Casino Curaçao). Two lovely restaurants are located in brand-new Sonesta Beach Hotel (see previous listing). Moderate to expensive.

* **Bistro Le Clochard**, 625666 (Rif Fort, Otrabanda). A rustic seaside dining room that offers French/Swiss specialities from veal to fondue and raclette. The restaurant also features sizzling-hot stone-cooked seafood, chicken, or meat dishes. Lofty desserts. Also try **Clochard's Harbour Side Terrace** for cocktails and hors d'oeuvres. Moderate to expensive.

* **A'louette**, 618222 (Orionweg 12). In a small house just outside of Willemstad, you'll find a warm welcome and changing menu of excellent, if rich, dishes from seafood to meat. Lots of fancy sauces. The plain grilled meats are fine, too. Expensive.

* **Rijsttafel Restaurant**, 612606 (Mercuriusstraat 13, Cerrito). The best Indonesian rijsttafel (the traditional rice table)—with 16 to 25 delicious side dishes—in Curaçao. Come with friends and make a party of it. Moderate to expensive.

* **The Wine Cellar Restaurant**, 674909 (Concordiastraat). Small restaurant in the country with Victorian decor, under the helm of owner/chef Nico Cornelissee. Select fine wines to sip with the well-prepared meat and seafood dishes that are always accompanied by the freshest vegetables available. Moderate to expensive.

* **El Marinero**, 379833 (Schottegatweg Noord 87-B). First-rate seafood from conch to lobster is served here. Basque-style sea bass and paella are favorites. Moderate to expensive.

* **Jaanchie's Restaurant**, 640126 (Westpunt). Fun and tasty local dishes like funchi, goat stew, conch creations, or fresh fish in a very casual open-air restaurant. Popular with locals and tourists alike. Inexpensive to moderate.

OTHER DEPENDABLE CHOICES

To rest between intervals of shopping in the Punda, everyone gathers at **The Downtown Restaurant** on Heerenstraat (no cars), for German or international fare. For a quick slice, go to **Cozzoli's Pizza** across from Spritzer & Fuhrmann. Good Italian food and pizza can also be had at **La Pergola** at the Waterfront Arches.

Rumour's Restaurant, 618100 (Lions Dive Hotel and Marina). This is a very popular restaurant with a lively atmosphere serving daily specials; good salad bar and fresh seafood selections as well. Moderate.

Cactus Club, 371600 (Van Staverenweg 6 on the outskirts of town). Come here for Mexican food—fajitas, tacos, nachos—as well as burgers, steak, and seafood. Great for families. Inexpensive to moderate.

Caribana Restaurant at Koral Agostini across from Otrobanda ferry landing serves Latin/Caribbean food. **Rodeo Ranch Saloon & Steakhouse** at the Seaquarium in Bapor Kibra has a casual western motif, including cowgirls and cowboys at the chuckwagon serving good steaks and seafood—another good place to take the kids. **Pisces Seafood**

Restaurant & Bar at the end of Caracasbaaiweg off Fisherman's Wharf, is good for lunches when sightseeing. All inexpensive to moderate.
Golden Star Restaurant, 654795 (Socratesstraat 2). This is another unpretentious but dependable spot dishing up good local and Créole food. Inexpensive.
Also try the local dishes prepared behind the **Floating Market**, a short walk from the Queen Emma Pontoon Bridge.

Recommended Shopping

Curaçao's main shopping district is called the **Punda**, a five-square-block area. The other prime shopping is at the **Waterfront Arches** boutiques nearby, and (across the floating pontoon bridge to the west) the Otrobanda in Willemstad, and easily can be covered in a morning or afternoon. Shops here are not as sophisticated as those in Aruba, St. Martin and the other French islands, or St. Thomas, but there are still some treasures and bargains to be found.

Art and handcrafts: Bamali, Arawak Clay Products (in the countryside), the open market, and The African Queen.

Cameras and electrical equipment: Boolchand's and Palais Hindu.

Crystal and china: Little Switzerland and Spritzer & Fuhrmann.

Fashions: Benetton, Bamali, and Little Holland.

Jewelry and watches: Gandelmann Jewelers, Boolchand's, Little Switzerland, Penha & Sons, and Spritzer & Fuhrmann.

Linens and tablecloths: Little Holland, New Amsterdam Store, and The Yellow House (Casa Amarilla).

Perfumes and cosmetics: The Yellow House and Penha & Sons.

Shoes: La Palestina and Little Holland.

The boutiques in most of Curaçao's many hotels carry resortwear, costume jewelry, and gift items.

For **gourmet foods,** especially reasonably priced Dutch cheeses and chocolates, go to **Zuikertuintje** on Zuikertuintjeweg.

Useful Information

Curaçao Holiday!, the island's yellow complimentary guide, should be kept at every traveler's side. The local English newspaper is *The Curaçao Gazette*.

Three well-known **car rental agencies** in Curaçao are **National**, (011-599-9) 683489; **Avis**, (011-599-9) 681163, and **Budget**, (011-599-9) 683466 or 683198. All have toll-free numbers in the U.S.

One-hour photo processing and film can be found at **Fugi Image Plaza** at the Waterside Arches, and **Palais Hindu** on Heerenstraat. You'll want to take lots of pictures of Willemstad's colorful architecture, the **Floating Market**, and the countryside.

Not to be missed is the beautiful **Mikve Israel–Emanuel Synagogue** in Willemstad, the oldest synagogue in continuous use in the Western Hemisphere, and the **Jewish Historical & Cultural Museum**. Also worth a visit are the **Curaçao Museum, Bolívar** and **Natural History museums**, the **Hato Caves**, the plantation houses (known as **landhuizen**), and the **Curaçao Seaquarium**. Tours of the **Amstel Brewery** and **Curaçao Liqueur Distillery** are offered as well.

Other important attractions are **Christoffel National Park** and the 12½-mile-long **Curaçao Underwater Park**, near the Princess Beach Hotel.

Curaçao also has several **casinos**.

≈ ≈

DOMINICA

ACCOMMODATIONS

DOMINICA'S BEST
Fort Young Hotel

NOTEWORTHY OPTIONS
Evergreen Hotel
Papillote Wilderness Retreat
Reigate Hall Hotel

RECOMMENDED RESTAURANTS

RECOMMENDED SHOPPING

USEFUL INFORMATION

≈ ≈

≈ ≈

Accommodations

DOMINICA'S BEST

Fort Young Hotel

Reopened after hurricane devastation in 1989, the Fort Young Hotel rests at the edge of Roseau in a seaside location among the ruins of the 1770 Fort Young. There is no beach here—the coastline waves lap at small, rocky cliffs. Still, Fort Young is the best place to stay in Dominica if modern-day creature comforts and a lively, friendly atmosphere are your primary concerns. Although the first-class, four-story Garraway Hotel opened recently just a few blocks away on the new Bayfront Drive, it's still trying to find a personality, and seemed to us a lonely, soulless place, empty as it was. Extra rooms in Roseau were badly needed for business travelers, so the Garraway ought to establish itself soon.

Fort Young's 33 conventional but comfortable well-kept rooms and suites, in a stone and masonry two-story building, curve in a half-circle around the public areas, which include a rectangular-shaped freshwater swimming pool with chaises, the Marquis de Bouille restaurant, bar, and lounge, and Hazel's Artcraft shop. Not all rooms have sea views, so be sure to request one with a water view when booking, as they always go first. All rooms do have air-conditioning and ceiling fans, cable TV with 11 channels, direct-dial phones, and balconies.

Fort Young is the first choice for business people, so the hotel also has conference and private meeting rooms. And additional guest rooms are in the hotel's future plans.

The Marquis de Bouille restaurant's vast stone-walled, wooden-beamed peaked-ceilinged dining room is invitingly attractive. Its tables are covered with white cloths and bouquets of flowers and have comfortable beige-upholstered wooden armchairs. Tasty lunch and dinner selections range from curried chicken salad with a cucumber vinaigrette and spaghetti with seafood and tomato sauce, to shrimp ajillo (shrimp with a herb, garlic, onion, olive, and white wine sauce) or grilled, steamed, or panfried fish of the day with a choice of garlic or lime butter or Créole sauce.

Fort Young is conveniently situated just across the street from La Robe Créole restaurant (see Recommended Restaurants section) and is a short stroll from the botanical gardens as well as from the center of Roseau. The hotel arranges tours and will rent cars for guests. Spend the day at the beach at Castaways, take day trips around the island, go hiking or diving—there's a lot to do and see in Dominica (see also Useful Information), and you'll find Fort Young an excellent home base to retreat to at the end of a long, exhilarating day.

FORT YOUNG HOTEL
P.O. Box 519, Victoria Street
Roseau, Dominica, West Indies
TEL: (809) 448-5000
FAX: (809) 448-5006

RESERVATIONS:
TEL: (800) 223-6510

Open all year.
Rates: Double occupancy. *January 1 to June 30:* Superior, $105; Deluxe, $115; Suite, $125. *July 1 to December 31:* Superior, $85; Deluxe, $95; Suite, $105. Extra person, $20 year-round. Children under 12 free if sharing room with two adults.
Meal plan: EP.
Service charge: 10%.
Government tax: 5%.
Children welcome.
Credit cards accepted.

NOTEWORTHY OPTIONS

Evergreen Hotel

Checking into Mena and Charles Winston's eight-year-old Evergreen Hotel, one mile from Roseau on a narrow strip of land along the coast road, is the equivalent of visiting family or old friends in their Dominican home. Jennifer, the Winstons' daughter and warm, efficient manager, and the gentle staff, are caring and helpful, whether it's to send a fax, bring extra pillows and hangers, or organize tours, dives, or a taxi.

Evergreen's two-story chalet-style main building houses the reception area, 10 simple but entirely adequate rooms (with porches or balconies), and a dining room, which serves breakfast, luncheon, and all-day snacks and has a veranda that overlooks the tropically planted lawn and the sea.

Prime lodgings here are the six balconied deluxe rooms in the new three-story white-and-yellow building across the lawn, right at the ocean's edge. The three top-floor rooms are delightful quarters for sea views and dramatic sunsets. The coastline below is pebble and rock, but Evergreen has a freshwater swimming pool with a Jean Desjoyaux water exercise machine, and a decent-sized terrace with chaise longues for sunning. (The Anchorage Hotel, a short walk to the north, has a good dive operation.)

Adjacent to Evergreen's pool is an indoor bar and a breezy, pretty dining room, the Crystal Terrace, where dinners are served. We sampled very good broiled fresh fish main courses served with excellent vegetable dishes, such as fresh grated carrots in a vinaigrette

Evergreen Hotel, Dominica.

sauce and coconut-batter-fried plantains. Sweet cakes and exotic fruit-flavored ice creams were the desserts. Our waitress gave me the coconut plantain recipe from the two chefs after I asked for seconds. Over coffee on the terrace by the pool, my husband and I listened to old standards softly playing — "Far Away Places" and "Slow Boat to China." Lulu, the Winstons' dog, escorted us back to room 6, the ground-floor corner room in the main building, where we had a peaceful eight-hour sleep.

All rooms are air-conditioned and neat, with 11-channel TVs (including HBO and CNN), telephones, tiled bathrooms, and a fresh bouquet of flowers.

During our stay, Evergreen was fully booked with American and European nature lovers, divers, and business travelers of all ages. Everyone appeared totally content here, just like we were. The hospitable Evergreen Hotel is warmly recommended for undemanding vacationers seeking tranquil, casual surroundings in beautiful Dominica.

EVERGREEN HOTEL
P.O. Box 309
Castle Comfort
Dominica, West Indies
TEL: (809) 448-3288/3276
FAX: (809) 448-6800

Open all year.
Rates: Double occupancy. Rooms, $100 to $125 year-round.

Meal plan: MAP (includes breakfast and dinner).
Service charge: 10%.
Government tax: 5%.
Children welcome.
Credit cards accepted.

Papillote Wilderness Retreat

Papillote Wilderness Retreat is an enchanting, rustic nature-lovers' inn set among more than 10 acres of tropical-rainforest gardens near 200-foot Trafalgar Falls, four miles east of Roseau. The winding, bumpy drive from town takes about 30 minutes, but the always fascinating Dominican scenery eventually transforms from pleasant countryside into a remarkable jungle wilderness, and almost before you want to be, you're there.

On our last visit we arrived just in time for another memorable lunch after the obligatory 15-minute climb to Trafalgar Falls. Thirsty from our hike, we immediately gulped down Papillote's delicious small but potent rum punches, and reminded ourselves next time to quench our thirst with something nonalcoholic beforehand.

The open-air, high-roofed pavilion dining room provided us with cooling breezes and shade while we savored a delightful meal of flying fish with curried onion sauce, light-as-air dasheen fritters, and a shredded raw carrot salad topped with tomato and cucumber slices and a creamy dressing. The healthful, organic menu always includes fresh provisions, such as root vegetables and fruits plucked from nearby trees, local seafood, mountain chicken (large landfrogs, called *craupauds*, when in season and available), fruit juices, and herbal and exotic tea infusions as curatives or simply refreshing drinks. Our dining companions included a few hotel guests and, parading the grounds, various cats, ducks, geese, and rare breeds of clucking chickens, like the amazing black-and-white-spotted roosters with wildly sprouting head feathers that the staff called rasta roosters.

Next to the restaurant is a hot mineral pool (one of several) for hotel guests. Papillote's excellent boutique features Dominican handcrafts and apparel, and, as of 1993, the owners opened a separate 60-seat restaurant in a handsome new stone building adjacent to the parking lot to accommodate the many day-trippers who naturally want to come to dine and see the falls. Hotel guests are much less interrupted from their private reveries now: outside visitors must make reservations for lunch and have to leave by 4 P.M. Dinner reservations are also taken.

The inn's eight rooms are modest lodgings in a two-story building called the Rain Forest Rooms. All are furnished with simple handmade furniture, locally-woven grass rugs, and adequate plumbing. No frills here except for the bold and charming hand-painted leaves, vines, and fronds of trees and plants that seem to grow across the walls and ceilings of the rooms. Papillote also rents a two-bedroom, two-bath cottage with a kitchen near the road and a wilderness trail.

Responsible for this "oasis in the rain forest," as the brochure accurately states, are New York–born amateur botanist Anne Jno. Baptiste and her Dominican husband, Cuthbert. Island residents for more than 30 years, they have made Papillote Wilderness

Retreat their Shangri-la in a labor of love. More than 110 rare horticultural specimens thrive in the nature sanctuary, including indigenous orchids, daturn "bella-donna," gaspo, soursop, breadfruit, heliconias, aroids, giant tree ferns, and bromeliads, plus more than 50 species of nesting birds that may be spotted, such as the Zenaida dove, the Caribbean elaenia, the red-necked pigeon, and the stolid flycatcher.

The hotel provides a map of the sanctuary for guests, guided nature walks, safari day tours, and will organize car rentals and scuba diving.

Other intriguing features of Papillote are granite and cement whimsical animal statues crafted by a guest, Lidee Climo, from Prince Edward Island. The moss-covered menagerie of iguanas, fish, swans, donkeys, and other creatures dot the garden grounds. Anne Jno. Baptiste posed for a photograph on the donkey, sipping one of her herbal infusions after lunch one day.

Papillote is a one-of-a kind hostelry and the Jno. Baptistes are welcoming, informative hosts.

PAPILLOTE WILDERNESS RETREAT
P.O. Box 67
Roseau, Commonwealth of Dominica, West Indies
TEL: (809) 448-2287
FAX: (809) 448-2285

Open all year.
Rates: Double occupancy. Rooms, $50 to $60; Two-Bedroom Cottage, $130, year-round.
Meal plan: EP. MAP (includes breakfast and dinner), add $30 per person per day.
Service charge: 10%.
Government tax: 5%.
Children welcome.
Credit cards accepted.

Reigate Hall Hotel

Ten-year-old Reigate Hall Hotel is a thirteen-room, two-suite renovated former manor house located on a hillside overlooking Roseau and the sea, about a mile and a half from town. The stucco, natural-stone, and wood-shingled compact complex has a small pool, tennis court, garden terrace under a giant flamboyant tree, indoor bar, lounge, and a second-floor restaurant with a small waterwheel that operates occasionally.

The combined white, redbrick, and wood-paneled room interiors are modestly decorated with wooden reproduction furniture, white bedcovers, and Caribbean oil paintings. Of the two suites, number 16 is preferred because of its second-floor corner location with lovely views overlooking Roseau and the sea. The suites, really only small rooms, feature four-poster double beds, wet bars, fridges, electric kettles, ice buckets, and early breakfast provisions of packets of instant coffee, tea bags, sugar, cream in the refrigerator, as well as pints of gin, Scotch, white rum, and tonic water. The suites also have telephones, clock radios, and cable TVs with video machines and a collection of cassettes. The large bathroom in suite 16 is equipped with a Jacuzzi, separate tub and shower, bidet, scale, and twin-basin sinks.

The regular rooms and bathrooms are very small. Beds are twins. All accommodations are air-conditioned and have tiny terraces or balconies. The corner suite's balcony is just large enough to accommodate two chaises with a small table in between.

Since December 1990, Reigate Hall has been owned by Guinness Reigate Hall, Ltd., a Dominican company. Its partners include Reginald Shillingford, Dominican born and London educated, who is the hotel's general manager and managing director and also owns the Reigate Waterfront Hotel (formerly the Sisserou Hotel) in Castle Comfort near the Evergreen Hotel. A recent visit revealed that much sprucing up is still needed at that property before it can be recommended. And, Reigate Hall, sadly, has lost some of its previous spirit and charm.

We were so looking forward to sampling some of our favorite dishes here for dinner. Still on the menu, we had hearts of palm au gratin and callaloo soup as starters, followed by mountain chicken (*craupaud*, a large land frog) in Créole sauce and fish in lime butter. Unfortunately, the food was only fair and much too salty.

Reigate Hall is still a pleasant little inn. And, aside from Castaways, it has the only other hotel tennis court on the island. Nights at Reigate are blissfully quiet and the views over town are expansive and the stars above twinkle brightly. Cool, smoky breezes and the sweet smells of frangipani are pure Dominican magic.

REIGATE HALL HOTEL
P.O. Box 356
Mountain Road, Roseau
Dominica, West Indies
TEL: (809) 448-4031
FAX: (809) 448-4034

Open all year.
Rates: Double occupancy. Rooms, $95; Suites, $180, year-round.
Meal plan: EP.
Service charge: 10%.
Government tax: 5%.
Children welcome.
Credit cards accepted.

Recommended Restaurants

DOMINICA'S BEST

* **Marquis de Bouille Restaurant**, 448-5000 (Fort Young Hotel, Roseau). Attractive, expansive dining room serving very good locally inspired food. (See hotel listing, page 151.) Moderate.

* **Crystal Terrace**, 448-6800 (Evergreen Hotel, Castle Comfort). Seaside terrace restaurant with a small menu of praiseworthy local food served by a soliticious staff. (See hotel listing, page 152.) Moderate.

* **Papillote Wilderness Retreat**, 448-2287 (Trafalgar Falls Road, four miles from Roseau). Local delicacies such as flying fish and mountain chicken are served for lunch and dinner in a brand-new restaurant with a delightful rain-forest hideaway. (See resort listing, page 154.) Inexpensive to moderate.

* **Floral Gardens**, 445-7636 (Floral Gardens Hotel in Concord near the Carib Indian Reservation). Friendly manager/owner Josephine Williams offers home cooking in a small dining room in a chalet-like, secluded little hotel near the rain forest. Open for breakfast, lunch, and dinner, although at night it's a long, dark drive. Reserve in advance for lunch, as Floral Gardens has become very popular with cruise-ship groups and bus-loads of day-trippers. Thankfully, they've added a pavilion across the road to accommodate large groups. We loved our meals of delectable agouti (a local pork/chicken-flavored rodent) and succulent crayfish. Both were attractively served with portions of sweet potatoes au gratin, creamy potato salad, fried banana slices, and tasty rice timbales. The homemade pies were mouth-watering. Try delicious hibiscus or other local juice beverages. Moderate.

* **Guiyave Restaurant and Pâtisserie**, 448-2930 (15 Cork Street, Roseau). This second-floor dining veranda serves delicious Dominican lunch specialities like baked fish with Créole sauce for lunch. The downstairs pâtisserie produces local confections and sandwiches. Both offer fresh local fruit juices—tamarind, soursop, etc. Inexpensive to moderate.

OTHER DEPENDABLE CHOICES

La Robe Créole, 448-2896 (3 Victoria Street, opposite Fort Young Hotel). Not as dependable as it used to be, this air-conditioned restaurant with wooden tables and pleasant decor for years was the best dining to be had in Dominica. On a recent visit we found slack service and uneven dishes coming out of the kitchen. We recently sampled unremarkable accras and lukewarm pumpkin soup, excellent chicken roti and average stewed chicken with ginger. The coconut rum punch was extremely sweet. It's still a lively gathering spot. Moderate. Outside, the attached **Mousehole Snackettes** is convenient for take-out rotis and other fast foods.

Other good dining choices in Roseau are **The Orchard Restaurant, Callaloo Restau-**

rant & Bar, **Pearl's Cuisine**, and **The World of Food Nice Place to Eat and Drink**, the latter, the former home of writer Jean Rhys. For pizza and buffalo wings go to **Famous Cathy's**. Unpretentious cafés offering good Créole food are the **Green Parrot** and **Créole Kitchen**.

Although we didn't eat there, the Chinese, Créole, and Continental food being served at the **Lauro River Hotel** looked excellent. There's a large swimming pool and the cool Lauro River for a swim before lunch. The hotel is managed by Taiwanese/Dominican owners.

Sunday's beach barbecue at **Castaways** (about 10 miles north of Roseau) is a popular local weekly event, but I can't recommend the food in the restaurant, and it's just so-so at the beach. Go instead to watch the action, snorkel, swim, and have a drink. There are shower and changing facilities on the beach at Castaways, Dominica's only real beachfront hotel, which also has a tennis court. If you're in Laudat, go to **Roxy's Mountain Lodge** for good local fare. At Portsmouth the two best selections are **Le Flambeau** at Picard Bay Hotel and **Coconut Beach Restaurant** for lunch.

Recommended Shopping

Tropicrafts, 448-7126/2747 (corner Queen Mary Street and Turkey Lane). The most important shopping stop in Dominica is this shop. Michael Pascal sells exquisite woven vetiver grass mats and rugs of all sizes that are featured in hotels throughout the Caribbean and the world. UPS and Federal Express delivery is available. Customers can watch local women expertly hand-stitching the mats together. Also on sale are locally produced food items such as hot sauces, nutmeg syrup, and jellies, along with wood crafts, handmade dolls, and pottery.

Caribana Craft Shop, 448-2761 (31 Cork Street), should be your next stop for locally handcrafted calabash bowls, miniature West Indian wooden stick houses, straw baskets made by the Carib Indians, and a lot more.

The **Old Mill Culture Centre** (near Canefield Airport) is a mini-museum with a shop featuring wood carvings.

Baroon Bijoux, 449-2888 (near Canefield Airport), manufactures and sells jewelry in 14K and 18K gold with semiprecious and precious stones, modest in design.

At the **Carib Indian Reservation**, north of Melville Hall Airport, several roadside stalls sell special Carib-styled baskets and handbags.

Agape Craft Co-Op (Delice). Handcrafts and beautiful handmade quilts (the nine-year-old one in our guest room is a prized possession), place mats, and pot holders. Usually, stock is limited, but they will ship orders.

Also visit the first-rate boutiques at **Papillote Wilderness Retreat**, **Floral Gardens**, and **Fort Young Hotel**.

The best book selection is at **Paperbacks** on Cork Street.

The **Forestry Division Offices** in the **Botanic Gardens** in Roseau sells a wide variety of inexpensive brochures and booklets on the natural wonders of Dominica, like the Cabrits National Park and the Morne Trois Pitons National Park of Dominica, plus attractive posters and a map of the island's wilderness trails.

The bustling **Old Market** in Roseau is a wonderful place to view and buy some of the island's superb produce.

Useful Information

Dominica has the living physical beauty of a Rousseau painting. The island's mountains, hills, and valleys are cloaked in the lush plumage of coconut palms, giant ferns, and banana trees, and hundreds of other species. At one point during a day of exploration, we paused to watch a pageant of orange-brown land crabs scurrying across low-lying fertile ground. The island is streaked with rushing rivers and gentle streams. Its rich volcanic soil produces vegetation with the speed and size of Jack's Beanstalk. You'll find rain-forest jungles, spectacular waterfalls, and the elusive Sisserou parrot, if you're lucky. Beaches are gray-black and caramel-colored sand.

Dominica is for nature lovers and the curious. Any visit here is strongly linked to discovering the island itself. Dominica is not a sophisticated, glamorous destination. Its hotels, found mainly in Roseau and its environs or along the west coast, with a few hidden retreats in the mountains, are on the whole modest or bare-bones lodgings.

Purchase copies of *The Dominica Story, A History of the Island* by Lennox Honychurch (Dominica Institute), *Caribbean Wild Plants and Their Uses* by Penelope N. Honychurch (Macmillan), and *Dominica Nature Island of the Caribbean,* put together by Hansib Publishing Limited of London, for excellent information and lovely photographs (all available at Caribana Handicrafts and other shops on the island).

Excellent local giveaway publications are *The Tropical Traveller* and *Discover Dominica.*

Among the many car rental companies are **Budget,** (809) 449-2030; **Valley Rent-A-Car,** (809) 448-3233 or 445-5252; and **Bonus,** (809) 448-2650.

Whether you rent a car (the roads, except for Portsmouth and mountain byways, are generally excellent), hire a taxi driver for the day, or join one of the many guided tours, be certain to see Dominica's outstanding sights: the **Botanic Gardens** in Roseau, **Ridgefield Estate, Trafalgar Falls,** the **Morne Trois Pitons National Park,** the **Carib Indian Reservation, Cabrits National Park,** the **Emerald Pool, Boiling Lake,** and many more. Two tour companies are Jacquot Tours (449-8026) and Hinterland (448-4850).

Other excellent activities on the island include hiking, birdwatching, and exploring the many excellent scuba-diving sites. There is no dearth of dive companies in Dominica, but two of the best are **Dive Dominica,** 448-6088 (Castle Comfort) and the **Anchorage Dive Centre,** 448-2638 (Anchorage Hotel, Castle Comfort).

Two tennis courts on the island available for travelers' use are at **Castaways Beach Hotel** and **Reigate Hall Hotel.**

The best beach for swimming is the long, calm gray-black sand strip at **Castaways Beach Hotel**, about seven miles north of Roseau on the coast road. Shower and changing facilities are located on the beach.

Excursions to Martinique and Guadeloupe can be arranged on **Caribbean Express's** fast passenger boats by booking through **H.H.V. Whitchurch and Co. Ltd. Travel Agency** on Old Street in Roseau, (809) 448-2181.

≈ ≈

GRENADA

ACCOMMODATIONS

GRENADA'S BEST
The Calabash Hotel
Rex Grenadian
Secret Harbour Resort

A NOTEWORTHY OPTION
Twelve Degrees North

RECOMMENDED RESTAURANTS

RECOMMENDED SHOPPING

PROVISIONS FOR YOUR ISLAND PANTRY

USEFUL INFORMATION

≈ ≈

≈ ≈

Accommodations

GRENADA'S BEST

The Calabash Hotel

It's impossible to resist Calabash, the island's best small authentic retreat, located on L'Anse aux Epines' lengthy beach, about 10 minutes from the Point Saline International Airport with its famous 9,000-foot runway. The Calabash is old-style island hospitality, welcoming and irresistible for those wanting a low-key yet pampered holiday. As one guest said, "It's more 'Bali Ha'i' than 'Yellow Bird.'"

All of the hotel's 28 rooms are attractively furnished in tropical fashion and have air-conditioning, ceiling fans, wall safes, adequate closet space, sitting areas, verandas, and tub-shower bathrooms, with the exception of the baths in the new quarters. These rooms are, of course, more bright and modern, each with a whirlpool.

Accommodations are named after flowers and trees and are found in 11 separate cottages — two- or four-unit, one- or two-storied buildings — that wind around each side of the public areas at the edge of the property. Every cottage has its own kitchen and a cook to prepare and serve breakfast at a prearranged time. There are no TVs in the rooms, but the small lounge room has one. Telephones are direct-dial. A note about the phone in my room read: "This apparatus is here for your convenience. If you do not wish for it in your room, please advise us and we will have it removed."

Eight suites have private pools — six are newer and ground level. Above them on the second floor are the whirlpool rooms. The other rooms with pools are 4-A Flamboyant, where I slept, and 11-A Calabash. The latter is the more desirable of the older rooms, as it has the bigger pool, terrace area, and open-air living room. Number 1-A Passion Flower, the honeymoon suite, a second-floor beachfront accommodation with a hand-carved mahogany four-poster bed, is the best room without a pool in the house. But all guests can enjoy laps in freshwater in Calabash's pretty pool.

The resort is spread over eight tropical acres bordering a western caramel-colored beach and calm sea. Lunches at Calabash are only available at the rustic seaside Calabash Beach Bar.

On my first morning at Calabash, after a fitful sleep, I took a dip in the pool, showered, and was toweling off when Elsa tapped on the door and asked how I'd like my eggs. She proceeded to cook breakfast in the adjoining kitchen. Seated at a table on the front patio, which was rimmed in a thick hedge of green-yellow-and orange-striped croton, I savored crisp bacon, fried eggs, a basket of toast, orange juice, a large, freshly picked banana, and rich, black coffee. It was sheer pleasure eating and peering out over a vast green lawn with a pond and a little humpbacked bridge, under a grove of coconut palms. The only activity was a slow parade of hotel staff picking flowers and carrying trays of breakfast ingredients to other guests' rooms. Mrs. Bubb, the housekeeper with the hotel for 21 years, stopped by to see if I needed anything, approved Elsa's presentation, and disappeared. Later in the morning the lounges lining the beach began to fill.

Time at the Calabash is a homecoming for the predominantly European clientele, overwhelmingly British, the rest Germans, Canadians, and some Americans. While I was visiting, guests ranged from a studious young Canadian man who read in the lounge all day, to several British couples of all ages, and a group of coworkers from London who were traveling together. One of the women, who possessed a voice exactly like Maggie Smith's at her most excited, recounted her first attempt at snorkeling: "It was haunting, simply haunting."

Windsurfing, scuba-diving, fishing, and snorkeling gear are available at the Calabash beach for a reasonable fee. The resort has one floodlit tennis court and a snooker and billiards room. A putting green is a few minutes' drive away.

Calabash's natural-stone, open-air restaurant, Cicely's, is situated off the bar and lounge area, partially covered by a long arbor draped in intertwined vines of delicate flowering thunbergia. The restaurant's award-winning cuisine includes a small selection of four courses of Continental dishes accented with Grenadian flavors. Meals are thoughtfully prepared by Cicely Roberts, who is celebrating her seventeenth year at the hotel. What makes dinner so enchanting is the graceful synchronized service of the waitresses dressed in flowing, long, green, floral-printed skirts and white blouses. Particularly good were pigeon-pea soup, dolphin (the fish not the mammal) cooked in coconut milk, roast leg of lamb with mint jelly, delicious crisp oven-roast potatoes, fresh steamed local pumpkin, and a sublime creamy vanilla ice cream laced with fresh guava slices and banana fritters.

The resort has a boutique and library room. Frills at Calabash come in the form of a gentle, caring staff.

Brit Leo Garbutt and Susan and Lyden Ramdhanny, co-owners of Calabash, continue to smoothly operate the thirty-one-year-old resort.

THE CALABASH HOTEL
P.O. Box 382, St. George's
L'Anse aux Epines
Grenada, West Indies
TEL: (809) 444-4334
FAX: (809) 444-5050

RESERVATIONS
TEL: (800) 528-5835

Open all year.
Rates: Double occupancy. *December 19 to April 3:* Beach/Garden View Rooms, $245

to $295; Whirlpool Rooms, $340 to $390; Pool Rooms, $425 to $475. Third person in room, $120 to $140 per person per day. *April 4 to December 18:* Beach/Garden View Rooms: MAP, $190 to $210; AP, $140 to $160. Whirlpool Rooms: MAP, $230 to $250; AP, $180 to $200. Pool Rooms: MAP, $295 to $315; AP, $245 to $265. Third person in room: MAP, $95 to $105 per person per day; AP, $70 to $80 per person per day.

Meal plan: MAP (includes breakfast and dinner) mandatory in winter and included in room rates. AP (with full breakfast) and MAP options for remainder of the year—rates given above.

Service charge: 10%.

Government tax: 8%.

Children over 12 welcome during winter season.

Credit cards accepted.

Rex Grenadian

A half a mile from Point Salines International Airport, six miles from St. George's, two new deluxe seaside resorts have recently opened—the Rex Grenadian and the upscale all-inclusive health-oriented La Source. After visiting both, my choice is the Rex Grenadian for several reasons. It has a much more sensible and diverse layout with expansive tropical lawns, little lakes with bridges, comfortable lounging areas, three pleasant dining options, and a wide selection of 210 first-rate accommodations for a range of budgets. Rex also has splendid beaches at Tamarind Bay (one for water sports, the other for swimming and lounging) and magnificent views of the sea and Grenadian coastline all the way to St. George's from an beautiful, imaginatively created elevated freeform pool and terrace. The staff is warm and welcoming, with manager Lawrence Samuel in charge.

The garden rooms have the fewest amenities, but cost only $145 a night per couple in season. They are small, cozy spaces with ceiling fans, telephones, radios, twin beds (separated or together), basic bathrooms, and balconies. The next class of rooms, ocean view and beachfront, have air-conditioning and hair dryers, as do all the remaining categories of rooms and suites. TVs come with the executive rooms up through the remaining variety of accommodations to the royal suites. The nine well-appointed royal suites have spacious bedrooms with a sitting area, full living room, and terraces overlooking the sea. Bathrooms have separate shower stalls and tubs, twin basins, and bidets, all for $310 a night for two in season. These are the most desirable places to stay at the resort.

Water sports include windsurfing, Sunfish sailing, and snorkeling, with equipment available. Scuba diving and deep-sea fishing can be arranged. Other activities include two all-weather tennis courts (small fee for night play), shuffleboard, table tennis, and volleyball. A fitness center is also available for workouts.

Sustenance at Rex Grenadian ranges from the Oriental Restaurant (which had not

Poolside at the Rex Grenadian in Grenada.

opened when I was there) and the International Restaurant, serving up good Continental fare, seafood, and barbecues, to my favorite, Spicers, a pool bar and restaurant that serves simple salads, sandwiches, and well-selected and -prepared snacks. The attraction here is not so much the food as it is the gorgeous surroundings—a large scalloped pool and seaside views. (The beaches are just below.) Tables and chairs are set under a covered red-tiled roof pavilion or out on the terrace under umbrellas. The large quarry-tile sundeck is dotted with chaises, freestanding Doric columns, planters, and potted plants. Room service is also offered 24 hours a day, and a great little beachside restaurant, Aquarium Beach Club & Restaurant, is located a short distance away from the Rex (see the Recommended Restaurants section).

The resort has conference facilities and future phases include the addition of several hundred rooms. For the time being, it's a terrific spot, though new as it is, it is still finding its way.

REX GRANADIAN
P.O. Box 893, Point Salines
St. George's
Grenada, West Indies
TEL: (809) 444-3333
FAX: (809) 444-1111

RESERVATIONS
Marketing & Reservations Inc.
1150 NW 72nd Avenue, Suite 377
Miami, FL 33172
TEL: (800) 255-5859 *or*
(305) 471-6170
FAX: (305) 471-9547

Open all year.
Rates: Double occupancy. *December 1 to April 10:* Garden Room, $145; Ocean View, $170; Beachfront, $220; Royal Suite, $310. *April 11 to November 9:* Garden Room, $105; Ocean View, $130; Beachfront, $180; Royal Suite, $270.
Meal plan: EP. MAP (includes breakfast and dinner), add $49 per person per day. For dinner only, add $35 per person per day. For buffet-style breakfast, add $14 per person per day.
Service charge: 10%.
Government tax: 8%.
Children welcome.
Credit cards accepted.

Secret Harbour Resort

Spanish Mediterranean-style Secret Harbour hugs a little hillside in a spectacular setting overlooking Mount Hartman Bay, four miles from the airport, on the southern tip of Grenada. The resort rests on 6½ wonderfully lush, peaceful acres and has a small, calm golden sand beach, reached by descending a stairway.

Secret Harbour's 10 white stucco and curved red-tile-roofed cottages have two units apiece, all suites, which form an undulating string around the middle of the property, with great land and sea views. A southern-facing beautiful freshwater pool sits under the hotel's spacious, multiroom restaurant, bar, and lobby/lounge. A lighted hard-surfaced tennis court is off to one side. Opened in 1972, owned and managed by Barbara Stevens, an Englishwoman, the hotel at first was a great success; truly a great romantic, uniquely decorated, secret hideaway. For a few years though, Secret Harbour had been in decline. That really was a shame, because the resort ought to have been one of the top ones in the Caribbean by virtue of the splendid setting, layout, and unusual roomy accommodations.

The S.O.S. is long over. Barbara Stevens sold Secret Harbour on February 3, 1989, to The Moorings, Ltd., the well-known, respected charter-boat and hotel operators, in business since 1969. The Moorings has facilities in Puerto Escondido in Baja California and in Tahiti and the Kingdom of Tonga. Club Mariner Resorts manages The Moorings hotels. Their other properties in the Caribbean are Marigot Bay Resort on St. Lucia and Treasure Isle Hotel on Tortola.

An added 50-slip marina now provides dockage for The Moorings' charter fleet, as well as space for visiting boaters. There's a full water-sports facility here, too. Shoppers, take note, Secret Harbour's boutique is first-rate.

Secret Harbour's suites contain sea-facing balconies, living rooms, and elevated bedrooms—each have two four-poster antique double beds, accents of stained-glass windows, Italian-tiled bathrooms with oversized sunken tiled tub/showers, vanities, hair dryers, and cabinet closet space. All rooms are air-conditioned and have ceiling fans as optional coolants. Quarry-tile floors are used throughout the premises. Planked wooden private sun terraces are splendid resting places. Redbrick arches with plantings separate the bedrooms from the sitting rooms. There are phones, mini-refrigerators, and coffee service.

The refurbished two-level main dining room, Mariner's, has arched brick walls and twinkling wrought-iron chandeliers. The menu offers international and West Indian cuisine. On Friday nights live entertainment is offered. Breakfasts and lunches are served on the casual terrace restaurant.

On my last visit, in February 1994, a new manager, Evelyn Cvetic, had literally just arrived.

Secluded Secret Harbour Resort is a good value and provides excellent, low-key lodgings on Grenada.

SECRET HARBOUR RESORT
P.O. Box 11, St. George's
Grenada, West Indies
TEL: (809) 444-4548
FAX: (809) 444-4819

RESERVATIONS
Club Mariner Resorts
19345 U.S. 19 North, Suite 402
Clearwater, FL 34624
TEL: (800) 334-2435 *or*
(813) 538-8760
FAX: (813) 530-9747

Open all year.
Rates: Double occupancy. *December 20 to April 15:* Rooms, $208. *April 16 to December 19:* Rooms, $125. Extra person, $20.
Meal plan: EP. MAP (includes breakfast and dinner), add $41 per person per day.
Service charge: 10%.
Government tax: 8%.
Children under 12 not admitted.
Credit cards accepted.

A NOTEWORTHY OPTION

Twelve Degrees North

If only there were more hideaways with idyllic tropical settings that were operated in the same imaginative style as Twelve Degrees North, a delightful accommodation located on the southeast coast of Grenada at L'Anse aux Epines. Ex–New Yorker Joe Gaylord built and opened Twelve Degrees North 27 years ago. Not exactly a hotel, apartment hotel, nor inn—there's no office or restaurant—Twelve Degrees North is run more like a super-deluxe bed-and-breakfast. Gaylord and his wife, Pat, rent eight reasonably priced apartments (six one-bedroom and two two-bedroom) in three two-story buildings, snugly spaced together across the crest of a little hillside facing west, adjacent to their home. What's so unusual about the place is that all guests are assigned a personal housekeeper/cook during the length of their stay. The housekeeper is available each day from 8 A.M. to 3 P.M. to cook and serve breakfast and lunch and keep the apartment spick and span, as well as tend to daily laundry and ironing. Guests dictate the housekeeper's schedule: If her presence is isn't desired for breakfast until 10, that's fine. If you want to dismiss her for the day after she tidies up, of course you can; if you'd like her to prepare your dinner before she leaves, she'll be happy to oblige. Guests state food preferences in advance of arrival. The requested supplies are purchased and the cost is added to the final bill. The experienced cooks excel in West Indian or Créole specialities, but will prepare anything within reason that you request.

Twelve Degrees' grounds are lushly planted with flowering gardens, lawns, and towering fruit trees. While I was there, the occupants of 4-B could pick grapefruits right off a bumper crop that dangled from the tree at their balcony. Amenities include a small freshwater swimming pool with a terrace and chaises next to a thatched-roof bar where you store your own fixings. A natural-stone pathway leads down to a narrow but private beach with good reef snorkeling along a lengthy pier. Local fishermen bring their day's catch of fish and lobster to the pier for consideration. Two gas barbecues are provided for grilling your own fresh catch or any food you like for lunch or dinner.

A bohio, built over the center of the pier with benches, is a coveted spot to repair to for sunset cocktails and await the green flash at sunset. Windsurfers and Sunfish are complimentary, as is the one tennis court.

Interiors are modestly furnished with a few pieces of local artwork, woven straw mats on quarry-tile floors with natural or white-painted rattan furniture with foam rubber cushions, and ceiling fans. Beds are twins placed together (they can be separated), and the bathrooms are standard with bath/showers. The second-floor apartments are prefer-rable for the extra spaciousness provided by peaked ceilings; the views are more expansive, too. Private covered balconies are favorite resting places, each fitted with chaises and a dining table and director's chairs. It wouldn't take much to brighten up the indoor spaces with colorful fabrics, throw pillows, plants, and artful Grenadian touches. To be honest, the quarters are a bit bleak.

Still, 85% to 95% of the clientele are repeat guests who are apparently more interested in Twelve Degrees' special personalized services, quiet surroundings, and the lovely physical outdoor setting than they are in decor, and besides, the price is right.

TWELVE DEGREES NORTH
P.O. Box 241, St. George's
Grenada, West Indies
TEL/FAX: (809) 444-4580

Open all year.
Rates: Double occupancy. *December 15 to April 15:* One-Bedroom Apartments, $175; Two-Bedroom Apartments (four persons), $280. Additional person, $70. *April 16 to December 14:* One-Bedroom Apartments, $125; Two-Bedroom Apartments (four persons), $200. Additional person, $60.
Meal plan: EP. A personal housekeeper is assigned to each apartment for service throughout the day, including cooking breakfast and lunches for guests. Guests pay for provisions that are stocked as directed in advance, if so requested. For an extra charge, cooks will also prepare meals.
Service charge: 10%.
Government tax: 8%.
Children over 15 welcome.
Credit cards accepted.

Recommended Restaurants

GRENADA'S FINEST*

* **Canboulay**, 444-4401 (Grand Anse Beach hillside in Morne Rouge). This is an unusually good contemporary island-inspired kitchen, with lovely views from the indoor restaurant or the veranda, especially at lunch. We sampled callaloo, excellent cashew-coated dolphin (the fish, not the mammal), crêpes with crab and shrimp, and nutmeg ice cream topped with fruit and spicy syrup. That day, the Grenadian Prime Minister and a large party were also contentedly dining here. Moderate to expensive.
* **Cicely's**, 444-4334 (the Calabash Hotel, L'Anse aux Epines Beach). This restaurant offers a delightful atmosphere and excellent service, matched by good food. (See hotel listing, page 162.) Moderate to expensive.
* **La Belle Créole**, 444-4316 (Blue Horizons Cottage Hotel, behind Spice Island). As the name suggests, Créole specialities plus traditional Grenadian food rated excellent are served here. Moderate to expensive.
* **La Sagesse Nature Center**, 444-6458 (St. David's parish). Lunches served in

beachside great house are simple and delicious soups, salads, seafood selections. La Sagesse has a few guest rooms, and an art gallery. Day visitors are invited to "come to spend a perfect day in the country" swimming, snorkeling, and windsurfing, hiking, birdwatching, relaxing, and chatting with Nancy and Michael Meranski, the owners. Cost: $26 per person; round-trip transportation provided. Moderate.

* **Morne Fendue**, 440-9330 (near Sauteurs). Start with a potent rum punch on the veranda and then dine inside among the family possessions on authentic Grenadian dishes—there's always pepperpot (a fragrant stew), callaloo, local vegetables like christophine, eggplant, and pigeon peas in Betty Mascoll's home in the northern part of the island. The rather awesome all-stone, two-story edifice enveloped in bushes of red poinsettia, was built by Mrs. Mascoll's father in 1912. It's a favorite tour-group stop, however, so when making a reservation (a must), inquire about the number of guests expected. Meals are graciously served on a variety of card-type tables if there's a crowd. Morne Fendue is not far from Douglaston Estates and the Nutmeg Cooperative, making it a convenient stop for lunch. (See "Useful Information," page 172.) Moderate.

* **Mamma's**, 440-1459 (on Lagoon Road a few minutes from St. George's). Insley Wardally's family carries on tradition serving 20-plus-course dinners, family style. An island institution. Dishes range from fragrant callaloo and lobster salad, to iguana, armadillo, and other stewed-up exotica. Unpretentious surroundings. Moderate.

* **Aquarium Beach Club & Restaurant**, 444-1410 (on a secluded beach near Point Salines Airport). An open-air, beachside find, Ulrich Kuhn's specialties include callaloo cannelloni and fresh grilled fish with a crunchy Dijon-mustard crust. At lunch we devoured super lobster-salad sandwiches and garlic bread. Rent sunbeds and deck chairs and spend the day at the beautiful beach. A lively lobster barbecue is held every Sunday from 12:30 to 9 P.M. This establishment is extremely popular with locals and American Embassy staff. Inexpensive to moderate. (**Dr. Groom's Beachside Bar & Restaurant**, 444-1979, on the beach, seemed similarly laid-back, also with a great location.)

OTHER DEPENDABLE CHOICES

In St. George's overlooking the harbor **Rudolf's**, **Nutmeg**, and **Delicious Landing** are suggested for lunch—all more for local atmosphere than food. In Grand Anse and Morne Rouge, for both lunches and dinners, worth trying are **Spice Island Inn** for weekly barbecues including roast suckling pig; **Ramada Renaissance's Terrace**, especially Grenadian Night; **Coconut's Beach**; and **Coyaba Hotel**. At L'Anse aux Epines: **Red Crab**, **Secret Harbour** (see hotel entry), **Horse Shoe Beach Hotel**, and the popular **Boatyard** with live music three nights a week. Go to **Spicers** at the Rex Grenadian for smashing views, and **Sur La Mer** on beautiful Marne Rouge beach.

Recommended Shopping

Shoppers in Grenada should be prepared to be harassed by vendors, especially at the cruise-ship dock area, where there are also stalls, along the harbor at The Carenage, and on beaches. On our last visit in February 1994, it was worse than ever. A friend and I were followed several times during our morning shopping in St. George's by pesky vendors, who eventually gave up. On a previous stay in Grenada, my husband was even awakened from sleep in his lounge chair on the beach by a man selling trinkets. The Tourism Board wants to set up special areas for vendors in town and at beaches. Assigning designated areas for vendors in kiosks has worked successfully in Barbados and in St. Thomas at the waterfront market. Here's hoping that Grenada's officials make a move soon.

Tikal, 440-2310 (Young Street one block up from The Carenage). American Jeanne Fisher stocks an excellent selection of imports and island arts and crafts. My favorite island footwear, called "no-shoes"—silver, gold, or white crocheted triangles of cloth that fit over the top of your foot, loop around one toe and tie behind the heel—are carried here. Tikal's flyer reads, "Where you are welcome just to browse without any sales pressure." It's true.

Yellow Poui Art Gallery, 440-3001 (Cross Street). This shop represents Caribbean and world art; oils and prints, etc.

Spice Island Perfumes Ltd., 440-2006 (The Carenage). Perfumes, spices, handcrafts, and batiks.

Other shops to look for are **Art Fabrik**, **Frangipani**, and **Noah's Arkade**, and on Saturdays, the lively, colorful **Market Square** for locally made straw hats, baskets, spices, fruits, and vegetables. Also check the boutiques in the **Ramada Renaissance**, **Spice Island Inn**, **La Sagesse Nature Center**, and **Grand Anse Shopping Plaza**. The **Duty-Free Shops** at the airport are worth a look for last-minute shopping.

Provisions for Your Island Pantry

The **Essentials Mini Market** at Spice Island Marine Services at Prickly Bay, Lance aux Epines, stocks a good variety of frozen and fresh food intended mainly for boat charters. It's conveniently located near Twelve Degrees North.

St. George's fabulous, bustling Granby Street **Market Square** is well worth a visit even if you're not cooking in. It's open every day except Sunday, but early Saturday morning is the best time to observe the action and buy everything from the biggest soursops I've ever seen, delicious local fruits and vegetables, herbs and spices, crabs, and cooking equipment, to wood coal made in *koalkeels* and baskets to carry all your treasures.

"D" Green Grocer on Main Road in Grand Anse sells fresh produce and staples; its connected sister store, **"D" Coffee Shop**, offers sweets and, of course, coffee.

You'll find fresh fish on Lagoon Road leading into The Carenage at **The Fish Shop**, as well as from local fishermen.

The best supermarkets are **Foodland** on Lagoon Road and **The Food Fair** at the Grand Anse Shopping Plaza.

Useful Information

Complimentary copies of *The Greeting Tourist Guide on Grenada, Carriacou, Petit Martinique* and *Discover Grenada* are excellent information sources. Also be certain to get hold of a good road map, if driving.

At least one full-day tour of Grenada is a must. Cars can be rented, while many roadways have been improved, many are not only rough going, especially in the north, but also unmarked. Car rental companies include **Avis**, (809) 440-3936 or (809) 440-2624 and **Budget**, (809) 444-1620.

Important sights to see are the **Grenada National Museum** and the **Botanical Gardens**, plus **Dougladston Estate** to visit the **Nutmeg Cooperative** (guides will show you the many spices, and sell some special packets, too), **Annandale** and **Concord Falls**, and **Grand Etang Forest Reserve and Lake**. There's plenty more, and en route you'll see some of Grenada's opulent nature — hills of bananas, cocoa, bamboo, breadfruit, papaya, and giant tree ferns.

For a very special experience, visit the restored historic great house called **The Tower**, three miles from St. George's in St. Paul's parish. It's a working spice and fruit plantation; the great house is a lived-in museum of interesting artifacts and memorabilia. Tours are arranged by appointment only; 440-3243.

A day trip to Grenada's sister islands, **Carriacou** and **Petit Martinique**, can be easily arranged. There's not much to see on backwater Petit Martinique — no restaurants or hotels for visitors, but Carriacou is highly recommended. It's the largest of the Grenadines, 13 square miles of hills and beautiful peaceful white-sand beaches, and located only 23 miles northeast of Grenada. Unfortunately, by boat it's a four-hour trip there and back, so a short flight is the preferred route for most. (Call **Airlines of Carriacou**, 444-4425.) Once there, you'll stroll through Hillsborough, the tiny capital, and see wooden-boat builders. Requisite stops are **Silver Beach Resort** at the edge of Hillsborough for a swim; arrange ahead to have lunch at renovated **Cassada Bay Resort** high in the hills, with spectacular 360-degree you-can-see-forever views.

Other dining possibilities in Carriacou are **Poivre Sel** and **Scraper's** for succulent seafood, including lobster and conch, both at Tyrrel Bay. For pastries, fried chicken, good rotis, or ice cream, try **Gramma's Bakery** and **What's the Scoop** on Main Street in Hillsborough.

GUADELOUPE AND LES SAINTES

ACCOMMODATIONS

GUADELOUPE'S BEST
Hôtel Hamak, St-François

NOTEWORTHY OPTIONS
Le Village Créole, Terre-de-Haut
Les Petits Saints aux Anacardiers, Terre-de-Haut

RECOMMENDED RESTAURANTS

RECOMMENDED SHOPPING

USEFUL INFORMATION

≈ ≈

Accommodations

GUADELOUPE'S BEST

Hôtel Hamak, St.-François

Hôtel Hamak, a five-acre resort in St.-Francois on the southeastern end of Grande-Terre island in Guadeloupe, about an hour's ride from the airport, opened in January 1978. It's private and self-contained—a perfect place for a discreet rendezvous. Perhaps that's why it was selected for the 1979 International Summit attended by Jimmy Carter, James Callaghan, Valéry Giscard d'Estaing, and Helmut Schmidt. The series of historic meetings took place at a round table in a room that is now appropriately named Kalumet, a circular, open-air dining pavilion and bar. A modest plaque commemorating the event hangs on a bamboo wall in back of the bar.

When we checked into Hamak, we were warmly greeted in English. Because Guadeloupe is a *département* of France, English isn't always spoken fluently or otherwise in small hotels on the island.

Each of Hamak's 28 cottages are divided into two rooms. Outside, a masonry wall with a wooden door separates the two lodgings' patios, which management will unlock on request for friends or families. Each side of the cottage has a gallery-covered front patio with a table and chairs and a fringed hammock, surrounded by ferns, bougainvillea, hibiscus, oleander, and many of the other 150-plus species.

Hamak's rooms are divided by a cleverly conceived, royal blue Formica and wooden wall unit, which divides the room into a small living room and bedroom. There is a drop-leaf desk and shelves in the living room, and a closet with sliding mirrored doors on the bedroom side, plus a wall safe and more shelving. Furniture consists of a desk, chair, and daybed sofa.

In the bedroom there's only room for two tiny end tables with lamps, a handsome leather-strapped luggage rack, and, of course, the king-size bed.

Bathrooms have tub/shower combinations and feature thick white towels stitched with hammock emblems, a blue Formica, single-basin vanity, a wall hair dryer, and a separate area with a toilet and bidet.

Although louvered doors and windows exist on the front and back sides of the units, and it was constantly breezy outside, we needed the air-conditioning in May. Every accommodation at Hamak has a totally private masonry-walled back garden patio. You can sunbathe here *au naturel* on lounges and refresh yourself in a large, tiled outdoor shower.

Rooms are simple, sedate, and functional. The French don't seem to ever mind small. I didn't mind it here either because I spent so little time in the room.

Beachfront cottages 25 through 29 are the most desirable and private, as they rest at the far end of the property, away from the public areas; they are the most expensive. Lowest priced are the garden rooms. Rooms have telephones but no TVs or radios. There's no swimming pool here, but a Jacuzzi is on the beach.

Hamak's glass-enclosed gift shop displays local art, Hamak-personalized Porthault bathrobes and bath sheets, locally crafted figurines, jewelry, casual clothing, and other odds and ends.

One of the delights at Hamak is sunning on lounges on one of several man-made sand-lined, small balconies perched right at the water's edge along the shore. Or you can opt to settle down on the small but lovely and well-maintained main beach, also man-made. (Since the beach is man-made it can only be used by the hotel's guests.) Here you'll be joined by Hamak's 80% European clientele, mostly French, with Italians, Swiss, and Germans; the remaining 20% are Americans.

From the beach we peered out over a brilliant canvas of aqua sea and baby-blue sky. A constant stream of windsurfers flew by. Hamak has its own windsurfers, but none of the guests were participating. The mesmerizing aquatic scene before us consisted of nimble guests from the 250-plus-room Méridien Hotel and 53-suite La Cocotierie just down the coast. At Hamak it's easy to cross the boundary from the sweet isolation of the resort to the kinetic energy of a Club Med—cum—St. Tropez atmosphere a few hundred meters away at the Méridien.

An 18-hole Robert Trent Jones golf course is directly across from Hamak, with guaranteed starting times for the hotel's guests. Three lighted tennis courts are shared with the Méridien. Hobie Cats, snorkeling equipment, and Yamaha water scooters are all available at Hamak. Specific chartered day trips to other islands can easily be arranged, as Hamak has its own plane and airstrip.

Jean-François Rozan, Hamak's reserved but gracious owner/manager, likes to think of the resort as having a congenial atmosphere that is informally elegant. He and his well-trained, attractive staff are always available, but not intrusive.

The cuisine at Hamak, in either the candlelit Kalumet or main dining room, is unpretentious but above average. Locally trained cooks present pleasing Créole- and French-inspired dishes of accra—saltfish fritters—spiced rice, sweet-and-sour scallops, creamy gratin dauphinoise, puréed pumpkin, marvelous fresh vegetables, salads, and seafood. The passionfruit and mango sorbets we sampled were wonderful. The small wine list offered a good selection. Outsiders can reserve for dinner at Hamak, but lunch is for hotel guests only, with occasional exceptions.

Nothing is grand at Hamak, but it's an appealingly understated French-flavored resort with plenty of diversions nearby for independent activity and entertainment.

HÔTEL HAMAK
97118 St-François
Guadeloupe, French West Indies
TEL: (590) 88.59.99
FAX: (590) 88.41.92

RESERVATIONS
Caribbean Inns, Ltd.
P.O. Box 7411
Hilton Head Island, SC 29938
TEL: (800) 633-7411 *or*
(803) 785-7411
FAX: (803) 686-7411

Closed September 1 to early October.
Rates: Double occupancy. *December 18 to January 2:* Garden, $340; Sea View, $400. *January 3 to April 3:* Garden, $300, Sea View, $350; *April 4 to October 29:* Garden, $200; Sea View, $250; *October 30 to December 17:* Garden, $230; Sea View, $250.
Meal plan: AP (includes full breakfast). MAP (open menu and wine included), add $50 per person per day.
Service charge: 15%.
Government tax included.
Children welcome.
Credit cards accepted.
Note: Honeymoon packages available.

NOTEWORTHY OPTIONS

Le Village Créole, Terre-de-Haut

If you're seeking an unpretentious but comfortable housekeeping apartment for a romantic interlude or a family retreat on a blissfully laid-back French island, Le Village Créole will more than adequately satisfy your needs. It's located at the foot of Fort Napoléon at Pointe Coquelet on the waterfront of Terre-de-Haut, a short walk to Bourge, the village town.

Set on 3⅓ acres, the hotel's 22 duplex apartments are strung along the waterfront or set into gardens. All have sea views and are furnished with fully equipped gallery kitchens, conventional rattan pieces, functional bathrooms, and outdoor verandas with tables and chairs. One special suite (designed with honeymooners in mind) has the most attractive decor and blue Courrèges bathroom fixtures. Regardless of where you unpack, everything is kept perfectly spick-and-span. There's no pool here, but lounge chairs are provided for sunning.

Open since 1987, Le Village Créole labels itself a residential hotel, offering air-conditioned bedrooms, wall safes, upstairs and downstairs direct-dial phones, transportation from and to the airport, and daily maid service. For an extra charge, TVs, mountain bikes, scooters, pedal boats, laundry service, and shuttle service to beaches or town are all obtainable. If you don't feel like going out or cooking, Le Village Créole will hire you a cook or order food to be brought in for you for a small fee. English-speaking owner

Ghyslain Laps has thought of virtually everything. He or his multilingual front desk staff will also be happy to make suggestions for dining, excursions to other islands, or local touring. Warmly recommended.

LE VILLAGE CRÉOLE
Pointe Coquelet
97137 Terre-de-Haut
Les Saintes, Guadeloupe, French West Indies
TEL: (590) 99.53.83
FAX: (590) 99.55.55

Open all year.
Rates: Double occupancy. *December 17 to April 15:* (Rates are based on 6 French francs (F) to U.S. $1.) Waterfront Suites, $140 to $165; Garden Suites, $106 to $130. Children 4 to 12, $20 to $25 each child per day; children 3 years or under, free. *April 15 to December 16:* Waterfront Suites, $93; Garden Suites, $76. Children 4 to 12, $15 each per day; children 3 years or under, free.
Meal plan: EP.
Service charge: None.
Government tax included.
Children welcome.
Credit cards accepted, except American Express.

Les Petits Saints aux Anacardiers, Terre-de-Haut

Resting on a hilltop in Terre-de-Haut overlooking the village of Bourg and the bay, less than half a mile to the beach, is the thoroughly charming ten-room auberge Les Petits Saints aux Anacardiers. Owned by Jean-Paul Colas and Didier Spinkler for only a couple of years, it has a singular Gallic personality, an interesting antique shop, a large freshwater pool with a sundeck, and a very good terrace restaurant. Meals focus on seafood creations like *soupe de poissons* and *navarin de langoustes*—the proprietors also own the restaurant Chez Deux Gros in Gossier on Guadeloupe.

It's not surprising that Les Petits Saints is the most coveted address on the island for travelers wanting hotel amenities and services. Only one of the owners is fluent in English. The staff and most of the clientele are French-speaking only, so be prepared.

Accommodations are modest but comfortable and sprinkled with antiques. Rooms are housed in a converted two-story home with a peaked red roof and dormers. The second-floor rooms, for singles, are quite small, and two rooms there must share a shower in the hall.

The pleasant air-conditioned rooms have telephones, TVs, mini-refrigerators, shower baths, toiletries, and hair dryers. The best and largest lodgings are on the first floor; two are by the pool.

Les Petits Saints guests spend their days at the beach, exploring the gentle island, sampling delicious Créole cuisine in small cafés (see both the Useful Information and Recommended Restaurants sections), or enjoying the sea view while contentedly ensconced at the pool.

Guests and locals gather at the bar and lounge to gossip and sip drinks before dinner. Occasionally someone plays the piano. Les Petits Saints is for undemanding escapists looking for an old-fashioned small French inn.

LES PETITS SAINTS AUX ANACARDIERS
97137 Terre-de-Haut
Les Saintes, Guadeloupe, French West Indies
TEL: (590) 99.50.99 *or*
(590) 99.54.55
FAX: (590) 99.54.51

Open all year.
Rates: Double occupancy. *December 15 to April 14:* Rooms with private baths, $93 to $130; single with bath, $120; single with shared bath, $83. *April 15 to December 14:* Rooms with private baths, $74 to $93; single with bath, $83; single with shared bath, $65.
Meal plan: CP (includes continental breakfast).
Service charge included.
Government tax included.
Children welcome, but not recommended for toddlers.
Credit cards accepted except American Express.

Recommended Restaurants

GUADELOUPE AND TERRE-DE-HAUT'S FINEST*

* **La Plantation**, 90.84.83 (Galerie Marina, Bas-du-Fort, Gosier). The decor in this second-floor dining room is not as wonderful as the cuisine. Smoked fish crêpe with red salmon caviar, sliced duck breast with caramel sauce, and zucchini spaghetti were perfection, as were scrumptious desserts. Superb wine cellar. Expensive.

* **Château de Feuilles**, 22.30.30 (at Campêche in Anse-Bertrand, Grande-Terre). In a lovely country setting with a pool is this local favorite. Go for a leisurely lunch (do not rush a meal here) and sample the superb seafood dishes; all original inspirations. Expensive.

* **Le Karacoli**, 28.41.17 (Grand Anse Beach at Deshaies). Lovely owner/chef Lucienne Salcede provides a relaxed beachside spot for dining on such Créole dishes as

accras, stuffed crab backs, and *boudin*. Bring your swimsuit and spend the day. Inexpensive to moderate.

* **Le Relais des Iles**, 99.53.04, Terre-de-Haut, on a hillside out of town. The best food served on the island comes from from owner/chef Bernard Mathiew. Creative seafood selections range from *soupe de poissons* to snapper in limey cream sauce. Celestial desserts. Expensive.

There are many, many fine restaurants in Guadeloupe. Here are a few of our favorites: **Rocher de Malendure** at Malendure Beach, 98.70.84, on a promontory overlooking Pigeon Island. **Les Oiseaux**, 88.56.92, in Anse-des-Rochers, for super seafood in a house adjacent to a swimming pool; seaside **Le Zagaya**, 88.67.21 and **La Louisiane**, 88.44.34—all in St. François. And **Chez Clara**, 28.72.99, in Ste-Rose on the beach is the place for excellent Créole food and fun.

OTHER DEPENDABLE CHOICES

Chez Mimi, 23.64.87 (corner of Rue Poincaré and Rue St-Jean), just north of St-Françgis. This tiny Créole establishment serves the usual accras, stuffed crab backs, and the like, always with delicious local vegetables. Mimi is always entertaining—literally. Moderate to expensive.

Chez Violetta, 84.10.34 (Gosier). Lots of tourists feel comfortable here in the pretty surroundings (waitresses wear Créole dress). The food is great. Moderate.

Chez Deux Gros, 84.16.20 (Gosier). A garden terrace room serving excellent seafood. Expensive.

In Terre-de-Haut, the restaurants at **Les Petits Saints** and **Joli Bois** are lovely settings where the food is always good. Also try **Le Foyal**, **Chez Line**, **Le Café de la Marine**, **La Saladerie**, **Le Blanc de Sahle**, **Relais des Isles Le Kanaoa**, **La Paillote**, **Le Case Croute**, and **Le Genois Sole Mio** and **Le Mambo** for delicious pizzas. **Centre Nautique** is a offers a pleasant lunch, usually with lots of action and divers around.

La Croissanterie de L'Ile at the Place de la Marine sells croissants, fresh bread, pastries, and beverages.

Recommended Shopping

All in Point-à-Pitre, **Rosébleu, Phoenicia**, and **Vendôme** sell a wide selection of fragrances and cosmetics. For jewelry, there's **Bijouterie Thomyris, Fritz Louis**, and **Danylor**. Fashion and resortwear possibilities include **Paul et Virginie, Bleue Marine**, and **Jennifer**. Try **Chez Claire, L'Habitation, En Temps Longtemps**, and **Le Culinarian** for crystal and china, household accessories, and kitchenware. There are many shops in Marina Bas-du-Fort, and inside the hotels in Gosier. St-François' port also has some shops as well as the boutiques, especially **Galaria Ayti**, in The Méridien hotel there. **Hôtel Hamak**'s boutique is worth a stop, too.

The **market** in Point-à-Pitre is a marvelous morning island experience. Vendors' stalls are stacked with produce, spices and herbs, handcrafts, tiny madras-clad market-women dolls (the latest styles are affixed on the top covers of baskets), costume jewelry, and unusual trinkets. A bottle of Vieux Rhum is a fine item to include on your shopping list.

In Les Saintes, you might want to buy the fabric-covered, hand-woven and stitched coolie-style straw salako hats, still worn on the island by fisherman and locals. These unique shade providers also make wonderful souvenirs. A colorful one is a splendid wall decoration.

Little shops line the harbor—look for **Yves Cohen's Maogany Artisanat, Perle des Iles, La Boutique Coconuts, Saccao, Tata Somba,** and **Galerie de la Baie.** Browse through the **antique shop** at **Les Petits Saints aux Anacardiers** for a one-of-a-kind memento.

Useful Information

Pick up an English edition of *Bonjour Guadeloupe* for helpful information. The tiny booklets *Ti Gourmet Guadeloupe* and *Ti Saintor's* are excellent restaurant guides. The **Tourist Bureau (Office Départemental du Tourisme),** 82.09.30, at 5 Square de la Banque in Point-à-Pitre, has other valuable brochures and booklets on the wide variety of excellent sights to see on Guadeloupe. If you're touring the island by car, purchase a good road map and don't miss the beautiful **Parc Naturel** on Basse-Terre, the left or west-island wing of the butterfly-shaped Guadeloupe. Also visit **Dashaies** beach and try some Créole specialties in simple local restaurants.

Car rentals in Guadeloupe include **Hertz,** (590) 82.00.14 or (590) 84.20.23; **Budget,** (590) 82.95.58 or 26.70.73; and **Avis,** (590) 82.02.71. All have toll-free North American numbers, if you wish to reserve in advance.

Guadeloupe has two casinos.

Air Guadeloupe has scheduled daily flights to Les Saintes, Marie-Galante, Martinique, St. Barts, St. Martin, and Dominica, and services other islands in the Caribbean as well; (590) 82.28.35 or (590) 91.12.25.

The eight-island archipelago of **Les Saintes** lies seven miles south of the Basse-Terre side of Guadeloupe. The largest island, Terre-de-Haut, offers the best hotel accommodations and facilities for travelers. People like to say the island is a miniature version of St. Barts the way it used to be—a laid-back, peaceful, thoroughly French hideaway. (See hotel listings and other information).

Visitors, many of whom are day-trippers, take either a short 15-minute flight from Point-à-Pitre, an express ferry from Point-à-Pitre's waterfront (it takes a little over an hour), or a ferry from Trois Rivières in Basse-Terre (about a half-hour cruise).

No cars can be rented on Terre-de-Haut, but there are a few vans for transportation to hotels and for two-hour tours. Most visitors walk—the island is about four miles across at its widest point—or rent bicycles, scooters, or mountain bikes. There are several wonderful beaches, such as **Petite Anse** and **Anse Devant**, set below **Pain de Sucre**, Terre-de-Haut's small version of Rio's Sugarloaf. Other alluring beaches are **Baie de Marigot** and **Plage de Pompierre**, which offer calm water and dreamy sun-drenched places for swimming.

Guadeloupe's **Fête des Cuisinères**, held annually on the second Saturday in August, is one of the Caribbean's most colorful and extraordinary events. It's a formidable competitive cookout that includes a parade of the all-women master chefs, dressed in fabulous Créole madras outfits draped in beads, gold necklaces, and bangle bracelets, and carrying elaborately decorated food baskets. The island is jammed during this festivity, so book way ahead and arrange with the hotel to secure required documents for the festival, which lasts about six hours.

≈ ≈

JAMAICA

(FALMOUTH, MONTEGO BAY, OCHO RIOS, PORT ANTONIO)

ACCOMMODATIONS

JAMAICA'S BEST

Good Hope Estate House, Falmouth
Half Moon Golf, Tennis & Beach Club, Montego Bay
Jamaica Inn Hotel, Ocho Rios
Round Hill Hotel and Villas, Montego Bay
Trident Villas and Hotel, Port Antonio
Tryall Golf, Tennis & Beach Resort, Montego Bay

RECOMMENDED RESTAURANTS

RECOMMENDED SHOPPING

USEFUL INFORMATION

≈ ≈

≈ ≈

Accommodations

JAMAICA'S BEST

Good Hope Great House

Good Hope Great House, built in 1755, has been elegantly brought back to life in its original Georgian style by a group of investors, headed by Tony Hart from Montego Bay. Open since late 1993, the 10-room hotel is a fascinating, luxurious destination for those who like the idea of a holiday deep in the heart of Jamaica plantation country.

Good Hope offers a multitude of diversions and amenities, including a freshwater swimming pool, two lighted tennis courts, and a stable of more than 20 horses with trails and 2,000 acres to explore. (Guests are charged $25 per ride; non-guests pay $30 for a one-hour ride and $40 for two hours.) The Martha Brae River (famous for river rafting, a 1½-hour experience that is easily arranged through the hotel) winds through the property's working farm, which produces akees, *uniq citrus* (ugly fruit), papayas, coconuts, and anthuriums. A papaya packaging plant is housed in the former sugarcane factory at Good Hope. To study the history of this extraordinary place and all of Jamaica, a library in the Great House has a wonderful collection that guests are welcome to peruse.

Although Good Hope is totally enveloped in verdant countryside and nature, it is only six miles from the coast and beaches at Falmouth, and 20 miles east of Montego Bay. The hotel will arrange transportation from the airport, or you can rent a car, which is recommended if you want your freedom.

You enter Good Hope at the top of a hill that leads to the twin staircases of the Great House. After warm greetings from Jamaican manager/chef Tammy Hall, her friendly staff, and even friendlier Labrador retrievers, you check into the following accommodations: one of four rooms in the two-story Great House; one of five smaller-sized rooms in an adjacent converted Coach House, complete with its own kitchen, dining area, and living room (an excellent choice for a family gathering or group of friends); or hope for the expansive separate quarters in the Palladian Counting House with a terrace and exquisite four-poster bed, referred to as the Honeymoon Suite. Rooms are beautifully decorated with handcrafted Jamaican antique furniture and attractive vibrant-colored fabrics. Lodgings have large louvered windows, stylish bathrooms with bath/showers and inlaid hardwoods, but there are no TVs or telephones. Good Hope has only one telephone line, in the office. Guests are welcome to use it to phone or fax.

Good Hope serves what it calls "Jamaican plantation-style food with a flair." Tammy Hall, who once was Al Pacino's personal chef, oversees the preparation of excellent meals featuring produce from the plantation with imaginative touches. Some of her creations include a steaming fresh pumpkin soup, snapper with a buttery lime sauce, and fresh Jamaican fruit or coconut confections. Tables are handsomely set with fine china and bouquets of flowers situated under a towering ceiling.

Bring a few books, a pair of jeans for riding, a tennis racquet, bathing suit, binoculars, cameras and film—or just bring along someone you love. Good Hope possesses many magical qualities and is an impossibly romantic hideaway.

GOOD HOPE GREAT HOUSE
P.O. Box 50
Falmouth
Jamaica, West Indies
TEL/FAX: (809) 954-3289

Closed from Mid-August to the first Sunday in September.
Rates: Double occupancy. *December 15 to April 15:* Rooms, $200 to $250. *April 16 to December 16:* Rooms, $150 to $175.
Meal plan: CP (includes continental breakfast). Lunch, $20; afternoon tea, $7; dinner, $30, each per-person-per-day.
Service charge: 10%.
Government tax: $12 per night.
Children welcome.
Credit cards accepted.

The Half Moon Golf, Tennis & Beach Club, Montego Bay

The Half Moon Club is a full-fledged 400-acre resort with a country club atmosphere, located six miles from Montego Bay's Donald Songster International Airport. Its various forms of lodgings—from comfortable suites and private villas with their own pools to deluxe rooms—are all terraced or balconied beachfront or have direct access to the resort's famous mile-long golden sand beach, only half of which is the half moon. The other half of the beach is a long strip lined with several stone jetties. The flourishing grounds are perfectly tended, and include a couple of small lakes; swans swim on one. The hotel also has two unusually attractive freshwater swimming pools.

Half Moon has about 200 accommodations, yet because of the layout and spaciousness of the property, guests rarely feel crowded, except at meals. Lunch and dinner aren't oppressive, but breakfasts, served in the Seagrape Terrace from only 8 to 9:30 A.M., can be overwhelmingly close at that early hour. (If you are staying in a villa or the studio apartments with kitchens, which are the best accommodations at Half Moon, a private cook will prepare your food when you want it. And you can always order room service.)

Half Moon's guests tend to eat early and head off for sports activities—that's the chief reason for coming to the resort. There are smaller, prettier resorts in the Montego Bay area, but none can match the range of sporting pleasures offered here.

Half Moon has 13 LayKold tennis courts (seven floodlit at night), four squash courts, an 18-hole Robert Trent Jones golf course, a Nautilus-equipped gym with saunas, massages, and aerobics classes available, plus snorkeling, windsurfing, fishing, sailing, horseback riding, and bicycling; also golf and tennis pro shops. It's no wonder that the black-strapped chaise longues on the beach are mostly unoccupied until the end of the day, when guests come to cool off with a swim and a drink at the beach bar.

The Half Moon opened in 1954 with only 30 rooms. Heinz Simovitsch, part owner and managing director for about 28 years, has overseen most of the additions and renovations, including a $3-million refurbishment a few years ago. Earl Levy, owner of Trident Villas and Hotel in Port Antonio, an architect and builder, was in charge of the improvements. The hotel's rooms are mostly furnished with Jamaican-made, wooden 18th-century reproductions; chintz fabrics are used, and mix well with the West Indian embellishments of rush rugs and fresh tropical flowers. The suite rooms on the beach, where I stayed, have Queen Anne tea tables in the sitting rooms along with comfy sofas and chairs, a writing table, and a cabinet-enclosed, unstocked mini-refrigerator. The living room is separated from the bedroom by columns. Twin beds placed together have two-poster headboards. The bathrooms are adequate, with showers and tubs. Toiletries and a little beaded necklace packaged in a basket are gifts from Half Moon.

The one- and two-bedroom villas are all individually decorated and different in configuration. Most have Jamaican reproduction furniture and standard decorations.

There are two dining rooms at Half Moon. One, the seaside Seagrape Terrace, serves average Continental cuisine. Entertainment is offered nightly during season—the Steel Drum Players, the Cabaret de Caribe Show with fire dancing and limbo, crab racing with pari-mutuel betting, and an orchestra playing "Yellow Bird" and similar tunes. Half Moon has a discothèque for late-night dancing and cocktails.

Additional dining is available at the Sugar Mill—a more elegant option. It overlooks the golf course near a 150-year-old water wheel and is open for lunch and dinner. Swiss chef Hans Schenk has developed his own Caribbean fare. Wines at the hotel are exceptionally good.

Half Moon's shopping arcade offers handcrafts, duty-free items, and resort wear. The shops are closed on Sundays. Be sure to visit the upstairs Images Gallery for interesting art exhibits.

The tour desk in Half Moon's lobby provides a full range of excursions, such as visits to the Rose Hall Great House, home of the famous "White Witch," or to the Tropical Bird Sanctuary, Dunn's River Falls, or rafting for 1¼ hours on the Martha Brae, to name only a few.

At Half Moon there's always plenty to do, and that's why the majority of the American and European repeat guests continue to return year after year. The resort is a haven for sports-minded sunseekers, but honeymooners and all ages of beachcombers can be happy here.

THE HALF MOON GOLF,
TENNIS & BEACH CLUB
P.O. Box 80, Montego Bay
Jamaica, West Indies
TEL: (809) 953-2211
FAX: (809) 953-2731

RESERVATIONS
Elegant Resorts International
810 North 96th Street
Omaha, NE 68114-2594
TEL: (800) 237-3237 *or*
    (402) 398-3218
FAX: (402) 398-5484

Open all year.
Rates: Double occupancy. *April 16 to December 14:* Rooms and Suites, $190 to $320; One- or Two-Bedroom Villas, $300 to $345 *per bedroom.* Winter rates not available at press time.
Meal plan: CP (includes continental breakfast). MAP (includes breakfast and dinner) mandatory in winter, add $60 per person per day; FAP (includes all meals) add $80 per person per day.
Service charge: 10%.
Government tax: $12 per person per day.
Children welcome.
Credit cards accepted.
Note: Special packages and all-inclusive Platinum Plan available.

Jamaica Inn Hotel, Ocho Rios

The Jamaica Inn Hotel elected not to become one of the "Elegant Resorts of Jamaica," characteristically setting itself apart in quiet independence.

The six-acre, 45-room blue and white two-story hotel is located two miles east of Ocho Rios on Jamaica's north coast Riviera, on a secluded cove with 700 feet of golden sand beach—a little gem. It's a 1½-hour drive from the Montego Bay airport and costs about $80 by taxi. With advance notice, the hotel will make suitable ground transportation arrangements for you.

Guests at the Jamaica Inn Hotel become accustomed to being spoiled. When you arrive, you are welcomed with a complimentary rum punch, an amenity offered to guests each evening during their stay. If you wake up thirsty in the middle of the night, a carafe of water is always waiting; ice cubes are stored in a silver-plate ice bucket. Every morning upon awakening, you will be served a silver pot of fresh-brewed Jamaican Blue Mountain coffee on the spacious balcony of your room. Accommodations at the inn are beautifully furnished, including the verandas filled with chintz-covered sofas, highback chairs and ottomans, and antique furniture. Views from the hotel rooms consist of the lushly landscaped garden lawn, the croquet court, the oval-shaped, freshwater swimming pool and bar. Personal attendants invisibly keep beds made and replace the thick, soft, white towels as needed. The staff, several of whom have been at the hotel since it opened 35 years ago, are first-rate.

The hotel was originally built as a private home in 1951. The Morrow family purchased it several years later, and tastefully converted the mansion into a country club inn. For over three decades, the hotel has been run by the Morrows, now Peter and Eric, who were in large part brought up by the hotel's staff.

The English, Canadian, and American middle- to upper-aged yearly repeaters are of a certain class or demeanor, so dignified and formal, in fact, that many couples wear black tie and long evening gowns every night for dinner, especially in season—the perfect cast for a British Colonial film. Jackets and ties are required for men in the evening, and there's nightly dancing in season to a five-piece orchestra. The Jamaica Inn will not suit everyone's tastes, which is just what the management intends.

The superior rooms on the second floor are my favorite choices for excellent views over the white balustrade balconies. Deluxe rooms are on the first floor, and every one can be recommended. Room 21, the White Suite, has an oversized living room, bedroom, and outside terrace and private pool. Winston Churchill vacationed here in the fifties.

All rooms have fairly standard tub/shower combination bathrooms, except for the newer beach wing rooms, which have more modern and elegant baths. Louvered windows, open doors, ceiling fans, and air-conditioning ensure desired temperatures. There are no TVs or radios, but all accommodations have telephones.

The resort provides snorkeling equipment and croquet. Sunfish, windsurfers, and waterskis are available for rental. There's free tennis available but the court is situated at the hotel next door. Golfers receive special rates at the 18-hole golf course at the Upton Country Club, a few minutes away. An offshore reef keeps boaters out, providing total privacy for the resort's guests as well as excellent swimming and snorkeling.

After a day in the sun and sea at Jamaica Inn, you'll want to relax with afternoon tea and retire to the ultimate luxury of your lovely room. Drinks in the wood-paneled bar are a nightly tradition, before candlelit dinners served in the romantic, open-air, two-level terrace dining room. Jamaica Inn's cuisine is a changing menu of Continental and Jamaican dishes, flawlessly served. One five-course meal consisted of exceptional cold lobster cocktail, pumpkin soup, broiled grouper with lemon butter, Lyonnaise potatoes, buttered gungo peas and sliced beets, a traditional tossed salad, and selections from the rather standard dessert table. Lunches are buffets and quite good, as is all the food. Room service is available 24 hours a day.

The Jamaica Inn is a tranquil, luxurious, clubby resort that the Morrows have preserved meticulously.

JAMAICA INN HOTEL
P.O. Box 1, Ocho Rios
Jamaica, West Indies
TEL: (809) 974-2514
FAX: (809) 974-2449

RESERVATIONS
Caribbean World Resorts
TEL: (800) 243-9420 *or*
(804) 460-2343
FAX: (804) 460-9420

Open all year.

Rates: Double occupancy. *December 16 to April 15:* Oceanfront, $395 to $475. *April 16 to December 15:* Oceanfront, $220 to $245.

Meal plan: FAP in winter (includes three meals). MAP in summer (includes breakfast and dinner).

Service charge: 10%.

Government tax: $12 per person per night.

Children under 14 not permitted.

Credit cards: American Express only.

Note: Special package available.

Round Hill Hotel and Villas, Montego Bay

Round Hill is one of the top luxury hotels in the Caribbean, and turns out to be quite a bargain when you compare its rates to those of other luxury resorts. The outgoing managing director Josef Forstmayr and assistant manager Mary Phillips have Round Hill operating seamlessly. A new addition is the "Back in Shape Spa at Round Hill."

Exclusive Round Hill is located approximately 10 miles west of (or a 30-minute drive from) Donald Sangster International Airport in Montego Bay on a hilly, lushly planted 98-acre peninsula on Jamaica's north shore, once part of Lord and Lady Monson's Round Hill Estate. Formerly a sugar plantation, coconuts and pimento (allspice) are produced here today.

Jamaican entrepreneur John Pringle, whose mother once owned and ran the former Sunset Lodge Hotel, founded and conceived the unique plan for Round Hill.

In 1954 Pringle subdivided 29 acres of the estate and invited prominent American and European socialites to become private shareholders, build cottages, and invest in the hotel. Stockholders have included Noël Coward, Adele Astaire, Bill and Babe Paley, Oscar Hammerstein, and Lady Rothermere. The original architecture was designed by William Ballard. The hotel's operations are currently directed by the chairman of the Board of Directors and owned by 26 Round Hill villa shareholders, each of whom may occupy their homes for up to two months each winter.

Today 27 private, whitewashed, shingle-roofed villas are perched on hillside gardens, all with sea views—some better than others—along a winding small road. The villas contain a total of 70 individual two-, three-, or four-room suites with separate entrances and private bathrooms. All villas have terraces, balconies, or patios. Forty of the 70 suites have access to the resort's 18 freshwater swimming pools. It is important to understand that unless you rent an entire villa, you share the living room areas, immediate grounds and, if there is one, the pool with other guests in the same villa. It's most desirable to rent all the suites (bedrooms) in the villa for family members and/or friends. The size, shape, and layout of each villa is one-of-a-kind. Most are lavishly decorated—the owners' form of friendly competition. Each villa has its own personal cook, maid, and gardener. Breakfasts are prepared on the premises and served on the terrace or patio. Only one villa, number 26, is actually beachfront—and it's next to impossible to book.

The remaining accommodations at Round Hill are in Pineapple House, a white-shingled and shuttered two-story building adjacent to the hotel's public areas and freeform freshwater swimming pool and terraced lawn, which overlooks the sea. Pineapple House's 36 rooms are handsomely put together with Jamaican-made mahogany four-poster beds—14 king-size and 22 twin-size. Rooms have adequate bathrooms; there are telephones but no TVs or radios. Paddle fans hanging from peaked ceilings circulate the air on the second-floor rooms. One drawback for guests staying in Pineapple House is that there are no seafront balconies, but there are terrific big windows.

A full-time staff of over 240 operate the hotel, more than half of whom have been at Round Hill for more than 15 years.

Round Hill is known for its many high-profile owners and visitors—the rich, famous, and powerful—who escape the northern cold climes in winter and migrate to Round Hill to continue socializing. Celebrities continue to flock here. And Ralph and Ricky Lauren have a beautiful winter home nearby. The Laurens recently redesigned the bar, and Harrison Ford checked in for Christmas 1994. But never mind the name-dropping, everyone is welcomed at the hotel. Round Hill has a spirited personality and is the least persnickety resort of its kind, if you don't mind that the Marchioness of Such-and-Such doesn't invite you to dine. You will be invited, just like everyone else, to Monday's Bonfire Beach Party with calypso music on the beach, Friday's Jamaican barbecue with folk and cultural group performances, and Saturday's formal dinner dance. (It's the only night jackets and ties are required.)

Lunches are extravagant buffets and dinners are served in the candlelit Georgian Colonial dining room overlooking Round Hill Bay. The cuisine—which consists of seafood and Continental fare enhanced with Jamaican fruits and vegetables and other local ingredients—is skillfully prepared and beautifully presented.

Round Hill has five LayKold tennis courts—two are lit for nighttime play. There are three championship golf courses in the area. The resort's golden sand beach is small and gets crowded in season, but the water is calm, protected by a reef. Snorkeling is good. Waterskiing, sailing, and other water sports can be arranged, as can horseback riding, and there is a fitness center on premises.

Have a delicious Planter's Punch, then retire to a chaise on the beach's balcony sunning shelf over the sea, near the pool, and watch entertaining vignettes of Round Hill's habitués, or take part in the new spa plan.

I can wholeheartedly recommend exquisite Round Hill.

ROUND HILL HOTEL AND VILLAS
P.O. Box 64, Montego Bay
Jamaica, West Indies
TEL: (809) 952-5150
FAX: (809) 952-2505

RESERVATIONS
Elegant Resorts International
810 North 96th Street
Omaha, NE 68114-2594
TEL: (800) 237-3237 or
(402) 398-3218
FAX: (402) 398-5484

Open all year.

Rates: Double occupancy. *December 15 to April 15:* Rooms, $300 to $380; Villas, $470 to $690. *April 16 to December 14:* Rooms, $190 to $230; Villas, $260 to $360. Extra person, $50 per person per day.

Meal plan: EP. AP (full breakfast only), add $20 per person per day, MAP (breakfast and dinner) mandatory in winter; add $60 to $65 per person per day; or FAP (three meals), add $80 to $85 per person per day; children 2 to 12, reduce Meal Plan charges by half. All meals are plus 10% service charge.

Service charge: 10%.

Government tax: $12 per person per day.

Children welcome.

Credit cards accepted.

Note: Special packages and all-inclusive Platinum Plan are available. Information and rates upon request. For "Back-in-Shape Spa at Round Hill," contact Marjorie Jaffe, (212) 245-9131 *or* (800) THE-HOST.

Trident Villas and Hotel, Port Antonio

Port Antonio, located on the eastern end of Jamaica's north coast, was once a prosperous, banana-trading port town, and it was also once one of the Caribbean's most sophisticated resort areas. Royalty, glamorous celebrities, and the wealthy, including J. P. Morgan, made their way to be seen on the scene. Port Antonio's twin harbors are surrounded by acres and acres of luxuriant tropical jungle, the most beautiful area in Jamaica.

After having passed through many years of decline since then, Port Antonio is now on an upswing. Thanks are due in large part to Jamaican architect and builder Earl Levy, the designer and builder of a number of exquisite homes here for the well-to-do and titled who have returned to Port Antonio in search of tranquility and the area's remarkable natural beauty. He also created one of Jamaica's most enchanting hotels—Trident Villas and Hotel.

Trident Villas is most easily reached by flying into Kingston and transferring to an interisland plane for a short flight to Port Antonio. If you drive from Kingston, it's a tedious two-hour journey. Port Antonio is about two and a half hours from Ocho Rios as well, but it's a more interesting trip. The hotel is about 15 minutes from the Port Antonio airport.

Trident Villas is a 14-acre fantasyland set along a rugged coral shoreline. Austrian pine topiaries line its pathways, and tame peacocks stroll the grounds. Fourteen whitewashed, shingle-roofed villa suites rest at the coast's edge in a meandering string. The bedrooms have desks, good lighting, and a sitting area placed in lattice-grilled bay windows. Each suite's private black-and-white-checkerboard slate-tile terrace has a whimsical gazebo pavilion where uniformed waiters serve guests breakfast overlooking a lawn and the crashing sea.

Aside from the villa suites, the hotel's other accommodations are eight junior suites located in an annex wing set off a courtyard fountain near the main building. Trident also has four luxurious tower suites. Two are very grand—the Prime Minister Suite and the Imperial Suite, a duplex with an immense living room and full dining room. The enormous bedroom upstairs has a magnificent antique four-poster bed.

All accommodations at Trident are uniquely furnished with antique or reproduction furniture and have individual appointments and ceiling fans. Chintz fabrics cover the sofas, chairs and bedcovers, and match the draperies. Fresh flower arrangements are placed throughout the rooms. Bathrooms at Trident are functional; the ones in the suites are the most lavish in the hotel. There are telephones in the suites, but no TVs or radios.

The resort's small but lovely beach is tucked away at the western end of the property in a private cove, where there are deluxe cushioned chaise longues, a thatched beach bar, and Sunfish. Scuba diving, deep-sea fishing, water-skiing, and a glass-bottom boat can be arranged at the famous so-called bottomless Blue Lagoon, a five-minute drive from the hotel. Suite 14 is closest to the beach and number 1 is the nearest to the public areas and pool.

Trident's two hard-surfaced tennis courts are across the road that borders the hotel, and the freeform freshwater pool sits majestically a few steps up on the hotel's vast lawn in front of the main building, which consists of the lobby/lounge, indoor bar, terraced open-air dining room, and adjacent indoor, formal, air-conditioned restaurant.

The clientele at Trident consists of predominately upper-crust Europeans with a sprinkling of knowledgeable and celebrity Americans.

During the day, Trident is totally relaxed and casual, but in the evenings, things change dramatically. Ties and jackets are required for men every evening, and ladies are expected to dress in proper attire.

Dinners in the small stately dining room are elaborately served by white-gloved, jacketed, and bow-tied waiters. Polished mahogany tables are splendidly set with red, white, and gold china, silver, and crystal, all on red fabric placemats with linen napkins. Silver candelabras light each table, and Oriental rugs and draperies help keep the din down. Trident's cuisine is a blend of Caribbean and international dishes. Soups such as carrot and pumpkin were perfect, duck à l'orange and poached snapper, lovely. A purée of akee, a local fruit, was palatable. First-rate vegetables, such as crisp roasted potatoes, fresh spinach, and cochoo, a local squash, complement main courses. Menus are set courses with desserts of crème caramel or coconut pie, followed by a silver pot of excellent local Blue Mountain coffee. Dinners always end with Jamaica's Tia Maria. Musicians entertain on the terrace each night in season.

Next door to Trident, Earl Levy has built and lavishly decorated a magnificent Loire-style castle, in which several fabulous suites are available for rent. Guests have cocktails here before dinner on Saturday nights. Information upon request.

TRIDENT VILLAS AND HOTEL
P.O. Box 119, Port Antonio
Jamaica, West Indies
TEL: (809) 993-2602
FAX: (809) 993-2590

RESERVATIONS
Elegant Resorts International
810 North 96th Street
Omaha, NE 68114-2594
TEL: (800) 237-3237 *or*
(402) 398-3218
FAX: (402) 398-4384

Open all year.
Rates: Double occupancy. *December 15 to April 15:* Deluxe Rooms, $350; Imperial Suite, $800. Extra Person, $100 per day. *April 16 to December 14:* Deluxe Rooms, $220; Imperial Suite, $500. Extra person, $50 per day.
Meal plan: EP. MAP (includes breakfast and dinner), add $65 per person per day.
Service charge: None.
Government tax: None.
Children welcome.
Credit cards accepted.
Note: Special packages and all-inclusive Platinum Plan available. Information and rates upon request.

Tryall Golf, Tennis, & Beach Resort, Montego Bay

Tryall Golf, Tennis, & Beach Resort's three greatest assets are the magnificent tropical grounds of the 2,200-acre plantation on which it's located; its challenging 18-hole, 6,800-yard golf course; and its 40 luxurious rental villas, situated on hillsides and along the sea. There's more, of course, like the refurbished, elegant, stone Great House with its towering, shuttered, peaked roof, originally built in 1834. The Great House has always been impeccably decorated with handsome mahogany antique pieces, the furniture chintzed, chandeliers sparkling, with floral arrangements adding further splendor to the lounge rooms. Tryall's freshwater swimming pool is one of the most inviting in the Caribbean, set below the restaurant with a shingled, flaring, peaked-roof pavilion swim-up bar. The resort also has nine LayKold all-weather tennis courts (five have lights), an expansive curved golden sand beach—it's not the greatest in Jamaica, but it's calm, and all water-sports facilities are offered here. The golf pro shop is adjacent to the beach restaurant.

Tryall is about 14 miles from Montego Bay's airport, and it takes 30 minutes to reach the hotel. I recommend renting a car if you want to stray from the hotel during your stay.

The resort's best accommodations are the villas. Each has one to four bedrooms and is specially decorated according to the owner's taste. Some have Caribbean-style furnishings, others traditional Jamaican trappings. All but one have pools. Each villa comes staffed with a cook, chambermaid, laundress, and gardener. Larger-sized villas can have a butler, bartender, and an extra maid, if so desired. If it's beginning to sound a little grand and stuffy, well it is. Tryall is a conservative country club, with capital Cs. Not everyone is straightbacked and swell, but if you're looking for a fun-filled, rousing holiday, this is not the place. Clothing styles range from Ralph Lauren to Lilly Pulitzer à la Palm Beach. Jackets for men are the only dress requirements, although most men wear ties in season. The ladies' hairstyles are created in the hotel's Impressions of Beauty Tryall salon. It's in a section of the hotel featuring the Great House Shops—including The Best of Jamaica (for some excellent handcrafts, although they are much cheaper down on the beach or in town), the Duty-Free Shop, and the Commissary (for sundry items).

Tryall is an enormous operation, and most of it is operated very well. It has 21 junior suites in this block of two-storied buildings, and several other Superior, Hibiscus, and Garden Terrace rooms—rooms 22 to 53. Rooms 38 through 45 have only walled garden views.

A little jitney will drive guests down to the beach; you can take that, drive your car, or walk. It's quite a distance. Lunch is served in the al fresco beachfront restaurant, where guests feast on curried goat, akee, and fish or jerk pork, for native fare, or select fettuccine with shrimps in garlic butter, or North Shore lobster salad served in a pineapple shell. The service is friendly, as is the staff.

Vendors have a special stall area just off of the beach. Local artisans sell clothing, hammocks, beautiful baskets, and fabulous hand-carved wooden items, from huge fish-shaped bowls to standing giraffes. Anthony Skippy carved scales on the bottom of my fish bowl while I lunched. Prices are reasonable.

Food in the Great House restaurant is quite impressive, seafood and meat entrées being the best. Complimentary afternoon tea and cocktails with hors d'oeuvres are served every day on the Great House Veranda.

Tryall offers enormous pleasures on a romantic magical old-world plantation.

TRYALL GOLF, TENNIS & BEACH RESORT
P.O. Box 1206
Montego Bay
Jamaica, West Indies
TEL: (809) 956-5660 *or* 956-5667
FAX: (809) 956-5673

RESERVATIONS
Icon Hotel Marketing
TEL: (800) 336-4571
    (305) 441-7996
FAX: (305) 441-8690

Open all year.
Rates: Double occupancy. Great House Rooms, *December 15 to April 7:* Deluxe Ocean View, $440; Junior Suite, Ocean View, $470; Junior suite, Ocean View with

Terrace, $510. Extra person, $70. *April 8 to December 10:* Deluxe Ocean View, $260; Junior Suite, Ocean View, $280; Junior Suite, Ocean View with Terrace, $310. Extra person, $55. Villa rates provided on request.

Meal plan: EP. MAP (includes breakfast and dinner) mandatory in winter, add $66 per person per day; children 2 to 12, add $33 per child per day.

Service charge: None.

Government tax: None.

Children welcome.

Credit cards accepted.

Note: Special packages and all-inclusive Platinum Plan available. Information and rates upon request.

Recommended Restaurants

MONTEGO BAY'S FINEST*

* **Norma at the Wharf House,** 979-2745 (waterfront west of Montego Bay). Dine on fresh fish such as snapper or special Jamaican creations of the day in the elegantly decorated lovely old home or on the dock terrace. Good salads. Moderate to expensive.

* **Georgian Colonial Room,** 952-5150 (Round Hill Hotel and Villas). Romantic, delicious, above-average dinners are elegantly presented in the raised terrace dining room. Informal lunches on the garden terrace adjacent to the sea. Monday night's barbecue with a bonfire on the beach is a delightful festivity. (See resort listing.) Expensive.

* **Tryall Golf, Tennis & Beach Resort,** 956-5660 (Tryall Golf, Tennis & Beach Resort). Dress up for dinner in the beautifully appointed Great House or lunch down at the casual Beach Cafe. (See resort listing.) Expensive.

* **The Sugar Mill Restaurant,** 953-2314 (Half Moon Golf, Tennis & Beach Club). Formal dining on Caribbean cuisine, akee, curried goat, and seafood. (See resort listing.) Expensive.

* **Marguerite's,** 952-4777 (Gloucester Avenue). Favorite seaside restaurant serving good to wonderful seafood—everything from fried lobster and Jamaican pepper shrimp to Marguerite's special chicken. Also try **The Beer Garden** for simple luncheon fare. Moderate to expensive.

* **The Pork Pit,** (Gloucester Avenue). The star is for Jamaica's best marinated spicy jerk chicken, pork, and pepper shrimp.. Sit at outdoor picnic tables or at the pavilion bar, have a Red Stripe beer, jerk, and a side order of roast yam, and enjoy. Inexpensive to moderate.

* **Good Hope Great House,** 954-3289 (about 20 miles from Montego Bay to Falmouth, then six miles farther north to Good Hope in Trelawny). If you do not plan to stay at this exquisite Great House retreat, take a late-morning drive here, perhaps after

rafting on the Martha Brae, for a fine Jamaican lunch served in a beautiful old-style plantation dining room. (See hotel listing.) Moderate.

OTHER DEPENDABLE CHOICES

Richmond Hill, 952-3859 or 952-5432 (Union Street). Spectacular views of town and ocean are available from this terraced poolside restaurant serving good, but not outstanding, seafood and standard Continental fare. Expensive.

Other possibilities are **The Cascade Room**, 952-3171, at The Pelican on Gloucester Avenue, **Gold Unicorn** on Queens Drive, and **Julia's** on Bogue Hill for an Italian dinner in a private home in the hills (reservations are a must here; 952-1772). Also try **Wexford Court; Coral Cliff Hotel**; the **Georgian House**; and the **Town House Restaurant**. Good Jamaican food at Jamaika Mi Krazy.

OCHO RIOS' FINEST*

* **Jamaica Inn**, 974-2514 (Jamaica Inn Hotel). Formal delicious dinners and casual lunches are graciously served here. (See resort listing). Expensive.

* **The Ruins**, 974-2442 or 974-2789 (Turtle River, DaCosta Drive). Stunning mountain waterfall setting wins a star. Food is Chinese with a Jamaican accent. Lunch or dinner here is memorable and fun. (Have a look in the boutiques.) Moderate to expensive.

* **Almond Tree**, 974-2676 (Hibiscus Lodge Hotel). Very good food is served on seaside terraces under a giant almond tree. Jamaican dishes, as well as wide selection of seafood, are featured. Inexpensive to moderate.

OTHER DEPENDABLE CHOICES

The Parkway Restaurant, 974-2667. Tasty, authentic Jamaican food at good prices. Inexpensive. East of Falmouth, try **Time 'N' Place** at Trelawny Beach.

If you happen to be shopping in this area, try **Harmony Hall Pub and Restaurant** on the road to Tower Isle. Other suggestions include **Nuccio** at Mantalent Inn in the hills for Italian food, and **Cutlass Bay Palm Terrace** at Shaw Park Beach Hotel on Great House terrace overlooking the sea.

On Main Street, look for **The Fruit Basket** in the Caribbean Complex for exotic fruit drinks and pretty good Jamaican food in funky kitchen-style dining room.

PORT ANTONIO'S FINEST*

* **Trident**, 952-5110 (Trident Villas and Hotel). Enjoy marvelous lunches on the raised terrace, or formal elegant dinners in the air-conditioned dining room. (See resort listing.) Expensive.

* **Jamaica Palace Hotel**, 933-3459 (on the main road, outskirts of town). Dine in new huge white monument of an hotel on Jamaican/Continental cuisine with a German accent. Have a cocktail in the bar before lunch or dinner. Moderate.

OTHER DEPENDABLE CHOICES

DeMontevin Lodge, 993-2604 (21 Fort George Street). Savor well-prepared Jamaican specialities in sea captain's restored Victorian-style gingerbread-trimmed home. Best for lunches. Inexpensive to moderate.

Admiralty Club, 993-2667 (Navy Island). Regular ferries run to and from the island. Lunch on lobster club sandwiches and other simple fare in the clubhouse gazebo, or take a stroll to Crusoe's Beach and have barbecued foods. Dinners of seafood and standard Continental cuisine in the main dining room overlooking the harbor and Port Antonio provide a pleasant evening's outing. Moderate to expensive.

Alternatives are the **Rafter's Restaurant** at the end of an exhilarating 2½-hour raft trip on the Rio Grande (an absolute must) for a refreshing fruit drink and unpretentious lunch of burgers, salads, or fish. Look for **Coronation Bakery** in town for delicious meat patties and sweets.

For the most authentic jerk pork and chicken, go to the Boston Bay area, about six miles east of Port Antonio. Bring along napkins—brown paper bags were all they had last visit.

Recommended Shopping

MONTEGO BAY

You'll find shops everywhere in Montego, from street stalls in the **Crafts Market and Park** selling Jamaican arts and crafts (including paintings, wood carvings, straw products, hammocks, and spices) to the **City Centre Building** for luxury duty-free merchandise. The **Holiday Village Shopping Arcades** and hotels such as **Wyndham Rose Hall, Round Hill, Half Moon Shopping Plaza**, and **Tryall** have some excellent shops and boutiques that aren't as crowded as those downtown. There is a very good crafts area set up adjacent to the beach at Tryall where I've purchased enormous carved fish-shaped bowls from Anthony Skippy. Prices are negotiable.

For unusually charming hand-painted animals, artwork, and excellent crafts, including pottery, head for **Gallery of West Indian Art**, 952-4547, on One Orange Lane.

Food lovers ought to consider bringing home fragrant Jamaican spices (particularly allspice, locally called pimento), jars of jerk sauces, and Blue Mountain coffee beans, all available at **Things Jamaican** branches at the airports.

OCHO RIOS

Harmony Hall, 975-4233 (four miles east of Ocho Rios on the A3 road to Oraca-bessa). It's worth a special trip here to see rotating exhibits of Jamaican artists in the gallery. The shop carries a wide selection of Jamaica's best handcrafts, from wood carvings and sculptures to ceramics, prints, and books.

Several shopping complexes in Ocho Rios offer a dizzying array of goods from duty-free jewelry, watches, and resortwear, to cameras, electrical equipment, and per-fumes. Whether you want locally made crafts or imported goods, you'll be in shopper's heaven at **Ocean Village** and **Coconut Grove shopping centers, Pineapple Place** (look for the duty-free shopping center here), the **Ocho Rios Crafts Market**, and **Frame Centre Gallery** in the Little Pub complex on Main Street. Also visit boutique and crafts shop at **The Ruins** restaurant, and the shop at Sans Souci. Make a special point of looking for beautifully designed colorful ceramic figurines of market women in crafts shops.

Jamaica-made ceramic market lady with a basket of akees.

PORT ANTONIO

Aside from the boutiques and shops in the **Jamaican Palace Hotel**, shopping is pretty much limited to downtown at the **Musgrave Market** in the center of town. There's everything from food vendors and handcrafts to tacky T-shirts and other souvenirs. Straw items, such as hats and baskets, are nice choices.

Useful Information

Useful complimentary guides are *Your Vacation Guide to Jamaica*, a newspaper called *Jamaica's Tourist Guide*, and *Stepping Out*.

The one thing travelers should do is *see* astoundingly beautiful Jamaica. Rent a car, go on tours, or hire taxi drivers for a morning, afternoon, or full day. Taxi tours are quite expensive, so it's more economical if two couples share the tariff. Jamaica's natural attractions are too many to describe here, but every hotel will be happy to supply guests with lists of these wonders, as well as guide you to important historical sights.

For car rentals contact: **Avis**, (809) 952-4543; **Hertz**, (809) 979-0438; **Budget**, (809) 952-1943—all at Montego Bay Airport or call their stateside 800 numbers.

Noël Coward's home, **Firefly**, has been restored and is open to the public. It's a 30-minute drive from Ocho Rios near Port Maria; (997-7201).

There are some marvelous excursions and things to see in the **Port Antonio** area. First and foremost is a three-hour rafting trip on the Rio Grande, an unforgettable, incredible downstream journey over rippling shoals, past forests of giant bamboo, tree ferns, breadfruit and mango trees, through a narrow passageway of moss-covered stone known as Lovers Rock, and past women and children bathing and washing laundry. The 30-foot bamboo raft seats only two and is expertly navigated by an experienced raftsman, a Caribbean gondolier, who gingerly maneuvers the raft that he built himself, through awkward twists and turns, over small falls and stones, with a long bamboo pole instead of an oar. Stops en route can be made for a swim in the cool water, and you can take along a picnic lunch or buy drinks and food en route. Arrange for a driver to pick you up at the drop-off point near Rafter's Rest, an attractive restaurant that has a souvenir shop and changing-room facilities. There is a shorter rafting trip near Falmouth (20 miles east of Montego Bay), on the Martha Brae River. It's about a 1½-hour trip over water.

Stop at the Jamaican Palace Hotel for lunch and be sure to see its pool—it's formed in the shape of Jamaica. You can swim from Montego Bay to Port Antonio in minutes.

MARTINIQUE

(BASSE-POINTE, LE FRANÇOIS, MARIGOT)

ACCOMMODATIONS

MARTINIQUE'S BEST
Habitation Lagrange, Marigot 🌴
Les Islets de L'Impératrice, Le François
Plantation de Leyritz Hotel, Basse-Pointe

A NOTEWORTHY OPTION
Fregate Bleue Hôtel, Le François

RECOMMENDED RESTAURANTS

RECOMMENDED SHOPPING

USEFUL INFORMATION

≈ ≈

Accommodations

MARTINIQUE'S BEST

Habitation Lagrange 🌴

On our latest trip, we fell in love with Martinique for many reasons. Its stunning, diverse geography includes beautiful beaches, lush tropical foliage, and opulent flower gardens, dramatic Mont Pelée, and tiny fishing villages. Delicious French/Créole food can be found everywhere. The shopping is superb, and the people are a mixture of graceful sophistication and great good humor. But perhaps the best reason is that we finally found an enchanting small well-run hotel that we'd like to return to whenever we need to unwind and be truly pampered in a tranquil atmosphere.

Habitation Lagrange is situated about a mile off the main Atlantic coast road on the

Habitation Lagrange in Martinique.

northeast side of the island, about 1¼ hours' drive from the airport, depending on traffic. After turning off the main road, we passed a crayfish farm and banana groves, which, after the journey, immediately made us hungry.

The four-year-old hotel is an imposing but welcoming complex of several restored buildings and similarly designed new ones that are made of stucco, stone, and brick ornamented with gingerbread and wraparound balconies and vast verandas. The two-story restored Great House, with exceptionally high ceilings, has an expansive formal dining room. One entire wall is covered with a hand-painted handsome nautical mural. The bar is wood-paneled with stools and wicker rocking chairs. Replicas of schooners are everywhere. There's a comfortable library room and a billiard table here, too.

Four large guest rooms are upstairs in the Great House. Six rooms are located in an opposite new two-story building, and the remaining two rooms are in a one-story structure adjacent to the breezy outdoor pavilion restaurant. Outside these rooms were peacock chairs and chaise longues.

All the buildings form a horseshoe around a sizable freeform swimming pool with tile and stone terraces lined with dark green fat-cushioned chaises and umbrellas. The tennis court is hidden behind plantings a short distance away. Another two-story building at the back of the property, almost completed when we were there, will provide six more guest rooms. Still, we preferred the rooms in the Great House or the one-story building with the long shaded gallery veranda.

Owners Jean-Louis and Isabelle de Lucy have decorated all spaces with refined good taste, reflecting the elegance of eighteenth-century plantation houses. They've collected antiques and reproduction furniture and used cheery, quality fabrics on the four-poster bedcovers, upholstery, cushions, and draperies. Bathrooms are lavish with brass hardware, claw-footed bathtubs, a basket of toiletries, and separate showers in some accommodations. The windows open wide, and there are also ceiling fans and air-conditioning throughout. Rooms have telephones and mini-refrigerators, but no TVs.

We headed straight for lunch with friends and were immediately served delicious tiny accras (salt-cod fritters). Chef Philippe Boffe's menus, though not expansive, are skillfully prepared. Our meals included steamed crayfish with red beans and sautéed bananas, stuffed crab, and snapper with a spicy sauce. The fresh rolls were yeasty and crisp. Portions at Habitation are on the small side until it comes to dessert or fruit: We had heaping servings of fruit sorbets and ice creams. A single serving of fruit contained eight whole fruits that were beautifully carved.

Managers Carole and Jérôme Guy, from Montpellier, France, will suggest an itinerary in the area, but all we wanted to do was relax at the pool, read, talk, take long walks in the thriving jungle surroundings, and after ti-punches, figure out when we could possibly manage to return to this splendid sanctuary.

HABITATION LAGRANGE
97225 Le Marigot
Martinique, French West Indies
TEL: (596) 53.60.60
FAX: (596) 53.50.58

Closed the month of June and September 1 to October 15.
Rates: Double occupancy. (All prices based on a currency exchange of 6 French francs to U.S. $1.) *December 20 to January 3:* Suite, $483; Rooms in Great House and Stable Wing, $433; New Rooms, $383. *January 4 to April 30:* Rates range from $316 to $416. *May 1 to May 31* and *October 15 to December 18:* $233 to $316. *July 1 to August 31:* $300 to $383.
Meal plan: CP (includes continental breakfast with fresh fruit).
Service charge included.
Government tax included.
Children welcome.
Credit cards accepted.

Les Islets de L'Impératrice, Le François

Two restored authentic wooden colonial homes are available as unique private rentals in Martinique on the island's east coast. Each is located on its own island (adjacent from the other) a short distance across the sea from the Fregate Bleue Hôtel (see page 204). The villas and hotel share the same management.

Islet Oscar's sanctuary is a five-bedroom, five-bathroom house situated at the water's edge on 20 landscaped acres. Islet Thierry's home boasts six bedrooms with four bathrooms, and rests on a 60-foot hill surrounded by 30 roamable acres. Breezes and paddle fans cool the inside premises; there is no air-conditioning or TV.

The villas' furnishings vary from new, light, and cheery, to standard tropical. Both are privately staffed, kept neat and in smooth running order by a house attendant and cook, plus a motorboat driver for transport.

Créole- and French-inspired meals, wine, beer, rum, and soft drinks are all included in the tariff. Windsurfing and waterskiing are available. A small motorboat, moored at each island's own dock, is always at guests' disposal for impromptu excursions and exploration.

The islands are rimmed with a few tiny sandy spots, not really beaches. However, the swimming is lovely, and I've heard there's good fishing.

Accommodations on Les Islets de L'Impératrice offer guests carefree, practical living and seclusion. They aren't at all grand or luxurious. Envision instead taking over *grandmère*'s second house while she's back home in Paris.

RESERVATIONS
Same information listed for Fregate Bleue Hôtel (see page 204).
Rates: *December 15 to April 15:* $1,200 per day for 2 to 6 adults; extra adults, $200 per person per day; child under 12, $100 per child per day. *April 16 to December 14:* $900 per day for 2 to 6 adults; extra adult, $150 per person per day; children under 12, $75 per child per day.

Plantation de Leyritz Hotel, Basse-Pointe

Plantation de Leyritz is for the adventurous traveler. You will reside in charming, eclectic accommodations on the beautiful grounds of an 18th-century plantation built by the Chevalier Michel de Leyritz. Guests must make a one-hour, winding drive from the airport through Martinique's magnificent lush tropical rain forest, Morne Rouge, to reach the hotel in the northern hills of the island. The bumpy road leading to the plantation cuts through masses of banana trees, many of which are covered with bright blue plastic bags to protect them from insects. The entire drive is a unique and enthralling experience, and so is the hotel.

Restored in 1970 by Charles and Yveline de Lucy de Fossarieu, the hotel consists of 16 rolling, verdant acres with a rum distillery, sugar mill, chapel, cottages, the mansion, a guardhouse, and workers' quarters.

While maintaining the 18th-century ambience, the hotel's various accommodations (there are 50 rooms) all have air-conditioning, in-room telephones, and private baths. No TVs, radios, or other frills here. The rooms are engagingly, if sparingly, decorated with family antiques. Lodgings are found in the mansion, an adjacent building, cottages, and former slave-quarter huts, authentically renovated with outer walls, roofs, and veranda coverings of bamboo. Bougainvillea drips over the verandas and lines the walls. The mansion's four superior rooms, all with four-poster beds, would be my choice for elegance and spaciousness. Bergère is the most captivating room. Cottage 13, known as the honeymoon cottage, is set off by itself and a real charmer.

The shuttered mansion has high-beamed ceilings, thick stone walls, and a large, Victorian-style parlor and dining room, chock-full of antiques and oriental rugs. A fantastic curved staircase leads up to the bedrooms. Former presidents Ford and Valéry Giscard d'Estaing met and dined at Leyritz's mansion in 1974.

One drawback at Leyritz Plantation is that the setting is so spectacular it draws lunchtime tour visitors who roam the grounds taking photos, just like you. However, I wouldn't let this stop me from going to Leyritz, because you can retire to your private quarters or escape to an isolated beach, about 30 minutes away, or visit Mont Pelée, a must anyway.

The hotel has a good boutique, freshwater swimming pool, and a single tennis court. There are no other sports facilities, but water-sports activities can be arranged if you have a car and are willing to do a little traveling. A car is a necessity unless you plan to remain at the resort during your whole vacation.

The food and service at Leyritz are excellent. Meals are served in several stone-walled, high-ceilinged rooms, on bright-red-cloth-covered tables, with white china, and, always, fresh flowers. Hibiscus blossoms are found even in chinks of the stone walls. The restaurant is famous for chicken cooked in coconut milk, which is superb, and Créole dishes like coquille of banana. A coconut crêpe dessert we sampled was heavenly.

End the day with a punch vieux—straight-up, strong, silky aged rum. Out on your terrace, surrounded by flourishing mango, avacado, and coconut palms, bask in the moonlight and sweet, fragrant earthy smells.

PLANTATION DE LEYRITZ HOTEL
Basse-Pointe 97218
Martinique, French West Indies
TEL: (596) 78.53.92
FAX: (596) 78.92.44

RESERVATIONS
Jacques de Larsay, Inc.
622 Broadway
New York, NY 10012
TEL: (800) 366-1510 *or*
(212) 477-1600
FAX: (212) 995-0286

Open all year.
Rates: Double occupancy. $125. Extra person, add $20 per person per day.
Meal plan: CP (includes continental breakfast).
Service charge: None.
Government tax included.
Children welcome.
Credit cards accepted.

A NOTEWORTHY OPTION

Fregate Bleue Hôtel, Le François

Travelers wanting to vacation in beautiful Martinique at an affordable small seaside inn with a quiet, bucolic setting will find contentment at Fregate Bleue Hôtel. The seven-suite hotel, open since the fall of 1990, is an unpretentious and enchanting treasure. To begin with, it's owner-operated by Madame Yveline de Lucy de Fossarieu, proprietor for many years of the delightful Plantation de Leyritz (see previous listing). The capable and ever-present Madame Fossarieu and her English-speaking staff will arrange water-sports activities and tennis when requested, as well as guide you to good local restaurants, shopping, beaches, and sights.

Fregate Bleue crowns a little hill on sprawling grounds above the sea overlooking several small islands. Two of the islands, Islet Oscar and Islet Thierry, are owned by the Fossarieus. For a real escapist's retreat, there's one private colonial home on each island available as a rental (see page 202).

The hotel is located about a 30-minute drive from the airport (you'll need a car), and a few kilometers from the town of Le François, where you'll be dining. The hotel has no restaurant, but provides full delicious breakfasts.

Fregate Bleue's architecture is simple, squarish white masonry saved by peaked red-orange tiled roofs trimmed in white lacy fretwork. The suites are all quietly but attractively decorated with four-poster beds, one-of-a-kind pieces, oriental rugs on white-tiled floors, comfortable chairs, and colorful draperies. Sliding glass doors lead out to private balconies with expansive views. All have air-conditioning and ceiling fans, cable TV, and telephones. Bathrooms are standard.

After a satisfying breakfast, guests can spend part of the day at the small freshwater pool on the wooden planked sundeck in chaises, then leisurely stroll the grounds, ending up at the hotel's private dock to indulge in aquatic activities.

FREGATE BLEUE HÔTEL	**RESERVATIONS**
97240 Le François,	Caribbean Inns, Ltd.
Martinique, French West Indies	P.O. Box 7411
TEL: (596) 54.54.66	Hilton Head Island, SC 29938
FAX: (596) 54.78.48	TEL: (800) 633-7411 *or*
	(803) 785-4111
	FAX: (803) 686-7411

Open all year.
Rates: Double occupancy. *April 16 to December 14:* Studio Suite, $96; Master Suite, $100. *December 15 to April 15:* Studio Suite, $170; Master Suite, $200. Extra person, $25 per day.
Meal plan: AP (includes full American breakfast).
Service charge: None.
Government tax included.
Children under 16 not permitted.
Credit cards accepted.
Note: Honeymoon special packages available. Information and rates on request.

Recommended Restaurants

MARTINIQUE'S FINEST*

Martinique has many fine restaurants, most featuring French and Créole cuisine, ranging from little seaside cafés and bistros to elegant dining rooms. It's also possible to find commendable Italian, Tunisian, Chinese, Vietnamese, and African food, but I recommend sticking with the "When in Rome" philosophy when dining in Martinique.

* **Habitation Lagrange** 53.60.60, (Basse-Pointe, at Habitation Lagrange hotel). Step back in island time and dine on Créole or French cuisine in a peaceful tropical garden setting in dining pavilion adjacent to a Louisiana-style Colonial mansion. (See hotel listing.) Expensive.

* **La Plantation**, 50.16.08 (Pays Mélé in Lamentin at Martinique Cottages). Gourmets might want to check into one of the cottages here to enjoy Chef Jean-Charles Bredas's unique version Créole/European/West Indian cuisine. Be sure to sample the foie gras napoleon. Expensive.

* **Le Colibri**, 66.91.95 (Morne des Esses). Stuffed crabs, conch fricassée, suckling

pig, and fresh crayfish from Mme. Clotilde Palladino's Créole kitchen are all first-rate. The open-air dining room overlooks the countryside. Expensive.

* **L'Amphore**, 66.03.09, (Anse Mitan, Trois-Ilets). Grilled lobster served with a variety of sauces and other delicious offerings from a French/Créole menu in sea-view dining room. Moderate to expensive.

* **La Villa Créole**, 66.05.53 (Anse Mitan, Trois-Ilets). This is one of the most popular restaurants in the area, so reserve in advance. Charming tropical setting with a waterfall where French/Créole specialties are served. Also a dance floor and guitar music. Moderate to expensive.

* **La Fontaine**, 64.28.70 (Route de Balata, Fort-de-France). Located in a Colonial house surrounded by antiques. Dine on lobster and basil fricassée, special Créole dishes, including curries; don't miss the melon au gratin. Expensive.

* **Yva Chez Vava**, 55.72.72 (Avenue du Général de Gaulle, Grand-Rivière). Tritis fritters, curried goat, christophine au gratin, and coconut custard in this simple Créole restaurant will tempt you back again and again. Inexpensive to moderate.

* **La Biguine**, 71.40.07 (corner Rue Captaine Manuel and Route de la Folie). Reservations are a must in this tiny, unpretentious gem offering innovative Créole dishes in a converted home. The dining room is on the second floor, with a tearoom offering desserts below. Moderate to expensive.

OTHER DEPENDABLE CHOICES

In Fort-de-France, try **Citron Vert** and **La Fontane**. In Anses d'Arlet, **Le Sunny, Ti Sable, Le Flamboyant des Iles**, and **Le Tamarin Plage**. At Le Prêcheur, go to **Chez Ginette** for extremely fresh seafood. In Vauclin, **Chez Julot** and **Sous les Cocotiers** are inexpensive and good French/Créole restaurants. Hôtel Bakoua's **Le Chateaubriand** is an elegant restaurant at Pointe du Bout in a seaside location. On the north side of the island **Plantation de Leyritz** and **L'Auberge de la montagne Pelée** at Mont Pelée are two unusual and good options.

Recommended Shopping

The excellent French-imported and locally made products in Martinique are found in shops and boutiques concentrated in Fort-de-France along the streets of Victor Hugo, Antoine Siger, Moreau de Jones, and Lamartine. There are also fine shops in the islands shopping centers in Bellevue, Dill, and Cluny, and at the shopping complexes **Place d'Armes** and **La Galleria Acajou** (with over 50 shops) in Le Lamentin. **Hôtel Bakoua, Le Méridien**, and **Leyritz Plantation** (which also has a lovely doll museum) have interesting boutiques as well. At Pointe du Bout look for **Bora Bora**, a small shop with some good local and Caribbean products. Ti-punch or other small glasses hand-painted with brilliant tropical flowers are especially nice.

Hôtel La Batelière, 61.49.49 (Schoelcher), has two excellent shops on its lower level. One has a charming collection of antiques and the other sells exquisite embroidered, lace, and plain white cotton blouses and skirts and other delicate creations.

At Lamentin Airport, stop at **Carambole** for locally related books, Créole lady dolls, and other handcrafts, especially the wooden Créole house reproductions.

The **Centre des Métiers d'Art** in Fort-de-France and the **craft market** in La Savane sell Créole dolls, pottery, wickerwork, jewelry, wood and bamboo bowls, trays, and other items.

Artisanat & Poterie, 68.18.01 (Trois-Ilets). Visit the pottery exhibition and purchase ceramics, paintings, ornaments, and handcrafts.

Basket-weaving workshop, 69.83.74 (Morne des Esses). Here you'll see the Carib Indians' natural dying and weaving techniques still in practice—baskets, handbags, hats, placemats, vases, and many other objects.

Cadet-Daniel, 71.41.48/60.26.57 (rue Antoine Siger, 72). This well-known store has an extensive collection of Créole jewelry, French crystal, china, and other treasures.

Other excellent sources for Créole jewelry are **Bijouterie Onyx** (73.65.05 rue Isambert, 26), **La Belle Matadore** at the Marina at Pointe du Bout, 66.04.88 and **Grain d'Or**, 50.21.40 (La Galleria in Le Lamentin).

Roger Albert, 71.71.71 (rue Victor Hugo, 7). This exclusive duty-free shop sells perfumes and cosmetics, jewelry, watches, and quality clothing and crystal, including Limoges, Lalique, and Baccarat.

Merlande, 71.38.66 (rue Victor Schoelcher, 10). This pleasant store carries excellent French fashions for every member of the family, plus leather goods, perfumes, jewelry, and watches. Also look for **Mounia**, a new designer boutique.

Thomas de Rogatis, 70.29.11 (rue St-Louis, 22). High-quality jewelry and watches. Also look for **La Maison Créole** for local gifts and treasures.

La Fontaine Fleurie, 60.23.21 (corner rues Victor Sévère and Gallieni). Beautifully packaged glazed produce, including sweet potatoes and gooseberries, plus chocolates, coconut bars, mints, and confections, all of which make wonderful gifts.

Travelers should consider bringing home a bottle of rhum vieux (rum), aged from six to twenty years and smooth as fine brandy. Rum distilleries to visit include **Distillerie La Mauny** in Pivière-Pilote; **Distillerie Trois-Rivières** in St-Luce; **Distillerie Clement**, l'Acajou, St-Francois; **Bally** in Le Carbet, and **Distillerie St. James**, in St-Marie.

You can also purchase rhum vieux, as well as local confections, foods, spices, and fruits bottled in rum, at **La Case à Rhum**, 73.73.20 (rue de la Liberté, 5).

Useful Information

Free helpful local guides, brochures, and booklets to look for are the English-language editions of *Bienvenue en Martinique, Martinique Historical Sites and Heritage, Une Histoire d'Armour Entre Ciel et Mer,* and *Ti Gourmet Martinique,* the last a wonderful little pocket-sized restaurant guide. Martinique's tourism office on boulevard Alfassa in Fort-de-France across from the waterfront (63.79.60), is well organized and has a friendly staff. Pick up a good map here with a plan of Fort-de-France and a map of the island.

Bring along a French/English dictionary and phrase book. Most shops and hotels in Fort-de-France have English-speaking employees, but you'll find that outside of the tourist areas most people speak only French or the local Créole patois. It's not easy to find an English-speaking taxi driver. If booking a half-day or whole-day tour by taxi, be certain to request an English-speaking driver. Robert Guiose, who drives an oversized '70s-model chocolate Mercedes, speaks fairly good English, is pleasant company, and is recommended; call (596) 79.32.16.

For mobility around Martinique, about 43 miles long and 18½ miles wide, a car is necessary. Three rental companies are **Budget**, (596) 63.69.00; **Hertz**, (596) 51.01.01; and **Avis**, (596) 51.26.86. All have toll-free 800 numbers in the U.S.A.

Regularly scheduled **ferry service** (*service de vedettes* in French) runs from Quai d'Esnambuc on the waterfront in Fort-de-France to the white-sand beaches in Trois-Îlets' Pointe du Bout, Anse Mitan, and Anse-à-l'Ane.

Madikera (rue Victor Hugo, 108), a large, sleek, fast car ferry, links Martinique with Guadeloupe and Dominica. It accommodates 352 passengers and 35 vehicles; (596) 91.60.87/70.08.50. **Caribbean Express** (rue Ernest Deproge, 18) also offers catamaran motorboat service to Guadeloupe and Dominica (596) 60.12.38.

Martinique has many attractions, but be sure to visit beautiful, expansive **Salines Beach** in the south; 4,586-foot-high **Mont Pelée's** neighboring village of St-Pierre and the volcano museum there, and **Le Jardin de Balata**, the Caribbean's most extraordinary botanical park, about a 20-minute drive north of Fort-de-France. The flower park in Trois-Îlets, **Macintosh Plantation** at Habitation Longchamps in Morne Rouge, and the **Botanical Garden** at Ajoupa-Bouillon are other stunning parks and gardens to visit. There are many museums, historical sites, and magnificent scenery and beaches in Martinique.

A beautiful 18-hole **golf course**, "Impératrice-Joséphine," designed by Robert Trent Jones, is located in Trois-Ilets, on the grounds of Habitation de la Pagérie (Empress Joséphine's birthplace). The facilities include caddy rental, a pro shop, and restaurant; (596) 68.32.81.

The Grand Folkloric Ballet of Martinique, musicians and dancers dressed in traditional Créole costumes, provides a colorful, enchanting show to the rhythm of the beguine on Thursdays at the Méridien, Fridays at the Bakoua, and Saturdays at the Batelière hotels. Performances begin at 8:30 P.M.

Martinique has two **casinos**—at the **Hôtel Méridien** on Pointe du Bout, and adjacent to the **Hôtel La Batelière** in Schoelcher, on the west coast just north of Fort-de-France (jackets and ties appreciated).

≈ ≈

NEVIS

ACCOMMODATIONS

NEVIS' BEST
Four Seasons Resort
The Hermitage
Montpelier Plantation Inn
Nisbet Plantation Beach Club

NOTEWORTHY OPTIONS
Mount Nevis Hotel & Beach Club
Oualie Beach Hotel

GREAT EXPECTATIONS
Cades Bay Beach Club

RECOMMENDED RESTAURANTS

RECOMMENDED SHOPPING

PROVISIONS FOR YOUR ISLAND PANTRY

USEFUL INFORMATION

≈ ≈

≈ ≈

Accommodations

NEVIS' BEST

Four Seasons Resort

Mention Four Seasons and travelers instantly envision first-rate accommodations, quality food, service, and staff. So, on our first visit, as we approached the 196-room Four Seasons Resort located on beautiful Pinney's Beach on Nevis, open since February 14, 1991, our expectations were high. Check-in at the resort's hospitality lounge in Basseterre on St. Kitts was graciously attended to; we were offered a beverage, then escorted to the *Spirit of Mt. Nevis* cruiser for the 35-minute sea voyage directly to the resort's private dock. Mount Nevis, encircled in puffy white clouds, soared in the distance as a magnificent backdrop.

Four Seasons' 12 cottages have been given Nevis estate names. Ten stretch along the beach and two are in the back with golf-course views—the beach rooms are preferred. When we first saw the two-story, boxy, balconied cottages, we were disappointed, but the appearance of the buildings has softened and changed since the plantings have grown and enveloped them. The cottages are constructed of vertical wooden boards and some masonry-covered exteriors, slightly pitched roofs covered in pale greenish asphalt, and thin white gingerbread trim. The entrance to the hotel has a high wooden-beamed structure reminiscent of Canadian lodge construction. The exterior of the main complex, with lounges, restaurants, boutiques, and conference rooms, is somewhat awkwardly designed, but the interiors are grand. The pool itself is pretty— between the beach and the main building complex, but a raised trilevel platform lined with chaise longues facing the building cuts off sea views and breezes. There's a large Jacuzzi whose fierce bubbling prompted my husband to comment, "It's time to put in the pasta." The Jacuzzi still wildly fizzes and bubbles, but a mother and her children were happily giggling inside.

There is good news: For the 1995 season, a second pool has been added, a 5,000-square-foot freeform beauty with two-lap swimming lanes—the ocean pool. Its terrace is beachside and nearest cottage 5. Views are sensational.

Best of all, the interiors of the Four Seasons remain elegant, distinct lodgings, if more decorator magazine than quaint Nevis in style. Inside, guests have every conceivable modern convenience: remote-control 25-inch color cable TV hidden in a dark wooden cabinet that also contains a VCR and a clock radio, plus air-conditioning, a comfortable king-size bed with excellent reading lights, an itty-bitty nightlight, a large sitting area, plenty of closet space with a safe and umbrella, an automatic icemaker, a mini-bar stocked with beverages and spirits, plus candy bars, nuts, and popcorn. One especially nice touch was a nutmeg grater with a whole nutmeg to top off tropical cocktails.

Bathrooms are huge and soothing, colored in pink and white with hanging lights over lengthy, marbled vanities with twin basins. Two carved-metal, wall-mounted hurricane lights further brighten the room. Large bathtubs have marble tops with tiled sides and adjacent separate glassed-in showers. Thick towels, bathrobes, toiletries, a hair dryer, and a lighted magnifying mirror are other amenities. The toilet is hidden in a private enclosure. A very convenient addition are washer/dryer areas in each cottage, stocked with detergent.

Breakfasts are bountiful buffets in the Grill Room. (There is also 24-hour room service in case you want to breakfast in bed or on your screened balcony.) For lunch, the Grill Room serves buffet and à la carte selections; guests also can dine at the al fresco Pool Cabana Restaurant—recently expanded, wrapping around the original pool, to accommodate up to 150 people.

Dinners served in the Grill Room or main dining room, inside or on the terrace, consistently excel. The indoor salon has high wooden-beamed ceilings that support enormous chandeliers. We've sampled excellent dishes here—coconut shrimp, perfect grilled lobster, and other seafood and meat offerings. Salads and vegetables are the freshest available, and desserts are always delectable, especially the ice creams and sorbets. Service is attentive.

The Four Seasons has plenty of activities to keep guests occupied. All water-sports facilities are available, as are seaboards, toobies, paddle boats, air mattresses, and underwater cameras. The health club has LifeCycles, StairMasters, treadmills, and much more. The resort also has 10 tennis courts, an 18-hole Robert Trent Jones course, croquet, volleyball, a horseshoe court, and shuffleboard. Billiards and darts can be played in the Tap recreation room in the main building's lower lobby. Nightly entertainment is also provided.

Four Seasons has an outstanding "Kids for All Seasons" activities program for youngsters from three to twelve. Programs include sports activities, crafts, cooking classes, science and nature walks, and picnics.

Shops at the Four Seasons sell island crafts and sundries, as well as upscale resortwear.

Independent guests should be aware that the Four Seasons is popular, deservedly so, with corporate incentive or convention holidays. During our first visit, three companies were having meetings throughout the day. On a recent visit, two groups were celebrating on the property. Nevertheless, the resort is large enough for everyone to find private space. Several guests we spoke with said they were in love with the place.

Beach service is so pampering, you may not even want to leave your chaise in the sand, except to plunge in the sea or have a bite of lobster salad. Mark Hellrung is professionally in charge of blossoming Four Seasons Resort of Nevis. Private villas open the summer of 1995.

FOUR SEASONS RESORT   RESERVATIONS
P.O. Box 565, Charlestown   TEL: (800) 332-3442
Nevis, West Indies
TEL: (809) 469-1111
FAX: (809) 469-1112

Open all year.

Rates: Double occupancy. *January 2 to March 31:* Deluxe Rooms, $500 to $550; One-Bedroom Suites, $950 to $2,200. *April 1 to May 31* and *November 1 to December 20:* Deluxe Rooms, $325 to $375; One-Bedroom Suites, $700 to $2,000. *June 1 to October 31:* Deluxe Rooms, $175 to $225; One-Bedroom Suites, $650 to $2,200. Two- and Three-Bedroom Suites available; rates upon request.

Meal plan: EP. MAP (includes breakfast and dinner), add $80 per person per day. FAP (includes breakfast, lunch, and dinner), add $95 per person per day. After sunset, in Library, Grill Room, and Dining Room, gentlemen are required to wear collared and buttoned shirts, full-length trousers, and closed-in footwear.

Service charge: 10%.

Government tax: 7%.

Children welcome.

Credit cards accepted.

Note: Seven different packages are available.

The Hermitage

The Hermitage Plantation inn is a gentle yet generous dose of inland tropical countryside. Ten miles from the airport on the southern end of Nevis, its physical address— Gingerland, St. John's Parish, Figtree—is as welcoming as the warm greetings we received from the owner/managers Richard and Maureen Lupinacci, and the peach-colored double hibiscus flowers we found tucked at our bed pillows upon arrival.

Originally from Quakertown, Pennsylvania, the Lupinaccis bought Hermitage, a former plantation with a crumbling 1740 Main House, in 1971. The small house was salvageable only because its frame and shingles were crafted from lignum vitae, an extremely hard tropical wood impervious to decay. While managing other properties, the Lupinaccis painstakingly renovated Hermitage's Main House. Then, in 1985, the restoration of the rest of the property began.

Since opening The Hermitage, Richard and Maureen have gained a reputation as congenial hosts with a willingness to please, embracing guests as part of their family.

The Lupinaccis will rent you a car, suggest island itineraries, or organize excursions to nearby islands. Transportation to several beaches is provided if you do not have a car. After a Sunday brunch at Montpelier Plantation Inn, about two miles away, we were unable to get a taxi back to the Hermitage because all drivers were glued to the TV or radio for an important cricket match between England and the West Indies. We called

A cottage at The Hermitage in Nevis.

The Hermitage for help and Richard collected us within minutes. On the way to our cottage, he invited us to see the thoroughbred stables and a dozen newly born, squealing piglets. It's not surprising that many of the inn's extended family of guests are yearly repeaters, the majority of whom are from England and America.

Hermitage's freshwater swimming pool, LayKold tennis court, stables, tackroom, carriage shed, fernery, gardens, and Main House with an adjoining terrace restaurant, and guest quarters in ten separate structures, sprawl across seven fertile acres. Once the residence of a colonial agricultural officer, the flourishing grounds are dotted with breadfruit, cashew, avocado, and mango trees. The inn rests 810 feet above sea level in the foothills of 3,232-foot Nevis Peak. The peak, directly to the north, is usually dramatically cloaked in dense, misty clouds. Lovely distant sea views are off to the south and west.

The inn's 14 accommodations, including a new manor house, are pretty-as-a-postcard, one- and two-story gingerbread-trimmed West Indian cottages that have been fully restored or newly created; the best are luxury-category Pink House, Blue House, The Loft, and White House. Each has a full kitchen, separate sitting room and bedroom, and is decorated with chintzes and antiques, including a four-poster canopy bed.

The hillside and deluxe cottages' interiors are plainer, but all have splendid vistas from private verandas (second-floor views are the best) with comfortable hammocks, tables, chairs, and lounges. All cottages have kitchenettes with mini-refrigerators and hair dryers. We unpacked in deluxe Tower-Down (meaning downstairs), overlooking the swimming pool. Our canopied four-poster was a newly crafted wooden-framed bed with a foam mattress that required two-step footstools to climb up onto. The room had a small sitting

214 | NEVIS

area, sufficient closet space, and a functional bath with a shower. Fragrant lily-of-the-valley soap was a nice amenity. We were perfectly comfortable here, but those more demanding should upgrade to luxury.

The ultimate residence at Hermitage, poised at the top of the property on its own half acre of gardens and lawns with a private swimming pool, is the two-story Yellow Manor House. It has two suites, large baths and dressing rooms, a dining room and full kitchen. Vast verandas wrap around each floor for a 180-degree panorama of rolling countryside and sea. It's an excellent choice for two couples or a family.

Life at The Hermitage is peaceful, whether you're hibernating in private quarters or lazing by the pool. Other diversions are horse-drawn carriage rides, tennis, hiking, or repairing to the Main House's antique-filled living room, which is the prime gathering place for reading, card or board games, taking afternoon tea, or watching TV in the small library. A guest during our stay wrote and read at a table on the adjoining porch each afternoon. The tiny bar next to the open-air dining terrace is open all day. If a ring of the little cowbell doesn't bring someone, you serve yourself, honor-system, and write up the tab.

Cocktails and hors d'oeuvres are served in the drawing room before dinner, which is announced promptly at 8 p.m. by a bell. Maureen and Richard normally dine with some of the guests and, if desired, they arrange compatible seating for other guests.

On Wednesday evenings, live music played by a local string band gets the rhythm going for a delicious West Indian buffet featuring a roast suckling pig.

The food we sampled at The Hermitage was good, often excellent, especially the dishes prepared with fresh vegetables and fruits grown in the inn's gardens or plucked from trees. We had a delicious hot pumpkin soup and cold eggplant salad for starters one evening, followed by tender veal scallops and well-seasoned mixed vegetables and sizable portions of a rich chocolate-and-whipped-cream dome-shaped cake. Our favorite lunch was breaded sautéed flying fish served with a huge crisp mixed salad and fresh picked tomatoes.

After dinner, I fell asleep in bed reading the "Things to Do Within Walking Distance" portion of the four-page information sheet, *Welcome to Hermitage*—something about the hike to Nevis Peak being strenuous. I turned out the light and promised to think about it the next day. Maybe I'll try that hike on a future visit to delightful Hermitage.

THE HERMITAGE
Nevis, West Indies
TEL: (809) 469-3477
FAX: (809) 469-2481

RESERVATIONS
Robert Reid Associates
500 Plaza Drive
Secaucus, NJ 07096
TEL: (800) 223-6510 *or*
(201) 902-7878
FAX: (201) 902-7738

Open all year.
Rates: Double occupancy. *December 15 to April 13:* Hillside, Deluxe, and Luxury

Cottages, $285 to $385; Manor House, $690. *April 14 to December 14:* Hillside, Deluxe, and Luxury Cottages, $190 to $270; Manor House, $690.
Meal plan: MAP (includes breakfast and dinner). Children 2 to 12, add $25 per child per day. Children under 12 can have dinner in Main House at 6 P.M.
Service charge: 10%.
Government tax: 7%.
Children welcome.
Credit Cards accepted.

Montpelier Plantation Inn

Montpelier Plantation Inn was host to Princess Diana and her family in 1993. She selected an unpretentious, British-owned and -operated respected inn tucked away in the Nevisian countryside, where the hounding press was held at bay. In advance of her arrival, five accommodations were refurbished and upgraded to premier, but aside from that, things have remained pretty much the same at Montpelier—even the handsome brochure the hotel has used for several years. Turn the translucent first page and the stone steps of a eighteenth-century shuttered great house leap out invitingly; huge-leafed potted plants line the steps; vines crawl up stone walls. What isn't pictured is the giant ficus tree at the center of a circular driveway, which transforms the area into a virtual arboretum.

The next page of the brochure shows the picture of a palm-fringed beach. It's the beautiful west-facing Pinney's Beach, a 20-minute drive from Montpelier Plantation. The inn transports guests there from its southern hilly location, through Charlestown, every morning, and makes pickups later in the day. The inn has its own designated area on the beach, and holds Tuesday barbecues at its new beach bar and grill. Guests, owners, and staff play a vigorous cricket match, which is fun for participants and spectators alike. Montpelier's 17-foot Boston whaler with an 85-hp outboard engine is geared up for waterskiing, snorkeling, and fishing.

At Montpelier you're up 650 feet above sea level, so annoying insects aren't a worry. You'll hear island sounds of donkeys, crickets, birds, crowing roosters, and barking dogs. The cottages that dot the spacious grounds create a pastoral feeling. Montpelier rolls over several acres with one tennis court and a large freshwater swimming pool bordered by an Arcadian mural-painted masonry wall adjacent to an elevated barroom. The old sugar mill, plantings, and gardens are charming embellishments.

Twelve accommodations, called Standard, are the original rooms, which are tidy and furnished with a cabinet closet, vanity, coffee table, two double beds, and two extra-comfortable, high-backed swivel chairs under a hanging light. Nosegays of flowers cheer up the rooms. The bathroom, which includes a shower, is all white except for a glass-topped table covered with a pink and white cloth.

The five refurbished premier rooms now have Italian inlaid tiles and restyled bathrooms. Tubs and showers have sliding glass doors, and the vanity basins have five-foot mirrors and makeup lights. Premier rooms have king-size beds; three are four-posters.

Rooms have ceiling fans, but no air-conditioning, TVs, radios, or telephones. Continental breakfasts can be taken on your small veranda or can be enjoyed in the yellow and white breakfast and lunch room adjacent to the pool.

Much of the food you'll consume at Montpelier is from the inn's orchards or grown in the organic farm. Guests and visitors gather in the stone-walled, chintz-decorated bar/living room lounge for cocktails and hors d'oeuvres. Repeat guests pitch in and help pass tidbits like Roquefort dip and crudités and nibble on chips with other English, Canadian, and American visitors, chatting amiably about what's happened between tea and dinnertime.

In the adjacent terraced dining room, guests sit down to wonderful meals composed of home-cured gravlax with mustard cream, red apple and celery soup, filet of lamb with wild mushroom tartlet, pommes Dauphinoise, baked butternut squash, and tiramisù, for example. Petit fours accompany coffee. Montpelier has an excellent, affordable wine list. A friend and I recently enjoyed a first-rate Sunday brunch featuring tender, crisp-skinned roast suckling pig.

Montpelier has been in the Gaskell family since 1964. The current family owners, warm and welcoming James and Celia Milnes Gaskell, conclude the inn's brochure with a handwritten message: "We made our home here and our life in the garden. We love it. You will, too." Indeed you will if you like the idea of a bit of "Caribbeanshire" in a tropical countryside setting with a restful atmosphere and caring, personalized service.

MONTPELIER PLANTATION INN	RESERVATIONS
P.O. Box 474	TEL: (800) 621-1270 *or*
Nevis, West Indies	(800) 243-9420
TEL: (809) 469-3462	
FAX: (809) 469-2932	

Closed from approximately last week in August to end of first week in October.
Rates: Double occupancy. *December 15 to April 15:* $220. Extra person, $70 per person per day. Children up to 12 years, $10 to $50 per child per day. *April 16 to December 14:* Room, $120. Extra person, $50 per day. Children up to 12 years, $10 to $35 per child per day. Add supplement of $60 per day for Premier Room.
Meal plan: CP (includes continental breakfast).
Service charge: 10%.
Government tax: 7%.
Children welcome.
Credit cards accepted, except for American Express.

Nisbet Plantation Beach Club

Thirty-five-acre Nisbet Plantation, five minutes from the airport and fifteen minutes from Charlestown, to the east of each, is only one of a handful of small inns on Nevis. The others are located mainly on the island's southern mountainside. Most are restored 18th-century great houses with sugar mills and are owner-managed. Travelers are welcome to visit these diverse places for a good island-style, home-cooked lunch or dinner (see Recommended Restaurants). Nisbet Plantation is part of Nevis' fascinating history. Fanny Nisbet lived here before her marriage to the illustrious Horatio Nelson. (Chapter 8 in James Michener's *Caribbean*, entitled "A Wedding on Nevis," provides a fascinating account of the lives of Nelson and Fanny Nisbet.)

Repeat clientele are still atwitter over the dramatic changes at Nisbet. No longer called an inn, it's been renamed a beach club. The new name suits the new Nisbet.

The transformation includes the total refurbishing a few years ago of the 13 existing duplex cottages; each of the 26 rooms have showers and baths, king-size beds, and screened-in patios. Twelve premier junior suites are housed in two-story pale yellow buildings. These white-tiled lodgings come with comfy sitting rooms, raised platform areas supporting king-size beds, full bathrooms with step-up tubs (take care, the tile can be slippery), and cotton robes. Furniture is lightly stained or painted tropical rattan pieces covered with jump-out-at-you jungle-style floral prints mixed with pastel-colored materials. Louvered windows, ceiling fans, and breezes through open patio doors cool the spaces. Pick the second floors for better scenery and high peak-roofed, white, wooden-beamed ceilings. All rooms at Nisbet have ceiling fans, telephones, mini-bars, safes, hair dryers, and tea- and coffee-making facilities.

The cottages and suite buildings are scattered over the expansive grounds off to each side of a wide lawn boulevard that runs from the Great House restaurant to the sea. Many of the resort's towering coconut trees were topped off some years ago by Hurricane Hugo. Those that survived blend in with newly planted specimens.

Gingerland, a small, pink, fretwork-trimmed West Indian house, once the resort's honeymoon cottage, has been converted into the Conch Shell boutique. It's just off the new reception building off the circular drive entrance.

Down at the beach there's been lots of activity, too. A freshwater pool and sun deck now sprawl below the Coconuts beach restaurant, an airy, bleached-pine pavilion where dinners are served. It's a nice option to the romantic, more formal Great House. Lunches or snacks of burgers, salads, or sandwiches are nibbled at the Beach Bar near the sea. Every Sunday there's a steak and lobster beach barbecue and Caribbean buffet, with a steel band sounds to get things swinging.

The graciously restored Great House is a magical setting in the evenings. Its screened terrace room has a view over the broad, open, sweeping green carpet to the sea. Candles shine on tables set with crystal and china. Food here, a set menu every night, has improved since our last visit. But since then a new chef has arrived.

The living-room-like lounge and expanded bar areas are welcoming, with inviting cushions on sturdy chairs and bamboo-based banquettes on polished, wooden-plank floors. Guests like to settle down here afternoons with a selection from the library and a cup of tea.

Nisbet has one hardcourt tennis court, croquet lawn, and complimentary equipment for snorkeling. Scuba diving, horseback riding, mountain climbing, sailing, and sports-fishing, not to mention golfing at a splendid course, are all activities easily organized on Nevis.

Nisbet still reflects casual, if upgraded, paradisical living, whether indoors or out. The changes here weren't a metamorphosis. Rather, I think, a happy renewal with a rearrangement of the order of the old mixed in with the new. Like any major addition or bold changes at a resort we love, it takes some getting used to. The uninitiated won't have to wait. And, by the way, Nisbet's Bermudian owner's other Caribbean resort is beachside The Reefs in Southampton, Bermuda.

NISBET PLANTATION BEACH CLUB	RESERVATIONS
St. James Parish	Jenkins & Gibson Ltd.
Nevis, West Indies	P.O. Box 10685
TEL: (809) 469-9325	Towson, MD 21285
FAX: (809) 469-9864	TEL: (800) 344-2049 *or*
	(410) 321-1231
	FAX: (410) 494-1910

Open all year.

Rates: Double occupancy. *December 21 to April 14:* Superior, $315; Deluxe, $375; Premier $415. Additional adult, $95 per person per day. *April 15 to December 20:* Superior, $215; Deluxe, $265; Premier, $295. Additional adult, $60 per person per day.

Meal plan: MAP (includes breakfast, afternoon tea, and dinner; also includes laundry, local phone calls, and postage).

Service charge: $15 per adult per day.

Government tax: 7%.

Children under 5 cannot be accommodated in Premier Suites. Children under 12 are served dinner at 6 P.M. in Great House, or special arrangements can be made.

Credit cards accepted.

Note: Special Honeymoon or Anniversary packages available.

NOTEWORTHY OPTIONS

Mount Nevis Hotel & Beach Club

Spread across just part of 14½ acres of Nevis' bucolic hillside in Newcastle is a reasonably priced, conventionally designed hotel complex called the Mount Nevis Hotel & Beach Club. What it has going for it are marvelous panoramic views across the sea to St. Kitts' undulating hills, a 60-foot angular-shaped, terraced freshwater swimming pool, and former Wall Street chef Jeff Debarbieri, who turns out quite good meals, especially from his nightly grill.

Mount Nevis has lots of other appealing features, like its second bar and restaurant (serving pizzas, salads, and other snack foods), a few minutes' drive from the hotel, at the Mount Nevis Beach Club. After breakfast, many guests head directly there to spend their days at the beach practicing their waterskiing, windsurfing, sea kayaking, or sailing on Sunfish. The Club's 55-foot air-conditioned cabin cruiser with an al fresco upper deck can be chartered.

Open since 1989, Mount Nevis Hotel attracts many repeat guests, both couples and families. What they're vying for are spaces in the 14 deluxe rooms and 14 suites in two-story whitewashed buildings with red peaked roofs—all with spacious covered terraces or balconies. The buildings are set apart at decent intervals on lawns among palms, crotons, blossoming bougainvillea and allemanda, and other plantings. It's not lush and jungly, but gardens are manicured and inviting.

The suites with ocean views are actually studios with full kitchens and queen-size trundle beds. Connecting doors to the deluxe rooms can turn the accommodations into one-bedroom, two-bath suites to accommodate four. Deluxe rooms also have private entrances and mini-refrigerators. All quarters come with direct-dial telephones, air-conditioning, ceiling fans, and cable TVs with VCRs and movie cassettes available for rent.

The immaculate rooms are furnished with white wicker and light-colored wood pieces with pastel covers as cushions. Though spartan, the rooms are welcoming lodgings.

Mount Nevis' owner, Dr. Adly Meguid, is an extremely hospitable on-the-scene director who obviously cares passionately about his hotel. His daughter, Noreen, acts as manager of sales from New York. They'll answer agreeably any question you might have about Mount Nevis, and, once you're ensconced, Dr. Meguid or one of his front-desk staff will help arrange any activity, such as golf nearby at the Four Seasons' 18-hole course, excursions, and so on.

There's nothing fancy at Mount Nevis, but it's well looked after and peaceful. I wouldn't mind returning for a holiday here anytime.

MOUNT NEVIS HOTEL & BEACH CLUB	RESERVATIONS
P.O. Box 494	TEL: (800) 75-NEVIS
	or
Nevis, West Indies	(212) 874-4276
TEL: (809) 469-9373 *or* 9374	
FAX: (809) 469-9375	

Open all year.
Rates: Double occupancy. *December 15 to April 15:* Deluxe Room, $170; Premier Studio, $210; Apartment, $380. *April 16 to December 14:* Deluxe Room, $120; Premier Studio, $150; Apartment, $250.

Meal plan: EP. Meal plan available upon request.
Service charge: 10%.
Government tax: 7%.
Children welcome.
Credit cards accepted.

Oualie Beach Hotel

Karen and John Yearwood's four-year-old Oualie Beach Hotel has become a successful small, comfortable seaside retreat. The hotel's white fretwork-trimmed one- and two-story cottages with green peaked roofs have recently increased in number to house 22 accommodations. Rooms now range from the standard original rooms with ceiling fans to the upgraded deluxe rooms and studios that can be transformed into one- or two-bedroom apartments. All deluxe lodgings have air-conditioning, cable TV, and queen-size mahogany four-poster or two double beds. The studios provide full kitchens with tables and chairs.

Baths are standard and functional. The water is heated by the sun, so guests bathe when the sun is shining, or shortly thereafter. There's no swimming pool here.

All the cottages face the sea and have screened verandas. The beachfront one-story cottages are preferred if you want to be only steps from the water. The two-story cottages are staggered in a back row, but contain most of the newer rooms. We particularly liked a second-floor studio with a peaked wooden-beamed ceiling.

The floors are tiled throughout and the furniture ranges from modest to early Ethan Allen–like reproductions. Fabrics are filmy cottons on windows and muted pinks and grays on upholstered sofas and chairs. In the new deluxe rooms, bedcovers are repeat-print fabrics with three-tiered flounces at the sides. The bundles of ruffles made me think of Scarlett O'Hara—she could have converted one of them into an amazing Southern belle gown.

But I like Oualie a lot for many reasons. Everything is kept neat and clean; the owners and staff couldn't be friendlier; and the indoor/outdoor restaurant and bar are right at the beach. (Food, alas, at Oualie is ordinary, featuring seafood, sandwiches, and salads. It's best to stick to the plain things, such as grilled fish.)

What also makes Oualie appealing is its unpretentiousness and quiet, very pleasant atmosphere. Locals as well as visitors like it here.

Nevis Water Sports is located on the property for dives and boat trips. The Tropical Treasure Boutique stocks a small collection of resortwear and gift items. And just in case you fall in love with Nevis, Oualie also has a real estate office as well.

Oualie is a old-style, laid-back kind of resort with comfortable rooms with modern facilities—a perfect spot for undemanding romantics or families.

OUALIE BEACH HOTEL
Oualie Beach
Nevis, West Indies
TEL: (809) 469-9735
FAX: (809) 469-9176

RESERVATIONS
TEL: (800) OUALIE-1

Open all year.
Rates: Double occupancy. *December 15 to April 14:* Rooms, $130 to $145; Studios and Suites, $170 to $320. *April 15 to December 14:* Rooms, $90 to $100; Studios and Suites, $120 to $230.
Meal plan: EP.
Service charge: 10%.
Government tax: 7%.
Children welcome.
Credit cards accepted.

GREAT EXPECTATIONS

Cades Bay Beach Resort

Eddy and Sheila Williams, owners of popular Eddy's Restaurant in Charlestown, have already cleared several acres on Cades Bay Beach (north of Pinney's Beach) to build a 30-room hotel. Cades Bay Beach Resort is slated to open in December 1995 in phases— the first 16 units will all have sea views.

Cades Bay will have a restaurant, plus a boutique, a freshwater swimming pool with a swim-up bar, a Jacuzzi, two lighted tennis courts, and a beach bar (that's already open). It sounds very promising. The Williamses are young, energetic, and creative.

For information, call Eddy's Restaurant at (809) 469-5958.

Recommended Restaurants

NEVIS' FINEST*

* **Four Seasons Resort**, 469-1111 (Pinney's Beach). The Four Seasons offers the most sophisticated dining on the island. Recommended are the buffet lunches in the Grill Room and simple beach food at the newly expanded Pool Pavilion overlooking the beach. Elegant dinners on the main dining terrace room are excellent. (See resort listing.) Moderate to expensive.

* **Miss June's**, 469-5330 (in new location at a restored home between Oualie Beach

Hotel and Prinderellas at Jones Bay). For an enchanting island experience, reserve a night of your stay for an excellent multi-course buffet of West and East Indian food at Trinidad-born Miss June Meister's residence. It's a dinner party atmosphere. Don't fill up on the wonderful tannia fritters, because there's lots more to come. A charismatic host, Miss June provides entertaining conversation. Oprah loved it! By reservation only. Expensive.

* **Hermitage Plantation**, 469-3477 (St. John's Parish in the hills to the southeast of Charlestown). Charming, historic island home at the inn owned by Richard and Maureen Lupinacci. Cocktails and hors d'oeuvres are taken in the antique-filled living room, followed by a lovely meal in the terrace dining room (see hotel listing). Friendly, pleasant ambience. Moderate to expensive.

* **Nisbet Plantation Beach Club**, 469-9325 (just east of the airport). Dine in the splendidly appointed great-house dining room in the evenings. At the beach, eat burgers and salads at Coconuts over the beautiful pool which adjoins the beach. Sunday lunch is a steak and lobster beach barbecue with live music. (See hotel listing.) Inexpensive to expensive.

* **Montpelier Plantation Inn**, 469-3462 (on the slopes of Mt. Nevis southeast of Charlestown). It's worth the trip to see the inn, have a pleasant cocktail hour, and dine on wonderful meals featuring many fresh ingredients grown right on the property. (See hotel listing.) Moderate to expensive.

* **Golden Rock Estate**, 469-3346 (Gingerland). Enjoy marvelous lunches in the outdoor courtyard in a blossoming garden. Dinners inside are okay, but the room is a little close. Moderate.

* **The Cooperage Dining Room**, 469-3445 (Croney's Old Manor Estate east of Charlestown in Gingerland). Vicki Knorr serves commendable West Indian/Continental lunches and dinners in her spacious dining room or garden terrace. Sunday brunch. Moderate to expensive.

OTHER DEPENDABLE CHOICES

Eddy's Restaurant & Bar, 469-5958 (located in a restored 19th-century home on Main Street). Go to this popular bar and restaurant with a veranda overlooking the goings-on in town for lunch, the happy hour, or delicious rotating Italian, Mexican, and West Indian dinners. Live music Saturday night. Inexpensive to moderate.

Cliff Dwellers, 469-0262 *or* 5195 (Tamarind Bay). Cliff Dwellers is back after closing for several years (eventually it will open as a condominium hotel). Savor well-prepared dinners from the stunning hilltop Sunset Terrace dining room. Sunset cocktails here are splendid. Sunday brunches are offered. Shuttle transportation is provided from parking area up steep hill road. Inexpensive to moderate.

Cla-Cha-Del, 469-9640 (Shaw's Road in Newcastle, on the way to Mount Nevis Hotel). Enjoy super local West Indian fare in an unpretentious roadside dining room. Inexpensive to moderate.

Fort Ashby Bar & Restaurant, 469-0135 *or* 3464 (near Cades Bay). An informal beachside open-air pavilion at the historic ruins of the fort is the place to sample such local dishes as chicken with honey and barbecue sauce and Créole-style fish. Sunday brunch with live music is a local favorite. Other days, lunch only. Inexpensive to moderate.

Callaloo, 469-5380 (Main Street). Here's a new air-conditioned restaurant that serves pizzas, burgers, and chicken and seafood with Créole accent. Inexpensive to moderate.

The Carousel has no phone but you can inquire details from the hotel; 469-3346 (Pinney's Beach at Golden Rock Estate). This is a casual, fun gathering place on a lovely beach for grilled burgers, fish, salads, and sandwiches. Inexpensive.

Unella's Waterfront Bar & Restaurant, 469-5574 (Charlestown Harbour). A terrific seaside location offering good ribs, conch, and West Indian specialities. Inexpensive to moderate.

Lunch at **Oualie Beach Club** and **Prinderellas** is simple, casual, beachside dining. **The Courtyard Café** at Caribbean Confections in Charlestown features quick foods and, of course, sweets from Confections. Also in Charlestown, try **Muriel's Cuisine** for delicious, authentic West Indian meals or **The Nook** for quick, good local food. **The Mariner's Wharf Restaurant & Bar** is another seaside location (near the airport) for fast food and pizza.

Recommended Shopping

The Plantation Picture House, 469-5694 (Main Street, Charlestown). This beautiful new gallery features Kate Spencer's still lifes, portraits, and island scenes in oil and watercolors. Also find her work on exquisite, immense silk scarves and pareos and on prints and cards. Ms. Spencer's studio and main gallery is on St. Kitts, adjacent to Rawlins Plantation.

Another gallery well worth a visit is **The Eva Wilkin Gallery**, 469-2673 (Clay Ghaut Estate in Gingerland). Go there to view the late Ms. Wilkin's paintings and drawings in a sugar mill gallery. Reproductions of her work, antique maps, works by Nevisian artists, plus cards and paper prints are sold in the lower-level shop.

Hidden away in the hills near Old Manor Estate is **Piscatorials Art Studio**, 469-2260, where you'll find enchanting hand-painted clothing, placemats, and other handcrafts. Observe the artist at work.

TMG Art Gallery has a marvelous collection of Caribbean paintings and prints and imported pottery, and **The Gallery of Nevis Art** carries island art; both are in Charlestown. **The Nevis Crafts Studio Cooperative** on Main Street below Craddock Road sells locally crafted pottery, wood carvings, bamboo wind chimes, coconut bird feeders, and more.

Newcastle Pottery (just east of the airport). The last time I flew out of Nevis at dusk, I saw the flames of a heap of burning coconut shells from my window. Almena Cornelius's potters were firing more whimsical bowls with birds fluttering at the rims, hurricane candle covers, vases, and other delightful primitive pieces. Visit and watch the potters at work.

The **Made in Nevis Shop** at the Museum of Nevis sells local products like Nevis honey and candles, jams, and jellies, baskets, prints, books, and other lovely items.

Sand Box Tree, 469-5662 (in a renovated 19th-century home a short stroll from Charlestown to the Park Ville Shopping Plaza). A prime destination for shoppers looking for antiques, art, unique souvenirs, and quality clothing.

The excellent boutiques at the **Four Seasons Resort** sell local and Caribbean hand-crafts and artwork, upscale resortwear, jewelry, hats, totes, footwear, and more.

Island Hopper, 469-2972 (The Arcade in Charlestown). This is a delightful contemporary boutique stocked with Caribelle batik clothing, T-shirts, resortwear, colorful ceramics, and terrific island designs on placemats, aprons, and dish towels. Other branches are located in St. Kitts and Antigua.

The Red Store at Croney's Old Manor has a very interesting shop featuring jewelry, ceramics, hand-painted T-shirts, and art.

Every Thursday the **Golden Rock Hotel** has an art and crafts exhibit.

Also visit the **Conch Shell Boutique** at Nisbet Plantation Beach Resort for resort wear and handcrafts.

The **Nevis Philatelic Bureau** is located off Main Street in Charlestown.

Marion Heights Plaza is a small shopping center conveniently situated if you're staying on the southern end of the island. Stores include **M&M Jewelry and Craft Store, Kids at Heart, Cal's Variety Store, Chief's Mini Cafe,** and **Candies Pastry Shop and Bar.**

Useful Information

Keep the free *Calabash Skyview Nevis Map* and *St. Kitts/Nevis The Traveller Tourist Guide* at your side for helpful information.

A trip to Nevis is not complete without a full tour around the island, 24 miles on both good and bumpy roads. Travelers can rent a car or hire a local driver. Three of the many car rental companies in Nevis are **TDC Rentals Ltd**, (809) 469-5690; **Noel's Car Rentals,** (809) 469-5199; and, for Jeeps and mini-mokes, **Nisbett's Car Rental**, (809) 469-9211.

Whichever you elect to do, be sure to visit the island's historic inns for a brief visit, a drink, or meal. Sights to see include not only the **Mineral Baths, Jewish cemetery, Alexander Hamilton House** and **Hamilton Museum** and the other special places that all the guides list, but also the vistas of beautiful countryside, especially in the south near **Mt. Nevis.** Saturday, Tuesday, and Thursday, be sure to visit the **market place** in Charlestown.

Nelson and Wendy Amory run **All Season Streamline Tours** in 10 comfortable air-conditioned Toyota vans. Call (809) 469-1138 for information.

Old-fashioned three-to-four-mile **carriage rides** through the Nevis countryside, seating four, depart from Hermitage Plantation at 9:30 A.M. Monday through Friday; $25 for adults, $12.50 for children. For reservations call 469-3477.

Nevis has several excellent hiking trails. The Golden Rock Hotel's **Monkey Trail & Source Trail** are particularly appealing. Green vervet monkeys can be observed a short distance from the hotel along the Monkey Trail. The Source hike is for those in good shape.

To visit the **Nevis Beekeeper's House** and view the honey-extraction facilities and beeswax candlemaking, call 469-5521, ext. 2086. J. Quentin Henderson's booklet *Beekeeping— The Nevis Way* is available at island museums. Also look for the *Nevis Great House Cookbook*.

For horseback riding call **Paradise Beach Stables**, 469-9577.

Two terrific **secluded beaches** on Nevis are **Indian Castle Beach** on the southeastern end of the island, and an unmarked, usually deserted stretch of white sand beach just to the west of the airport: following directions for the Yamseed Inn, turn north off the coast road. Both are marked on the free Calabash Skyview Nevis Map.

For Swedish/sports massages, make an appointment with massage therapist **Tracy Rigby** at 469-9690.

≈ ≈

PUERTO RICO

(RINCÓN AND OLD SAN JUAN)

ACCOMMODATIONS

PUERTO RICO'S BEST
Casa San José, Old San Juan
The Horned Dorset Primavera Hotel, Rincón 🌴

A NOTEWORTHY OPTION
Galería San Juan, Old San Juan

RECOMMENDED RESTAURANTS

RECOMMENDED SHOPPING

USEFUL INFORMATION

≈ ≈

≈ ≈

Accommodations

PUERTO RICO'S BEST

Casa San José

A three-story 17th-century mansion in the heart of seven-square-block historical Old San Juan has been converted into an elegant ten-room inn called Casa San José. It's only steps away from the Plaza de Armas and the City Hall building, and within walking distance to numerous art galleries, museums, restaurants, shopping, and the governor's residence, La Fortaleza.

Owners Jag and Simone Mehta, with combined expertise, dedication, and over a million dollars spent on renovations, opened Casa San José in December 1991 to rave reviews. Jag Mehta is a prominent island hotelier. Mrs. Mehta's refined skills as an interior decorator are evident throughout the beautifully decorated hotel.

You enter the pale yellow townhouse from a sidewalk only a few feet wide off busy, narrow Calle de San José, and step into a blissfully peaceful chandeliered reception area. Floors throughout the hallways and most of the rooms are a checkerboard pattern of light and dark gray marble. Doorways are gracefully arched.

We stayed in Room 103 on the first floor with brand-new quarry-tile floors. Small white tiles lined our bathroom and large shower. Bathrooms in the suites are wall-to-wall marble or oversized tubs set into white tile. Toiletries are provided.

Our sitting room was furnished with an antique sofa, a side table, comfortable chairs, and plenty of lighting. In the bedroom two queen-size beds had Spanish-style green-painted and gilded wooden headboards. The bedcovers were Ralph Lauren Charlotte pattern quilts. Ceilings throughout are wooden beamed, and are especially high in the hallways. At the center of the hotel is a stone courtyard patio with a square green-tiled pool surrounding a bubbling fountain. Potted plants are strategically placed everywhere.

Rooms on the second and third floors, off balconies, can be reached by tile-lined staircases or an elevator.

There are four double rooms, four one-bedroom suites, and one two-bedroom suite. All are air-conditioned and uniquely furnished with European and local antiques, new pieces, oriental or other carpets, and a collection of interesting artwork. Mrs. Mehta enjoys and possesses a gift for mixing things. She bought the enchanting figurine-based

Guestroom at Casa San José in Old San Juan, Puerto Rico.

lamp in our room for next to nothing at a sale, then painted it gold and topped it with a pretty shade. Rooms have telephones, but no TVs.

Guests gather in the second-floor grand salon, a handsome, expansive room overlooking the street below, for complimentary afternoon tea and cocktails. The cheerful, sunny room has a grand piano, sofas, a settee, and overstuffed chairs. After a day of visiting galleries, sightseeing, and shopping, it's a splendid place to relax. Small business and private receptions or dinners are occasionally held here.

Breakfasts at Casa San José are served in a small dining room near the salon that is decked out with cloth-covered tables, and loveseats and chairs upholstered in a matching red and white *toile de Jouy* fabric.

Although physically our room was a delight and totally comfortable, it got noisy at night from the activity on the street outside and the music coming from next door. I highly recommend all the other accommodations, especially the suites, at the otherwise quiet, luxurious Casa San José. Service, under the supervision of manager Joanna Cartagna, is first-rate.

CASA SAN JOSÉ
159 Calle de San José
Old San Juan, Puerto Rico 00901
TEL: (809) 723-1212
FAX: (809) 723-7620

RESERVATIONS
TEL: (800) 223-6510

Open all year.
Rates: Double occupancy. *April 16 to November 30:* Double Rooms, $170 to $190; One-Bedroom Suite, $270; Two-Bedroom Suite, $475. *December 1 to April 15:* Double Rooms, $225 to $245; One-Bedroom Suite, $355; Two-Bedroom Suite, $600.
Meal plan: CP (includes continental breakfast, as well as evening cocktails).
Service charge: None.
Government tax: 7%.
Children 12 and over welcome.
Credit cards accepted.

The Horned Dorset Primavera Hotel, Rincón

Tastefully creating, developing, administrating, and maintaining a small exclusive luxury resort in the Caribbean, the dream of so many, is a formidable task. On-the-premises owner/managers Kingsley Wratten and Harold Davies, Americans, Colgate University graduates, and friends, have met the challenge triumphantly. The hotel's unusual name, The Horned Dorset Primavera Hotel, is a combination of a special breed of English sheep that the owners once bred in upstate New York, and the former name of the property before they bought it—La Primavera Beach Hotel.

The Horned Dorset Primavera Hotel, open since May 1988, remains Puerto Rico's best small seaside luxury retreat, secluded on four lush tropical acres with a 70 × 35-foot terraced Roman-style freshwater swimming pool, a classical Spanish-style two-story hacienda (which serves as the great house), sophisticated restaurant, and, with the addition of eight new suites, has grown to 32 exquisitely decorated accommodations. It's located about 75 miles west and light-years away from the congestion of San Juan's high-rise hotels and casinos. One of about a dozen daily scheduled 30-minute flights from San Juan will bring you into Mayagüez's Eugeno M. de Hostos Airport. The Horned Dorset is just eight miles north of Mayagüez. Rent a car, hire a taxi, or arrange to have the hotel collect you for the drive north through tropical pastures and sugarcane fields to the serene foothills south of Rincón on the island's west coast.

If your only port of call in Puerto Rico has been San Juan, then you will have missed the extraordinary and diverse natural beauty of the island. Puerto Rico's special attractions include a magnificent rain forest, El Yunque, east of San Juan; the fabulous Camuy Caves, with the world's third-largest underground river; and a lot more. (See Useful Information, page 236.)

The Horned Dorset, a Relais & Châteaux member since November 1993, is an intimate inn, not a full-fledged resort, as it has no tennis courts or sports facilities. There's marvelous swimming and snorkeling off the hotel's speck of caramel sand beach, which rests a few feet below the seaside rooms, a sunning terrace, and the great-house lobby and lounge. After about a 15-minute walk along the rocky shore to the north, or a short drive there, the beach broadens to miles of uninhabited, palm-lined sand, and one called Anasco Beach. Just north of the town of Rincón, a 10-minute drive away, are the famous surfing beaches where the world surfing championships were held in 1968. Deep-sea fishing and other water-sports activities and golf are available in the area.

Most of the discriminating young to middle-aged Puerto Rican and American guests who have found The Horned Dorset appear thoroughly content to hibernate on the hotel's beautiful grounds.

From the second-floor private patio of Room 21, we gazed out through creamy-white fragrant frangipani blossoms, hibiscus, bougainvillea, and a grapefruit tree over brilliant green lawns. A rare brazil nut, giant breadfruit, mango, and almond trees; royal, sago, and traveler palms; and a stately Norfolk pine are only some of the splendid tropical wonders here. From our patio we also overlooked the pool and white-masonry, red-tile-roofed great house with its massive pair of curved, open-arm staircases leading to the main dining room with its black-and-white-checkered marble floor. The backdrop panorama is green hillsides to the left and, off across the sea to the right, the shoreline of Mayagüez, which sparkles at night like Marbella on the Costa del Sol.

After purchasing the property, Wratten and Davies retained one of Puerto Rico's leading naturalists and restoration architects, Otto Octavio Reyes Casanova, to redesign and create a complex of classic two-story Spanish buildings on graduating levels with arched patios and wooden-screen-louvered windows to house the original 24 spacious suites.

The terra-cotta-tiled accommodations have all been stylishly decorated by the owners, who combined oriental rugs, reproduction Chinese ceramic lamps, rattan loveseats, desks and chairs, and magnificent hand-carved and -turned mahogany four-poster beds, end tables, and bureaus, crafted by a Puerto Rican father and son. Handsome handcrafted armoires from the Dominican Republic act as closets, and the fabrics used throughout are colorful bold prints and stripes. Bedrooms have air-conditioning, plus ceiling fans in each room. There's even a fan in the skylighted, gray-and-white-streaked marble-tile bathrooms. The marvelous bathrooms have French white porcelain basins, toilets, bidets, and old-fashioned brass-footed tubs. Horned Dorset has its own signature "natural" toiletries from Dominica. There are no TVs, radios, or phones, but there are mini-refrigerators, and mineral water is complimentary.

The excellent news at Horned Dorset is that by February 1995 it will have expanded. The new addition is a two-story villa called Escondida ("Hidden," in English), composed of eight new deluxe suites and a small conference room—enveloped in gardens located to the north of the original suite accommodations buildings. The four garden suites of Escondida have private plunge pools.

Horned Dorset's cozy lounge and bar on the first floor of the great house is an airy spot to curl up in a chair or loveseat, have a rum punch, and select a magazine or book from a well-stocked library. Taped classical music is played, and tapas are served here with cocktails before dinner. Open to the public, dinners are elegantly set, à la carte menus or six-course affairs, served skillfully by black-bowtied waiters. The wine list is a small but well-balanced selection.

The large 60-seat air-conditioned dining room is indirectly lighted with tangerine-colored, multishaded European chandeliers, wall sconces, and candlelit hurricane globes. The well-spaced, white-clothed tables are set with silver, gold-rimmed white china, and crystal. Emphasis is on classic French cuisine accented with island ingredients. The menus change daily and a new chef from New York's Areole has just arrived. One dinner (before the new chef arrived) consisted of vichyssoise, superb lobster medallions with grapefruit sections, and artichoke hearts with a light vinaigrette sauce and fresh basil. Soursop sorbet cleared the palate, tart and perfect. Entrées are presented covered with silver cloches. Ours revealed rare tender tournedos, crisp carrots, delicious okra and tomatoes, and cheese-laced mashed potatoes. Extra-fresh mixed salads followed, accompanied by three small wedges of cheese, then a rich, vanilla-frosted rum cake, accompanied by excellent strong coffee. In season on Saturday nights a guitar player and singer perform.

Breakfasts are served on the first floor of the great house on a charming, breezy veranda facing the elevated pool. Lunches here are light seafood dishes served with rice and beans, vegetable salads, and sandwiches. Room service is available for continental breakfasts only.

Apart from the countryside, the local sights consist of the Mayagüez Zoo and the Tropical Agricultural Research Station for self-guided tours.

There isn't any shopping to speak of in the area, but the hotel's small boutique carries such Puerto Rican craft items as hand-carved santos (small wooden religious figures) and mundillos (handmade lace products).

The Horned Dorset Primavera Hotel, which just gets better and better, is a unique hideaway in Puerto Rico, where you can totally relax and luxuriate. You'll hear bleeping coquí frogs and rooster crows and you can converse with Pompidou, Horned Dorset's stunning scarlet macaw, in the bar or poolside. You'll certainly have a romantic, unforgettable holiday.

THE HORNED DORSET PRIMAVERA HOTEL	**RESERVATIONS**
Reservations Manager,	Caribbean Inns, Ltd.
Apartado 1132	P.O. Box 7411
Rincón, Puerto Rico 00743	Hilton Head Island, SC 29938
TEL: (809) 823-4030	TEL: (800) 633-7411 *or*
FAX: (809) 823-5580	(803) 785-7411
	FAX: (803) 686-7411

Open all year.

Rates: Double occupancy. *December 15 to April 15:* Deluxe Suite, $325. *April 16 to December 14:* $190. Rates for new Escondida plunge-pool suites upon request.

Meal plan: EP. For six-course dinners add $45 per person per day, plus 15% service charge.

Service charge: 3% on EP rates.

Government tax: 7%.

Children: No cribs or facilities for children here; not recommended for youngsters under 12.

Credit cards accepted.

A NOTEWORTHY OPTION

Galería San Juan, Old San Juan

There are 10 eclectic rooms and suites in Galería San Juan, a combination inn, gallery, private restaurant, and home and studio of exuberant Connecticut-born, Bennington- and Yale-educated artist Jan D'Esopo and her husband Manuco, a Puerto Rican Olympic equestrian-team trainer and the gallery manager. Manuco concocts a mean cocktail, if he's around for your welcome. And that's the distinctive thing about the Galería: after a brief orientation, you're left on your own.

The Galería is a restored 18th-century complex of several connected buildings that originally served as officers' quarters for the Spanish Artillery. The Galería rests on a hillside street across from the Atlantic Ocean halfway between Fort San Cristóbal and Fort El Moro in historic Old San Juan. It's a marvelous location for viewing interesting Spanish architecture, visiting local sights, indulging at good neighborhood restaurants, and doing a bit of shopping (see Recommended Restaurants and Shopping).

As we drove up to the Galería, Jan waved to us through the open window of her front studio. She unlocked the front gate and warmly greeted us, wearing shorts and leg warmers, her hands coated with plaster. We were invited into her studio while she cleaned off, all the while briefing us with background on the inn and her other artist friends. We were then shown up a narrow spiral staircase to our second-floor room. Guests are given a key to the back door which leads to a cobblestoned street, enabling them to come and go as they please. It's a lively Bohemian atmosphere.

The complex consists of a series of plant-filled open-air or covered courtyards with benches and sitting areas and a gallery. The entire place is chockablock with paintings and sculptures by Jan and other artists. Many of Jan's works can be purchased.

The rooms with telephone and air-conditioning (two rooms have only ceiling fans) vary from extremely basic and small to sizable antique-decorated suites. Ours was of the plain variety, but we did have a covered outdoor sitting room leading to a rather unattractive yet large roof deck. Our view extended over the rooftops of town out to cruise ships docked at the port. An embellishment directly in our vision was a nearby rooftop satellite dish, which we pretended was a contemporary piece of sculpture.

The favored suite at Galería is a spacious, carpeted hideaway with a kitchenette, a ceiling of wooden beams, and a four-poster bed. Bathrooms are mostly motel variety. Nothing at Galería can be labeled luxurious and the inn certainly isn't for everyone. Friends who recommended the hotel to me come because they like Jan (and who wouldn't?), the artistic atmosphere, and, best of all, the easy access to Old San Juan.

One final word concerns Galería's restaurant, the San Sebastián Dining Room, with black-and-white terrazzo floors, high ceilings, and beautifully set tables with unique centerpiece arrangements of small sculptures reclining in a nest of tropical flowers. The sad news is that no meals are provided for guests, except morning continental breakfasts, which are fragrant feasts of homemade bread and guava and other tropical jellies, fruit juices, and Puerto Rican coffee. Jan, who along with her Puerto Rican cook also excels in culinary matters, hosts occasional special banquets and meals for small groups of visiting or local corporations, or for anyone celebrating an event with a minimum of 20 to a maximum of 50 people. We awakened to the scent of sautéing garlic and pork permeating our room. That evening, wives of a stateside company were expected for cocktails and an authentic Puerto Rican dinner. Since festivities to which you aren't invited can continue into the evening, be forewarned; it can be noisy but merry.

Guests at Galería San Juan can enjoy a self-service bar, and two roof gardens with wonderful views of the ocean and Old San Juan. There is studio space for trying your hand at silk screening and sculpture. If you are interested in serious study here, call the inn.

Multitalented Jan D'Esopo has created her very special place in the sun, with a lot of hard work, good humor, and endless energy. She is delighted to share it with anyone who's genuinely interested.

GALERÍA SAN JUAN
Jan D'Esopo
boulevard del Valle 204–206
Old San Juan, Puerto Rico 00901
TEL: (809) 723-6516 *or*
725-3829
FAX: (809) 724-7360

Open all year.
Rates: Rooms, $85 to $95; Suites, $110 to $175 year-round.
Meal plan: CP (includes continental breakfast).
Service charge included.
Government tax included.
Children welcome. However, keep in mind that there are stairways, statues, and works of art everywhere, plus dogs.
Credit cards accepted.

Recommended Restaurants

The island of Puerto Rico, including San Juan, has hundreds of very good restaurants. Only a handful can be included here. Do consider excellent hotel restaurants like Don Juan and Dar Tiffany in the El San Juan Hotel and La Scala in the Ambassador Plaza Hotel.

If traveling around the island, be certain to obtain a list of 45 Gastronomicas (small restaurants specializing in Puerto Rican dishes) outside of San Juan. Call (800) 223-6530 for information.

PUERTO RICO'S FINEST*

* **Criollissimo**, 767-3344 (avenida F. D. Roosevelt 300, Hato Rey). Excellent Puerto Rican cuisine served in a pretty dining room. Moderate to expensive.

* **Ailli Mojili**, 725-9195 (Clemenceau 6 at the corner of Joffre in Condado). Family-style Puerto Rican food is the specialty in this pink stucco dining room. Try the goat fricassée and the excellent house beans. Moderate.

* **La Mallorquina**, 722-3261 (calle San Justo 207, Old San Juan). Founded in 1848, this standby still produces mouthwatering arroz con pollo (chicken with rice) and fabulous asopaos (chicken or seafood stews). A lovely pink, high-ceiling dining room, plus a handsome bar. Moderate.

* **Il Perugino**, 722-5481 (calle Cristo 202, Old San Juan) A pretty restaurant serving first-rate Italian food. Moderate to expensive.

* **Amadeus**, 722-8635 (calle San Sebastián 106, Old San Juan). Delicious, inventive nouvelle Puerto Rican tapas dishes featuring seafood are served in this attractive dining room with a great bar. Owners José and Ramón Ramírez are hospitable hosts. Moderate.

* **La Zaragozana**, 723-5103 or 725-3262 (calle San Francisco 356, Old San Juan). The three dining rooms here are always bustling. Our order rarely changes — black bean soup and paella valenciana — but the menu offers many other Spanish/Cuban/Puerto Rican dishes. Reservations are necessary. Expensive.

* **La Tasca del Callejon**, 721-1689 (calle Fortaleza 317, Old San Juan). This is a welcoming, popular casual restaurant serving first-rate Spanish tapas as well as entrees. Inexpensive to moderate.

* **The Horned Dorset Primavera**, 823-4030 (8 miles north of Mayagüez at The Horned Dorset Primavera Hotel in Rincón). Excellent food inspired by local ingredients, served in an elegant dining room (see hotel listing). Expensive.

OTHER DEPENDABLE CHOICES

Amanda's, 722-1682 (corner of calle Sol and calle Norzagaray, Old San Juan). Here's a cheery, colorful dining room dishing up delicious Mexican creations. Seafood dishes are especially good. Moderate.

Bistro Gambaro, 723-4592 (calle Fortaleza 320, Old San Juan). This new and popular, gaily decorated restaurant serves nouvelle seafood and salads. Moderate.
La Bombonera, 772-0658 (calle San Francisco 259). This island institution is really nothing more than an oversized coffee shop serving reasonably priced decent breakfasts and foods such as pork sandwiches or seafood asopao. It also serves a delicious buttery, sugared sweet roll (toasted on a press grill) called a *Mallorca*, apparently named after that island's incredible, light-as-air confection called an *ensaimada*. Inexpensive to moderate.
Delicious, generous portions of Cuban food are served at an unpretentious restaurant near the airport called the **Metropol**, 751-4022, on avenida F. D. Roosevelt in Hato Rey. For the best Mexican fixings and margaritas, go to **Casa María**, 758-8987 (avenida F. D. Roosevelt 1344).

Recommended Shopping

There are hundreds of shops and boutiques in San Juan that sell quality merchandise. Included here are just some of the shops in Old San Juan, the most historically interesting area of San Juan. Do consider the shops in the better hotels as well, especially the El San Juan, and the abundance of stores in the Condato and Isla Verde sections of town.
Among the many galleries in Old San Juan, those deserving special mention are **Fenn Studio Gallery, Galería W. Labiosa, Aguadilla, Galería Botello**, and **Galería San Juan.**
Rainbow Jewelry, 723-3725 (calle Fortaleza 105). Special fine jewelry from local designers.
Bared 724-4811 (branches on calle Fortaleza in Old San Juan and at the El San Juan Hotel). China and crystal, plus jewelry and watches.
Joyería Riviera, 725-4000 (calle Cruz 205, Old San Juan). Another option for fine jewelry and watches.
The Book Store, 724-1815 (calle San José 255, Old San Juan) is the source for reading needs, including a number of books on the Caribbean islands.
Polo Ralph Lauren Factory Store, 722-2136 (calle Cristo 201). Good buys from the designer's collection.
The Butterfly People, 723-2432 (calle Fortaleza 152). Brilliant butterfly specimens in plexiglass boxes, plus other treasures. There's a restaurant here, too.
Java Wraps, 725-7654 (calle Cristo 206). Hand-batiked resortwear, jewelry, and so on.
Spicy Caribbee, 725-4690 (calle Cristo 202). Puerto Rican coffee, Caribbean spices, herbs, teas, preserves, and handcrafts can be found here.
Puerto Rican Arts and Crafts Shop, 725-5596 (calle Fortaleza 204). Local artists' handcrafts are sold.

Useful Information

¿Qué Pasa?, the complimentary official visitors' guide to San Juan and Puerto Rico, is an invaluable booklet filled with just about everything you need to know. Also look for **Sun Spot** and **Quick City Guide**. **The Other Puerto Rico** by Kathryn Robinson is a detailed insider's guide worth purchasing, especially if you're traveling around the island.

Car rental companies: **Hertz**, (809) 791-0840; **Avis**, (809) 721-5212; **Budget**, (809) 791-3685.

Note: As of June 1994, the *San Juan Star* reported that San Juan held the title as the island's carjacking capital. It led all major U.S. cities in carjacking on a per capita basis. So, keep cars locked at all times and try to park your cars where there are attendants in San Juan.

The Calling Station at calle Tetuán 357 in Old San Juan has air-conditioned booths with direct-dial phones for long distance calls. Fax and copy service as well.

Puerto Rico is 110 miles long and 35 miles wide, and has a population of over three million. There's much to do and see beyond San Juan. Historically and geographically, Puerto Rico is a fascinating country to discover. All the attractions, including concerts and entertainment are covered in the guides mentioned above, but inquisitive travelers might want to consider day trips to the little known islands of **Culebra** or **Vieques**. There are ferries from Fajardo on the island's southeast coasts. The islands have beautiful beaches, and a welcoming old-island atmosphere. And, keep in mind, **St. Thomas** is only a 30-minute flight away.

SABA

ACCOMMODATIONS

SABA'S BEST
Juliana's
Willard's of Saba

NOTEWORTHY OPTIONS
Captain's Quarters
The Cottage Club
The Gate House

GREAT EXPECTATIONS
Queens Gardens Resort

RECOMMENDED RESTAURANTS

RECOMMENDED SHOPPING

PROVISIONS FOR YOUR ISLAND PANTRY

USEFUL INFORMATION

≈ ≈

Accommodations

SABA'S BEST

Juliana's

Juliana and Franklin Johnson's 10-room guest house in Windwardside, Juliana's, should win an award for consistency, hospitality, and neatness. The gardens surrounding the property, which spreads across a little street, are composed of well-groomed speckled crotons, bright red hibiscus, blood-red ginger clusters popping out of salad greens, and buttercup-yellow allemanda that seem like delicately placed oversized bouquets.

The simple but very nice rooms are housed in storybook wooden cottages with front porches or balconies and capped with red corrugated roofs and fretwork. Leafy plants hang along entranceways. The tidy knotty-pine interiors have tile floors, good lighting, and standard baths and furnishing. Fabrics are floral prints.

Also available is a little prize called Flossie's Cottage, a refurbished Saban cottage with two bedrooms, a living room, fully equipped kitchen, and dining room. Flossie's boasts two porches with views of the Saban countryside, Mount Scenery, and the sea.

New in 1994 is a 2½-room apartment with a kitchenette.

Repeat guests at Juliana's, of which there are many, come for a peaceful holiday spent at their old friends' small guest house.

All guests can cool off with a dip in Juliana's inviting rectangular swimming pool, then have breakfast or lunch at the inn's terrace restaurant, the Tropics Café. The Johnsons' son, Griffin, prepares light lunches of burgers, sandwiches, and salads. The food is good and inexpensive.

Juliana's seems to improve every year, because Juliana really cares. She's an on-the-scene owner/manager, with a "How can I improve the place?" philosophy. Warmly recommended.

JULIANA'S
Windwardside Saba, Netherlands Antilles
TEL: (011-599)-4-62269
FAX: (011-599)-4-62389

RESERVATIONS
International Travel & Resorts
TEL: (800) 223-9815
For Dive Packages, contact Go Diving
TEL: (800) 328-5285

Open all year, unless the owners go on holiday.
Rates: Double occupancy. *December 16 to April 15:* Room, $95; Flossie's Cottage,
$125; Apartment, $125. *April 16 to December 15:* Room, $75; Flossie's Cottage,
$100; Apartment, $100. Extra person, $20 per person per day year-round.
Meal plan: EP.
Service charge: 10%.
Government tax: 5%.
Children welcome.
Credit cards accepted.
Note: Dive packages are available.

Willard's of Saba

William (Brad) Willard, Jr., grandson of the founder of Willard's Hotel in Washington,
D.C. (H. A. Willard), opened Willard's of Saba early in 1994. When I called the hotel
to arrange a visit, the manager/chef, Philippine-born Corazón de Johnson, said, "Come
immediately, you must see our beautiful hotel." She went on to list the amenities, which
sounded especially luxurious for the tiny island of Saba. Among the items mentioned
were a heated 20 × 40-foot heated swimming pool, a cliffside hot tub/Jacuzzi, a tennis
court, two luxury rooms and a VIP room in the main building, and four bungalow rooms
in two separate cottages. I booked a flight.

A few minutes' drive out of the village of Windwardside, up a curved steep driveway,
guests arrive at Willard's white-stucco-and-red-roof two-story main building under a
porte cochère with natural stone columns. Corazón de Johnson, a charming, gracious
host, led me on a tour of the property, dramatically situated 1,700 feet above sea level,
set at the edge of a sheer cliffside at Booby Hill on the southeastern side of Saba. Brad
Willard, a worldwide real estate investor, certainly met his challenge when he built this
hotel in such a precarious location. But in real estate it's location, location, location that
counts, and Willard's property is spectacular. The views are a magnificent sweep of the
open sea with the islands of St. Eustatius, St. Kitts, and Nevis as a backdrop.

The enormous rectangular pool is surrounded by a white-tiled terrace with thick-
cushioned chaise longues and tables and chairs. An oversized black-and-white checkerboard is set whimsically into the terrace floor tiles. Up a staircase, in a roost of its own,
is the kidney-shaped hot tub/Jacuzzi with striking day views, and a canopy of stars
overhead at night. Two duplex cottages, a few steps up beyond the Jacuzzi, also in prime
locations, were in the final stages of decoration and would open soon after my visit.

Inside, the luxury and VIP rooms were furnished with quality rattan chairs and
curved-reed coffee and end tables stained pale pine. Fabrics are bold floral prints of
yellow-gold, red, and green or aqua, gold, and orange. Paddle fans throughout hang
under wooden-planked ceilings. The hotel has no telephones, but TVs were on order.

The bathrooms are modern with white tiled shower stalls. The VIP room's extra-large
bath has a tub/shower and a bidet. All baths are supplied with a tray of toiletries.

Willard's bar is on the second floor with a balcony overlooking the pool with tables
and chairs. There's a small sitting area for TV viewing.

Pool and sea view from Willard's in Saba.

The hotel's restaurant is on the first floor in a large room off the pool terrace and is pleasingly decorated with round tables and rattan chairs. Framed original old prints of Willard's Hotel in Washington hang on the walls. Corazón, previously in the catering business, prepares meals skillfully with attractive presentations. Her rainbow snapper is a steamed flavorful filet covered with rows of minced cooked egg yolks and whites, parsley, and other garnishes. The diverse menu includes succulent beef, chicken, pork, or shrimp cooked and served sizzling on individual stones; delectable Shanghai rolls with Zosette sauce, a sweet tangy concoction; a variety of pasta dishes; saffron chicken over almond rice; and a special dessert of fried banana and jackfruit topped with whipped cream. For lunch, highlights include a crab and celery salad with a yogurt dressing served in a bread bowl or chicken tenderloins with a red pepper sauce.

Willard's is a delightful new hideaway where guests can hibernate, play tennis, swim laps in the pool, and enjoy the natural beauty of Saba, expansive ocean views, and excellent food. It's the most luxurious hotel on the island, and Corazón de Johnson and her small staff will pamper you.

WILLARD'S OF SABA
P.O. Box 515
Windwardside
Saba, Netherlands Antilles
TEL: (011-599)-4-62498
FAX: (011-599)-4-62482

RESERVATIONS
International Travel & Resorts
TEL: (800) 223-9815 *or*
(212) 251-1800

Open all year.
Rates: Double occupancy. *December 15 to April 14:* Luxury Room, $180; Bungalow, $250; VIP Room, $300. *April 15 to December 14:* Luxury Room, $150; Bungalow, $200; VIP Room, $250.
Meal plan: EP.
Service charge included.
Government tax: 5%.
Children 4 and over welcome.
Credit cards accepted.

NOTEWORTHY OPTIONS

Captain's Quarters

For many years *the* place to stay on Saba was Captain's Quarters, located at the end of a small sloping road at the edge of the village of Windwardside. The hotel's main two-story building was constructed at the turn of the century as the home of Captain Henry Hassell, one of Saba's many fine mariners. The main building now houses four accommodations, reception, and a library/living room lounge. The other six rooms at Captain's Quarters are in a motel-like, two-story balconied building across the driveway from the small freshwater swimming pool. All the buildings are white with red roofs, like all of the residences and structures on the island.

Captain's Quarters is set in a garden of tropical trees, including two giant mangoes, and a profusion of flowers. Interiors include standard furnishings with some antiques, including several four-poster double beds. Bathrooms are functional, and all rooms have verandas or balconies. Rooms vary in size with garden or sea views.

Captain's Quarters has always been a congenial place, like the island itself, with a cordial staff and a simple but good restaurant situated in a screened pavilion dining room. The hotel has a separate covered bar and dining area off the pool where light lunches are served and where dances are sometimes held.

On a recent visit to Saba, we found Captain's Quarters closed for remodeling and work on the swimming pool. We stayed at the inn a few years ago. Since then, there's a new Saban owner, Calvin Holm, who, in view of new competition on the island, was busy making some improvements.

We look forward to returning to see what changes have been made and sampling a meal. Meantime, Captain's Quarters is still a good choice for undemanding travelers looking for a peaceful spot to unpack in the village.

CAPTAIN'S QUARTERS
Windwardside Saba, Netherlands Antilles
TEL: (011-599)-4-62201 *or* 62522
FAX: (011-599)-4-62377

Open all year.
Rates: Double occupancy. *December 15 to April 14:* Room, $125. *April 15 to December 14:* Room, $95. Extra person, $35 per day.
Meal plan: CP (includes continental breakfast).
Service charge: 15%.
Government tax: 5%.
Children welcome.
Credit cards accepted except American Express.
Note: Package rates are offered for groups or extended stays.

The Cottage Club

The Cottage Club, another new lodging in Saba, partially opened a few lodgings in early 1994 at the eastern edge of Windwardside. It's a collection of 10 newly built Saban-style gingerbread cottages with balconies, plus countryside and sea views. Inside, the rooms have fully equipped kitchens with a dining area, queen-size and twin beds, modern bathrooms, cable TVs, and telephones.

New landscaping has been planted along brick pathways leading to each cottage. These little nests are spick-and-span and should be excellent choices for travelers wanting to settle into a neighborhood location and do a little housekeeping on Saba.

The centerpiece of the cottages is a handsome Colonial two-story balconied stone building, which houses reception and a lobby room furnished with antiques.

The hotel should be fully operational by press time. Some of its first guests report that they were extremely satisfied and comfortable at The Cottage Club—so much so that they planned to return next year.

THE COTTAGE CLUB
Windwardside Saba, Netherlands Antilles
TEL: (011-599)-4-52486 *or* 62386
FAX: (011-499)-4-62434

Open all year.
Rates: Double occupancy. *November 1 to March 31:* Cottage, $136.50. *April 1 to October 31:* Cottage, $105.
Meal plan: EP.
Service charge included.
Government tax included.
Children welcome.
Credit cards accepted.
Note: Special Dive Package or extended-stay rates available upon request.

The Gate House

Young-at-heart travelers looking for reasonably priced lodgings in a new bed-and-breakfast guest house on Saba will be delighted to discover Jim Siegel and Kym Rabbito's The Gate House.

The handsome, energetic young couple fell in love with Saba, whose conical shape they refer to as the pyramid, after Jim's mother bought a home in May 1993 in Hell's Gate.

Jim and Kym, both looking for a career and a geographical change after 10 years in New York's fashion business, learned that Danny Hassell's large contemporary Saban-style Hell's Gate home, resting on a stone-walled embankment, was on the market. On December 15, 1993, they signed the papers. Working feverishly, the creatively talented duo transformed the house into a modest but charming six-room guest house with a small, gaily decorated restaurant and lounge, named it The Gate House, and opened doors to guests on February 12, 1994.

The result is a two-story white balconied building with red gabled roofs and gingerbread trim. Shutters on the windows are dark green and white. Two rooms are upstairs on the same floor as the restaurant and lounge; four are below. All rooms have private outdoor entrances. The simple but extremely pleasant, well-kept rooms have French doors, short gauzy curtains with Riviera blinds, quarry-tile or painted wooden-planked floors, bright striped or checkered cotton comforters on twin or queen-size beds, and walls adorned with colorful Caribbean artwork. Two rooms have kitchens and bathtubs with showers; the other four have shower stalls. There are no TVs or telephones here.

The couple discovered that a neighbor, Beverly Hassell, had once worked as a cook at super-luxurious Petit St. Vincent Resort in the Grenadines. After tasting one of her delicious meals, they persuaded her to take over The Gate House's six-table restaurant (open only for dinner). Not surprisingly, Ms. Hassell has turned The Gate House Café into a great success, using locally caught seafood, Saban home-grown garden vegetables, and hours-old fresh eggs. Shipments from St. Maarten supply any missing ingredients. The Créole-inspired menu changes daily. A recent one offered a choice of cream of broccoli soup or a green salad, followed by curried goat, grilled chicken, or poached snapper, and, for dessert, a rich chocolate cake. The restaurant also serves buffets for up to 20.

Outside is a small deck and balcony with tables, chairs, and benches. A freshwater swimming pool may be in The Gate House's future. For the time being, the inn and its freshly planted gardens are maturing and Kym and Jim are becoming masters at the art of innkeeping.

The informal Gate House is particularly appealing to scuba divers, hikers, and nature lovers or anyone interested in a comfortable environment on a quiet island. Views from the inn face east over a wide-open panorama of the sea to St. Eustatius and St. Barts, across tiny red-roofed homes and to the little airport down below. Tradewind breezes here are nearly constant, so there's no need for ceiling fans, especially at night, when guests gratefully snuggle under their fat comforters.

The Gate House is a refreshing, most welcome addition to Saba.

THE GATE HOUSE
Hell's Gate
Saba, Netherlands Antilles
TEL: (011-599)-4-62416
FAX: (011-599)-4-62415

RESERVATIONS
In U.S.
Tel: (708) 354-9641

Open all year.
Rates: Double occupancy. *December 16 to April 15:* Room, $80. *April 16 to December 15:* Room, $70.
Meal plan: CP (including continental breakfast). Meal plans available; rates upon request.
Service charge: 10%.
Government tax: 5%.
Children: Not recommended for children under 12.
Credit cards accepted.
Note: Special rates available for dive packages, groups, or extended stays.

GREAT EXPECTATIONS

Queens Gardens Resort

The much-anticipated opening of Queens Garden Resort, a deluxe resort of 40 one- and two-bedroom apartments clustered on a hillside above Saba's tiny capital town, The Bottom, has, alas, been postponed. At press time, it was in foreclosure. Informed locals expect a new buyer to take over the project soon.

Queens Gardens Resort was an enormous undertaking, especially on the remote, one-hairpin-turn, hilly road island of Saba. When and if the resort opens it will be the largest and grandest hotel on the island.

When I visited Queens Gardens recently, buildings were erected and the resort was indeed well on its way to completion. With the hope that a buyer is found and that Queens Gardens opens within the next year, here is a short list of some of the amenities and features promised in the original plans. All the apartments come with private plunge pools, full kitchens, and cable TVs. Facilities include a restaurant and two bars, a large main freshwater swimming pool and a Jacuzzi, an entertainment center, museum, fitness center, and a tennis court.

Prospective guests should keep in mind that Queens Gardens is in an inland location, perched on the lower side of a hill facing west over the little village of The Bottom. In back of the resort, the hillside towers above.

For information on the current status of Queens Gardens Resort, contact Glen Holm, head of the Saba Tourist Board (011-599)-4-62231.

Recommended Restaurants

SABA'S FINEST*

* **Willard's**, 62498 (Booby Hill at Willard's of Saba). Delicious food with an Asian accent blended with local ingredients created by Corazón de Johnson, manager/chef of the lovely new hotel (see hotel listing). Moderate to expensive.

* **Lollypops Restaurant**, 63330 (off The Road on a hillside leading into The Bottom). Wilbourne and Carmen Caines' small indoor/outdoor restaurant serves up great fish cakes, stuffed crabs, roti, seafood, and other well-prepared fare. (Free transportation is offered.) Moderate.

* **The Gate House Café**, 62416 (The Gate House guest house, Hell's Gate). Local cook Beverly Hassell is in charge of this tiny restaurant serving appetizing home-style Créole-flavored and Continental foods (see guest house listing). Moderate.

* **Scout's Place**, 62205 (central Windwardside). Diana Medero's unpretentious, friendly restaurant (also a 15-room modest inn with a pool) is a popular place for excellent breakfasts or a cup of coffee, while enjoying the view from the great al fresco terrace or the indoor dining room. My last dinner there was a tender broiled lobster (you can also have lobster Newburg) so huge its claws fell off the platter onto the table. Inexpensive to moderate. Also at Scout's is **Scout's Stop and Snack**, where you can get quick foods and ice cream.

* **Captain's Quarters**, 62201 (Captain's Quarters Hotel). A new chef reigns here, but the restaurant is always recommended for better-than-average food in pleasing surroundings on a screened terrace pavilion. Moderate.

OTHER DEPENDABLE CHOICES

Brigadoon Restaurant, 62380 (central Windwardside). This small restaurant in a Saban cottage features seafood, Caribbean, American, and Continental cuisine. Lobster tank. The seafood is highly recommended. Moderate.

Try **In Two Deep**, (Fort Bay Harbor) for a laid-back pub atmosphere in an air-conditioned dining room. Open daily for breakfast and lunch; dinner on Saturdays only. Popular with the diving set. Sandwiches, salads, and beer on tap. While I was there the owner was advertising for a cook — "Certified Chef Wanted." Inexpensive to moderate.

In the village of Windwardside, other choices are **Guido's Pizzeria, Tropics Café** at Juliana's, and **Saba Chinese Bar & Restaurant** at two locations (the second is called **The Family Restaurant**). For take-out, go to the **Gourmet Deli** for pastries, sandwiches, rollmops, or whatever the cook has prepared that day. Don't miss **The Serving Spoon** in The Bottom for tasty local dishes.

Recommended Shopping

Shopping in Saba is rather limited, but things are definitely picking up. There is a growing number of boutiques in Windwardside. One of the best shops is Jean MacBeth's **Around the Bend**. Jean, who lived for many years in St. Thomas, says she came to Saba a few years ago for a peaceful life, "the way it once was in St. Thomas." Her delightful boutique carries "gifts, oddments, and pretties," including clothing, books, and an interesting collection of handcrafts from neighboring islands. Worth a visit.

Other shops in Windwardside are **Wild Orchid Studio** in a small complex confusingly named the **Breadfruit Gallery**, where a local artist makes glass beads and turns them into pretty, whimsical jewelry. **The Little Shop**, also at Breadfruit Gallery, has another sign on an outside wall that reads **"Lambee's Place."** In any case, go and have a look at the watercolors, prints, and featured works of local artists. You can also find ceramics, beautiful lacework handkerchiefs, placements, and other items created by Saban women. Jeanne Simmons's **Cotton Pickins'** is a lovely new addition at Breadfruit as well. She has a collection of pretty cotton and knit tops and resortwear. In town, check out **The Yellow Store** and stop in at the **Square Nickel Store**. It's basically a five-and-dime, but a real Saban experience.

Go to **Peggy's Boutique** for the island's brew, Saba Spice. Pass through Scout's Place and visit Windwardside and **Lynn's Galleries**.

In The Bottom two shops that shouldn't be missed are the **Handicrafts by Saba Artisan Foundation**, where lovely silkscreen cottons are produced and sold by the yard or made into garments. Sometimes beautiful, simple caftans are in stock. The Artisan Foundation also sells Saba Spice and lace works, souvenirs, books, and postcards.

Visit **Heleen's Art Gallery** to view Heleen Cornet's lovely watercolors and pick up a copy of her book *Saban Cottages* (see Useful Information).

Provisions for Your Island Pantry

The place to shop for groceries, staples, and cooking supplies is **The Big Rock** market on the corner in the center of Windwardside. Big Rock also carries liquor, candles, and just about everything else. Just look for the big rock in the front yard.

Also in Windwardside is the tiny **Corner Grocery Store**, selling a modest amount of produce and canned goods. Another source for produce and groceries is **The Unique Shop,** across the street from **Saba Liquors**, where you can pick up rum-based Saba Spice and duty-free liquor.

The **Saba Farmers Market** near the Tourist Bureau in Windwardside sells vegetables. **Murray's Saba Hydro Gardens** has excellent Bibb lettuce. The latter is near Guido's Pizzeria.

The **Corner Deli and Gourmet Shop** has dependable take-out pastries, salads, sandwiches, and other items.

The **Morning Star Shop** carries delicious homemade bread and fresh produce.

Useful Information

After a visit to Saba, the late Alec Waugh wrote in *House and Garden* in 1952, "I should not be surprised if in fifty years Saba is uninhabited. The young people will get restless and go away."

Mr. Waugh would be astonished to learn that only a few years short of his prediction for human extinction on Saba, several new hotels have just opened, and a couple of luxury resorts are in the island's future. The Saba Medical School opened last year at The Bottom's new facility and hospital, adding over 60 students plus doctors, professors, and staff to the island's population. The former hospital, sitting on a rocky ridge between the small villages of Windward and the island's capital, has been attractively remodeled and expanded to serve as Saba's public school.

Some young people might be leaving the island to obtain educations and seek new challenges, but others are returning, along with a growing number of expatriates. The population of this five-square-mile, mountainous, dormant volcano island, a Gibraltar lookalike, is 1,200.

Waugh could not have predicted that in the nineties a worldwide concern for the environment and physical fitness would draw visitors to tiny Saba to explore its many natural treasures. Although the rocky island has no beaches, it does have a series of excellent nature trails, both easygoing and arduous. One scales the nearly 3,000-foot Mount Scenery with a stairwell surrounded by a secondary rain forest of beautiful flora like elephant ears, tannia, bromeliads, heliconia, and breadfruit, mountain mahogany and palm, fig trees, and immense tree ferns, not to mention the fauna, like tiny speckled lizards, *Anolis sabanus*.

The deep waters surrounding Saba have more than 25 fabulous dive habitats in a protected marina park for scuba divers of all levels. There are several dive operations on Saba, and most hotels offer dive packages.

The hearty ancestors of this Dutch island's early inhabitants, a compatible mixture of Dutch, Irish, Scotch, English, and African decendents, still populate the island. I counted over 75 Hassells in the phone directory. Saba's gentle, friendly permanent residents, who have a keen sense of humor, seem amazed that so many people are suddenly coming to visit and increasing numbers are trying to rent apartments or buy homes. The government keeps a close check on the number of residents and is slow to approve development. Officials are determined to preserve the island's quaint atmosphere and its traditions of hospitality, fishing, lace-making, and producing the potent rum-based brew Saba Spice. After all, 28 miles to the north on the Dutch/French island of St. Maarten/St. Martin they see a glaring example of how a beautiful island can be damaged by rampant development in the name of tourism.

Saba is one of the last vestiges of quiet, relaxed, safe island living left in the Caribbean. Local authorities do not tolerate the use of drugs, and no serious crime exists here. There is only one way to cross the island, on a man-made serpentine seven-mile road that took 20 years to build over the rough terrain. Everyone on the island knows everyone else. In fact, even if you come to Saba on a day trip, you'll know several residents' names before you leave. There's no way to get here except by plane, by ferry, or by private boat at Fort Bay. The most common route to Saba is a 12-minute flight on Winair from St. Maarten. The landing takes place on an aircraft-carrier-size runway (1,300 feet) at Juancho Yrausquin Airport built on Flat Point, the flattest place on the island.

In recent years, ungainly, difficult-to-reach Saba has transformed itself from a frog into a prince. It's a singularly captivating island paradise, though admittedly not for everyone.

Will Johnson's book *Saban Lore: Tales from My Grandmother's Pipe* is an excellent source of historical information. Another book worth buying is local artist Heleen Cornet's collection of enchanting watercolors, *Saban Cottages*; Ruth Hassel and Frans Brugman supplied architectural and historical information for the book. Both books are widely available on the island, but a trip to Heleen's Art Gallery in The Bottom is worth a visit to meet the artist and have her autograph your copy of *Saban Cottages*.

After checking into your hotel, your first stop in Saba should be the **Saba Tourist Bureau**, located in a cottage in the center of Windwardside. Ecelicia Simmons or any of the staff will be glad to provide you with brochures, maps, and everything you need to know about the island. Particularly useful is a brochure, *Walking Tour Guide of Windwardside*.

Taxis are the easiest form of travel. Fares are reasonable and the drivers, who know every nook and cranny of the island, are accustomed to dropping passengers for a hike, meal, or a dive, and returning at a prearranged time for a pick-up. My favorite taxi driver is congenial Garvis Hassell, Taxi #18, telephone 62358, but all are accommodating and friendly.

Car rentals are available at **Scout's Place**, (011-599) 4-62205, and **Johnson's Rent A Car**, (011-599) 4-62269, in Windwardside. Scooters can be rented at **Sandra's Salon & Boutique**, (011-599) 4-62507.

≈ ≈

ST. BARTHÉLEMY

ACCOMMODATIONS

ST. BARTHÉLEMY'S BEST

Castelets
Guanahani
Hôtel Carl Gustaf
Hôtel Filao Beach
Hôtel St. Barth Isle de France
Le Toiny 🌴
Sibarth

A NOTEWORTHY OPTION

Tropical Hotel

RECOMMENDED RESTAURANTS

RECOMMENDED SHOPPING

PROVISIONS FOR YOUR ISLAND PANTRY

USEFUL INFORMATION

≈ ≈

≈ ≈

Accommodations

ST. BARTHÉLEMY'S BEST

Castelets

Castelets is an enchanting slice of French countryside snuggled on top of St. Barts' Mt. Loren. This peaceful and secluded haven is comprised of a cluster of four buildings (including ten rooms), a tiny triangular-shaped swimming pool, a profusion of plantings, incredible vistas, and a first-rate restaurant.

Geneviève Jouany, a petite Gallic bundle of energy, has discriminatingly managed Castelets since 1974. (For two years, the hotel became Sapare di Mare, but is, thankfully, back in the competent, caring hands of Ms. Jouany, who has a home nearby.)

Although Castelets is a mere 1.7 miles from St. Jean Airport and 7/10 of a mile from Gustavia, the tiny capital of St. Barts, it's located in a quiet residential neighborhood. You feel on top of the world, but a Mediterranean world. You'll never hear a live steel band or experience a West Indian carnival here. St. Barts is nine square miles of France, which is the very reason that so many people flock here every year. Castelets' clientele is 99% American, with many repeaters, especially in high season. The French stay in beach hotels; after all, there are plenty of quaint auberges back home.

The hotel's main building houses the small lobby, bar, restaurant, reception, and kitchen, with two small double rooms, called Club Rooms, on the second floor. Each room has a double bed and a private bath.

The other accommodations are situated in three villas. Villa 1 is L-shaped with four rooms: A, B, and D (the largest, with a sitting area) have king-size beds made by connecting twin beds, and C has a pair of stationary twin beds. All the rooms have private baths, and share a sizable furnished terrace.

Villa 3 is a duplex with two carpeted bedrooms with a loft entrance upstairs; twin beds in one, a queen-size in the other, and one bath. The living room, kitchen, and terrace make this a great family selection.

Villa 2, where we were, is the choicest residence. Again, it's a duplex with a loft, with one bedroom (king-size bed) and bath with a bidet, tub, and shower upstairs, and a queen-size bedroom and bath on the ground level. All the villas have tape decks and stocked refrigerators. There are no phones, TVs, or radios. Every bedroom in the hotel

250

has an air conditioner, but the wide arched windows and doors let in the breeze throughout.

Interiors of the rooms are tasteful individual combinations of French Provincial fabrics, leather chairs, velvet sofas, antique armoires, chests, coffee tables, wall sconces, prints of still lifes, and amusing caricatures. You might very well be in *tante*'s house. *Petit déjeuner* is included in the price of the room. At a prearranged time, there's a tap on your door. A waitress carries a covered basket out onto your terrace or into your room and sets out pretty blue and white china for a feast of oversized warm croissants and toast, sweet butter, strawberry preserves, fresh orange juice, and excellent strong coffee.

There is no place to roam at Castelet, and you'll need a car to get about. St. Barts has many glorious beaches. Two favorites, Gouverneur and Petite Galet (also called Shell Beach for obvious reasons), are only five minutes from the hotel, in opposite directions.

You'll surely want to browse or shop in St. Barts' duty-free elegant or funky boutiques and chic shops in Gustavia, Villa Créole in St. Jean, and at the shopping center across from the airport.

One of the main events of St. Barts is sampling the island's marvelous restaurants. The hotel's restaurant, always one of the finest on the island, is now open for dinner only, under the direction of two new young French chefs. According to Ms. Jouany, "At my place, now, cooking is serene, unpretentious, appetizing, and simple." We haven't yet sampled the new chefs' work, but recent guests report that it's superb. Be sure to book a reservation well in advance, even if you're a guest in the hotel.

CASTELETS
P.O. Box 60
97133 St. Barthélemy, Cédux,
French West Indies
TEL: (590) 27.61.73
FAX: (590) 27.85.27
June through October contact:
Geneviève Jouany
TEL: (590) 27.83.19
FAX: (590) 27.78.08

RESERVATIONS
Ralph Locke Islands, Inc.
TEL: (800) 223-1108
FAX: (914) 763-5362

Closed June through October.
Rates: Double occupancy. *November 1 to December 18:* Club Rooms, $70 to $100; Villas 1A through 1D, $90 to $190; Villa 2, Suite 2, $250; Room 2A, $100; Villa 3, $300; three to four people, $400. *December 19 to April 3:* Club Rooms, $105 to $155; Villas 1A through 1C, $135 to $265; Villa 2, Suite 2, $420, Room 2A, $155; Villa 3, $470; three to four people, $570.
Meal plan: CP (including continental breakfast).
Service charge: 10%.

Government tax included.
Children welcome.
Credit cards accepted.

Guanahani

The pastel-colored, gingerbread-trimmed cottages spread over several hillside acres at the western end of Grand Cul-de-Sac Bay give Guanahani the feeling of a cozy resort complex in the south of France. I like Guanahani because it's a beachfront hotel with a great pool, luncheon restaurant and bar, and comfortable deluxe, if small, accommodations. It's located on the eastern end of St. Barts, about 15 minutes from the airport. Transfer to and from the hotel is included in the room rate. Mini-Mokes can be rented right at the hotel, and on St. Barts, you need a car.

Although Guanahani's white sand beach is perfect for sunbathing, and dotted with palm trees, it's not St. Barts' best. It has surf at times and is a little reefy. However, you can take your towel and walk to a path to the left, where you'll find a lovely curved beach next to a forest of coconut palms. A host of other activities or restaurant options are only a short drive or walk away, since there is a whole cluster of resorts and restaurants lining the opposite end of Grand Cul-de-Sac.

Guanahani opened in December 1986 and has grown to 96 units, in 50 cottages, a combination of double rooms and junior and one-bedroom suites, all with air-conditioning and ceiling fans, remote-controlled color TVs, radios, telephones, wall safes, small but excellent bathrooms, and private terraces, where you'll enjoy the marvelous complimentary breakfast. Best are the junior and one-bedroom suites with kitchenettes and private pools. The junior suites' pools are shared. The regular double rooms are small, with just enough closet space, but all have large writing tables, firm king-size beds (a few have twins) covered with paisley bedspreads, matching draperies, and good reading lights. In the 76 original units the wooden furniture is painted white and sits on cool terra-cotta floors. Toiletries are arranged in ceramic seashells. Decoration is tasteful and pleasing. The new quarters have dark wood furniture and whimsical decor. I prefer the old lodgings for their locations and prettier interiors.

The location of your room is important at Guanahani. Request oceanfront or ocean-view accommodations away from the tennis courts, road, and public areas. As only a few rooms are beachfront, there's climbing involved to reach the restaurant, main pool and Jacuzzi, two lighted tennis courts, and the chic boutique. Guanahani's personalized T-shirts, bathrobes, beach bags, and linens are elegant and expensive.

Windsurfing, Hobie Cats, and snorkeling equipment can be rented on the premises; all other water sports can be arranged.

The sun shines and the sea sparkles during lunches at open-air L'Indigo Café, which is raised up a few steps and adjoins one of the prettiest freshwater swimming pools in the Caribbean. As you dine on a large platter of succulent lobster salad with fresh vegetables, a cold glass of wine, and fresh fruit or sorbet, you'll hear the lively chatter of young to middle-aged French, Italian, and American visitors.

Room service is offered for continental breakfasts from 6:30 to 10 A.M. and light meals from 6:30 to 8:30 P.M.—smoked salmon, salads, or cold roast chicken.

Bartholoméo Restaurant has become the pride of Guanahani. The restaurant has dark-stained wood chairs and tables, banquettes, creamy yellow walls, and a bright aqua-blue painted ceiling. Starfish sconce lights adorn the walls. Dining is available out on the terrace as well. I've had some very good meals in Bartholoméo, like cold fish consommé with saffron, tuna carpaccio with Parmesan cheese shavings, sautéed veal medallions and yam purée with a lime ginger sauce, and noisettes of lamb with thyme, caramelized tomato, and Provençale vegetables. The cold pineapple soufflé, hot apple tart with vanilla ice cream, and palette of fresh tropical fruit sorbets were outstanding. I haven't sampled the new chef's creations.

GUANAHANI
P.O. Box 109
97133 St. Barthélemy, Cédux,
French West Indies
TEL: (590) 27.66.60
FAX: (590) 27.70.70

RESERVATIONS
Leading Hotels of the World
747 Third Avenue
New York, NY 10017-2847
TEL: (800) 223-6800 *or*
   (212) 838-3110
FAX: (212) 758-7367

Closed September 1 through October 31.
Rates: Double occupancy. *January 5 to April 5* and *January 27 to March 8:* $400 to $700. For other periods, call the toll-free 800 number.
Meal plan: CP (includes continental breakfast).
Service charge included.
Government tax included.
Children welcome.
Credit cards accepted.
Note: Special packages available.

Hôtel Carl Gustaf

As of July 1, 1991, sojourners able to foot the bill could stay in one of St. Barts' most luxurious hotels, Carl Gustaf. The pretty-as-a-postcard, sprawling complex contains twelve units, six one-bedroom and six two-bedroom suites in pink stucco buildings, topped with red, corrugated roofs. Each unit is accented with four white columns supporting an A-frame front gallery covering the flat sides of which are roofless structures open to the sky for sunning and views.

Hôtel Carl Gustaf cascades down and sweeps across a hillside just south of Gustavia. The view from each accommodation is a captivating picture of the island's enchanting harbor, countryside, and sea.

All small but charming suites have two satellite TVs and a VCR, two direct-dial telephones, a fax machine, two stereos, air-conditioned bedrooms and ceiling paddle fans throughout, king-size beds, bathroom hair dryers and magnifying mirrors, a comfortable living room with a bar, a dining area, and a kitchen. Small sun decks all have private plunge pools. Decor is composed of quality rattan pieces covered in floral prints or stripes.

Guests at the hotel can enjoy a fitness center and sauna as part of the tariff, and be given preferential rates on the hotel's cruiser, *Carl Gustaf I*, for day tours or fishing trips. All water sports, tennis, horseback riding, car rental, and French lessons can be arranged. Since a car is essential, notify the hotel well in advance if you want to reserve one.

Shell (Petite Galet) beach is only a short distance from the hotel, and my favorite St. Barts beach, Gouverneur, is a few minutes' drive to the south.

All suites are bordered by quarry-tiled walkways and staircases (considerable climbing is involved), and multi-tiered, straight- and curved-walled planters are generously filled with palm trees, blooming allamanda, bougainvillea, hibiscus, oleander, and other tropicana.

Pampered guests will be served continental breakfasts in their suites. Elegant French buffet lunches and dinners are served alfresco at the top of the hotel in the spacious poolside aerie – the food is first-rate.

Hôtel Carl Gustaf has become one of *the* places to stay and dine on St. Barts. Even if you don't register here, try a meal and experience the exquisite view at impressive Carl Gustaf.

HÔTEL CARL GUSTAF
Rue des Normands, Gustavia
97133 St. Barthélemy Cédux, French West Indies
TEL: (590) 27.82.83
FAX: (509) 27.82.37

Closed September 1 to October 15.
Rates: Double occupancy. *December 20 to January 7:* One-Bedroom Suites, $950; Two-Bedroom Suites (four persons), $1,200. *January 8 to April 14:* One-Bedroom Suites, $770; Two-Bedroom Suites (four persons), $1,000. *April 15 to December 19:* One-Bedroom Suites, $500; Two-Bedroom Suites (four persons), $660. All include transportation from and to airport.
Meal plan: CP (includes continental breakfast).
Service charge included.
Government tax included.
Children welcome.
Credit cards accepted.
Note: Packages for seminars and groups available.

Hôtel Filao Beach

Baie de St-Jean is St. Barts' Champs-Elysées, the most popular beach promenade on the island. The north-facing white strand spans a mile from the western end at the tiny airport's runway to the opposite end, at Eden Rock, a rustic, red-roofed inn and restaurant perched on a rocky promontory. (Eden Rock was St. Barts' first hotel. Recently renovated, it's a great elevated spot for breakfast, lunch, or sunset cocktails.) Lining St. Jean Beach are a few French bistros and small seaside hotels. The best is Hôtel Filao Beach. Filao is among the nearly 400 hotels, inns, and restaurants from around the world included in the prestigious Relais et Châteaux, a highly regarded French publication whose selectors adhere to strict criteria based on quality of service, lodgings, and charm. While Filao meets the requirements, there is nothing lavish here. Filao's outstanding feature is its prime beachside location, as well as good service, a pleasant raised and terraced seaside freshwater swimming pool, and a good restaurant and bar (open for breakfast and lunch only). Mario, the amiable bartender, is an island institution. Upon introduction you'll immediately be added to his repertory of friends.

The majority of guests at Filao are French and American families and young and middle-aged couples on repeat visits. It's next to impossible for a newcomer to book a room over the Christmas holidays, but you can always try—sometimes there are cancellations.

What everyone is vying for are the 30 neat, comfortable rooms with front porches in 15 single-story two-unit bungalows set in gardens that run perpendicular to the beach on the western side of the property and swing around in back of the restaurant. The only actual beachfront room is number 10, the most coveted. Number 11 is the next-best choice for seaside fanciers.

Owned by Societé SAIT and managed by Pierre Verdier, all the quarters have been redecorated and pepped up with standard but pretty tropical furniture in sitting areas, with desks, bureaus, and twin or king-size beds. Accommodations have air-conditioning and ceiling fans, direct-dial telephones, TVs, and small refrigerators. Tiled bathrooms have bidets, shower/tubs, and wall-mounted hair dryers. Robes and toiletries are supplied.

Lunches at Filao's covered open-air restaurant, adjacent to the pool deck, feature inviting selections like red snapper with sea urchin purée, conch-stuffed quail, fillet of beef with rosemary and pine nuts, and a dessert—I especially liked the chilled coconut-and-chocolate soufflé. Meals are efficiently served. Both local businesspeople and guests love the place.

Filao has no boutique but sells its attractive T-shirts, cards, and sundries in the totally redesigned, attractive reception lounge. Although boutiques and shops are never far away in St. Barts, for browsing, restaurant-hopping, and independence you'll need to rent a car, which the hotel will arrange. Shuttle transfers to and from the airport are included in the rates.

From your Filao chaise on St. Jean Beach you're the audience to a great spectacle of people-watching. It's St-Tropez in the tropics, where going topless is still in. The sun and swimming are wonderful in the pool or sea, and St. Jean Beach is a windsurfer's delight. A rental shop is adjacent to the hotel. Any water-sports activity can be arranged, and a court is provided for tennis buffs.

The pleasures of Filao are simple. You can find contentment here if you are undemanding and want to be on the beach where all the action is.

HÔTEL FILAO BEACH
P.O. Box 667
97099 St. Barthélemy Cédux,
French West Indies
TEL: (590) 27.64.84
FAX: (590) 27.62.24

U.S. RESERVATIONS
(800) 67 RELAIS

Closed September 1 to October 15.
Rates: (Rates are based on 5 French francs to U.S. $1, so they are only approximate.) Double occupancy. *December 20 to January 6* and *the month of February:* Deluxe Beachside Room, $640; Deluxe Room, $500; Superior Garden, $420. *January 7 to January 31* and *March 1 to April 5:* $350 to $560. Other times of the year: $200 to $420. Extra person, $60 per person per day, year-round. Rates include complimentary shuttle service from and to the airport, with advance notice of arrival time.
Meal plan: AP in winter (includes full American breakfast); CP in summer (includes continental breakfast).
Service charge included.
Government tax included.
Children welcome.
Credit cards accepted.

Hôtel St. Barth Isle de France

Anse des Flamands, one of the premier beaches in St. Barts, on the northwestern coast of the island, hosts a few small inexpensive, humble beachfront hideaways like White Sands Cottages; a 24-room old-timer, Hôtel Baie de Flamands, with a terrific restaurant, Le Frégate (see Recommended Restaurants); and Taïwana, a small, outrageously expensive resort at the far eastern end of the strand. Next door to Taïwana is four-year-old Hôtel St. Barth Isle de France, which, if you can snare the right room, is the best beach resort on the island.

The resort has 30 first-rate, quietly luxurious air-conditioned accommodations with patios or balconies, antique and reproduction mahogany furniture, including some four-poster beds (all king-size), with mosquito netting, sitting areas, cable TVs, stocked mini-fridges, and electric coffeemakers. Bathrooms are all tan-colored marble, and on the stark side but generous-sized, with twin basins, tubs (some with whirlpools), separate shower stalls, plus toiletries and robes. Private safes are placed in closets that provide ample space. Floors throughout are marble, which has a cooling effect but can get very slippery.

The twelve prime lodgings are the nine rooms and three suites in the main building, all beachfront. Any on the second floor are better choices for privacy as well as spectacular beach and sea views.

Isle de France's remaining rooms and suites are housed in bungalows sprinkled in back gardens across a tiny street among a virtual forest of sky-high lantanier palms. Meandering, raised boardwalks lead to private entranceways.

One of the hotel's two lovely freshwater swimming pools, the tennis court, fitness center, squash court, and a lounge with a billiards table and bar (open only in the evening), are also located in the back gardens. "In the back" has been a problem with the hotel's layout since opening day. The restaurant, originally off the pool terrace in the back gardens, wasn't where guests or visiting diners wanted to be, since the gorgeous beach has always been the chief draw anywhere on Flamands. Correcting the error, the owner built an attractive new beachside pavilion adjacent to the main building and pool and moved the boutique and its restaurant, La Case de l'Isle, here in November 1993—open only for breakfast and lunch.

We recently sampled a good, but not great, lunch at La Case de l'Isle of light salads and seafood dishes accompanied by superb crusty rolls, ending the meal with a lofty chocolate mousse cake, fruit sorbets, and a plate of well-selected cheeses. Green-and-cream-tinted French bistro tables and chairs were covered with cloths and service was agreeably tended to by a young, ponytailed French waiter. Here you'll find perfectly adequate tropical-clime sustenance in a fine spot for guests not wanting to leave the premises.

The main building, with a small reception room and front veranda, has a grand long central marbled floor hallway that leads to the rectangular swimming pool and terrace raised up over the sea. Guests have only to walk a few steps to the marvelous crescent beach, where they can laze away their days in chaises, do laps (the area in front of the hotel is protected by a reef), snorkel, jog, or build castles in the sand.

Hotel St. Barth Isle de France's director is Céline Renaud, who supervises a competent, if not overly welcoming, staff. Still, if it's a luxurious hotel you want on an excellent St. Barts beach, book into one of Isle de France's twelve beachfront accommodations.

HOTEL ST. BARTH
ISLE DE FRANCE
P.O. Box 612
97098 St. Barthélemy Cédux,
French West Indies
TEL: (590) 27.61.81
FAX: (590) 27.86.83

RESERVATIONS
Crown International Marketing
12 Route 17 North, Suite 203
Paramus, NJ 07652
TEL: (800) 628-8929 *or*
       (201) 265-5151
FAX: (201) 712-1279

Closed September 1 to November 1.
Rates: Double occupancy. *December 20 to January 6:* Rooms and Suites, $350 to $700.

January 7 to April 30: Rooms and Suites, $315 to $660. *May 1 to December 19:* Rooms and Suites, $240 to $500. Third person year-round, $70. Transfer from and to airport included.

Meal plan: CP (includes continental breakfast).
Service charge included.
Government tax: None.
Children welcome.
Credit cards accepted.

Le Toiny 🌴

On the way to the car one morning at Le Toiny, I witnessed a young woman doing graceful arabesques down the little driveway leading to her cottage. Unwittingly, she was aerobically expressing my precise sentiments. Remarkable Le Toiny has the capacity to stimulate the senses to soaring proportions. Physically, it's been intelligently designed and exquisitely decorated. Owner Michael Shen has thought of practically every amenity. The cuisine is sublime; the service professional yet personalized, headed expertly by manager Laurie Smith and assistant manager David Henderson.

Twelve-suite Le Toiny opened in October 1992 on a peaceful southeastern St. Barts hillside. Views from every 1,076-square-foot cottage (each with its own 10 × 20-foot freshwater swimming pool and quarry-tiled deck with cushioned chaises, tables and chairs) has views over a palm-tree-dotted savanna, a small salt pond, and out to a

Private pool at Le Toiny, St. Barthélemy.

shoreline and endless sea. Surfers riding the waves are distant daily entertainment. Although Le Toiny is not on the beach, several beaches, including first-rate Saline, are only minutes away. All sports are easily arranged on St. Barts. Aside from private pools and a large communal crescent-shaped one adjacent to the restaurant in the great house, the one thing Le Toiny doesn't offer is sports facilities. You'll also need a car for mobility.

Le Toiny's cluster of pale pastel wooden and stucco West Indian–style cottages with peaked mint-green corrugated roofs are scattered at various levels and angles across a sloping hill. All are air-conditioned and have ceiling fans. Plumbago, casaurina pines, palms, morning glories, hibiscus, and bougainvillea enshroud the property and each bungalow.

Interiors, inspired by plantation homes in the French Caribbean, are stylishly put together with quality appointments, including comfortable sofas and fine artwork. Fabrics on the draperies, cushions on furniture, and pillows throughout are various shades of cotton *toile de Jouy*. Chairs are reproduction plantation designs, as are the four-poster, king-size mahogany beds.

The spacious bathrooms are glorious tiled havens with step-down open showers, separate bathtubs, bidets, twin basins set in wide tiled counter space, cotton robes, an abundance of toiletries artfully displayed in enchanting boxes and straw baskets garnished with hibiscus blossoms. All elegant personalized Le Toiny toiletries and other items, like the *étui cathy*, a delicate cotton case with tiny silk ribbons covering the tissue box, can be bought in the hotel's tiny boutique. Inside the enormous walk-in closets are wall safes.

Each villa is supplied with two satellite TVs (one enclosed in an armoire in the living room, the other bedside on a stand), a VCR (a small video library is available), a stereo, telephones, and a fax machine. A *TimesFax* is delivered with breakfast in season.

Although room service is only a call away, the cottages are equipped with essentials, including a stocked mini-refrigerator with an automatic icemaker, stove, microwave oven, sink, Wedgwood and Limoges china, glassware, cutlery, and linen. Hors d'oeuvres chilling in the refrigerator and a basket of fruit await arriving guests.

It is unlikely, however, that many guests will be doing much cooking. Le Gaïac, under the direction of twenty-eight-year-old Jean Christophe Perrin, formerly with Mas d'Artigny, Michel Rostang, and Troisgros in France, excels. Lunch in the poolside, quietly refined restaurant includes such choices as a spectacular lobster salad composed of medallions of local lobster, slices of chicken sausage, thin strips of smoked salmon, grapefruit and orange sections surrounded by endive spears filled with couscous. Also extraordinary is the *crépinette fondante de poisson des îles au colombo*, celestial seafood-stuffed crêpes with a curry sauce. Dinners are wondrous selections like pâté of pigeon with seasoned fruits, pan-fried duck breast slices with fennel sauce served with a purée of sweet potato, and an assortment of desserts from a sublime hot banana tart with crème de menthe to coconut follies or a soursop soufflé.

The restaurant, in the great house at a circular driveway near the entranceway, connects to a wood-paneled bar and small lounge that leads up a few steps to the reception area and boutique.

I found Le Toiny flawless. If it were on the beach, it would deserve a place on the Top

Ten Super-Luxury Resort list—a beachside location is a prerequisite. So Le Toiny is awarded the next best, a "Palm Tree," for being one of the Caribbean's Top Ten Special Hideaways.

LE TOINY
Anse de Toiny
97133 St. Barthélemy Cédux,
French West Indies
TEL: (590) 27.88.88
FAX: (590) 27.89.30

RESERVATIONS
WIMCO
P.O. Box 1461
Newport, RI 02840
TEL: (800) 932-3222 *or*
(401) 849-8012
FAX: (401) 847-6290

Closed from the end of the first week in September to the end of October.
Rates: Double occupancy. *October 29 to December 16:* Villa Suite, $400. *December 17 to April 17:* Villa Suite, $720. *April 18 to September 6:* Villa Suite, $450. Third person in room, $90 per night year-round. Rates include transportation from and to airport.
Meal plan: CP (includes continental breakfast).
Service charge included.
Government tax included.
Children welcome.
Credit cards accepted.

Sibarth

Brook and Roger Lacour's Sibarth Real Estate is the largest villa rental agency on St. Barts. Totally familiar with each accommodation, they book over 150 properties for everyone from first-timers to repeat celebrities. Villas and apartments are located on all areas of the island, ranging from practical housing in a beachside apartment to ultra-luxurious living in a trilevel villa sprawling across the top of a hillside. Villas and apartments have from one to four bedrooms, most with pools and magnificent views. Villa or apartment living in St. Barts is easily managed for travelers by the Lacours, and suits the independent. Household help come regularly in most cases. Cars are essential. Either Sibarth or Wimco can arrange for cars, baby-sitters, or cooks.

Those interested in a rental villa or apartment should consider purchasing a copy of the latest edition of St. Barthélemy's *Vendôme Guide*. It's a thick, glossy magazine containing color photographs and particulars of many of the island's rentals, accompanied by a rate sheet and map pinpointing locations of all properties with one-line descriptions. For information about obtaining a copy, contact WIMCO (West Indies Management Company) at the toll-free number given below.

The Lacours' La Calèche Yacht Charter Agency can also arrange half- or whole-day boat charters, including a special sail around St. Barts, an excursion to neighboring islands, or a snorkeling safari. (Same phone number as Sibarth's.)

SIBARTH	**RESERVATIONS**
P.O. Box 55	U.S. Representative
Gustavia	WIMCO
97133 St. Barthélemy Cédux,	P.O. Box 1461
French West Indies	Newport, RI 02840
TEL: (590) 27.62.38	TEL: (800) 932-3222 *or*
FAX: (590) 27.60.52	(401) 849-8012
	FAX: (401) 847-6290

Note: Weekly rates range from $1,000 for a 1-bedroom apartment to $9,000 for a 4-bed-room villa in winter. Summer rates are substantially less. Information and rates upon request.

A NOTEWORTHY OPTION

Tropical Hotel

Tropical Hotel, snuggled into a lower hillside of St-Jean, is a good choice for travelers who want an affordable, pleasant hideaway on St. Barts. This unassuming 20-room hotel lies only 40 yards from beautiful, lengthy St. Jean Beach. The hotel's location is also ideal for shopping in Villa Créole and for restaurant-hopping to the many informal dining spots in the area. A car is not necessary, and transportation from and to the airport is provided if requested in advance.

Tropical's neat little rooms, in one-story fretwork-trimmed cottages, are strung around a garden. Nine rooms have sea views; the remaining eleven, garden views. Seaview rooms are reserved first, so book as far in advance as you can. Mind you, the views aren't a wide-open ocean panorama, but any one of the small patios is a peaceful retreat surrounded by tropical shrubbery. A small road at the hotel's entrance leads up a steep hill, so there are motor sounds.

As for the accommodations, expect charming little nests recently redecorated with white rattan furniture. Painted white wooden headboards on the twin or king-size beds sprout carved pineapples at the top. Mosquito netting hangs overhead. Rooms have tile floors, air-conditioning and ceiling fans, direct-dial phones, TVs, and radios. Light is sufficient, and as small as the bathrooms are they include a basin vanity, hair dryer, toilet, bidet, and tiled shower stall. Minimal closet space, shelves, and a mini-refrigerators are tucked away behind white doors.

Tropical's small, rectangular freshwater pool is framed by a quarry-tiled deck lined with chaises. Breakfasts and light meals are served throughout the day on the adjoining covered terrace or inside a spacious lounge area, the center of which is a redbrick-and-wood square bar.

Marithé Weber manages the hotel with care and concern for all her guests. Water sports, deep-sea fishing, and excursions are no problem to arrange. Tropical offers just the right quotient of creature comforts for unfussy guests.

TROPICAL HOTEL
P.O. Box 147
97133 St. Barthélemy Cédux,
French West Indies
TEL: (590) 27.64.87
FAX: (590) 27.81.74

Closed June 1 to August 1.
Rates: Double occupancy. *December 22 to January 4:* Ocean View, $260; Garden View, $240; extra bed, $55. *January 5 to April 20:* Ocean View, $230; Garden View, $160; extra bed, $55. *April 21 to December 21:* Ocean View, $145; Garden View, $95; extra bed, $55.
Meal plan: CP (includes continental breakfast).
Service charge: None.
Government Tax: None.
Children welcome.
Credit cards accepted.
Note: Special summer packages available March 1 to December 21.

Recommended Restaurants

ST. BARTS' BEST*

* **Le Gaïac**, 27.88.88 (Anse de Toiny, Hôtel Le Toiny). Jean Christophe Perrin's masterful creations are a must for serious diners. The elegant dining room overlooks the pool terrace on a bucolic hillside out to the sea. (see resort listing). Expensive to very expensive.

* **La Tocque Lyonnaise**, 27.64.80 (El Sereno Beach Hotel, Grand Cul-de-Sac). Select a Gourmande, Menu Dégustation, or an à la carte menu exquisitely executed. Very expensive.

* **Castelets**, 27.61.73 (Lurin hillside on road leading to Gouverneur Beach). Two new young French chefs (as yet untried by me) reign here—the reports I have received are excellent. Expensive to very expensive.

* **Maya's**, 27.73.61 (beachfront between Gustavia and Corossol). Créole and seafood

dishes are excellent at this casual, trendy, cheerful restaurant. Background music doesn't interfere. Expensive.

* **Lafayette Club**, 27.62.51 (Grand Cul-de-Sac). Lunch is served on covered terrace or at tables set right on the beach. The fresh grilled fish and salads are especially recommended. Models show fashions during meals. Be prepared: Very expensive.

* **La Frégate**, 27.66.51 (Hotel Baie des Flamands). Jean-Pierre Crouzet from Le Sapotillier has moved here and turned this terrace (preferred) and indoor restaurant into a major contender for lunch and dinner. Superb seafood dishes and spectacular desserts. Moderate to expensive.

* **Carl Gustaf**, 27.82.83 (Hôtel Carl Gustaf). A beautiful dining room with an exquisite view of the harbor serves excellent fare (see hotel listing). Expensive.

* **Le Tamarin**, 27.72.12 (Grande Saline). Catherine Cent and her eccentric macaw, Cooky, will charm you in this rustic, countryside setting. A favorite. The food is superb. The roquefort flan with figs and the grilled yellowtail served with plantain preserves and mashed sweet potatoes are our favorites. Desserts include addictive crème brûlée and double chocolate tart cake. Linger over lunch sipping a chilled rosé. Hammocks hanging under a giant tamarind tree await satiated customers. Expensive.

OTHER DEPENDABLE CHOICES

Marigot Bay Club, 27.75.45 (beachside Marigot). An old friend who spent several years in St. Thomas, St. Barts–born Michel Ledee has had a success on his hands for several years now. His casual seaside restaurant serves wonderful fresh seafood, including lobster, crayfish, and Créole dishes. It's just the kind of relaxing spot travelers look for in the Caribbean. Bring along bathing suits and towels if you go for lunch. Moderate to expensive.

La Banane, 27.68.25 (Lorient). Jean-Marie Rivière serves commendable French food, then joins in the restaurant's cabaret at dinner's end. An amusing evening. Also has a small hotel. Moderate to expensive.

La Marine, 27.68.91 (Gustavia, west side of harbor). This is an unpretentious café serving fresh seafood on the waterfront. On Thursday night, order steamed mussels, pomme frites, and wine. Moderate.

Topolino, 27.70.92 (St. Jean). Lunch and dinner are served in this garden restaurant with pool for guests' use. Favorite with families dining out on barbecued foods, homemade pastas, pizzas, and seafood. Moderate.

Hôtel Filao Beach, 27.64.84 (St-Jean). *Emince de saumon cru au citron vert,* grilled lobster, entrecôte, or a simple ham sandwich and salad are possibilities in this friendly beachside restaurant. See hotel listing, page 255. Moderate to expensive.

New Born, 27.67.07 (Flamands). Créole specialties and seafood can be sampled in this laid-back garden setting. Moderate.

La Crêperie, 27.84.07 (Gustavia). Delicious crêpes, snacks, and ice creams are featured here. Inexpensive.

Pasta Paradise, 27.80.78 (rue du Roi Oscar). Italian fare from carpaccio to homemade pasta with innovative and traditional sauces is dished up here. Moderate. There are many more restaurants worth seeking out. Among the best are **Bartolomeo** and **L'Indigo restaurants** at Guanahani, **Le Sapotillier, L'Entrecot, Eddy's Ghetto, Hôtel Eden Rock, L'Iguane, Chez Jo Jo, L'Entr'act, Le Bistrot des Arts, Chez Francine, L'Orchidée** (at Christopher Hotel), **Le Steak House, La Crémaillère, La Gloriette, Restaurant Saigon, Les Lauriers, La Case de l'Isle, La Luna, Taïwana,** and **Giacomo's.** Also useful is **Santa Fe** for hamburgers and snacks at hillside turnoff leading to Gouverneur Beach. Just down from Santa Fe is the hot new disco **Why Not.** Another disco is **Le Petit Club** in Gustavia.

Popular bars are **Le Bar de l'Oubli** and **Le Sélect** (the charm of this run-down joint has always escaped me) in central Gustavia and **S.O.S. Chez Ginette** close to Anse des Cayes.

Recommended Shopping

There are three main shopping areas in St. Barts: **La Villa Créole** and **Galerie du Commerce** shopping centers in St-Jean, and a shopping complex adjacent to it by the **Sodexa** market; **La Savane Center** across from the airport; and throughout the streets of Gustavia. Many fine shops and boutiques are in a mall here called **Le Carré d'Or.** Some resorts and hotels, such as Guanahani, have small boutiques, and there are art galleries and shops in other locations on the island.

In French St. Barts there's plenty of high-quality merchandise, particularly clothing and jewelry, and regular T-shirt shops. It will only take a morning or afternoon to visit the major shopping centers.

Special shops are:

Jean-Yves Froment, 27.61.72 (Colombier). Original tropical ceramics, tiles, murals, and fashions hand-blocked on soft cottons. Hummingbirds and island fauna are featured here.

The New Art Studio (Corossol). Paintings on silk and cotton.

La Galerie 20, 27.68.22 (Villa Créole, St-Jean). Marie-Christine Toussaint's latest paintings, as well as those of other local artists.

Papaguyo, 27.78.04 (rue du Général-de-Gaulle). You'll find Haitian arts and crafts, T-shirts, and paintings here. It's a great shop to visit with kids.

Stéphane and **Bernard,** 27.65.69 and 27.69.13 (Gustavia and La Savane across from the airport). These two fine fashion boutiques carry Sonia Rykiel, Kenzo, Escada, and Ungaro, plus jewelry, accessories, and more. Ask for Diane Young's assistance in La Savane shop.

Loulou's Marine, 27.62.74 (rue de la République, Gustavia). Nautical supplies, gear, and resortwear; insiders purchase Loulou's famous personalized canvas tote bags, which for some reason have become a worldwide status symbol. Interesting collection of books as well.

Souleiado, 27.69.46 (rue de Général-de-Gaulle). Fabulous French Provincial repeat print and other designs in cotton fabrics by the yard or turned into bags, tablecloths, placemats, napkins, and so on are featured here. Fabulous prices.
Diamond Genesis, 27.66.94 (rue du Roi Oscar II). Designer jewelry and watches.
Kornérupine in Villa Créole features same designer, Dominique Elie. Beautiful baubles, especially contemporary charm bracelets and necklaces.

Other fine shopping at **Gianni Versace, Manuel Canovas, Black Swan, Blue Marine, Hermès, Cartier, Gucci, Little Switzerland, Oro del Sol, Carat**, and **Privilège**. Also look for **Fabyshoes, KoKonuts, Sophie Laurent, Libertine, Peace and Love, Java, Hookipa**, and the **Pati de Saint Barth Tee-Shirt Factory**, 150 yards past L'Escale restaurant by the port.

For locally made, delicately hand-woven straw hats, clutch purses, baskets, and other products, go to the **Corossol** beachfront and weavers will appear with their wares.

Provisions for Your Island Pantry

Match 27.68.16 (across the street from the airport). Excellent large supermarket with a selection of French and U.S. imports, meat, seafood, produce, staples, household supplies, and wines and liquor.
Alain Magras, 27.60.09 (Gustavia Harbor). Supermarket with a bakery, a French deli carrying pâtés, cheeses, prepared foods, as well as fresh produce and staples.
Unic Plus, 27.71.98 (across from the airport at Les Galeries du Commerce). Useful general supermarket that also carries prepared take-out dishes. Open seven days a week from 8 A.M. to 8 P.M.
La Rôtisserie, 27.63.13 or 27.73.46 (in Gustavia on rue du Roi Oscar, at St. Jean's Villa Créole and in Pointe Milou). Roast chickens, quiche, pâtés, salads, imported Fauchon products, tinned delicacies, breads and pastries are the specialties. Reliable and very good.
Carambole, 27.90.05 (on rue Jeanne d'Arc at rue du Centenaire, Gustavia). Shop for excellent baguettes and pastries here.
Stalactite Pâtisserie, 27.78.61 (across from airport). Wonderful croissants (plain or chocolate), French bread, special snacks, and fresh fruit sorbet.
Anna Banana, (rue de Roi Oscar). Go to this tiny little streetside ice-cream parlor for Häagen-Dazs, frozen yogurt, and homemade sorbets.
Régal Glace (St-Jean, Villa Créole). Little hole-in-the-wall scooping up delicious ice creams and sorbets.
Cuisine de Michel, 27.90.47 (Grand Fond Road). A great find, this oceanside place prepares wonderful French take-out food—*blanquette de veau, coq au vin*, and *tarte tatin*. Mostly French traditional foods are featured, but great thin-crusted pizzas are also available. The blackboard menu changes daily and food disappears quickly.
For fine French wines try Daniel Passeri's **Grands Vins de France**, 27.77.44, in new

266 ST. BARTHÉLEMY

quarters on rue du Roi Oscar. Vieux rhums and port are available, as well as wine accessories—lovely decanters, corkscrews, and so on.

La Cave, 27.63.21 (Marigot). Excellent vintage wines, tinned foie gras, pâtés, cigars, and some local produce, which usually includes fresh herbs. sometimes tomatoes are available in this well-known establishment.

Useful Information

St. Barth Magazine, Tropical St. Barth, Le Journal de St. Barth and *Ti Gourmet Saint Barth* are free publications that are widely distributed throughout the island and packed with information.

Car rental agencies include **Henri Greaux's Hertz,** (590) 27.60.21 or 27.71.14; **Turbe Car Rental,** (590) 27.71.42; and **Europcar's Caraïbes Car Service,** (590) 27.73.33.

There are two taxi stands on St. Barts—one at the airport and the other in Gustavia in front of Loulou's Marine.

Ferry service to St. Maarten on **St. Barth Express,** departing from Gustavia's dock, is a little over an hour one-way journey. For reservations call (590) 27.77.24.

Richard Photo, 27.68.97 (quai de la République, Gustavia), is the source for film and one-hour photo processing.

Colombier Beach is accessible only by boat or a half-hour climb over hill and dale, along and through rugged cliff boulders. The hike begins at the end of Flamands Beach road. Take a picnic lunch and beverages, as there's nothing at the beach except a spectacular wide boulevard of sand. David Rockefeller's estate is perched at the southern end of the beach.

Librairie Barnes, 27.71.55 (rue du Général-de-Gaulle, Gustavia), carries stateside and international newspapers, Caribbean books focusing on the French islands, and stationery supplies.

ST. KITTS

ACCOMMODATIONS

ST. KITTS' BEST
The Golden Lemon Inn and Villas
Ottley's Plantation Inn
Rawlins Plantation 🌴
The White House

A NOTEWORTHY OPTION
Palms Hotel

RECOMMENDED RESTAURANTS

RECOMMENDED SHOPPING

USEFUL INFORMATION

≈ ≈

Accommodations

ST. KITTS' BEST

The Golden Lemon Inn and Villas

The Golden Lemon is Arthur Leaman's love letter to St. Kitts. This charming, intimate inn has eight uniquely furnished rooms in the great house (all highly recommended), a reconverted 17th-century storehouse, six spectacular contemporary condominium apartments with private pools in an adjacent building, The Lemon Court, and, The Lemon Grove, where 10 condominiums with private pools on the palm-columned, black sand beach nearby. One (unlighted) hard-surface tennis court is located there.

Let me say at the outset that The Golden Lemon is not for everyone. It is not an isolated exclusive hotel on a private beach. The black sand beach few steps away is public, and might include strolling cows.

The hotel sits on a cul-de-sac at the end of a narrow street in the small village of Dieppe Bay. As you check in, you may see children holding donkey races gallop past the stone-walled entrance gate, Arthur Leaman watching them with smiling approval, as he welcomes you. He believes that St. Kitts is the hotel's greatest asset, and he wants visitors and guests to discover St. Kittitians and appreciate the natural beauty of the island. That natural beauty includes 3,792-foot Mount Liamuiga nearby.

Non-guests are welcome for lunch and dinner with reservations, but children under 18 are never permitted as guests in the hotel. The island ambassador/proprietor's rules are a formula that best suits him and makes the hotel "work," for he sincerely wants guests to enjoy their holiday, and he wants to enjoy his guests' company in return.

All the rooms' elegantly casual interiors are assembled with the eye of an expert. Mr. Leaman, a former *House & Garden* decorating editor, has combined antiques with contemporary pieces of furniture, enlivened with vibrantly colored fabrics, imported bric-a-brac, and Caribbean paintings and handcrafts, all set against stark white or pastel-painted walls, geometric stained-glass windows, and plants and bouquets of flowers everywhere.

The bathrooms (all with showers) are good-sized, fluffy towels are plentiful, have hair dryers, and the water is always very hot. Each bathroom style and layout is intriguingly different. There are ceiling fans, but no phones, TVs, or radios.

My favorite accommodation is in Lemon Court 6, a two-bedroom, two-bath duplex (one bedroom and bath upstairs, the others on the first floor) with a cathedral-ceiling living/dining room and full kitchen. From the arched doorway of the dining area you literally take just one step down into a small swimming pool. A living room door leads to the pool's terrace area, which is furnished with yellow-cushioned chaise longues and table and chairs, facing northeast, fronted with an embankment of rocks and accompanied by sounds of crashing waves. The islands of Saba and St. Eustatius appear in the distance. The terrace area is enclosed by a natural wall of lush papaya, banana, breadfruit, and soursop trees, sea grape, fragrant frangipani, bougainvillea, and fauna—a delightful place for breakfast every morning. Every apartment in the Lemon Court and all rooms in the Great House are lovely.

On a recent visit, Arthur Leaman was searching for a new chef, so I can't report on the food. However, knowing his good taste, he's sure to find a skilled replacement for the season. In the past, the food at The Golden Lemon has always been quite good.

Tea is served at 5 P.M. in the interior garden patio near the raised freshwater swimming pool and surrounding arboretum.

Dinner in the antique-filled main dining room lit by candlelight is served from 7:30, with most of the guests gathering on the veranda or in the bar around 7 P.M. Everyone grouped together on the nights we were there, exchanging stories of the day's adventures and gossiping with our host. The lounge has been moved to a chaired and banquetted area across from the dining room.

The old bar terrace and inside room were transformed into The Golden Lemon's excellent shop, A Slice of Lemon, carrying everything from resortwear, handcrafts, and pieces of antique silver, to ceramics and sundries.

The separate building that once housed A Slice of Lemon at the entranceway to the hotel is now The Lemon Library for the local children, thanks to Mr. Leaman.

At Golden Lemon, you'll hear morning rooster crows and an occasional yipping dog. But that's the idea. Come here to experience St. Kitts and one of the Caribbean's most celebrated inns.

**THE GOLDEN LEMON
INN AND VILLAS**
Dieppe Bay
St. Kitts, West Indies
TEL: (809) 465-7260
FAX: (809) 465-4019

RESERVATIONS
Caribbean Inns, Ltd.
P.O. Box 7411
Hilton Head Island, SC 29938
TEL: (800) 633-7411 *or*
(803) 785-7411
FAX: (803) 686-7411

Open all year.
Rates: Double occupancy. *December 16 to April 15:* Great House Deluxe Rooms, $350; Lemon Court and Lemon Grove Villas, including Seaside Deluxe Room, Mountain View Studio and One-Bedroom Apartments with Pools, and Seaside One- and Two-Bedroom Apartments with Pools, $380 to $865. *April 16 to December 15:*

Great House Deluxe Rooms, $280; Villa Apartments, $310 to $700. Extra person, $85 per person per day year-round.
Meal plan: MAP (includes breakfast, afternoon tea, and dinner).
Service charge: 10%.
Government tax: 7%.
Children under 18 not permitted.
Credit cards accepted.
Note: Special plans and rates are available for villas on long-term rentals.

Ottley's Plantation Inn

My husband and I don't always agree on my hotel and resort appraisals. We often end up agreeing to differ. I know in advance that he always prefers seaside living with water-sports facilities, so if I'm smitten with a inland hotel, I begin mentally preparing my case in favor of it. This was not necessary at Ottley's Plantation Inn. We both fell in love with the place, so much so that we immediately talked about returning for a real holiday here—a time together when the sole purpose of the visit wasn't research.

Ottley was the family name of the English owners of the sugar plantation that thrived on the 35-acre property 300 years ago. The inn is a 15-minute drive to the north from St. Kitts Golden Rock Airport on the windward coast road. As we drove up the winding, bumpy road leading to the estate, we encountered a braying donkey and rich fertile land with fields of sugarcane, mango and bushy banana trees, and sweet potatoes and peas. As we approached the inn, our taxi driver that first time told us that Ottley's new owners had added a second floor to the Great House. You'd never guess it from the perfect symmetry of the stately white house trimmed with bright yellow shutters, Brazilian green heart louvered windows and doors, and topped with a massive shingled peaked roof. Sweeping verandas encircle both floors of the Great House.

Some years back, Art and Ruth Keusch, bookstore owners from New Jersey (Titles Unlimited) who'd been vacationing in St. Kitts for years, learned that the plantation was for sale, made inquiries, and before they knew it they were out of the book business and owners, along with their daughter and son-in-law, Nancy and Marty Lowell, of a plantation. After several months of planning, it took about a year of hard work and dedication and considerable dollars to reconstruct and renovate. Not surprisingly, the 15-room inn opened to quiet raves in 1989. The once-neophyte innkeepers are pleased that the incubation period is over.

Arriving guests pass through columns of majestic, royal palms lining the road leading to the inn. As we climbed out of the van, the sweet smell of fresh-cut grass greeted us. Congenial Marty Lowell showed us to our room, number 6, the most outstanding accommodation in the house. It's a second-floor front room with mountain and full sea views, overlooking the expansive, well-tended garden grounds. The spectacular panorama includes giant Norfolk pines and a flamboyant tree adjacent to the 66 × 22-foot spring-fed swimming pool with a vast terrace of red interlocked paving stone, chock-full of chaise longues, tables, and chairs, that connects to the bar and open-air restaurant, all set in the preserved sugar mill ruins 50 yards or so below the Great House.

Six rooms are located upstairs and three down in the Great House. The other six lodgings are found in neighboring stone cottages. Every one is delightfully decorated with antique pieces or quality white rattan. Our enormous room, with white-painted wooden-plank floors, walls, and high, beamed ceiling, proved to be a most comfortable living space. Two queen-size beds were covered with thick bedcovers of blue and red tropical fronds, flowers, and parrots, with blue-and-white-striped dust ruffles. Closet space is ample, and rattan chairs with a table, bureau, floral island prints, and vases filled with lobster claw, croton, and green leaves enlivened the room. Rooms have telephones, air-conditioning, and ceiling fans. No mini-bar or TV in the rooms, but room service is available and there's a TV with a VCR in a small library nook off the Great House's first-floor living room. The well-lit bathroom has a separate vanity and basin area with an adjoining large room for the tub, shower, and toilet that has floors of black and white tiles. Complimentary toiletries are English imports.

Days are spent strolling the lawns and inspecting the rain forest trails, swimming laps in the pool, sunning, reading, or touring the island by car; you'll need one. The inn does provide transportation to and from Frigate or Friar's Beach each day. And, for those interested, an orientation briefing on St. Kitts and the hotel is offered. Sports facilities, including golf and tennis, can easily be arranged.

Meals are under the supervision of Pamela Hope Yahn, a Culinary Institute graduate from Massachusetts. She works with imported foods from the States and fresh vegetables, including lettuces, squash, and tomatoes, and fresh herbs that are grown in the plantation's own garden. Soursop, mangoes, papayas, bananas, coconuts, and other tropical delights are picked right on the grounds. Not only is the food quite good, it's also beautifully presented. Our crisp, succulent coconut shrimp arrived in a fresh coconut shell on a plate garnished with magenta bougainvillea and tiny speckled croton leaves. The accompanying sauce was a tangy mixture of orange marmalade and horseradish. Main courses of pasta with seafood sauce, including chunks of lobster, and a pork tenderloin sauté with side dishes of rice timbales and fresh yellow squash, served with herbed bread and with butter sculpted into roses, were first-rate.

Because Ottley's restaurant welcomes outsiders, on certain evenings groups of travelers from Four Seasons Resort in Nevis arrive for special dinners. We just missed one of those evenings, but it's so tranquil at the inn, the activity would probably provide a welcome change.

Chirping birds woke us in the morning, and after a delicious fresh fruit platter, coffee and tea, we really hated the thought of having to pack and leave.

OTTLEY'S PLANTATION INN
P.O. Box 245, Basseterre
St. Kitts, West Indies
TEL: (809) 465-7234
FAX: (809) 465-4760

Closed September.
Rates: Double occupancy. *December 15 to April 15:* Rooms, $300 to $350; Two-Room Cottage $385. *April 16 to December 14:* Rooms, $240 to $255; Two-Room Cottage, $285. Rates for Gatekeeper's Cottage upon request.
Meal plan: MAP, (includes breakfast and dinner), except in Gatekeeper's Cottage, where both EP or MAP rates are available year-round.
Service charge: 10%.
Government tax: 7%.
Children under 10 discouraged.
Credit cards accepted.

Rawlins Plantation

After about a thirty-minute 15-mile drive from Golden Rock Airport to St. Kitts' northwest side near Dieppe Bay, you'll turn down a bumpy, sugarcane swathed dirt road. A few turns on the trail and a couple of minutes later, you will encounter emerald-green lawns, bushy crotons, and majestic breadfruit and African tulip trees. What you see is not an illusion—it's Rawlins Plantation, a one-time sugar estate that is the Caribbean's finest small English countryside inn. Finest because it is impeccably run by Paul and Claire Rawson, the owner/managers, and their small, loyal staff. The public and private rooms are immaculate, homelike, and welcoming. Brilliantly colored flowers that flourish on the immediate property also fill vases and seashells and decorate the dining tables everywhere. The food at Rawlins, some of which is grown in the inn's own gardens, is outstanding for its simplicity, presentation, and flavor.

When you arrive at the inn you immediately gain a sense of peace, as if all were right with the world. The atmosphere is serene and pastoral, yet the setting is quite dramatic. Not far behind the hotel to the south is 3,792-foot Mount Liamuiga. Intrepid climbers can ascend to the lip of the crater at about 2,600 feet. Off in the distance to the northwest are the islands of St. Eustatius and Saba.

The first thing you might want to do after checking into the plantation house, cottages, or sugar mill, is to adjourn to the veranda of the house to enjoy a glass of the hotel's special rum punch, the best I've had in the Caribbean. It's made with fresh orange juice, rum, and fresh grated nutmeg, plus secret ingredients.

When you stay in one of the 10 delightful rooms at Rawlins, you become temporary beneficiaries of part of the legacy left to Philip Walwyn by his English ancestors, who took title to the plantation in 1790. Although the original main house burned down, in 1970 it was replaced, along with some new buildings, and carefully designed to blend into the plantation's ruins, including the old molasses boiling house, stone sugar mill, and smokestack. The round mill is an enchanting two-story lovenest that is often used as a honeymoon suite. The bridal bed is upstairs.

Rawlins Plantation is 25 splendid sloping acres of pastures and meticulously tended tropical gardens with a croquet court and grass tennis court. The inn's swimming pool is fed by the Rawlins' own mountain stream and sits in the ground a few steps below

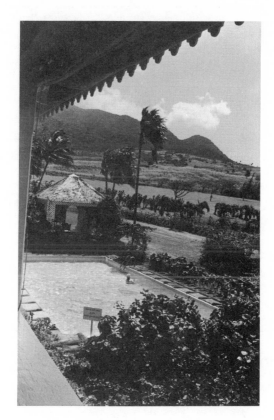

Rawlins Plantation on St. Kitts.

a latticed, shingle-roofed gazebo and the stone tower smoke stack. Adjacent to the pool is the plantation house's raised gallery and bar, along with the living room lounges, including a significant library, some guest quarters, and the indoor and open-air dining rooms. The entire hotel is furnished with antique mahogany pieces mixed with Caribbean, chintzed rattan, and wrought iron. Baths are showers or tubs, small and just fine. Amenities here include toiletries and hair dryers.

Rawlins has no TVs, radios, or telephones. Paddle fans and fresh air are the only necessary cooling elements here at 350 feet above sea level.

Rawlins' guests, many of whom have been annual visitors for years, are for the most part upper-class English, Canadians, and Americans of all ages. It's essential that you like the quiet life to be happy at Rawlins.

Service at the inn is exemplary and meals are prepared with doting care. Lunches are West Indian buffets with a selection from fried fillets of flying fish, Rawlins' special rice,

274 | ST. KITTS

and candied sweet potatoes with raisins and nuts to coconut meringue pie. Guests preferring lighter fare are accommodated with delicious salads or sandwiches. Whatever you choose, you're served on the alfresco terrace overlooking the pool and lawns. Dinners are more formal candlelit affairs, romantically exquisite, especially if there's a moon. You'll dine privately or with other guests (it's your decision) on local specialties such as red pepper and marjoram soup, breast of duck with passion fruit sauce, fresh local vegetables, and bananas in pastry with a sour orange sauce.

Adjacent to Rawlins, in the restored Mount Pleasant House, is The Plantation Picture Gallery, where Kate Spencer's superb oil and watercolors are displayed (see Recommended Shopping).

Conversation is the main form of entertainment. Bring along the books you've been wanting to read, a diary in need of updating, walking shoes, a bathing suit or two, and casual elegant clothing for the evening. Be prepared to be independent but well looked after.

RAWLINS PLANTATION	RESERVATIONS
P.O. Box 340,	J. D. B. Associates
St. Kitts, West Indies	P.O. Box 16086
TEL: (809) 465-6221	Alexandria, VA 22302
FAX: (809) 465-4954	TEL: (800) 346-5358
	FAX: (703) 548-5825

Open all year.
Rates: Double occupancy. *December 15 to April 15:* Rooms, $375. *April 16 to December 14:* Rooms, $245.
Meal plan: MAP (includes breakfast, afternoon tea, and dinner).
Service charge: 10%.
Government tax: 7%.
Children welcome.
Credit cards not accepted.

The White House

The White House, a restored 250-year-old great house and stone cottage compound set in the foothills above Basseterre, St. Kitts' capital, made its debut in January 1990. When we arrived at the inn, we were held at bay at the front gate entrance by four large, friendly but barking boxers. Janice Barber, owner/manager of the inn, along with her husband, Malcolm, originally from a tiny village outside of Cambridge, England, came bouncing down the lawn to greet us. Aside from occasional barking, the knocks of croquet mallets, and tennis balls being batted back and forth on the grass court, The White House is a blissfully quiet retreat, although en route to the inn, you'll pass through a growing local community.

Guests at The White House are overwhelmingly English, and have flown a long way to St. Kitts to enjoy the inn's serene and pastoral setting, quality lodgings and food, amiable service, and to soak up the island's almost constant daily sunshine. Most come for a two-week holiday.

The White House has eight accommodations. Four are located in a two-story converted carriage house; the rest in small stone cottages nearby. All rooms have been carefully and tastefully renovated and updated with modern conveniences like the super, tiled step-up and down tub/showers with brass towel racks, faucets, and spigots. Natural stone walls, as well as antique vanities, bureaus, fainting sofas, end tables, and four-poster beds covered with Chinese embroidered white coverlets and piles of pillows, decorate some of the rooms. Mosquito nets hang over beds, and ceiling fans stir up breezes. There are no telephones or TVs. Hairdryers are supplied in each room, and lighting is good. Every room has a private balcony. The second-floor rooms of the Carriage House would be my choice for views.

Outdoors, the spacious, well-groomed grounds and gardens are cloaked with everything from tall palm trees, hibiscus, bougainvillea, allamanda, and croton to oleander, asparagus, and other ferns and leafy greenery. The lovely Roman-style pool, surrounded by a quarry-tiled terrace, is set off from the rooms and public areas in a private section of lawn enclosed behind a white picket fence. The dogs aren't allowed inside.

Lounging areas are an outdoor, wicker-filled porch and the handsome, antique-filled great-house living room. Breakfasts and buffet lunches are taken in a newly designed, cheerful open-air gallery or in one of the two formal dining rooms inside the great house. Tables are beautifully set. Just where Mrs. Barber decides to serve the candlelit dinners depends on the weather and number of guests. (Outsiders are welcome strictly by reservation.) If there are only eight for dinner, it's likely everyone will dine at one table in the great-house main dining room.

Food at The White House consists of a changing array of interesting first courses, soups, salads, and good fish and meat entrées, accompanied by fresh island vegetables. Desserts offered are daily pastries and rich, tropical-flavored ice creams.

The Barbers or their helpful staff will happily organize any activity. The inn provides daily transportation to local beaches and Basseterre for shopping, but a car really is necessary here.

THE WHITE HOUSE
P.O. Box 436, St. Peters,
St. Kitts, West Indies
TEL: (809) 465-8126
FAX: (809) 465-8275

RESERVATIONS
Clayton Thomas
P.O. Box 800
Waccabuc, NY 10597
TEL: (800) 223-1108
FAX: (914) 763-5362

Closed July and August.
Rates: *December 15 to April 14:* Double, $350; Single, $250. *April 15 to December 14:*

Double, $250; Single, $150. Also included are transfers from and to airport, and daily transportation service to beaches and shopping.
Meal plan: MAP (includes breakfast, afternoon tea, and dinner).
Service charge: 10%.
Government tax: 7%.
Children: Not appropriate until independent age.
Credit cards accepted.

A NOTEWORTHY OPTION

Palms Hotel

I'm including Palms Hotel, open since September 1993, because for as little as $85 for two in season, a perfectly decent hotel room can be booked right in the heart of Basseterre at The Circus.

Intended for business travelers, the Palms Hotel happily welcomes vacationers to its friendly second-floor hotel.

The Palms' eight carpeted accommodations include five rooms called junior suites; the remaining are one- and two-bedroom suites. All are on the small side, with new but conventional hotel furnishings. Lodgings have air-conditioning, modern standard bathrooms, mini-refrigerators, direct-dial phones, 24-channel cable TV with VCR facilities (the desk has literally hundreds of films to rent), electric coffeemakers, and daily laundry service.

Ferguson's Bar (formerly the popular Shorty's), across the balcony from reception, rests on an alfresco terrace with open views of the action below. Conveniently, the taxi stand is on the street near the entrance to the hotel. Guests can grab a cab any time of the day for a tour of the island or a trip to one of St. Kitts' lovely southern beaches for the day (see Useful Information).

At Palms you're also within walking distance of a variety of restaurants, shops, and the ferry dock, where you can book passage to Nevis—an excursion I highly recommend.

There's no restaurant at the hotel, but once you've brewed your morning tea or coffee, you can walk down the steps to any number of local cafés for breakfast. The Palms Hotel is clearly not for everyone, but it's a bargain hunter's find.

PALMS HOTEL
P.O. Box 64, The Circus
Basseterre
St. Kitts, West Indies
TEL: (809) 465-0800
FAX: (809) 465-5889

Open all year.
Rates: Double occupancy. *December 16 to April 15:* Junior Suites, $85; One-Bedroom

Suites, $105; Two-Bedroom Suites: $150. *April 16 to December 15:* Junior Suites, $75; One-Bedroom Suites, $88; Two-Bedroom Suites, $110. Extra person, $15 per person per day year-round.
Meal plan: EP.
Service charge: 10%.
Government tax: 7%.
Children: Not recommended until independent age.
Credit cards accepted.

Recommended Restaurants

ST. KITTS' FINEST*

* **The Golden Lemon**, 465-7260 (Dieppe Bay). Island/Continental cuisine. Lunch on the veranda or dine after dark in candlelight in the elegantly appointed formal dining room. Moderate to expensive.

* **Rawlins Plantation**, 465-6221 (near Dieppe off Northern Coast Road). At the foothills of Mt. Liamuiga, lunch on a delicious West Indian buffet in a gracious terrace dining room overlooking pool and beautiful plantation grounds. Dinners are deliciously romantic candlelit affairs. Moderate to expensive.

* **The Royal Palm**, 465-7234 (Ottley's Plantation Inn about halfway between airport and Black Rocks on coast road). Pamela Yahn serves reliably good Caribbean-inspired food on a poolside dining terrace. Lunch or dinner highly recommended. Moderate to expensive.

* **The White House**, 465-8162 (foothills above Basseterre). Enjoy the buffet lunch in the terrace pavilion, evenings, or feast in the pavilion or the plantation's formal dining room. English hosts provide delicious food. Moderate to expensive.
(See the hotel listing for each of the finest above.)

* **The Patio**, 465-8666 (Frigate Bay). Dine in the Mallalieus family home on Helen's fresh lobster, seafood, or meats, and garden-fresh vegetables, all skillfully prepared Caribbean style. Reservations are a must. Moderate.

* **Blue Horizon**, 465-5863 (Bird Rock, outskirts of Basseterre). Unpretentious but quite good food is served in this delightful "in" indoor/outdoor restaurant perched at seaside—sparkling views of Basseterre and Nevis. Great spot to watch the sunset. Seafood is the feature. Dinner only. Moderate.

* **Turtle Beach Bar & Grill**, 469-0986 (Southeastern Peninsula with spectacular panorama of Nevis across the Narrows). A wonderfully isolated location on windswept beach to spend the day. There are water sports here, including scuba instruction and rental equipment—windsurfers, kayaks, masks and fins, sailing, and deep-sea fishing. Bicycles are available to pedal to other beaches. We got an unusually close look at a green vervet monkey who came for a drink of orange juice and a banana. An open-air dining

pavilion serves honey mustard ribs, Calypso chicken salad with orange and fresh basil, and barbecue chicken Créole style. Try a mango monkey cocktail. Open from 10 A.M. to 10 P.M. weekdays. Saturday is gourmet night—grilled swordfish steak, grilled or fresh lobster salad, or coconut shrimp are the stars. A live steel band plays at Sunday's island beach buffet. Old island atmosphere and fun. Inexpensive to moderate.

OTHER DEPENDABLE CHOICES

Ballahoo, 465-4197 (north side of The Circus). The most popular restaurant in Basseterre, on a second-floor veranda, serves good local fare—seafood, salads, and sandwiches. Inexpensive to moderate.

Fisherman's Wharf, 465-2754 (on the harbor at west end of Basseterre). Dine on conch chowder, fresh seafood, BBQ ribs, chicken, and steaks. Open for dinner only. Where the action is. Entertainment. Shop in boutique, too. Moderate.

Chef's Place, 465-6176 (Church Street, central Basseterre). Delightful island dining can be had on the porchfront of this local house where Oliver Peetes serves up West Indian dishes like pumpkin soup, fresh fish, and goat water, a tasty stew. Inexpensive to moderate.

Also try **Arlecchino** at Amory's Mall for Italian fare; **The Lighthouse Gourmet Restaurant** for fine food overlooking the harbor; **Rafters Restaurant and Lounge** at the Pelican Mall, **Stone Walls** on Princes Street, **QT's Delight** in Shoreline Place on waterfront, **Tracy's Corner** on the outskirts of town, and **J's Place** at the foot of Brimstone Hill (also an art gallery) for West Indian dishes. **Cisco's Place** on New Street will satisfy cravings for Chinese food. **Coconut Cafe** offers grilled seafood on beautiful Timothy Beach at Frigate Bay (open for breakfast, lunch, and dinner).

Recommended Shopping

The Plantation Picture House, 465-7740 (at Mount Pleasant House, adjacent to Rawlins Plantation). Kate Spencer's studio and gallery features her enchanting watercolors and oil still lifes and island scenes in this restored Colonial plantation home. Ms. Spencer's beautiful silk pareos and scarves, particularly a large square white-and-claybrown West Indian coalpot print, are exceptional treasures. (Another gallery is also in Nevis.)

Island Hopper, 465-2905 (The Circus, Basseterre). First-rate Caribbeanana from minature dolls, colorful aprons, totes, hats, and T-shirts to ceramics and art. (Also branches in Nevis and Antigua.)

Caribelle Batik, 465-6253 (the Circus in Basseterre and at Romney Manor). The beautifully restored Romney Manor Great House in the country about halfway between Basseterre and Brimstone Hill is well worth the visit. It's both a showroom and artist's workshop. The artisans will explain and demonstrate their ancient batik technique. There are 35 different selections of batik clothing for men, women, and children, plus framed artwork and pareos—lengths of batik cotton that come with instructions for 13 styles of body wrappings.

A Slice of the Lemon, 465-2889 (Palms Arcade, Fort Street, Basseterre). Duty-free gift shop for china, crystal, jewelry and watches, and perfumes. Portmeirion China collection includes charming placemats, tablecloths, etc.

Lemonaid, 465-7359 (The Golden Lemon). Expensive but lovely antiques, jewelry, clothing, and gift items. Check in advance about hours.

Palm Crafts, 465-2599 (Palms Arcade). Caribbean handcrafts, clothing, jewelry, Sunny Caribbee spices, perfumes, and other products, and John Warden's resortwear. Great shop for gifts.

The Spencer Cameron Art Gallery, 465-4047 (North Independence Square). Shop for good collection of prints and paintings by Caribbean artists. Same-day custom framing service.

Wall's Deluxe Record & Book Shop, 465-2159 (Corner of Fort and Princes streets). A local store with an excellent selection of Caribbean books, magazines, stationery, and maps, plus a wide selection of local music, too.

The Pelican Shopping Mall at the harborfront is a two-story shopping complex with many boutiques and stores including **Little Switzerland, Island Style, Linen & Gold, The Palm Leaf, Smoke 'n Booze,** and **Windjammer & Caribbean Scents**. The **St. Kitts Philatelic Bureau** has moved here. Other shopping centers to visit are **Amory Mall** on Cayon Street, **TDC Mall**, and **Palms Arcade**. There are some interesting shops on **Liverpool Row**, one street back of Bay Road.

Useful Information

St. Kitts' free information publications are first-rate, so pick up copies of *St. Kitts/Nevis the Traveller Tourist Guide* and *The Official Tourist Guide for St. Kitts & Nevis* the minute you arrive.

Car rental companies include **Avis**, (809) 465-6507, and **TDC Rentals, Ltd.**, (809) 469-5690. Limousine service is available in St. Kitts at **Sincerely Yours**, (809) 465-8225.

Jack Tar Village has an 18-hole championship **golf course** and a **casino**, 465-8631.

The southern peninsula of St. Kitts has been opened by Dr. Kennedy Simmonds Highway, which loops around the scenic, hilly area on 6.5 miles of curved, smooth blacktop. Twelve secluded, white-sand beaches, formerly reached only by boat, are now accessible by car. Several new hotels are in planning stages and should be built within the next couple of years. Meantime, pack a lunch and head for this tranquil, unspoiled sanctuary. Nevis, only a few miles across the sea, is a stunning view from Cockleshell, Banana, or Major's bays. A **day trip to Nevis** is a must, and easily arranged via ferry, catamaran, or plane.

Also worth visits are the volcanic **Black Rocks** and **Brimstone Hill**, a massive eighteenth-century fort, called the Gibraltar of the West Indies. On clear days, from up top, you'll see Statia, Saba, St. Martin, and St. Barthélemy.

Rain-forest and mountain hikes, especially to 3,792-foot Mt. Liamuiga, make fine day trips. Two **tours** are recommended: **Rain Forest and Cave Trek** by Kriss Berry, 465-4042, or **Greg's Safaris**, 465-4121 *or* 5209.

ST. LUCIA

ACCOMMODATIONS

ST. LUCIA'S BEST
Anse Chastanet Hotel, Soufrière 🌴
Jalousie Plantation Resort & Spa, Soufrière 👑
Ladera Resort, Soufrière
Le Sport, Castries

GREAT EXPECTATIONS
Etwelle de Mer, Soufrière

RECOMMENDED RESTAURANTS

RECOMMENDED SHOPPING

USEFUL INFORMATION

≈ ≈

Accommodations

ST. LUCIA'S BEST

Anse Chastanet Hotel, Soufrière 🌴

Anse Chastanet (Chastanet was the name of an aristocratic 18th-century French family that settled on St. Lucia; *anse* is Old French for "bay") is a rare nesting spot for undemanding romantics to reflect, recharge, and recreate in historical, breathtakingly beautiful geography. You feel as if you're in the Caribbean Alps. Over St. Lucia itself, one always feels compelled to wax lyrical.

Secluded on its own quarter-mile-long silver-gray black sand beach (only part of the 400-acre property, which includes another private beach) rests this entrancing Créole West Indian escapist's retreat. Anse Chastanet's 48 accommodations are divided among the 20 original 1968 hillside octagonal-shaped gazebos, one- and two-bedroom suites, and 12 deluxe beachside rooms and 12 hillside deluxe aeries, and four new immense premium rooms with dramatic sweeping views. Canadian owner and managing director Nick Troobitscoff, an architect, designed these handsome new dwellings, fitting them with inlaid furniture that he created out of local breadfruit, red cedar, teak, and purple heart. (Karolin Kolcuoglu Troobitscoff, his wife, is the resort's delightful and competent marketing director.) Within the next two years, 24 more rooms will be added.

Anse Chastanet is "upstairs downstairs." It is 100 steps down to the beach, where the luncheon restaurant Trou-au-Diable, the all-day bar with a soaring, cone-shaped, thatched roof, two boutiques, the sports center, and one unlighted tennis court are located. If you're renting a car (and most guests do) you can drive down to the beach area.

Upstairs is reception, the Pitons Restaurant for breakfast and dinner, a breezy bar, game room, and the Treehouse dining area and library.

If you're staying upstairs, there's a further climb up from the Pitons Restaurant to your quarters. Nevertheless, I prefer the new deluxe or premium rooms for their sweeping views, cool breezes, and easier access to morning and evening meals.

The 18 × 18-foot octagonal rooms have either a magnificent view of both Gros and Petit Pitons or the beach and sea. The simple rooms, with exposed-wood-beam ceilings and paddle fans, exuded a cheerful, inviting Caribbean aura. Branches of vividly colored bougainvillea lay on every surface, even across the wooden bed headboard. The draperies, comfortable rattan chair cushions, and king-size spread and bed skirt (the bed is two twins pushed together), were all covered with cotton Créole red, green, and yellow madras plaid. Batik prints of fish and parrots decorated the walls. New, intricately woven vetiver grass rugs rested on quarry-tiled floors. Small closets fit into a wall next to the small, two-section, white-tiled bathrooms.

The deluxe rooms all have either views of the Pitons or of wide open ocean. Still a favorite is Charconia 7C (all rooms are named after flowers and trees), a two-bedroom suite with a kitchenette. The huge gallery-covered outdoor living room has a balcony with a bunting of greenery and is unquestionably one of the most splendid panoramas in the Caribbean, with the Pitons as the centerpiece. The new rooms dotting the hillside are spacious lodgings (ranging from 900 to 1,200 square feet) with individual configurations and king-size beds. All rooms have mini-refrigerators, electric tea/coffeemakers, and hair dryers. Upper rooms have sky-high ceilings. In some instances, units had to be built around giant ancient trees to preserve them, which now naturally enhance interiors. Baths are large with bidets, twin sinks, and open showers. Many have fabulous views. The premium rooms are extra-roomy, spectacular spaces.

There are no radios, TVs, telephones, or clocks. Nature is your wake-up call.

Lunch down on the beach is international Créole food—fish kebabs, vegetable roti, and grilled foods. You can finish lunch with a banana split, if you can possibly still be hungry. Servings are generous.

Anse Chastanet's new chef, British-born Nigel Ravenshear, intends to create dishes based on luscious local ingredients that are light, low-calorie, and delicious, like dorado with a mustard, ginger, and caper sauce and brochette of snapper with lime and green peppercorn sauce. Meals continue to be served with warmth, charm, and eagerness by smiling young waitresses, dressed in white peasant blouses, madras plaid flounced skirts, and matching little handkerchief hats.

Anse Chastanet has extensive diving programs for all levels, managed by Michael and Karen Allard, originally from California (Michael's a PADI Master Scuba Diver Trainer). The team has an experienced and professional staff and a fleet of dive boats. Crystal-clear water and reefs and caves offer spectacular underwater adventures. The hotel has no pool.

It's not surprising to find that about 25% of the young to middle-aged clientele, 70% North American, are divers; the other guests are mostly English, German, and Swiss. Anse Chastanet has become popular with honeymooners. There are six to eight weddings a month.

Beyond scuba diving, you can windsurf, mini-sail, deep-sea fish, take a scheduled boat trip from the hotel for shopping in Castries, or simply recline on lounges under dense thatched bohios on the beach.

The hotel will provide boat service to its second romantic deserted beach at Anse Matin. It's a walkable journey, too, taking about 10 minutes along the coastline bordered by a forest of towering palms. Anse Matin was an 18th-century French Colonial sugar plantation that once thrived on these grounds. Guests can investigate remains of the estate's ruins: the house, sugar works, a giant water wheel, and a viaduct system. Tropical fruit and other trees, flowers, and other extraordinary vegetation flourish on the property.

Live entertainment at the resort includes rotating bands, either "shak shak," reggae, or rock'n'roll, and music at beach barbecue dances, among other surprise festivities. (The Troobitscoffs are opening another hotel nearby—see Great Expectations.) Richard and Lynda Barnett, the young managers, are welcoming, and have added energy to this romantic old-island charmer.

ANSE CHASTANET HOTEL
P.O. Box 7000, Soufrière
St. Lucia, West Indies
TEL: (809) 459-7000 *or*
    (809) 459-7554
FAX: (809) 459-7700

RESERVATIONS
Ralph Locke Islands, Inc.
TEL: (800) 223-1108 *or*
    (310) 440-3225
FAX: (310) 440-4220

Open all year.

Rates: Double occupancy. *December 20 to April 15 (MAP):* Standard, $310; Superior, $360; Deluxe, $410; Premium, $500. *April 16 to May 15* and *November 1 to December 19 (EP):* Standard, $160; Superior, $210; Deluxe, $250; Premium, $350. *May 16 to October 31 (EP):* Standard, $130; Superior, $170; Deluxe, $210; Premium, $290.

Meal plan: MAP (includes breakfast and dinner) in season. Off-season, add $50 per person per day.

Service charge: 10%.

Government tax: 8%.

Children under 2 years not accommodated.

Credit cards accepted.

Note: Special Scuba, Honeymoon, and Escape Packages available; information and rates upon request.

Jalousie Plantation Resort & Spa, Soufrière ◣◢

> Bordered by a secluded beach and a tropical rain forest, Jalousie Plantation Resort & Spa was carefully designed to compliment the natural beauty of its setting. An exclusive hideaway resort, Jalousie gives its guests some of the finest in dining, accommodations and recreation in the Caribbean. Jalousie is the jewel of the Caribbean.
>
> A. PASCAL MAHVI, PRESIDENT AND CEO

I knew before arriving at 325-acre Jalousie Plantation Resort & Spa, secluded on the southern west coast of St. Lucia, that its setting was arresting—spread among the hillsides of a sweeping canyon between the spectacular Les Pitons peaks, bordered by a long and expansive protected beach. We'd cruised by the coastline a few years before the resort's development began, searching for the sole occupant of the former sugar planta-

Jalousie Plantation grounds on St. Lucia.

tion, Bupa the elephant (more about this famous pachyderm later). I did not, however, expect to like the young resort so much.

Building a super-luxury hotel starting from scratch is a tremendous undertaking that requires extraordinary organization, especially in such a remote jungle wilderness. It was further complicated by critics concerned that construction would destroy the delicate ecology of this precious natural habitat. The criticism was eventually appeased by the resort's commitment to environmental preservation, which includes saving original flora and fauna, nurturing plant growth, preserving the delicate coral reefs, maintaining a hydroponic garden, recycling, independent sewage and incinerator operations, managing flood control, and, important in the equation, decreasing local unemployment. Jalousie Plantation has about 340 employees; 30 are full-time gardeners. The resort took four years to build at a cost of $55 million.

Jalousie's sensational property had been owned for some time by Lord Glenconner (a.k.a. Colin Tennant), the eccentric British visionary who had owned and created Mustique, the exclusive private Grendaine island. Glenconner, now a St. Lucia resident, conceived the idea for Jalousie and found partners for the project. Before Jalousie Plantation opened on October 1, 1992, Lord Glenconner had sold his shares but still owned adjacent beachfront property, called Beau Estate, where he has a home and is currently in the process of privately developing his land. The first stage opened a week before my visit. One of the joys of staying at Jalousie is patronizing his enchanting little village that has an open-air West Indian restaurant, rum bar, and gift shop right along the sparkling sea.

The road leading to Jalousie from the terrible, bumpy western main road (you can elect to arrive here by helicopter) is a million-dollar steep, serpentine-smooth driveway. Guests are greeted in the beautifully appointed Jacquot Great House at reception. Also housed in the rambling Great House complex are an activities desk and separate tour desk, two fine boutiques, a conference room, a ballroom, two restaurants, two bars, and The Lord's Great Room, designed by Lord Glenconner, which is eclectically furnished with a collection of his antiques from around the world.

After check-in, guests are transferred to one of the hotel's 115 one-bedroom cottages, cottage suites spread about the hillsides. Transportation is by open-air safari buses that circle the resort.

The architecture of the building's exteriors are modest, fade-into-the-landscape painted brown wood bungalows with white trim, set among mature and young palmy gardens. Most lodgings are a good distance from the public areas, restaurants, beach and pool, with the exception of the 12 Sugar Mill junior suites, situated in attractive light-colored stucco buildings in two clusters across from the Great House, only a stroll from the pool and beach. There are no plunge pools in the Sugar Mill accommodations, but the location is more convenient to the public areas and the beach and pool.

I unpacked in luxury deluxe Cisseau Cottage 604, midway up in the hills, containing a comfortable, large bedroom with an oversize queen bed, a small living room, and a huge, wonderful bathroom with a separate shower and tub, bidet, and double sinks set into a green marble countertop. Through French doors I had ocean views and a terraced private sizable plunge pool (some pools are small dunkers) with an outdoor wet bar and stocked refrigerator with an automatic icemaker, all surrounded by banana plants and green foliage. It took fifteen minutes to read Jalousie's information directory. How could one not fall for a resort with a phone extension designated "Desire to Please" for extra towels or next to anything, including room service for any meal?

All-inclusive Jalousie has a first-rate full spa facility with free massages (treatments are extra) and a fitness center, aerobics classes, an air-conditioned squash court, plus a beauty salon, adjacent to a vast terrace called the Sun Splash Deck. Views here are a framed picture postcard of the sea and Pitons' peaks. Weddings are often celebrated from this glorious location. Jalousie also boasts a four-hole golf course, a croquet court, and four Plexicushion tennis courts. Three are lit, but the lights detract from the nighttime ambience, especially at Ladera Resort, perched up above (see resort listing).

Jalousie's lovely, enormous freshwater swimming pool is only a few yards from the sea and water-sports facilities—everything from waterskiing, kayaking, windsurfing, Sunfish and catamaran sailing, to snorkeling and scuba diving. Horseback riding is also available, and the resort offers numerous interesting excursions for an extra charge. There are four boutiques, including a tiny convenience store. The extensive activities program includes Patois language, Caribbean cocktail mixology, St. Lucian history classes, tours of Jalousie's hydroponic vegetable greenhouses, a children's program, live entertainment, a weekly carnival "jump-up," and teatime every day—just to mention a few.

Iranian owner A. Pascal Mahvi and general manager Patrick R. Fortemps are sincere in their efforts to satisfy guests by offering every possible amenity, from gifts of an artist's charming watercolor maps of the resort, prettily boxed Jalousie Plantation jigsaw puzzles and signature Coco-Mango toiletries to plastic packets of threaded needles. Guests have hair dryers, digital wall safes, and quality, lightweight, personalized white cotton robes, which can be purchased for only $35. Rooms have electric coffeemakers, clock radios, and cable TV with four channels including CNN.

I found the quarry-tiled rooms attractively furnished with dhurrie throw rugs, comfortable rattan or reproduction wood furniture with light-toned floral-print and striped material, but they're more stateside than island in style. Ever eager to please, Jalousie's decorator, Sam Rosenberg Design of West Palm Beach, Florida, is already redesigning interiors of a number of the cottages with handsome West Indian plantation house interiors: four-poster beds hung with mosquito netting, terra-cotta lamps, Caribbean artwork, and so on.

Joined by friends at the resort, we felt a certain energizing euphoria here from the moment we arrived. We had difficulty deciding where to go and what to do with so many choices at hand. First, we headed for the lovely gray-black sand beach for a refreshing swim. Although some may be disappointed that it's not white sand, the water in the bay is calm and crystal-clear. We imagined the sand composed of rare, finely crushed Tahitian South Sea black pearls—a multimillion-dollar beach.

We enjoyed breakfasts on the expansive terrace of the Verandah Restaurant—a buffet of tropical fruits, cereals, eggs any way, bacon, sausage, croissants, sweet rolls, and on and on. Guests place slices of bread in a large revolving toaster so they always have it piping hot. Vistas from the Verandah looking over a green lawn dotted with 75-foot-high coconut palms out to the ocean are mesmerizing. Below the Great House a giant chess board with child-sized kings and queens is set into a vast terrace. We thought it was grand.

Down between the pool and beach with bohios (more are needed) at the Bayside Bar and Grill, a buffet of salads and grilled entrées are offered at lunchtime. Food at the cheerfully decorated alfresco bar and dining room was satisfactory but unimaginative.

The breezy pavilion Pier Restaurant, overlooking the sea at the southern end of the resort, served quite good Créole and seafood dishes for dinner. Lunches can be taken here, too, and are buffets. There's a dance floor and evening entertainment.

I missed dining in the formal, elegant Plantation Room in the Great House, but my friends reported that they'd enjoyed a fine meal there.

Jalousie Plantation is all-inclusive; all food and drinks and afternoon tea are covered in the room rate.

We couldn't resist repeatedly visiting Lord Glenconner's Beau Estate. The entrance is next to the Pier Restaurant. The first thing you see upon entering the compound's courtyard is an enchanting, two-story pink and white renovated island home with gingerbread trim. At night a chandelier twinkles inside. This is the home of Glenconner's young twin daughters, May, who's an art student in London, and Amy, who manages the operation. The village, seaside Bang Between the Pitons, includes Ye Olde Jerk Pit serving up delicious grilled coconut chips, fried plantains, conch fritters, stamp and go (salted fish cakes), spicy jerked chicken, and pork with peanut sauce—all delicious. The rum bar mixes a potent rum punch, and there is nightly entertainment and dancing. Customers rest in funky striped tents with banquettes or at tables and chairs. The Bupa

Gift Shop, in a little cottage, has been stocked with imported elephant objects from statues, clothing, belts, and artwork to jewelry, including custom-made bangle bracelets from India that feature "Bupa" emblazoned in rhinestones. Glenconner brought Bupa here about 20 years ago after saving his life in some sort of transportation mixup. The celebrity elephant roamed Jalousie's grounds, looked after by human friends, until his death just before the opening of Beau Estate. Beau Estate is one of the most original, fun, and spirited watering holes and dining spots in the Caribbean. It's wonderfully quirky and old-island with a sense of humor. (Visitors not staying at Jalousie must pay a fee to the resort for parking and transportation.)

Only 75 acres of Jalousie Plantation have been developed. Thirty more bungalows may be added in future phases, which also include private residential homesites.

My friends and I spent a delightful holiday here, luxuriously pampered in elegant accommodations. We found the staff warm and welcoming, the service great, and agreed that we'd like to return as soon as possible—next time with my husband, Tully, who I know would love the place.

**JALOUSIE PLANTATION
RESORT & SPA**
P.O. Box 251, Soufrière
St. Lucia, West Indies
TEL: (809) 459-7666
FAX: (809) 459-7667

RESERVATIONS
Sterling Hotel Group
TEL: (800) 392-2007

Open all year.
Rates: Double occupancy. *December 19 to April 3:* Sugar Mill Room, $275; One-Bedroom Cottages and Suites, $300 to $450. *April 4 to December 19:* Sugar Mill Room, $240; One-Bedroom Cottages and Suites, $250 to $385. Round-trip airport transfers included.
Meal plan: FAP. (All meals and unlimited drinks and wine with meals included.) Also included are two massages per person during a week's stay.
Service charge included.
Government tax included.
Children welcome.
Credit cards accepted.
Note: Special packages are available.

Ladera Resort, Soufrière

Throughout the day and evening at Ladera, guests gather 1,000 feet above sea level on a long stretch of deck perched on the crest of a hill. From cushioned chaise longues or chairs with ottomans, they gaze out to the sea through an enormous valley below, flanked by the dramatic Piton peaks, and search for apt metaphors—a verdant jungle Grand

Canyon; an arboretum between a pair of Rio Sugarloafs; a singularly magical retreat-with-a-view like no other in the world.

Thoroughly enchanting Ladera, originally named Dasheen, was built as an unusual natural habitat condominium hotel in the 1970s. After management problems, it closed in the late eighties. To the delight of many Dasheen devotees, a new owner took over and made extensive renovations, and renamed the hotel **Ladera** (Spanish for "hillside"), and reopened it in November 1992 to unanimous raves. After a recent visit, I am amazed that there is ever a vacancy in this captivating hideaway.

Alone on this trip, I found myself eavesdropping on a young couple on the sun deck who were listing all the shades of green they spotted in the lush landscape — emerald, jade, forest, mint, olive, pine, bottle, lime, pea, sea, and grape. Seeing the sun shining through a newly sprouted banana leaf, I blurted out (embarrassingly), "Chartreuse." "Yes," they kindly agreed, "that leaf is definitely chartreuse." They called me Chartreuse during the balance of our stay.

Ladera's very special, comfortable multi-level thirteen suites and six three-bedroom villas are "eco-green," open-air, tropical drawing-room aviaries surrounded by leafy gardens, terraces, and lawns. One wall of each accommodation is wide open for the stunning Piton and valley views, yet protected from the elements by overhead coverings and face away from any inclement weather. Each suite or villa has been creatively fashioned with exterior side walls, plantings, vine-covered lattice, or wattled twig pannels for privacy from next-door neighbors, whom you might hear but never see. The rooms sit at the edge of a precipice that plunges several hundred feet below. Ladera is not for young children or anyone jittery about heights.

Lizards silently patrolled my quarters in three-bedroom Villa E. Frogs croaked, birds chirped, and cicadas trilled me to sleep. Because of the altitude there aren't any no-see-ums, and during my stay, no mosquitos, although I slept under sheer mosquito netting.

Six one-bedroom suites and four of the three-bedroom villas have private, immaculate plunge pools. Ladera also has a lovely main freeform swimming pool set on a terrace garden below the alfresco restaurant, Dasheen. The romantic setting is famous as a location site used in the film *Superman II*.

All the rustic lodgings are constructed of natural stone, varnished hardwoods, and tile. Furnishings are a combination of locally made wooden pieces, pretty antiques, wicker and bamboo with appointments of local woven grass mats, hand-carved wooden animals and fish, gaily colored prints hanging on walls, and bouquets of fresh flowers.

In Villa E, my stone-walled living room was an enormous area with a huge white cushioned, wood-framed sofa, a stone-based wooden-topped coffee table, a table and chairs, full kitchen, and an inviting plunge pool. Two steps through the open wall lead to a deck with chaises and a lawn bordered by a small hedge, banana plants, scarlet hibiscus, and other dense greenery.

Thick round wooden beams supported the second-floor master bedroom that was also open-air with railings set under a high, angled beamed ceiling. From the four-poster queen-size platform bed I had another striking bird's-eye view of the Pitons and the sea. The bathroom had an open shower and Caswell-Massey toiletries. Nothing fancy, but perfectly adequate. Behind, through a central staircase, were two other bedrooms and a full bath with a shower. The three-bedroom villas are ideal for a family or friends sharing accommodations. (Villa C has a Jacuzzi.) Rooms have no telephones, TVs, or radios.

Ladera's amenities include a bar and lounge, a library and game room with a TV and VCR. A video camera can be rented to film your own version of *Superman II*. The hotel's small, well-stocked boutique off the front office carries clothing, sundries, and handcrafts, including hand-printed products from Bagshaw's (see Recommended Shopping). The five-acre property also has interesting botanical, fruit, and cutting gardens to explore.

Ladera is only a short distance from the village of Soufrière, where boat service is provided to Anse Chastenet's beach. (See the hotel listing; for a $5 fee you can rent a lounge chair for the day.) The Sulphur Springs, the so-called drive-in volcano, is nearby, as is the ultra-luxurious Jalousie Plantation (see resort listing). Unfortunately, lights from Jalousie's tennis courts mar Ladera's view in the early evening, as it rests on a ridge above the elegant beachside resort.

General manager Frode Sund or longtime staffer Rosemary in the front office staff will gladly help organize car rentals, island tours, taxis, scuba diving, fishing trips, or local guides for rain-forest walks or other hikes.

One of the highlights of staying at Ladera is the treehouse restaurant Dasheen, supervised by the talented young chef David Carrington. (Guests and visitors tend to make early dinner reservations to get the front tables with the best sunset and moonlit views.) Chef Carrington combines Créole, California, and European traditional cuisines with his own light touches in tasty dishes like christophene and coconut soup with callaloo, chilled tuna Créole, shrimp with pineapple and Stilton, and duck breast with an orange and ginger sauce. Entrées are served with local vegetables, spicy rice or pastas, and exceptionally good fresh baked dinner rolls. Live entertainers perform at Ladera twice a week in season, one night a week off-season.

Breakfasts are exhilarating from the top of this primordial tropical world—simple but delicious fresh squeezed juices, assortments of tropical fruits, and addictive breads such as coconut and banana muffins. Service is most agreeable.

Ladera is a stunning revival of the way many of us always want the Caribbean to be— friendly, low-key, welcoming, and, above all, luxuriously natural. Highly recommended for nature lovers and romantics.

LADERA RESORT
P.O. Box 225, Soufrière
St. Lucia, West Indies
TEL: (809) 459-7323
FAX: (809) 459-5156

RESERVATIONS
TEL: (800) 841-4145 *or*
(607) 273-9484
FAX: (607) 273-5302

Open all year.
Rates: Double occupancy. *December 18 to April 15:* One-Bedroom Suite, $300; One-

Bedroom Suite with Pool, $350; Three-Bedroom Villas, $475 to $650. *April 16 to June 30 and November 5 to December 17:* One-Bedroom Suite, $250; One-Bedroom Suite with Pool, $275; Three-Bedroom Villas, $375 to $525. *July 1 to November 4:* One-Bedroom Suite, $175; One-Bedroom with Pool, $200; Three-Bedroom Villas, $295 to $450. Extra person, $25 per person per day. All rates include transportation from and to Hewanorra Airport.
Meal Plan: CP (includes continental breakfast). MAP (includes breakfast and dinner), add $40 per person per day.
Service charge: 10%.
Government tax: 8%.
Children welcome.
Credit cards accepted.
Note: Special packages and Executive Retreat Programs are available.

Le Sport, Castries

More and more travelers today are seeking out Caribbean resorts that feature health, exercise, and special sports facilities. Le Sport, transformed from the former lackluster Steigenberger Cariblue Hotel into an elegant, slightly Moorish, 102-room, 15-acre health-spa retreat, is an agreeable resort. Its slogan is "The Body Holiday."

Le Sport is situated on a secluded cove on a hillside on St. Lucia's northwestern tip at Cap Estate, 20 minutes from Castries, the island's capital. Transfer from and to Hewanorra International Airport, included in the rate, takes about 1½ hours. After the bumpy trip, you'll discover a delightful beachside haven to vacation in, whether you are a health or exercise addict or just plain curious. It would be a mistake not to partake of the various therapies and treatments offered, because when you depart you will feel better, if not thinner, and will have had some fun along the way.

First of all, Le Sport is all-inclusive with a capital *A*. When you consider what's included, it's relatively reasonable. Here's what you get: Deluxe accommodations, all meals (either *cuisine légère*—light, low-fat meals fashioned after France's three-star chef Michel Guérard's innovative nouvelle cuisine—or regular meals), all bar drinks, a weekly barbecue, nightly live entertainment plus dancing, and all body and beauty treatments, such as thalassotherapy (rejuvenation treatments) for men and women, seaweed nutrient wraps, massages, Swiss needle showers, jet-hose massages, hydro pool, loofah rubs, and saunas. Aerobics, yoga, and stretch classes are also given. Instruction and equipment are available for snorkeling and scuba diving, waterskiing, windsurfing, Sunfish sailing, tennis on the resort's one lit court, archery, fencing, weight lifting, horseback riding on English saddles, golf on a nine-hole course nearby, cycling, volleyball, and Ping-Pong. There's also relaxation therapy.

Le Sport has two swimming pools, one freshwater, the other saltwater, and a beautiful stretch of beach and seawater in which to exercise naturally.

The resort has a boutique, pharmacy, and hair salon. Manicures, pedicures, sets, and cuts are extra, as is laundry service.

The staff is amiable and helpful, with good intentions, which doesn't necessarily mean speed. Still, the lodgings are prettily put together with island trappings, and have air-conditioning. There are mini-bars, wonderful marble bathrooms with hair dryers, and private balconies or terraces.

After checking in, you're given a quick check-up by a doctor or nurse. Guests can be as active in daily scheduled routines as they desire, but no one insists that you fill up your spa card.

The treatment center is housed in an adjacent Spanish-style red-tile-roofed building complex with breezy arched walkways. There is a good deal of walking and climbing at Le Sport, so be prepared.

Meals, low in fat and calories, include slimming buffets and dinners of snapper terrine, lobster with mango sauce and grilled pineapple, lots of julienned vegetables, and fresh fruit dishes and drinks. It's nice to alternate low-fat meals with tastier regular food, be it salads, steak, pork, or chicken, and chocolate cake or other "guilty" desserts.

After an invigorating holiday at Le Sport, you can't help but feel refreshed.

LE SPORT
P.O. Box 437, Cariblue Beach
St. Lucia, West Indies
TEL: (809) 450-8551
FAX: (809) 450-0368

RESERVATIONS
TEL: (800) 544-2883

Open all year.

Rates: Le Sport has eight different rate schedules throughout the year, with five different rate structures ranging from Garden View, Ocean-View, Ocean-Front, Suite, and Plantation House. Only winter rates are given here. Daily rate per person for Rooms, $200 to $450.

Meal plan: FAP (three meals and bar drinks, plus all spa and sports facilities and airport transfers).

Service charge included.

Government tax included.

Children welcome.

Credit cards accepted.

GREAT EXPECTATIONS

Etwelle de Mer, Soufrière

Nick and Karolin Troobitscoff, owners of Anse Chastanet Hotel, are building an affordable small inn (about 20 rooms, exact number undecided at press time), on the side of a nearby hillside. When I visited recently, I was startled to see an incredible pavilion roof high atop a structure well into construction. I later learned from Anse Chastanet's manager, Richard Barnett, that this was the top of the five-story inn—less than 500 yards from a small, private, but rocky beach. Guests here will be able to use the expansive gray sand beach and facilities at Anse Chastanet.

A local couple will be engaged to manage Etwelle de Mer and its Créole restaurant and bar, which will serve breakfast, lunch, and dinner.

The building hugs the side of a hill, so five stories means that there are five levels from which to reach rooms by pathways. The standard and superior rooms will be spacious with simple Créole decor and amenities—no phones, TVs, or radios, but each will have an extraordinary view of the twin Pitons peaks and the sea. The superior rooms on top will certainly be the most coveted.

Opening is slated for the winter of the 1994/1995 season. Interested parties should contact Anse Chastanet Hotel, (809) 459-7000 or (809) 459-7554, for information.

Recommended Restaurants

CASTRIES' FINEST*

* The Bistro, 452-9494 (waterfront at Rodney Bay Marina). Pat and Nick Bowden, original owners of San Antoine, are back with a delightful restaurant offering homemade pastas, Cornish pasties, fresh seafood, steak and kidney pie, and "Chicken Wellington." Moderate to expensive.

* The Great House Restaurant, 450-0450 or 450-0211 (worth the drive beyond Gros Islet to Cap Estate near Club St. Lucia). This elegant French Créole restaurant serves Xavier's delicious creations—like pumpkin soup and rack of lamb with thyme and rosemary—in a splendid setting. Moderate to expensive.

* San Antoine, 452-4660 (Morne Fortune). Have lunch or dinner in this renovated historic great house and enjoy the expansive views high up over Castries and Pigeon Point. The elegantly served Italian, Continental, and West Indian Créole menu is good but not great. Expensive.

* Bon Appétit, 452-2757 (top of Morne Fortune). Stunning views from this very pleasant little newcomer, and the seafood and steaks are well prepared. Moderate.

* Rain, 452-3022 (Derek Walcott Square). Head upstairs for the view or dine in the courtyard of this green-and-white gingerbread-trimmed Colonial mansion on good West Indian fare or pizza throughout the day. Inexpensive to moderate.

* Jimmie's, 452-5142 (Vigie Cove Marina). Lots of good island food and fun in a great harbor location. Owner/chef Jimmie James's wonderful sense of humor makes it work. Whatever you order—fresh soups, seafood, fritters, fish-and-chips—will be very good. Locals love the place. Inexpensive to moderate.

OTHER DEPENDABLE CHOICES

In Castries, **Paul's Place**, serving Créole and Asian cuisine, and **The Pink Elephant Grill and Bar**, offering grilled fish and meat and island specials, are unpretentious and recommended. **D's** and **Coal Pot** at Vigie Beach and Marina are both informal and fun and serve excellent, reasonably priced meals. At Rodney Bay, try **Capone's** for good Italian food (**Capone's Pizzeria** has opened next door); **The Mortar & Pestle**, for Caribbean fare, such as lambi (conch), casareep pepper pot, and lobster Créole; **The Lime Restaurant & Bar**, for grilled seafood, chicken, pork, steaks, and ribs; **Key Largo!**, for gourmet pizza and salads; **Ginger Lily**, for Chinese; and the always dependable **Chart House**, for American and Créole cuisine.

Also consider dining at **Le Sport's** restaurants (see resort listing) and **Jammers** at Windjammer Landing—both about twenty minutes from Castries. **Eudovic's Art Studio** in Goodlands, Morne Fortune, operates a guest house with a small Créole restaurant. At Marigot Bay, about a 45-minute drive south of Castries, **Dolittles** and **The Rusty Anchor** at Marigot Bay Resort are set in picturesque Hurricane Hole. The food is pretty standard, but the setting's delicious.

SOUFRIÈRE'S BEST*

* Jalousie Plantation's **Plantation Room** and **Pier Restaurant**, 459-7666, are lovely dining rooms and worth a trip to have a look at the beautiful resort if you're not staying there. A must for some West Indian Créole fixings is Lord Glenconner's funky **Bang Between the Pitons**, 459-7864, for lunch or dinner or late-night action—at **Beau Estate** next door to **The Pier Restaurant** at Jalousie Plantation, also the site of **Bupa Gift Shop** and **Ye Olde Jerk Pit**. Jalousie Plantation charged outsiders a $10 fee last time I was there. Bang is moderately priced, so go for it. (See all the above restaurants in the resort's listing.) Jalousie's restaurants are moderate to expensive.

* **Dasheen**, 497-7323 (Ladera Resort). The view is intoxicating from this mountain-top, small open-air restaurant set between the Pitons overlooking the sea. The food and service is fine in this casual, friendly environment. (See the Ladera Resort listing.) Moderate.

* **Pitons Restaurant**, 459-7000 or 459-7700 (Anse Chastanet Hotel). Old-island atmosphere and gentle service in lovely restaurant serving good food. Also beachdiving for lunch at *Trou-au-Diable*. (See the hotel listing.) Moderate to expensive.

* **The Hummingbird**, 459-7232 (beachfront, at northern edge of Soufrière). Take a dip in the sea or the pool at this small hotel's delightful terrace restaurant. For lunch or dinner, try lobster coquilles St-Jacques, fish Créole style, or grilled entrecôte with garlic butter. Joyce's rum cheesecake, named after owner Joyce Alexander, is one of the best desserts. This place is popular with locals and visitors. Have a look at Joyce's boutique here, which sells batik and art. Moderate to expensive.

* **The Still**, 459-7224/7060/7261 (outskirts of Soufrière). The Still, a spacious converted rum distillery, has improved and expanded by adding ten nice-looking studio and one- and two-bedroom apartments with a freshwater swimming pool. The complex

Bang Between the Pitons private house in St. Lucia.

has an excellent boutique, too. Although popular with cruise-ship groups, independent travelers and guests of the hotel are well looked after by manager Desmond du Boulay and his staff. The airy, big homey dining room serves savory pepperpot, curried lamb or pork, fresh fish dishes, salads, and sandwiches. Inexpensive to moderate.

OTHER DEPENDABLE CHOICES

On the main road past Ladera are two excellent local restaurants — **Barbican**, run by a St. Lucian couple, and **Jacquot's Restaurant & Bar**, serving great garlic prawns, roti, and other curried dishes and Créole food; the owners are from Brooklyn, New York.

In Vieux Fort, near the airport, go to **Chak Chak Cafe** for some delectable local food.

Recommended Shopping

CASTRIES

Bagshaw Studios, with many branches—including those at Pointe Seraphine, Anse Chastanet in Soufrière, and Hewanorra International Airport—produces the late Sydney Bagshaw's original hand-printed silkscreen designs on fabrics made up into a variety of enchanting items on display in the main showroom and separate workshop outside Castries, next to Sandals, overlooking the sea and beach. You'll find surprisingly reasonable prices on everything from tea cozies and placemats to clothing and cosmetic bags. Excellent shop to stock up on gifts created and sold only on St. Lucia.

Eudovic Art Studio, Restaurant, & Bar, 452-2747 (Goodlands, back of Morne Fortune). Beautiful hand-carved wood sculptures in all price categories can be purchased here. Also a small guest house with a tiny restaurant.

Artsibit Gallery, 452-7865 (corner of Brazil and Mongiraud streets, Castries). Come here for an interesting selection of pottery, sculpture, and Caribbean handcrafts and art.

Book Salon, 452-3817 (corner of Laborie and Jeremie streets in Castries). Good selection of books, fiction and nonfiction, periodicals, maps, stationery, postcards, and gift items.

Caribee Batik, 452-3022 (Old Victoria Road). This factory outlet workshop and showroom sells batik clothing, wall hangings, and more.

Pointe Seraphine (at deep-water dock in the harbor). This sprawling duty-free shopping complex (bring your passport and airline ticket) has about 20 shops and boutiques including **Noah's Arkade, Colombian Emeralds, Bagshaw Studios, The Gallery, Images, Little Switzerland**, and **Island Connection. The Sunshine Bookshop** is also located here.

In Castries, **Rain** on Derek Walcott Square has a nice resortwear collection. **Y. De Lima** on William Peter Boulevard is another source for fine jewelry, perfume, and gift items.

Other shops and boutiques are located at the **Gablewoods Shopping Mall, Rodney Bay Marina**, and at various resorts and hotels.

Visit Saturday's **market** in the newly built pavilion where the island's produce, herbs, spices, and handcrafts are on display.

SOUFRIÈRE

You'll find boutiques at **Anse Chastanet, Ladera, Jalousie Plantation**, and **Bupa's** at Beau Estate there, along the streets in town, and at **Hummingbird's Batik Studio** and **The Still**. In the little village of Choiseul, between Hewanorra International Airport and Soufrière, there's a **Handcraft Center** that sells baskets, straw rugs, furniture, and carved wooden objects created by apprentices. Inexpensive for the most part. The only problem is finding enough suitcase space to carry the items home.

Useful Information

Try to reserve window seats on the left side of the aircraft when flying into St. Lucia's Hewanorra International Airport to get a glorious view of the dramatic Piton Peaks that dominate the island's terrain like a twin verdant version of Rio's Sugarloaf. It's quite a welcome.

Rocky, our taxi driver, entertained us with a narrative of facts, figures, and a bit of St. Lucia's history during the hour-long 18-mile serpentine drive to Soufrière. (The second airport, Vigie, for small planes, is 1½ hours away on the north side of the island in Castries.) Rocky's recitation ended with a list of all the movies that have been made on St. Lucia, including *Dr. Doolittle, Fire Power,* and *Water.*

It's no wonder that filmmakers come to St. Lucia for genuine tropical beauty. The rugged hills and mountains are an infinity of majestic coconut palms, bamboo, papaya, giant mango, cocoa, breadfruit, avocado, almond, and banana trees.

A film director would need many days to re-create the scenes we encountered in only a few moments' time—grazing cattle, horses, and donkeys in open fields, caravans of goats crisscrossing the road in their usual scrambled fashion, women striding slowly along with substantial loads of fruit, baskets, or packages balanced on their heads, river and stream banks carpeted with drying laundry, scampering children, handsome senior citizens lost in thought in open window frames, and miniature houses and villages active in the slow, Caribbean-style choreography of life.

Sightseeing by tour, taxi, or car, especially from the south of St. Lucia all the way to the north on the serpentine west coast road, is an enchanting island experience despite the curvy, potholed thoroughfare. Some of the special things to do are hike through the **Moule-à-Chique rain forest**; see St. Lucia's drive-in volcano (**Mount Soufrière**)—you'll be expected to hire a licensed guide; and the **Diamond Mineral Baths**. Bring binoculars if interested in birdwatching.

If spending a day in St. Lucia's largest working plantation to see historic buildings, banana harvesting, or whatever's currently appeals to you, book a tour to the immense **Marquis Plantation**. Visitors receive a welcome drink, and ride in a canoe from the Marquis River through the plantation. Unfortunately, you're not allowed to see the plantation on your own. Your hotel will make arrangements.

Every Friday night there's a "jump-up" street party in **Gros Islet** just north of Castries. Leave valuables home, and party into the wee hours along with locals. There are steel bands, vendors, and lots of tasty island food. If you don't have a car, make sure you've organized transportation back to the hotel.

St. Lucia's lovely Roman Catholic church, **The Cathedral of the Immaculate Con-**

ception in Castries, was visited by Pope John Paul II in the early eighties. The cathedral's interiors combine traditional and Caribbean artwork. **VISIONS** *Tourist Guide of St. Lucia* and *St. Lucia's Tropical Traveller* are free publications filled with valuable information.

Car rental companies include **National,** (809) 454-6699 at Hewanorra Airport, (809) 452-3050 at Vigie Airport; **Avis,** (809) 454-6325 at Hewanorra Airport, (809) 452-2046 at Vigie Airport; **Hertz,** (809) 454-9636 at Hewanorra Airport, (809) 451-7351 at Vigie Airport.

ST. MAARTEN/ST. MARTIN

ACCOMMODATIONS

ST. MARTIN'S BEST

Hotel L'Esplanade Caraïbes, St. Martin
La Samanna, St. Martin 👑

RECOMMENDED RESTAURANTS

RECOMMENDED SHOPPING

PROVISIONS FOR YOUR ISLAND PANTRY

USEFUL INFORMATION

≈ ≈

Accommodations

ST. MARTIN'S BEST

Hôtel L'Esplanade Caraïbes, St. Martin

Grand Case, the tiny seaside village on the northern coast of French St. Martin, is an enchanting remnant of old-island living on this overdeveloped two-nation island that includes Dutch St. Maarten. Little West Indian cottages, a dozen or so excellent restaurants and lolos (native roadside eateries specializing in grilled foods; see Recommended Restaurants), a scattering of boutiques, markets, and modest, mostly small hotels line Grand Case's long crescent beach. Until late 1992, there were no luxury hotels here.

The caption of Hôtel L'Esplanade Caraïbes' brochure reads, "On the hill, above the rest," a fitting double entendre for this stunningly beautiful 24-apartment complex that spills across a hillside at the eastern edge of the village.

The handsome Mediterranean white stucco buildings have red-corrugated-steel peaked roofs and ballustraded ocean-view balconies. The entire complex is accented with lovely imported French and Portuguese ceramic tiles that embellish walkways, steps, walls, staircases, planters, and are set in a geometric design at the bottom of the large swimming pool. The Brazilian artisans who installed the tiles also masterfully created delicate mosaic wall murals, large and small, throughout the hotel.

There are 16 studio and loft apartments, and eight one-bedroom apartments, four of which are the prize accommodations at the hotel, with oversized loft duplexes with towering ceilings and balconied bedrooms. All the living rooms in the one-bedroom apartments have sleeper sofas, providing lodging for four.

L'Esplanade is surrounded with gardens of palm trees, hibiscus, aloe, and ginger. Venezuelan landscape architect Alfonso Utrilla has two full-time assistants who continually plant and prune back the allamanda and bougainvillea that overflows planters, arbors, and staircases.

Guests enter the hotel up a rather steep winding driveway to the open-air reception area at the center of the hotel. One of the directors, Marco or Sally Tramoni (a competent husband/wife team—he is French, she is American), escort you to your room and explain the layout of the property. After that, you're pretty much on your own. L'Es-

Poolside view at Hotel L'Esplanade Caraïbe in St. Martin.

planade has no restaurant, although there may be one in the hotel's future. In season, continental breakfasts are available. Arrangements can be made in advance for a welcome basket of food and beverages, so you have refreshments in the refrigerator the moment you step into your apartment. Just about everything you'll need for total comfort, aside from food, is inside.

Interiors are decorated with quality rattan furniture. Doors, wooden-beamed ceilings, and stairways are Brazilian hardwoods. The air-conditioned rooms have ceiling fans, TVs, private safes, direct-dial telephones (with a punch-in wake-up call that on my visit rang right on time), and fully stocked kitchens, including white china, cutlery, pots and pans, toasters, and electric coffeemakers. You can food-shop at the well-stocked Grand Anse Superette, a short walk away (see Provisions for Your Island Pantry).

Bathrooms are large, with open stall showers, hair dryers, lots of counter and storage space, and lighted makeup mirrors.

Life at the hotel centers on your comfortable apartment and the gorgeous freshwater pools and garden area set below on the left side of the property. One pool is sizable and angular-shaped with a swim-up bar. The other pool is a small, shallow round one for toddlers. The bright-blue-roofed bar pavilion is open throughout the day and evenings in season. Lounge chairs dot the terrace.

The hotel has a 44-foot Davis deep-sea boat for dives and fishing, and any water-sports activity can be found on the beach at Grand Case Beach Club. A sloping pathway lined with round stones set into grass leads down to a small road with access to Grand Case Beach for swimming. It's a five-minute walk from L'Esplanade. Without a car, I made the trip up and down several times to shop for food, dine out, browse in the boutiques, stroll on the beach, and swim.

Grand Case's small L'Esperance Airport is a short distance to the south, but no night landings are permitted, and so few small planes appear here that I barely noticed its existence during my stay. Actually, if booking at L'Esplanade, arranging to arrive at this airport would be wonderfully convenient.

L'Esplanade is a great addition to Grand Case, and it's one of St. Martin's most beautiful small apartment hotels. Highly recommended.

HÔTEL L'ESPLANADE CARAÏBES
P.O. Box 5007, Grand Case
97150 St. Martin
French West Indies
TEL: (590) 87.06.55
FAX: (590) 87.29.15

Open all year.
Rates: Double occupancy. *December 15 to April 14:* Deluxe Studio, $190; Deluxe Loft, $225; One-Bedroom or Oversized Loft, $260. *April 15 to December 14:* Deluxe Studio, $110; Deluxe Loft, $130; One-Bedroom or Oversized Loft, $150.
Meal plan: EP.
Service charge: 10%.
Government tax: 5%.
Children welcome.
Credit cards accepted.
Note: Honeymoon package is available.

La Samanna, St. Martin ◢◣

At La Samanna, we are fully committed to earning an international reputation as the finest luxury resort in the Caribbean and one of the best in the world. To achieve this distinction, our staff works together as a team, always placing guests' needs and comfort as the highest priority.

ULRICH KRAUER, MANAGING DIRECTOR

Recently I sat in the bar at La Samanna sipping one of the resort's signature, frosty pineapple daiquiris, waiting for a table in the adjacent Poolside Grill. It was packed with gregarious souls dining on wonderful salads, pastas, seafood, and burgers and pommes frites. Below, at the beautiful tile-bordered pool, bronzed guests were relaxing on handsome teak chaise longues with thick blue cushions—gone were the uncomfortable plastic pipe contraptions that were formerly a fixture at the hotel. I was happy to see the Indian wedding tent still draped overhead decorating the ceiling in the bar. It was one of the late James Frankel's favorite decorative touches at the hotel.

There have been some dramatic changes at La Samanna since its creator, James Frankel, died in April 1989. Frankel's family, who now owns the hotel, turned the operation and management over to highly respected Rosewood Resorts and Hotels of Dallas, which undertook a multimillion-dollar renovation completed in November 1992. Rosewood's interior-design partner, Vision Design, transformed the fading beauty into a rejuvenated, exclusive star resort once again. Although the renovations, new furnishings and appointments were essential, the resort's glorious 55-acre location, set along one of St. Martin's best beaches, Baie Longue, has always been outstanding.

La Samanna (an acronym for Frankel's three daughters, Samantha, Anouk, and Nathalie) opened on December 5, 1973 on the southwestern shore of St. Martin. The resort is an attractive group of Mediterranean-style buildings designed by the late Robertson (Happy) Ward. The white-stucco and red-tiled-roofed main building sits on a bluff overlooking the sea. The main restaurant and lobby, library, intimate bar, Pool Grill, pool and terrace, and ten rooms, including the newly designed and coveted multi-veranda Terrace Suite, are housed here.

Of the remaining one- to three-bedroom suites and villas, a total of 80 rooms, a few are cliffside with ocean views; the rest are oceanfront prize spaces strung along Baie Longue Beach.

The elegant villas have fully equipped kitchens with new tile countertops, living rooms, dining areas, and spacious patios. Interiors have been upgraded substantially. The standard tropical decor has been replaced with quality classic Caribbean artwork, designer oversized pieces, including sofas with wooden arms and legs, zambale-peel wicker lounge chairs and ottomans, all with fat cushions and pillows covered with cheerful cotton solids and prints. Especially appealing are the blue and coral fabrics covered with patterns of seashells and monkeys. Mahogany desks and chairs, hand-carved wooden floor lamps, and coffee tables featuring bamboo bases wrapped with leather and glass are only a few of the many enhancements. (In the Caribbean, Rosewood also operates super-luxury resorts Caneel Bay in the United States Virgin Islands and Little Dix Bay in the British Virgin Islands.) Under Rosewood guidance, Little Dix recently underwent a highly successful renovation and Caneel Bay's facelift is in progress; see resort listings.

If price is no object, guests can find complete seclusion at La Samanna's new luxury villa that comprises two master bedrooms, a living room, full kitchen, satellite TV, a vehicle, personal butler, 24-hour security, and a private swimming pool on a nearby hillside overlooking the resort and the coastline. Villa residents enjoy all the services of the resort.

Guest amenities at La Samanna meet 1995 expectations — stocked bars and refrigerators, a welcome gift basket of fruit and pastries, a daily *TimesFax,* fresh flowers, bathrobes, hair dryers, and beautifully packaged La Samanna toiletries. The air-conditioned rooms have telephones but no TVs. However, VCRs and movie cassettes are available for in-room entertainment.

La Samanna has a fully equipped 40 × 20-foot fitness pavilion, aerobics instruction, and a television and movie room, as well as an upscale boutique. Massages and beauty treatments can be organized.

Three tennis courts are set in a botanical garden near the redesigned entrance gate. Other sports available are complimentary waterskiing, Sunfish sailing, windsurfing, and snorkeling equipment. Scuba diving lessions, diving and fishing trips, and other excursions can be arranged.

One of the best attributes of La Samanna is its open-air restaurant that sits on a balconied terrace with magical day or night views of the entire Baie Longue and the glistening sea.

Executive Chef Marc Ehrler (whose impressive credentials include Maxim's de Paris in New York and K Club in Barbuda) combines classical French provincial cuisine with new California/Caribbean cuisine, turning out dishes like hot and cold California foie gras, lobster risotto, and Norwegian salmon with seedless red-flame grape sauce. We sampled a succulent roast butterflied Cornish game hen with fresh herbs snipped from La Samanna's gardens and a superb crème brûlée. The fresh-baked breads, Caribbean fruit sorbets, and ice creams are outstanding. La Samanna's vintage wine cellar is the best on St. Martin. (Beach and pool lunch and bar service is provided, as well as 24-hour room service for all meals.)

Guests at La Samanna are mostly wealthy Americans of all ages, both repeaters and first-timers. Well-known personalities, famous politicians, and stars continue to flock to La Samanna, where they can be assured that earnest managing director Ulrich Krauer and his now friendlier, attitude-free youthful staff respect their privacy to the utmost — always a feature here.

It is difficult for anyone who knew La Samanna from its first days not to associate the resort with its founder, the mercurial seventies pioneer in the industry, James Frankel. He liked his guests to think of La Samanna as a home, not a hotel. Passionate about his home, Frankel had a gift for compressing all the luxury of a well-managed, top resort into a totally comfortable, magical, and intimate setting. His heirs and Rosewood have exceeded his wishes beyond expectation.

LA SAMANNA
P.O. Box 4077
97064 St. Martin Cédex,
French West Indies
TEL: (590) 87.51.22
FAX: (590) 87.87.86

RESERVATIONS
Rosewood Hotels & Resorts
TEL: (800) 854-2252

Open all year.
Rates: Double occupancy. *December 18 to April 9:* Superior and Deluxe Rooms, $480 to $540; Suites and One- to Three-Bedroom Accommodations, $680 to $1,650. *October 29 to December 17* and *April 10 to May 31:* Superior and Deluxe Rooms, $390 to $450; Suites and One- to Three-Bedroom Accommodations, $550 to $1,350. *June 1 to August 31:* Superior and Deluxe Rooms, $295 to $375; Suites and One- to Three-Bedroom Accommodations, $475 to $1,275. Additional person in room, $70 per night. For information on Villa, contact Rosewood Hotels & Resort.
Meal plan: AP (includes full breakfast). MAP (includes breakfast and dinner), add $65 per person per night.
Service charge included.
Government tax: $4 per person per night.
Children welcome.
Credit cards accepted.
Note: Special-Interest Weeks (Culinary and Literary) debuted in 1994.

Recommended Restaurants

More gastronomic satisfaction can be found on this shared two-island nation of Dutch St. Maarten and French St. Martin than perhaps on any other island in the Caribbean — St. Barts would come in second, followed by Martinique. There is an enormous variety of cuisines available on St. Maarten/St. Martin, from Chinese and Indonesian to Caribbean, Créole, Italian, American, and Mexican to its outstanding French cuisine. Prices range from reasonable to fantastically expensive. The best offerings are on the French side, but St. Maarten's ever-growing roster of fine restaurants warrants serious consideration.

ST. MAARTEN'S FINEST*

* **Spartaco**, 45379 (Almond Grove, Cole Bay). Reserve several days in advance for delicious northern Italian dinners like carpaccio with Parmesan shavings and olive oil, tagliatelle of swordfish with pink peppercorns and rosemary, or rich veal Vesuviana,

306 I ST. MAARTEN/ST. MARTIN

served in a dining room engulfed in jungle greenery and statues. Good wine selection. Very expensive.

OTHER DEPENDABLE CHOICES

L'Espadon and **La Terrasse**, 45222 (Port de Plaisance, Cole Bay). Both restaurants are positioned on elevated terraces that overlook the mega-expensive yachts tethered at docks outside. We prefer the seafood and other menu selections, especially foods grilled on hot rocks right on your table, at the more casual, nautically decorated L'Espadon. La Terrasse has a champagne Sunday brunch. Moderate to expensive.

Da Livio, 22690 (159 Front Street). Traditional, but very good Italian dishes— lobster fra diavolo, linguine with clam sauce, and grilled veal chops—are served by the sea. Moderate.

Pink Pearl, 32127 (39 Front Street) or **Dragon Phoenix**, 22967 (Back Street). If you have a yen for Chinese, these are two good options. Moderate.

The Wajang Doll, 22687 (137 Front Street). This restaurant is recommended for those who want to enjoy a multicourse Indonesian rijsttafel in a simple setting. Moderate.

Lynette's Grill, 52865 (at the end of the airport runway). The directions sound a bit ominous, but a taxi driver steered us here for casual dining in a very popular, friendly local restaurant serving delicious seafood and Créole dishes. Everyone munches away, ignoring the planes. Moderate.

Also for consideration in the top category in St. Maarten are the following: **L'Escargot**, 22483 (84 Front Street) and **Le Bec Fin**, 22976 (119 Front Street), for French fare; the **Passanggrahan** dining room, 23588 (15 Front Street) for an escape from the mob to a modest hotel restaurant with menu to match; still, it's seaside and pleasant. **Le Perroquet**, 54339 (72 Airport Road), is popular for exotic and French creations.

Old-timer **Mary's Boon**, in an unpretentious small hotel near the airport at Simpson Bay, rests on a beautiful beach—usually fun for cocktail conversation and a decent, inexpensive dinner. Reservations a must; call 54235.

Rick and Kathy Hetzel from Dallas, Texas, opened **Ric's Place** (Front Street next to Colombian Emeralds), an American café and sports bar. The place is jumping with informally clad statesiders downing big American burgers, Philly steaks, nachos grande, and burritos—your own backyard in Dutch St. Maarten; take-out available. Also in Philipsburg is **Callaloo** on Front Street in the Promenade Arcade for a lively atmosphere, moderately priced food, and hours from breakfast until late. **Cheri's Cafe** at the Cinnamon Grove Shopping Center at Maho Beach is an entertaining place with a huge, reasonably priced menu for families and young folks.

ST. MARTIN'S FINEST*

* **La Samanna**, 87.51.22 (La Samanna Hôtel, Baie Longue). Located in a spectacular setting overlooking a wide expanse of beach and sea, this cliffside open-air terrace restaurant's fine cuisine is always worth a detour. Fine wines. The casual grill terrace restaurant at La Samanna serves lunch only: offerings include super salads, pastas, and more. Try La Samanna's luscious fresh pineapple daiquiri. (See the resort listing.) The main restaurant is expensive to very expensive; the grill is moderate.

There are over 20 restaurants in Grand Case, not counting the numerous *lolos,* little roadside eateries serving grilled chicken, ribs, fish, and lobster. Meals in *lolos* include homemade side dishes lined up on a big table like a potluck dinner—which is what your delicious meal really is. There is a concentration of *lolos* along the northern side of the eastern end of Grand Case Boulevard jutting out over the sand on stilts—**Talk of the Town** is considered the best, but several others were barbecuing up some crayfish that looked pretty tempting. In any case, apart from the *lolos,* here are some favorites both elegant and casual in Grand Case:

* **Chez Martine,** 87.51.59 (also a small hotel, on boulevard de Grand Case). I had a delectable lobster Charlotte, fragrant red snapper fillet served on curry and fruit sauce, and a perfect crème brûlée in the small oceanfront dining terrace. Very expensive.

Also star-quality in Grand Case, but too numerous to describe separately, are * **Le Tastevin,** * **Sebastiano,** * **L'Escapade,** * **Fish Pot,** * **Il Nettuno,** * **Key Largo,** * **Hevea,** * **L'Auberge Gourmande,** and * **Rainbow.** Prices at all verge on exorbitant, except for L'Auberge Gourmande and Hevea.

OTHER DEPENDABLE CHOICES

More reasonably priced options in Grand Case include **Cha Cha Cha** for Caribbean/Créole tapas and entrées in the garden or old-island stone home; **La Canne à Sucre** for French/Créole dishes; **Le Balaou** for good, inexpensive seafood seaside; **Café Panoramique,** set out on a promontory at the end of the beach in the 72-room Grand Case Beach Club on a spectacular site; **Bye Bar Brasil** is the place for authentic Brazilian cuisine; and **California,** for good pizzas and seafood. **Blue Moon,** on the right at the fork in the road to Grand Case or Orient Bay, is one of the best values in the area—*soupe de poissons,* $5; *aile de raie, capres, beurre noisette* (poached sting ray with capers and nut butter), $11.

Following are other options in French St. Martin:

Le Mini-Club, 87.50.69 (Marigot near the waterfront). A Marigot institution of old-fashioned, owner-managed, reliable fine dining served on an expansive second-floor terrace with sea views. French/Créole specialities—superb lobster, conch, fresh pasta and fish dishes, plus French cheeses and pastries. Moderate to expensive.

La Veranda, 87.67.00 (Méridien L'Habitation Le Domaine at Anse Marcel). This young restaurant rests along the beach near a lovely swimming pool in the private section of a large hotel complex. The Créole gingerbread cottage's veranda is prettily set with French bistro chairs and colorful dinnerware. Salad niçoise and other salads, pastas, seafood, and pizzas are delicious. Moderate to expensive.

Here are some new and long-standing restaurants that are worth visiting for good food and/or lovely locations (prices range from low to very high): **Mark's Place, Le 1er Etage, Le Cotonnier, Le Jardin Créole, KaKao Restaurant, Tropicana, Don Camillo,**

L'Astrolabe, Jean Dupont, La Vie en Rose, La Calanque, Alizéa, La Provence, Messalina, La Résidence, and Drew's Deli.

Bistro Nu in Marigot, on a side street off rue Hollande, is fun for local atmosphere and Créole/French fare at bargain prices.

Le Bar de la Mer, 1 rue du Gouverneur Felix Eboune near the Market, is a very useful bistro offering reasonably priced salads, seafood, pizzas, pastas, and desserts. **Le Bateau Lavoir**, on rue du Palais de Justice, is an inexpensive garden café in central Marigot open for breakfast, snacks, and lunch. Try the conch sausage, curried goat, croque monsieur, or omelette, frites, and salad.

One of the locals' favorite Sunday activities is the midday barbecue buffet at modest beachfront **Coralita Beach Hotel**, not far from Oyster Pond. Swim in the sea or huge pool, dine well, dance to live music, and enjoy the camaraderie.

Etna Ice Cream Per Dolce Vita, in Port La Royale in Marigot, is the place to go for 27 flavors of delicious ice cream, plus espresso and cappuccino with pastries or croissants for breakfast.

Recommended Shopping

ST. MAARTEN

Duty-free shopping in waterfront Philipsburg, the capital of the Dutch side of the island, on Front Street or the Old Street mall, continues to be one of the most unpleasant, exasperating experiences in the Caribbean. When cruise ships are in, and in season they often are, taxis jam the dock debarking area's small square (lined with street vendors) and one-way Front Street. The town's narrow sidewalks, many in disrepair, are a crush of perspiring ill-tempered people. A recent visit revealed that the situation remains the same, and that several stores were vacant. Overflowing small garbage cans were surrounded by litter on the ground.

Another unpleasant aspect of visiting Philipsburg is the foul-smelling Salt Pond that borders the fringe of downtown. I asked a local for directions to a certain place and part of her directions were "go past Stinky Pond."

My advice is to stay away from Philipsburg entirely, and shop on the French side of the island. However, if you happen to find yourself in Philipsburg, there are some good shops. Here are a few: **H. Stern Jewellers, Gold Mine** and **Diamond Mine, Colombian Emeralds International, Boolchand's, New Amsterdam Store, Ashburry's, Bye-Bye, La Romana, MaximoFlorence, Diamonds International, Gurlink, Java Wraps, Little Switzerland, Lil' Shoppe, Shipwreck Shop, Gucci, Dalila, Artistic, Loulian's, Summer Times, The Yellow House**, and **Beach Stuff**.

There are some fine shops in Cole Bay at **Port de Plaisance's Casino Atrium**. Look for **Le Cigar Shop, La Perla, Angelique, Guerlain, Linnz'e, Hello Dolly, Vacation Club Boutique**, and **Ted Lapidus**.

ST. MARTIN

Shopping in Marigot in French St. Martin is a decided improvement over the crunch at Philipsburg, although traffic can bottleneck and motor scooters zoom by. The stores listed below are but a few in Marigot's **Marina Port La Royale** and Marigot center streets stretching east to rue de La République and the waterside market and ferry dock. There are scores of lovely shops and boutiques in hotels like **La Samanna, L'Habitation**, and **La Belle Créole**, plus the **Mullet Bay** and **Maho shopping complexes**, and **Port de Plaisance** and **Simpson Bay shopping centers**.

First, a few of my favorite shops, then the listings in categories.

Passions Joaillier, 87.59.53/87.58.02 (Marina Port La Royale). Here you'll find an exclusive jewelry and watch collection. The "les anneaux Chaumet," puffy gold rings, are exquisite.

Animale, 87.00.87 (Marina Port La Royale). This tiny shop carries a unique line of resort and sportswear fashioned in St-Tropez.

Souleiado Factory Outlet (corner rue Felix Elboue in Marigot). Enchanting French Provincial repeat print and other brilliant-colored designs in cotton fabrics or turned into bathing suits, clothing, tablecloths, placemats, and scarves.

Ecotel, rue St. James, one block up from rue Kennedy. The island's source for professional cooking equipment from knives and whisks, quality pots and pans, to baking and soufflé dishes, tart pans, tocques, aprons, and menus. Serious cooks shouldn't miss it.

Art and handcrafts: Gingerbread Gallery, Mahogany, Galerie Minguet, Camaieu Art Gallery, American West India Company, Jessie's Art Workshop, Roland Richardson, The Lynn Studio.

Cameras, videos, and electronic equipment: Maneks.

Cosmetics and perfumes: Beauty and Scents, Lipstick, and La Romana.

Crystal and china: Oro de Sol and Little Switzerland.

Fashions: Boutique Donna, Boutique Ted Lapidus, La Romana and Genesis, Beach Stuff, and Gucci.

Jewelry and watches: Carat, Oro de Sol, Maurella Senesi, Little Switzerland, Goldfinger, Colombian Emeralds, European Jewelers, La Coulée d'Or.

Tablecloths and linens: Oro del Sol.

Provisions for Your Island Pantry

Housekeeping travelers will find fantastic one-stop food shopping at **Match**, 87.92.36, a giant supermarket, in the Howells Center shopping complex on the eastern fringe of Marigot. You will find every possible ingredient needed for your larder from produce to excellent pâtés, cheeses, meats, imported canned and frozen foods, wines and liquors, to household and beach accessories. Across from Match is a small bakery selling crisp-crusted baguettes and sweets. There are many small pâtisseries all around the island selling fresh-baked French bread, croissants, brioches, and pastries.

Food Center, St. Maarten, 43489 (Cole Bay; a second store on Bush Road, phone 22315). Another enormous supermarket stocked with groceries, fresh produce, meats, beverages, and sodas. Has a good pastry shop, Dutch cheeses, and chocolates. Also in Cole Bay Shopping Center, look for **Mike's Deli**.

L'Epicerie, 87.17.69 (at Marina Port La Royale, St. Martin, and at Port de Plaisance, Dutch side, 42353). Petrossian and Hédiard gourmet products—smoked salmon, fine caviars, foie gras, jams, mustards, honeys, vinegars, teas, coffees, and chocolates—are stocked in this superb speciality food emporium, along with wines, spirits, champagnes, and a small selection of prepared light meals and sandwiches.

There are small markets all over the island, but if you're staying in Grand Case at L'Esplanade, the **Grand Case Superette** is well stocked and convenient.

Drew's Manhattan Style Deli, 87.32.47 (in French Cul-de-Sac, near turn-off to L'Habitation). Drew's Deli is a restaurant, but also a wonderful source for takeout and catering—roast chickens, seafood, meats, sandwiches, salads, and homemade desserts.

La Boulangerie Parisienne (Coin de la Poste in central Marigot) sells excellent pâtisserie, special breads, wonderful baguettes, quiches, mini-pizzas, salads, grilled foods, pastries, ice creams, and beverages. It's a great place to put together a picnic for the beach or a meal taken on the veranda of your room.

The **Outdoor Market** at the parking lot and waterfront in Marigot is an excellent source for fresh produce, herbs and spices, crabs, fresh opened coconuts, and handcrafts, trinkets, and T-shirts. It's open every day except Sunday, but Wednesday and Saturday mornings are the busiest and best days.

A service called **Shoppe-Ease** will do your food shopping for you and deliver it right to your hotel. Call 54207, ext. 22.

"Le Saint Séverin," 87.97.00 (Les Portes de St. Martin). A small restaurant and fine food boutique that also sells wines and spirits. A personal catering service can arrange anything from intimate meals to cocktail parties; place order by 3 P.M. and have it delivered for dinner. Roast duck with orange sauce, $17; cold lobster plate with vegetables, $22; many other dishes to go.

For wines and liquor, try **Le Gout du Vin**, 87.25.03, rue de l'Anguille, Marigot; **La Maison du Vin**, 87.88.97, Zac del Bellevue, Marigot; **La Cave du Savour Club**, 87.58.51 (1, rue de la Liberté).

Useful Information

Complimentary publications to look for in St. Maarten/St. Martin are *Discover, St. Maarten Holiday!, St. Maarten Events, TODAY*, and *Reflets Saint Martin*.

St. Maarten/St. Martin, a physically beautiful island with over 30 splendid beaches, is no longer unspoiled; huge multiroom hotels, casinos (on the Dutch side only), and condominiums abound and continue to spring up. St. Maarten/St. Martin is half French and half Dutch, but there are no formalities at border crossings and travel is unrestricted. Marigot is the French side's charming meandering port capital on the eastern side of the island. Philipsburg, on the historic, more citified south coast, is the capital of the Dutch side—a frustrating maze of one-way streets.

Car rental companies in St. Martin are **Hertz**, (590) 87.73.01; **Avis**, (590) 87.50.60; and **Roy Rogers**, (590) 87.53.31.

I've had some excellent and dependable **taxi** service and drivers from **U.C.T.S.M.** (the union of taxi drivers of St. Martin based in Sandy Ground); 87.08.08. Fax, 87.78.87.

For a day trip to **St. Barts** by sea, take the 75-foot motorized catamaran *White Octopus* from Bobby's Marina, St. Maarten. It departs at 9 A.M. and returns to St. Maarten at 5 P.M.; Days (599-5) 24096, evenings (599-5) 23170. **St. Barth Express**, (599-5) 87.99.03, offers the same jaunt.

Island-hopping flights to any of the nearby islands of **Anguilla, St. Barts, Saba, St. Eustatius, Nevis**, and **St. Kitts** are easily arranged by **Winair** at (599-5) 52002; or contact your travel agent. **Irish Travel Tours**, in conjunction with Winair, organizes several day trips and dive packages to the above-mentioned islands, plus **Domenica**; 53663 (Safari Building, Airport Road, Simpson Bay). Flying time to these island ranges from six to forty minutes.

There is regularly scheduled ferry service to and from the lovely island of **Anguilla** from Marigot. The trip takes about 20 minutes. Anguilla has magnificent beaches and many excellent restaurants. If you have the time, don't miss it (See Recommended Restaurants, Shopping, and Useful Information for Anguilla). Ferries depart Marigot every half hour from 8 A.M. to 5:30 P.M. Return from Anguilla every half hour until 5 P.M. There's also a 7 P.M. and 10:30 P.M. ferry and a 6:15 P.M. and 10:15 P.M. return. One-way fare is $10 per person (children under 12, half price), plus $2 departure tax.

Mullet Bay Resort & Casino has an 18-hole **golf course**.

The Dutch side of the island has several **casinos**.

≈ ≈

ST. VINCENT AND THE GRENADINES

(BEQUIA, MAYREAU, MUSTIQUE, PALM ISLAND, PETIT ST. VINCENT, UNION ISLAND, AND YOUNG ISLAND)

ACCOMMODATIONS

ST. VINCENT AND THE GRENADINES' BEST

The Cotton House Hotel, Mustique
The Mustique Villas, Mustique
Palm Island Beach Club, Palm Island
Petit St. Vincent Resort, Petit St. Vincent
Plantation House Hotel, Bequia
Saltwhistle Bay Club, Mayreau
Young Island, St. Vincent

NOTEWORTHY OPTIONS

Firefly Guest House, Mustique
The Frangipani, Bequia
Petit Byahaut, St. Vincent

RECOMMENDED RESTAURANTS

RECOMMENDED SHOPPING

USEFUL INFORMATION

≈ ≈

≈ ≈
Accommodations

ST. VINCENT AND THE GRENADINES' BEST

The Cotton House Hotel, Mustique

Mustique's bamboo airport terminal looks like the extended backyard of a Caribbean villa, with neat lawns, potted palms, and flags waving majestically. Guests at Cotton House are met and transported to the resort, a five-minute drive from the terminal.

Since new manager Warren W. Francis, Jr., arrived in November 1993, there has been some serious upgrading at the charming 20-room hotel, the only resort on the island. All furniture has been recovered with soft earth tones. Floors have been tiled and bathrooms redone in natural-colored marble. Eight formerly superior rooms have been converted into four double-sized, deluxe two-room suites. New outdoor furniture graces the swimming pool. The Mill Boutique, in a stone sugar mill, has been totally refurbished and stocks upscale resortwear, sunglasses and toiletries, local foods, souvenirs, and sundries.

Three accommodations are located in small individual white-shuttered bungalows with orange-scalloped shingled roofs. Back verandas are roomy and overlook a coconut grove—Mick Jagger's beachfront fortress, and L'Ansecoy Bay. It's about a five-minute walk to reach this spectacular northern beach. Endeavour Beach is smaller but just as splendid, and right on the hotel's property. It faces west for all-day sun.

The rooms at Cotton House are simple elegance. You sleep beneath mosquito netting and a ceiling fan. Hibiscus are tucked at the pillow folds each day. Rooms have writing tables and bookcases that include a diverse selection of books in several languages—guests at Cotton House are an international mix.

Bathrooms have hair dryers and toiletries. There are telephones and room safes, but no TVs, radios, or air-conditioning.

Other lodgings are sprinkled around the lushly planted tropical grounds in four two-story Caribbean Georgian-style dwellings, and a one-level, reconverted stone villa. All rooms have similar amenities and balconies or verandas with lovely views.

The main building at Cotton House is a restored eighteenth-century stone and coral estate warehouse with cedar shutters and huge louvered doors leading out to a wrap-around veranda. New tiles have gone in here. The late Oliver Messel, the renowned decorator/architect and stage designer, originally designed and coordinated all of Cotton

House. He decorated the huge lobby with overstuffed sofas and chairs covered in fabrics that he designed, combined with an eclectic collection of furniture and objets d'art. The romantic open-air terrace dining room is off to one side, overlooking the lawn and out to sea. The restaurant's candlelit seafood dinners are good Créole/international specialities, featuring local vegetables, fruits, spices and herbs.

Mr. Messel designed a beautiful pool and surrounded it with Roman-style ruins. Next to it is a gallery area where breakfasts and buffet lunches are served. The food at midday combines selections of vegetable salads, island fruits, chilled seafood, and the chef's hot-dish special of the day. The pool bar serves tropical treats such as paw paw punch, soursop cocktails, or nonalcoholic lime squash. Service is very friendly.

Our favorite meal—and the whole island's, judging by the size of the crowd—was Saturday night's Flambeaux Beach Barbecue at Endeavor Bay Beach. Magical torches light a path down to the beach, ending in a wide circle. Inside the circle are the bar, barbecue, buffet tables, dining areas—cement circles, each with a built-in table, chairs under a thatched roof, and a round dancing platform. A Vincentian band plays island and popular music. The hearty meal consists of superb callaloo soup, as much fresh grilled lobster, steak, and barbecued chicken as you can eat, baked potatoes, rice and beans, shredded cabbage salad, and freshly baked bread. Dessert might be a wonderful old-fashioned pineapple upside-down cake and fruit salad.

Snorkeling, swimming, and tennis (two courts, no lights) are all free. At an additional cost, horseback riding, fishing, day sails, waterskiing, scuba diving, and jaunts to neighboring islands can be arranged. Guests can visit Mustique's other beaches, of course. Macaroni Beach is the most popular.

We surrendered to the charms of Endeavour Beach, swam, snorkeled, and read under giant palm fronds, and became contented chaise papayas—couch potatoes gone Caribbean.

Privileged Mustique is a casual, pastoral playground. It's genteel England, Southampton, and France with a little spice from Hollywood and the West Indies, and Cotton House is a little gem.

THE COTTON HOUSE HOTEL
P.O. Box 349
Mustique
The Grenadines, West Indies
TEL: (809) 456-4777
FAX: (809) 456-5887

RESERVATIONS
Prima Hotels
TEL: (800) 447-7462 *or*
    (212) 223-2848
FAX: (212) 644-6840

Open all year.
Rates: Double occupancy. *December 16 to January 5:* Deluxe Room, $575; Junior Suite, $660; Deluxe Suite, $760. *January 6 to April 15:* Deluxe Room, $550; Junior Suite, $630; Deluxe Suite, $730. *April 16 to December 15:* Deluxe Room, $325; Junior Suite, $450; Deluxe Suite; $550.

Meal plan: In winter, FAP (includes three meals and afternoon tea); in summer, MAP (includes breakfast and dinner).

Service charge: 10%.

Government tax: 7%.

Children welcome.

Credit cards accepted.

Note: Special summer honeymoon and summer seventh night free packages available. Rates upon request.

The Mustique Villas, Mustique

Of the more than 70 exclusive private villas scattered along the shorelines and throughout the Arcadian hills of Mustique, 42 are available for rental when the owners are not in residence. Belonging to aristocrats, royalty, and celebrities in the arts and business worlds, the distinct villas, with two to six bedrooms, are suitable for four to twelve guests. Decor and amenities vary, depending on the owner's tastes. Most are exquisite homes with glorious sea views and pools. Each villa has 24-hour direct-dial telephones.

The Mustique Villas provide splendid holiday lodgings for honeymooners, families and friends, those wanting a special fantasy home to celebrate a birthday or anniversary, or anyone seeking ultimate privacy and luxurious pampering.

In season, December 1 to April 30, prices range from $3,500 to $13,000 a week, including a vehicle, a Land Rover or Jeep, and household staff—room attendants, a gardener, and a cook. Guests arrange for specific meals or food and drink preferences with their cook, who obtains supplies from the island's general store at the renter's expense. Accounts can be opened at the store, or at the Cotton House and Basil's Beach Bar, the island's only restaurants.

Princess Margaret's Villa, Les Jolies Eaux ("Pretty Waters"), with five bedrooms, costs $8,000 for the week. It's a lovely Messel design with marvelous views and a pool set in gardens below the house. From May 1 to November 30, rates range from $2,900 to $12,000 per week.

For information on renting a Mustique Villa, contact:
RESORTS MANAGEMENT, INC.
The Carriage House
201½ East 29th Street
New York, NY 10016
TEL: (800) 225-4255 *or* in New York (212) 696-4566
FAX: (212) 689-1598

On Mustique, contact:
THE MUSTIQUE COMPANY, LTD.,
P.O. Box 349
The Grenadines
St. Vincent, West Indies
TEL: (809) 458-4621. Telephone exchange is open from 7 A.M. until 10 P.M. only.
FAX: (809) 456-4565

The minimum booking for a villa is one week.

Palm Island Beach Club, Palm Island

You might say that John and Mary Caldwell *are* Palm Island. They transformed their 130-acre private island, formerly called Prune Island, from swampland and brush into a palm-studded, laid-back resort; this was accomplished with the help of sons Johnny and Roger and a corps of West Indian workers. The project was begun in 1966 after the Caldwells retired from their adventurous life of sailing around the world. When you arrive at Palm Island you'll get a copy of their story—called *One Couple's Paradise*—so I won't spoil it for you. John also wrote a book about his exploits called *Desperate Voyage*.

After the flight to Union Island (generally from Barbados), Palm Island guests are taken on a 10-minute cruise to the island aboard the resort's launch.

Accommodations at Palm Island are homespun quarters in double-unit, natural stone and wood cottages. The 24 rooms have king-size or twin beds, each with private bath (water is heated by solar panels on the roofs), unstocked refrigerator, ceiling fan, and an outside, walled-in sun patio with a fixed coconut-frond-covered gazebo where a simple tea is served every afternoon promptly at 4 P.M.

Inside, rattan furniture blends with the original handmade wooden pieces. There are closets with drawers and a shelf storage area. Mosquito netting is positioned over the beds, and vertical louvers swing open to verdant tropical scenery surrounding the cottages. The craggy hills of Union Island across the sea to the west provide the backdrop. There are no TVs, radios, air-conditioning, or swimming pool.

Bathrooms have showers and are on the small side. They are stocked with Palm Island toiletries and all the bath towels needed, plus large beach towels emblazoned with a nautical motif. An umbrella is provided but probably won't be necessary as Palm Island claims at least 300 days of sun a year.

The welcome at Palm Island begins with a complimentary cocktail and a buffet lunch in the high wooden-beam-ceilinged dining pavilion. Chef Prince's dinners are candlelit multicourse meals featuring lobster twice weekly, plus such favorites as roast beef with oven-roasted potatoes, and seafood or Créole specialties. Soups are good—cream of carrot was our favorite. Desserts are always delicious—we had an unusually good trifle with nuts, raisins, and pineapple. Room service is available for all meals.

In season, Palm Island has a Saturday night steak and fish barbecue with a steel band and "jump-up." A manager's Punch Party is held on the beach on Wednesdays, followed by a fish and chicken barbecue. A calypso band entertains.

Full water-sports gear and activities offered include scuba diving, resort dive courses, windsurfing, snorkeling apparatus (coral groves are abundant), small boats, offshore fishing, and day-sailing parties on Palm Island's fleet of boats.

Palm Island's five beautiful beaches make it possible for guests to cast away on Petit Martinique Bay, Tamarind, Wreck Bay, or Coral Bay beaches, but the more-than-a-mile-long Casuarina Beach is the most stunning. The glorious talcum-powder sand beach winds around the shoreline from the north to the south, shaded by Casuarina pine trees, croton, sea grapes, and coconut palms.

A nice diversion comes in the form of exercise. Jog or walk around Palm Island's one-mile Highway 90 — John's "road to health, fitness, and longevity" trail. John gives fitness sessions three times a week, too. The diverse clientele, young and old, joins in the fun.

Palm Island has one lighted tennis court located next to the guest lounge, where you'll find a TV, video, Ping-Pong, table games, and reading materials.

La Boutique sells charming beachwear, local handcrafts, jewelry, beach towels, thongs, and sundries. The shop is attached to the dive shop on the beach, adjacent to the open-air, circular-shaped bar and patio.

A small rustic grocery store, Halfway Mart, carries staple foods, beverages, produce, notions, drugstore items, and snacks.

Palm Island is an active, yet gentle, touching getaway. The Caldwells, and a friendly West Indian staff, do everything they can to make your stay at Palm Island the low-key tropical-paradise vacation that the doctor ordered.

PALM ISLAND BEACH CLUB
Palm Island, The Grenadines
St. Vincent, West Indies
TEL: (809) 458-8804
FAX: (809) 458-8804, ask for fax

RESERVATIONS
Paradise Found, Inc.
TEL: (800) 776-7256 *or*
(301) 990-0277
FAX: (301) 990-0290

Open all year.
Rates: Double occupancy. *April 15 to December 20:* $245 to $345. *December 21 to April 14:* Rooms range from $265 to $345.
Meal plan: FAP (includes breakfast, lunch, afternoon tea, and dinner).
Service charge: 10%.
Government tax: 7%.
Children welcome.
Credit cards accepted.

Petit St. Vincent Resort, Petit St. Vincent 👑

I am proud to announce that 25 years ago, on December 22, 1968, I welcomed our first guest to Petit St. Vincent Resort. We have maintained our original concept of offering luxury accommodations, fine cuisine, and excellent service, in an atmosphere which offers the maximum in privacy and serenity, with just 22 private cottages."

HAZEN K. RICHARDSON II, OWNER/MANAGER

The excellent news at Petit St. Vincent, also called PSV, is that there is still no news. No *TimesFax*, no televisions, and no telephones. The 55% winter repeaters keep pleading— "Please, don't change a thing." Subtle changes are made here, of course, like continual refurbishing, the addition of more thatched-roof beach shelters with hammocks dotting the beaches, plantings, hair dryers, lighted cosmetic mirrors in cottage dressing rooms, and set-up bars stocked with liquors and sodas in the cottages. The resort is producing garden-fresh lettuce, and a small chicken farm here provides hours-old fresh eggs.

On a recent visit, I arrived unscheduled at Union Island and had just missed Petit St. Vincent's Grand Banks private motor-yacht. I called the resort and owner/manager Haze Richardson cheerfully offered, "If you don't mind a small boat, I'll be there in 20 minutes." He was at the dock at Union in 15 minutes. The trip to PSV, four miles away, on Richardson's small, fast motor skiff was an exhilarating journey, especially for a non–boat person like myself. Captain Richardson skillfully steered us through waves like a bullet, passing fish glistening in leaps through the air en route to the resort.

Petit St. Vincent, shaped like an elongated mitten, is located 40 miles south of St. Vincent in the windswept Grenadines. The only development on the 113-acre private island is the quintessential Caribbean hideaway resort bearing the same name. Petit St. Vincent is a jeroboam of champagne for anyone looking for remote island seclusion, superior accommodations (only 22 cottages—three are double units, the rest individual bungalows), efficient service, and an informal atmosphere with an Arcadian environment. Astounding panoramas greet you at every turn, and silky white sand beaches, rimmed in coral, almost circle the two-mile perimeter of the island with plenty of beaches for swimming.

The best route to the resort is from Barbados. There you transfer to a commuter plane or a charter flight, which PSV will organize, to Union Island. At Union Island, Petit St. Vincent's Grand Banks collects guests for an entrancing 35-minute crossing to PSV. Whales are spotted in the channel occasionally. You will pass a tiny islet, an oasis composed entirely of sand, with thatched bohios. The island is affectionately named Petit St. Richardson, after Hazen K. Richardson, who has masterminded and managed PSV from ground-breaking ceremonies to the present.

With 24 hours' notice the resort will drop you off at Petit St. Richardson for a box-lunch picnic and total privacy, except for passing boats. A PSV motorboat will return to pick you up after a few hours of reverie. If you go, bring sunblock, sun hats or visors, and snorkeling gear.

At PSV's dock you are welcomed with piña coladas. Within minutes, a Mini-Moke has delivered you to your cottage. Number 20 is the closest to the public area: the restaurant, bar and open-air terrace lounge, excellent boutique, and reception. Although only a three- or four-minute walk to the dining room, the bungalow is a quiet haven of privacy, with a south-facing terrace overlooking the dock, the boat-filled harbor, and the nearby island of Petit Martinique. Check-in comes later, when it's convenient, and checkout can be arranged in your own quarters.

Other cottages are situated on hilltops, sides of cliffs, and on the beach. The ideal rooms for seaside living on the Atlantic side are numbers 6 through 11. Cottage 1 is the most secluded, facing north; number 18, another favorite, sits on a tiny bluff at the island's southwestern tip—a staircase leads down to a beach that's virtually private. Two others have stairways leading directly to the beach.

All the keyless cottages, surrounded by tropical plantings, have patios, sizable living rooms with two daybed-sofas that sleep extra guests, a bedroom with two queen-size beds with outstanding lighting, a dressing room, a bath with a round, natural-stone, curtained shower stall and either twin-sink vanities or two separate sink and counter areas. Enough closet and storage space, fold-up beach chairs, roll-up beach mats, and umbrellas are provided. So are two blue-trimmed white terry-cloth robes, and a heaping basket of toiletries. Thick-pile towels, a Black & Decker Spot Liter, a CD player (bring your own CDs), and a constantly filled ice bucket are more of the amenities at PSV.

PSV has no air-conditioning, but attractive vertical wooden louvers, sliding screen doors, and ceiling fans cool the rooms nicely. The cottage's natural stone walls and dark hardwood peaked roofs (newly reshingled) create a further cooling effect, combined with the pastel fabrics used throughout. Bouquets of flowers, framed prints, and khus-khus rugs on quarry-tile floors all add up to stylish Caribbean comfort.

Communicating service needs to the staff from the phoneless cottages, many at some distance from the main building, is solved with flair and ingenuity. At the pathway entrance of each bungalow stands a bamboo flagpole with two flags on a pulley. The yellow flag means that you have a request—this can be anything from extra towels or a transportation pickup to room-service orders or afternoon tea. A red flag means *Do not disturb under any circumstances.* An attendant rides the trails in an almost silent Mini-Moke checking the signals.

If ordered the previous evening, early-morning coffee or tea is left on a shelf outside the stone wall gate of your cottage, so that no one is disturbed. At a specified time, a sumptuous breakfast is delivered. Lunches aren't elaborate, but are perfectly satisfying salads, cheeses, and cold cuts accompanied by a hot dish or two.

Chef Slick's dinners are selections like escargot and lobster en croûte in coquille, and broiled kingfish with lime. A flan, chocolate cake, and freshly made soursop ice cream are all very good.

Water-sports activities are many. Swim or snorkel over the reefs right off the shore. Hobie Cats, Sunfish, windsurfers for all levels, and snorkeling gear are free. Waterskiing, deep-sea fishing, day sails on PSV's charter boat and scuba diving and instruction are available for an extra charge.

PSV has one lighted tennis court, racquets, and an oscillating ball machine free to guests. There is no swimming pool.

A 20-station, self-paced, self-guided exercise and jogging trail winds along the beach through savannas and into the woods. Guests also can take long walks with seven gentle yellow Labradors, island denizens who will become your pets-away-from-home, if encouraged.

A luncheon and evening barbecue is held on the beach every week, and musicians entertain several nights a week. The only other entertainment are the passengers and crews from the continually arriving boats that anchor off the island. PSV is a "must" stop in the Grenadines for drinking, dining, and socializing. Outsiders are restricted to the public areas, but the resort wouldn't be as much fun or as interesting without the lively banter. It's all part of the fluidity of Petit St. Vincent, an aristocrat of private island resorts, that Haze and Lynn Richardson run with tender loving care and expertise.

PETIT ST. VINCENT	RESERVATIONS
RESORT	Petit St. Vincent
Petit St. Vincent,	P.O. Box 12506
The Grenadines	Cincinnati, OH 45212
St. Vincent, West Indies	TEL: (800) 654-9326 *or*
TEL: (809) 458-8801	(513) 242-1333
FAX: (809) 458-8428	FAX:(513) 242-6951

Closed: September and October.
Rates: Double occupancy. *November 1 to December 18:* Cottage, $430; additional adult, $125. *December 19 to March 12:* Cottage, $680; additional adult, $205. *March 13 to April 10:* Cottage, $555; additional adult, $170.
Meal plan: FAP (includes breakfast, lunch, and dinner, plus afternoon tea, room or beach service).
Service charge: 10%.
Government tax: 7%.
Children welcome.
Credit cards not accepted.
Note: Special summer packages are available.

Plantation House Hotel, Bequia

The best accommodations in Bequia stand in a 10-acre palm grove on the waterfront at Admiralty Bay in Port Elizabeth at the 25-room Plantation House Hotel. Fifteen charming little cabanas in the grove have twin beds, a shower room, and ceiling fans. The remaining, more spacious deluxe rooms are located on the second floor of the two-story peach-colored Plantation House, with air-conditioning; or the jewels on the oceanfront with ceiling fans and verandas.

Nothing on Bequia is ultra-luxurious, but Plantation House comes as close to superior as it gets here.

The Plantation House's pretty, cool veranda evening restaurant serves well-prepared local dishes, pastas, and very good seafood. The hotel's location between the Frangipani and Mac's Pizzeria, and near other restaurants and shopping, is excellent. Still, it's an extremely tranquil atmosphere, and living is comfortable in this well-run hotel. Laundry and room service are available.

Dive Bequia is at the water's edge for water sports. There is a lighted tennis court, a sizable freeform swimming pool, a beach grill and bar restaurant, and lawns with luxuriant tropical gardens. Plantation House's 600-foot beach is a great plus, and gorgeous Princess Margaret Beach is within walking distance.

PLANTATION HOUSE	RESERVATIONS
P.O. Box 16, Bequia	E & M Associates
St. Vincent and The Grenadines,	211 East 43rd Street
West Indies	New York, NY 10017
TEL: (809) 458-3425	TEL: (800) 223-9832 *or*
FAX: (809) 458-3612	(212) 599-8280
	FAX: (212) 599-1755

Open all year.
Rates: Double occupancy. *December 15 to April 20:* Cabana, $300; Deluxe, $330. *April 21 to December 14:* Cabana; $180; Deluxe, $190.
Meal plan: MAP in winter. Summer, room only.
Service charge: 12%.
Government tax: 7%.
Children welcome.
Credit cards accepted.
Note: Packages are available.

Saltwhistle Bay Club, Mayreau 🌴

Sometimes a resort's greatest disadvantage can also be its greatest asset. This is true of eight-year-old Saltwhistle Bay Club on the enchanting 700-acre island of Mayreau in the Grenadines, located roughly halfway between St. Vincent and Grenada. Mayreau has a population of about 250, mostly fishermen.

Saltwhistle Bay's main drawback is its inaccessibility, as Mayreau can only be reached by boat. But the resort's unique isolation, tranquil and beautiful natural surroundings, its perfect long curve of white sand beach, transparent, gentle sea, tasteful accommodations, decent food, and welcoming staff make this small resort a special kind of deluxe rustic retreat. There are no real roads, cars, or airport on the island.

To reach Mayreau, guests ordinarily fly from Barbados to the newly extended airport at Union Island (interisland transfers can be arranged by the resort), clear customs, and are met by the crew of the hotel's motor launch for a 20-minute cruise to the resort. This method of transfer is standard procedure for remote small island resorts.

Owner/manager Undine Potter greets guests with rum cocktails. Mrs. Potter and her husband, Tom, built the hotel from scratch over a period of ten years.

The natural stone lodgings at Saltwhistle Bay sit a few yards back from the beach, separated only by an expansive palm grove and a scattering of hammocks. (It is a falling coconut zone, so choose your path carefully.)

We were in Hibiscus, half of one of the resort's cottages. Each has two good-sized bedrooms and private bathrooms. Connecting doors through an outside hallway in the back lead to a stairway. The occupants of the cottage share an upper, open-air, roof-covered aerie with tables, chairs, and a hammock. It's a great spot if you're with friends or family.

Other rooms, in a single building, are small and would be the second choice. There are 20 rooms in all.

The abundance of flowers in our room came fresh in vases and in pictures on framed batik cloth hangings on the wall. The comfortable rooms have cool, brown-tiled floors, a ceiling fan, purple-heart and green-heartwood louvered windows, and some hand-crafted wood and new rattan furniture, including a writing table with a selection of books. Bedtable lamps and a hanging one over a sitting area provide plenty of reading light.

Floral-printed spreads covered king-size beds. A wooden cabinet closet was an adequate size.

The bathroom has a round open, stone-walled and white-tile-floored shower, a wooden vanity with drawers, a brightly lit sink area, and stack of bath and beach towels. Water is heated by the sun.

Insect repellent, floats, and umbrellas for the beach are supplied. You'll find no TV, radio, phone, or swimming pool here.

The outstanding man-made feature of Saltwhistle Bay is the cluster of round, stone, cushioned banquettes with center circle tables under wooden and thatched rooftops that actually serves as the dining room. There's a sizable open-air bar pavilion nearby.

The food at Saltwhistle is mostly a choice of fresh seafood and daily specials, depending on availability. A tasty lentil soup, roasted stuffed Cornish game hens, boiled potatoes, vegetables, and apple crisp were very good. A generous portion of plain lobster salad at lunch was superb, as were the freshly made dinner rolls and firm white bread.

Snorkeling gear, windsurfers, and fishing rods are included in the room rate. Scuba diving, "Champagne" nighttime sailing, "Sundowner" cruises, or "Robinson Crusoe" picnics and fishing jaunts can be had at an extra cost. The unspoiled, uninhabited Tobago Cays are adjacent to Mayreau and worth a visit.

For an adventure take a 30-minute trek through the bush and bucolic countryside along a trail to the top of the hill. Here you can visit the school, church, and little village. (There are two small dining options on Mayreau now. See Recommended Restaurants.) The magnificent view is a full panorama of the Grenadines. Sometimes, a cruise ship anchors off a western beach of Mayreau. Passengers are tendered to the beach for a swim and picnic. Standing on the crest of the hill next to a grazing donkey, the sight can be surrealistic—as if modern-day pirates were invading paradise. We retreated back to the seclusion of Saltwhistle Bay, where aside from guests and staff, the only people one sees are occasional fishermen and boaters. The resort is a favorite stopover for lunch or dinner and overnight anchorage. The day we arrived, a group of Frenchmen had come ashore from their sailboat to play a game of *boule* in the palm grove.

On the windward side of the resort's 16-acre property is another beach, good for a stroll and a few snapshots, but not for swimming because of the strong surf.

Saltwhistle's mini-boutique carries T-shirts, cover-ups, other casual clothing, jewelry, and sundries.

Table tennis, volleyball, darts, backgammon, cards, chess, and other available games can occupy the time, but the varied clientele here all tend to prefer just luxuriating in the peaceful serenity of the place. At idyllic Saltwhistle Bay everything comes to a quantum standstill.

SALTWHISTLE BAY CLUB
Mayreau
St. Vincent and The Grenadines,
West Indies
TEL: (800) 561-7258
  or in Canada
  (613) 634-7108
FAX: (613) 384-6300

Closed September and October.
Rates: Double occupancy. *December 15 to March 31:* $490; extra person in room, $160.
  April 1 to August 31: $300; extra person in room, $100. Children under 18, half
  price.
Meal plan: MAP (includes breakfast and dinner).
Service charge: 10%.
Government tax: 7%.
Children 5 and above welcome.
Credit cards not accepted.

Young Island, St. Vincent

I have a special affinity for the seclusion and intimacy of private island resorts. Young Island is singular in several other appealing ways as well, especially for those who appreciate, as I do, true West Indian ambience, and a relaxed and casual atmosphere in a natural setting.

Young Island is a 10-minute drive from the airport, then a five-minute cruise across the 200 yards of sea that separate it from St. Vincent. The vessel of transport, a curious mix of motorized skiff and the *African Queen,* is indigenous to St. Vincent. We came to grow very fond of its putt-putt crossings during our sojourn here.

Stepping onto the dock, we were welcomed by a waiter delivering a potent, hibiscus-capped rum punch, and an attendant who accompanied us up a maze of natural stone stairways, shrouded in tropical foliage, to our cottage, number 27. I'm not sure which was more intoxicating—the drink, or the view from the roomy open-air terrace gallery.

Peering out over Young Island's own jungle and across the sparkling necklace of sea to the smoky hills of St. Vincent, bathed in the intense golden light of the late afternoon, one immediately felt enveloped in this 25-acre Shangri-la. You want to kick off your shoes, and that's just what you are encouraged to do by owner/manager Vidal S. Browne.

This resort has the natural luxuries of outdoor enclosed stone showers attached to quarters, gaily hand-painted friezes bordering the room ceilings, local artwork, vases of fresh flowers, a basket of fresh fruit in your room upon arrival in the mini-refrigerator, with no distracting phones, TVs, or radios. Attractive, oval-shaped, vertical, wooden window louvers provide cross-ventilation, and ceiling fans promote continual cool comfort.

The cozy, homey rooms include firm king-size beds and sturdy chairs, desks and chairs, and adequate bathrooms (and outdoor showers, as mentioned). The bathrooms in the luxury suites are much larger and grader. Thick terry-cloth robes and oversized, fluffy, blue beach towels are provided, as are wall safes and toiletries. No hair dryers.

The 29 cottages and suites, of varying sizes and layouts, some with tiny plunge pools, are threaded along the white sand carpet of beach, beyond to the rocky coast, and up onto the hillside. It's a trek to the upper units, but I like these locations best for their marvelous views, especially suites 27 and 29.

Drowsy days can be spent in hammocks under thatched roofs on the beach, or lounging by the spacious, freeform saltwater pool set in an almost ridiculous wealth of flora. (One thing the hotel needs—by the pool and on the beach—are new chaise longues with thick cushions. The ones on our recent trip were hard and uncomfortable.) If thirst interrupts idleness, simply wade or swim out to the floating Coconut Bar a few yards offshore for a banana daiquiri and fresh coconut strips. (It's open only between 10 A.M. and 2 P.M.)

For diversions from inactivity there is a tennis court (you must pay a fee to light the court at night), and the hotel's yachts are available for chartered day sails in the area. Or you can visit other islands, Bequia and Mustique—overnight trips aboard can also be arranged. Young Island Dive St. Vincent will organize expeditions to explore the underwater wonders nearby.

Young Island has its own assigned taxi drivers, who, with a little advance notice, will meet you at the dock on the St. Vincent side, and take you sightseeing or shopping.

We never ventured off Young Island at night. After cocktails in the sprawling Captain Bligh Bar, dinner is served in the adjacent thatched roofed hut pavilions or in the tiered, Polynesian-style dining room. The meals on our last trip were excellent. Banana pancakes, eggs, bacon, or a West Indian breakfast with delicious snapper and johnnycakes rated A-1. Dinners were offerings from a buffet of smoked salmon, roast beef, pork, turkey, and a variety of vegetables and first-rate desserts.

At lunch and dinner a giant bread board, laden with five whole loaves of freshly baked warm bread, are offered: coconut, banana, whole wheat, raisin, and white. Generous slices of your selections are cut tableside before meals or served at the buffet table.

One night a week, interested guests are ferried to Fort Duvernette, Young Island's 250-foot-high annex island, where English cannons and ruins of the fort still exist.

There's live music during a torchlit cocktail party, replete with hors d'oeuvres, before you head back for dinner.

Young Island's Dock Shop, located next to the French Restaurant at the dock right across from the resort, carries sea-island cotton batiks, silk screens, swimwear, T-shirts, and handcrafts.

When you wake up in the morning at Young Island, you'll hear barking dogs or rooster crows from distant St. Vincent, reminders of reality from your privileged perch. Young Island is not for the finicky. Service can be uneven. It doesn't always seem as caring as in the past. Owner/manager Vidal S. Browne is building a small hotel called Browne's, across from Young Island in St. Vincent at the shoreline, which should open for the 1995 season.

Communication at Young Island can be frustrating. We had to leave early in the morning, and although we'd notified the office for a bellman at 6:30 A.M., none arrived. We couldn't carry all our luggage, so we had to climb down and find someone to collect the bags, which made us late for the airport. A flag system like Petit St. Vincent's would be an improvement.

YOUNG ISLAND
P.O. Box 211, Young Island
St. Vincent, West Indies
TEL: (809) 458-4826
FAX: (809) 457-4567

RESERVATIONS
Ralph Locke Islands, Inc.
TEL: (800) 223-1108 *or*
(310) 440-3225
FAX: (310) 440-4220

Open all year.
Rates: Double occupancy. *December 14 to February 28:* Superior, $430; Deluxe, $500, Luxury, $590. *March 1 to April 14:* Superior, $335; Deluxe, $405, Luxury, $495. *April 15 to December 17:* Superior, $275, Deluxe, $345; Luxury, $435.
Meal plan: MAP (includes breakfast and dinner), with 17% government tax and gratuities.
Service charge: 10%.
Government tax: 7%.
Children under 5 not permitted January 15 to March 15.
Credit cards accepted.
Note: Packages are available.

NOTEWORTHY OPTIONS

Firefly Guest House, Mustique

A most pleasant and inexpensive alternative to one of Mustique's pricey villas or the Cotton House is the four-room Firefly Guest House. Owned and run by Billy Mitchell, the Firefly overlooks Britannia Bay. Guests only have to walk a few minutes to the beach, Basil's Bar and Restaurant, and the Cotton House. Mrs. Mitchell's daughter, Gala, who helps out at the inn and also gives massages and yoga classes on the beach, suggests that guests rent a scooter, buggy, or Jeep from Kurt Meyers after arriving if their budget allows. This is good advice, unless you like walking up and down hills.

All four rooms are neat, with white walls, white upholstery, and cushioned furniture, interspersed with a few antique pieces. The choice two rooms are in the front where, as Mrs. Mitchell says, the lovely views are the walls. Louvered doors close across these enchanting views at night to give you privacy. Every room has a ceiling fan, adequate bathroom with shower, mini-refrigerator, and balcony.

Full breakfasts at Firefly are savored in a large upper terrace room. This aerie is open all day and evening as a comfy lounge/library with cable TV and an honor-system bar. Tropical flowers and shrubbery abound at Firefly, inside and out. The staff is friendly, and the charms of this guest house are plentiful enough to satisfy undemanding vacationers.

FIREFLY GUEST HOUSE
Mrs. Billy Mitchell
P.O. Box 349
Mustique
St. Vincent and The Grenadines
TEL: (809) 456-3414

Open all year.
Rates: Double occupancy. *December 1 to December 21:* $107. *December 22 to January 3:* $150. *January 4 to April 30:* $107. *May 1 to November 30:* $80. Add $5 per day for air-conditioning.
Meal plan: AP (includes full American breakfast).
Service charge: 10%.
Government tax: 7%.
Children not recommended.
Credit cards accepted.
Note: Special discounts for lengthy stays. Rates on request.

The Frangipani, Bequia

The small, waterfront Frangipani terrace is Bequia's equivalent of Rome's Via Veneto. Everyone on the island seems to pass through at least once a day—mothers with babies, expatriates, fishermen, travelers, salty sailors, Rastafarians, giggling children, starry-eyed lovers, cruiseship passengers, and elegant Europeans from luxury sailboats. Still, the Frangipani is the favorite place to be. It sits right on the seafront shoreline of Port Elizabeth, the island's only town, on beautiful, protected Admiralty Bay, which is a popular port stop for boaters in the Grenadines.

The red-roofed Frangipani opened in the late sixties. It was once the family home of the current Bequia-born owner, James "Son" Mitchell, who is the prime minister of St. Vincent and the Grenadines. Marie Kingston manages the modest 15-room hotel.

Accommodations are located in five rooms on the second floor of the stone and shingled two-story main building. Downstairs is the lobby, reception, and restaurant. One of the rooms upstairs is furnished with antiques, including a four-poster bed. The room has a private bath. The other four lodgings here share baths. There's a common outdoor terrace for guests that overlooks the hotel's front patio and out over the harbor. With the exception of the specially furnished room, the best thing about these spaces is their low rates. The choice, quieter rooms at Frangipani are set in the back of the hotel across a lawn of frangipani, croton, palms, hibiscus, and sea grape. Two two-story cottages built of natural stone and hardwood contain four units each—two up and two down. One of the buildings was constructed in 1990, and because its accommodations are slightly larger and have newer furnishings, I'd book a room there. A two-bedroom house with a shared living room sits next door. Each accommodation has a private bathroom with a shower, a dressing room, and a private sundeck. Two twin beds are placed together under mosquito nets. Louvered windows and doors and an electric fan cool the air; closet space is sufficient. Several shelves provide extra storage space. Rooms are very plain but comfortable and have rush rugs and terra-cotta floors. There's no pool, phones, TVs, or radios. The second-floor lodgings are better for privacy and views.

The Frangipani has a single hard-surface tennis court, but no other sports activities.

Dining pleasures on Bequia are as simple as the general lifestyle. Frangipani's fare has improved considerably since Mr. Mitchell's daughter took over the kitchen. The menu focuses on seafood and local produce. Service is pleasant, as is the atmosphere. No room service is available at Frangipani.

On Bequia, water taxis are more common than ground transportation, with an endless parade of numbered launches searching for passengers along the waterfront and beaches.

Frangipani has a Thursday night "jump-up" barbecue with a steel band playing on a covered bandstand. You'll be joined by locals and the hotel's melting pot of guests for the fun.

Frangipani has no real boutique, but T-shirts and a few items such as Cuban cigars are on sale. Shops, markets, and boutiques wrap around the shoreline to and beyond the hotel from the village.

At the end of the evening you can sit on Frangipani's terrace on Caribbean versions of Adirondack chairs, listening to lapping water, sipping a nightcap, and overlooking the peaceful harbor. Bequia still offers the stress-free island living of yesteryear, and Frangipani is a delightful unpretentious hostelry.

THE FRANGIPANI
Bequia
P.O. Box 1,
St. Vincent and The Grenadines, West Indies
TEL: (809) 458-3255
FAX: (809) 458-3824

Closed September to early October.

Rates: Double occupancy. *December 16 to April 14:* $50 to $120. *April 15 to December 15:* $40 to $80. Extra person in room, $20 year-round.

Meal plan: EP. MAP (includes breakfast and dinner), add $20 per person per day.

Service charge: None.

Government tax: 7%.

Children welcome.

Credit cards accepted.

Petit Byahaut, St. Vincent

Accessible only by sea, Petit Byahaut is a 50-acre valley, beachfront naturalist's retreat on the southwestern coast of St. Vincent. Guests can arrive only by sea, a short four-mile cruise from Kingstown, in a ferry or water taxi.

Life at the resort is comfortable, bivouacking in one of seven 10 × 13-foot tent shelters stationed on roof-covered wood platform decks on a hillside location overlooking the sea. Beds are queen-size and showers solar heated. There are no phones, no electricity, or traditional amenities like hair dryers in this secluded jungle sanctuary. The sun and breezes will dry your locks organically.

The resort's alfresco restaurant provides all meals with an emphasis on vegetarian cuisine, using the island's extraordinary vegetables and exotic fruits. Dinners are candlelit affairs. Sundries and T-shirts can be found in a small boutique, and Petit Byahaut has an abundance of water-sports facilities, including snorkeling and sail- and rowboats. The young owners, Sharon Schrama and Charles Meistrell, will organize scuba dives, as well as other nature excursions on sea or through nature trails.

Boat service is included for guests who book in this lush tropical cocoon for three or more nights; otherwise, it's $50 round trip per person. Moorings and air-fills are available for rental for independent boaters. Outsiders are welcome to come and spend the day if they make reservations in advance. Meals start at $10.

Petit Byahaut is a supreme "green," laid-back hideaway for campers and the adventurous who desire close contact with nature in St. Vincent's voluptuous, unspoiled wilderness.

PETIT BYAHAUT
Petit Byahaut
St. Vincent and The Grenadines, West Indies
TEL/FAX: (809) 457-7008
VHF 68

Open all year.

Rates: Double occupancy. Year-round: Hilltop, $250; Hillside, $290. Round-trip ferry from Kingston at the Grenadine Pier free for guests.

Meal plan: FAP (includes breakfast, lunch, and dinner).
Service charge: 10%.
Government tax: 7%.
Children welcome.
Credit cards accepted are Mastercard and VISA only.
Note: Special group and five-day package rates and scuba packages are available.

Recommended Restaurants

ST. VINCENT AND THE GRENADINES' FINEST*

The majority of the top restaurants and most charming dining options in St. Vincent and the Grenadines are at the excellent private island resorts in the region. Read the restaurant descriptions in the accommodations listing for each of the following resorts: *Saltwhistle Bay Club in Mayreau; *The Cotton House Hotel in Mustique; *Palm Island Beach Club on Palm Island off Union Island; *Petit St. Vincent Resort on Petit St. Vincent; and *Young Island just off the coast of St. Vincent. Reservations are requested at all restaurants.

OTHER DEPENDABLE CHOICES

BEQUIA

The Old Fort Country Inn, 458-3440 (hilltop Mount Pleasant). Dine in a remote stone fortress or adjoining airy terrace in Otmar and Sonja Schaedle's restaurant on Mediterranean/Créole cuisine that includes spring lamb, barbecued barracuda, and other commendable seafood dishes. Delightful candlelit dining. Moderate to expensive.
Le Petit Jardin, 458-3318 (Back Street, Port Elizabeth). Artfully presented meats, seafoods, and salads complemented with imported and island produce are offered here. Nice wines. Moderate to expensive.
Mac's Pizzeria & Bake Shop, 458-3474 (waterfront to west of Frangipani Hotel). This informal two-tiered, wooden-decked café serves fabulous lobster pizza, conch fritters, quiche, sandwiches on freshly baked pita bread, and other selections. Mac's bakery produces bran muffins, a variety of breads, cookies, cakes, and sweet rolls. Inexpensive to moderate.
Gingerbread Restaurant & Bar, 458-3800 (waterfront to the east of Mac's Pizzeria). This second-floor terrace restaurant with lovely views of Admiralty Bay serves good seafood and quick foods. Inexpensive to moderate. (Also at Gingerbread, you'll find grilled barbecued chicken and seafood you eat at shoreline picnic tables.)
Spring on Bequia, 458-3414 (10-minute ride from Port Elizabeth on hillside over-

looking Spring Bay). Casual, open-air dining room of the Spring on Bequia hotel, serving three meals in pastoral, tropical atmosphere. Sunday brunch, excellent curry is featured. Inexpensive to moderate.

Frangipani and **Plantation House Restaurant** (and **Coco's Grill** there) on Admiralty Bay are pleasant dining choices (see resort listings). Moderate.

Friendship Bay Restaurant, 458-3222 (southwestern side of island at Friendship Bay Resort). The Saturday night "jump-up" barbecue dinner at the beach with lobster, beef, and chicken is lots of fun. Other nights dinners are served in the hillside restaurant. Moderate.

For West Indian seaside dining, go to **De Reef** on Lower Bay, **The Whaleboner**, next to Frangipani, **Old Fig Tree** and **Green Boley** on Belmont Beach south of Gingerbread. And don't miss **Maranne's Ice Cream** at Boley's, made with fresh fruits.

Fernando's Hideaway (locally known as Nando's, on hill at Lower Bay), is *the* place to go for Wednesday and Saturday night entertainment and terrific local fare like goat water (a stew). **Theresa's** on Lower Bay serves rotating international cuisines for dinner.

MAYREAU

Other than **Saltwhistle Bay Club**, these are the only two other options in Mayreau:

Dennis' Hideaway, 458-8594 (Saline Bay). A tiny inn, supermarket, and restaurant that serves fresh fish and seafood in laid-back surroundings. Inexpensive to moderate.

Island Paradise, no phone (above Dennis' Hideaway). James Alexander, formerly at Petit St. Vincent, has opened a small café serving seafood and island fare with splendid views.

MUSTIQUE

Basil's Bar & The Raft, 458-4621 (Britannia Bay). The only restaurant on Mustique other than that at **The Cotton House Hotel**. Everyone eventually shows up for the merriment here to drink or dine on excellent seafood. Wednesday is the weekly "jump-up" barbecue, but the mood is pretty uninhibited all the time. Don't miss the central-casting mix of characters socializing—chic home-owners, first-time renters, movie stars, industrialists, royalty, local workers, and fishermen, hosted by towering charmer, Basil Charles. This impresario also owns the bakery, general store, gift shop, and a water-sports center. Basil has another bar and restaurant in St. Vincent (see following listing).

ST. VINCENT

French Restaurant, 458-4972 (Villa Beach, across from Young Island). This casual garden terrace restaurant at the seaside's edge serves food that is a mix of French and local cuisine. It's very popular, but the food isn't as great as it once was. Still, go for the pleasant atmosphere, decent fare, and fine service. Moderate to expensive.

Lime N' Pub, 458-4227 (Villa Beach, south of French Restaurant across from Young

Island). Very casual garden and elevated terraced restaurant by the sea serving flavor-packed Vincentian-style flying fish, pigeon pea, pumpkin, lobster, callaloo, and crayfish soups. Sample entries: scallops of grouper Provençale, deviled crab back, and a large assortment of seafood dishes; for dessert, Black Forest cake, fresh lemon cheesecake, and bananas flambée. Moderate to expensive.

Cobblestone Roof Top Restaurant, 456-1937/1177 (in Cobblestone Inn on Bay Street, Kingstown). This is a quiet terrace courtside second-floor restaurant that serves West Indian daily specials and burgers, sandwiches, and so on. Friendly service. Inexpensive to moderate.

Basil's Bar & Restaurant, 457-2713 (downstairs at the Cobblestone Inn on Bay Street, Kingstown). Sister restaurant to Basil's on Mustique, but this one's not as much fun. Popular, of course, but dark and air-conditioned, with a smoky atmosphere. Moderate.

Petit Byahaut, 457-7008 (VHF 68) (southwestern coast of St. Vincent, four miles from Kingstown). For an unforgettable adventure, spend a day at this private, totally secluded retreat (see resort listing) and lunch al fresco on vegetarian or local specialties with other nature lovers. Expensive to reach. Hotel-arranged ferry costs $50 round trip, so try to find your own transportation. Reservations are a must. Food is moderately priced.

Vee Jay's Rooftop Diner & Pub, 457-2845/1395 (Upper Bay Street above Rogers' Photo Studios). Worth a visit for some wonderful rôtis, burgers, salads, and fish and chips as well as some real island atmosphere and sea views. There's another restaurant downstairs, so make sure to go to the rooftop. Inexpensive to moderate.

Browne's Hotel, no phone at press time (across from Young Island, with same owner). The new seaside hotel's restaurant will feature West Indian specialities. Since Young Island's food has improved considerably, it should be worth checking out. Moderate.

Following are some other interesting alternatives: **Grand View Beach Hotel**, above Kingstown, **The Dolphin Restaurant** next to the Lime N' Pub, and, a drive 30 minutes away to the northwest, **The Valley** at the Emerald Valley Resort and Casino.

UNION ISLAND

Anchorage Yacht Club Restaurant, 458-8221 (Clifton, dockside near airport). Here you'll find a very good French/Caribbean menu featuring accras, lobster pie with cardinale sauce, conch stew, superb grilled fresh lobsters, and duck breast with mango sauce. Desserts range from chocolate mousse and profiteroles to a gratin of fresh fruits. There's also a take-out section with quiche, pizza, and excellent baguette sandwiches. Be sure to take a look at the front pool filled with slithering live sharks. Inexpensive to expensive — if you select lobster.

Lambi's Restaurant, 458-8549 (dockside off southwestern pier). A funky, shell-lined indoor eatery dishing out local specials like mutton stew, shark, chicken, and conch. Dine on second floor for pleasant views. Inexpensive to moderate. Close by are truly rustic

Clifton Beach Restaurant in the hotel of the same name, Casablanca, and Bool Head Bar & Restaurant for chicken and beef roti and fish and chips.

Recommended Shopping

The shops at the private island resorts of The Cotton House on Mustique, Palm Island Beach Club on Palm Island, and Petit St. Vincent Resort on Petit St. Vincent have fine collections (especially Petit St. Vincent Resort's Boutique) of colorful, casual clothing and swimwear, personalized items and T-shirts, visors, Caribbean gift items, and beach necessities from flip-flops to sunglasses.

Young Island's Dock Shop, directly across from the resort on St. Vincent, sells clothing, local products made of coconut, bamboo, and woven straw, including the resort's attractive cloth-lined straw menu folders, condiments, spices, and books.

BEQUIA

Tiny Bequia has become an island shopper's bazaar. For the most part, the treasures available to visitors are created by local artisans—everything from jewelry and model boats to hand-painted and silk-screened clothing. Boutiques, shops, and vendors selling brilliant colored T-shirts and clothing line the Admiralty Bay waterfront. A new shopping complex and covered outdoor market at the tender dock (used by small cruise ships) are worth perusing, and there is a handful of gift shops in the two-story Bayshore Mall, including a bakery and liquor store.

Nearby are two of Bequia's top shopping destinations—Mauvin's and Sargeant Brothers—master model-boat builders. These two families carry on the tradition of handcrafting exquisite miniature vessels in minute detail, from small Bequia fishing boats to impressive commissioned pieces like the HMS *Britannia*. The boats can be taken apart and safely packed for travel. Instructions for reassembly are provided. Prices range from reasonable to hundreds of dollars. (Ask anyone for directions.)

Artists Sam and Donna McDowell's Banana Patch Studio, (809) 458-3865 (at Paget Farm on the south side), are seen by appointment only. The McDowells' lovely folk art and marine objets d'art are on display. The McDowells specialize in "sailor's valentines"—enchanting replicas of nineteenth-century octagonal-shaped wooden boxes inlaid inside with intricate, fanciful designs in tiny seashells.

Bequia Bookshop, 458-3905 (on Front Street opposite the dinghy dock). This shop is renowned throughout the Caribbean for its excellent collection of island-related books, rare old volumes, and new. Also "sailor's valentines" (mentioned on the previous page), scrimshaw, West Indies charts, maps, Caribbean courtesy flags, prints, and Sam McDowell's captivating, oversized postcards depicting Bequia scenery can be found here.

Other interesting shops are the Crab Hole, famous for silk-screening and handcrafts, and Melinda's, for one-of-a-kind designs hand-painted on lightweight cotton apparel;

Sprotties, just off the waterfront for island clothing and gifts; nearby **Local Color** for casual resortwear, accessories, and souvenirs; and **Noah's Arkade** at the Frangipani Hotel for books, excellent local handcrafts, teas and other food products, and jewelry, as well as casual clothing. Also have a look at the **Whaleboner** and **Plantation House** shops.

A small emporium at the **Gingerbread Complex** on the waterfront stocks locally produced chutneys, jams, and jellies, hot sauces, delicious St. Vincentian bottled peanuts, and other goodies.

MUSTIQUE

Aside from **The Mill Boutique** at the Cotton House Hotel, there are three other shopping choices: **Basil's Caribbean Classic Boutique** (at Basil's Bar & Restaurant on Britannia Bay). Basil's personalized T-shirts are prized collectibles, and he has also assembled Bali batiks, cotton and silk shirts, other clothing, and lots more.

Also on Britannia Bay, two quaint gingerbread cottages (great photo opportunities) are first-rate, if pricey, boutiques. The pink house, **Treasure Boutique**, is stocked with beach items—masks, fins, snorkels, sunscreens, Mustique T-shirts, sunglasses, hats, and water toys. The purple cottage, **Treasure Fashion**, sells upscale resortwear and accessories for men, women, and children.

ST. VINCENT

Noah's Arkade, 457-1513 (Bay Street). Best shopping in Kingstown for arts and crafts from throughout the Caribbean, including baskets, ceramics, West Indian dolls, straw and bamboo placemats, handbags, ceramics, spices and condiments, T-shirts, and a good selection of island-related books.

St. Vincent Handicrafts (fringe of central Kingstown). I never miss visiting this small showroom to buy hand-woven and -stitched table or floor mats, wall hangings, handbags, carved wooden pieces, and so on.

Other shops are **Y. de Lima**, 457-1681 (corner of Bay and Egmont streets), where you'll find jewelry, watches, and electronics. **Stechers** (in the Cobblestone Arcade, Lane Bay Street), is stocked with duty-free crystal, china, colorful ceramics, watches, jewelry, and imported perfumes. **T&M Limited** (in the Heron Hotel Complex) sells wines and specialty foods.

The **Wayfarer Bookstore**, 457-1137 (Upper Bay Street), is a source for books, periodicals, postcards, and stationery supplies.

St. Vincent Philatelic Services, 456-2383 (Bay 43 Building, Lower Bay Street). Travelers are welcome to visit the "World of Stamps" showcase and sales office.

UNION ISLAND

Head to **Castello Art Designs** in a little blue cottage on the waterfront for enchanting works by local artists, from paintings to pottery.

Anchorage Yacht Club Boutique (next to the airport, in a hotel) offers a very good selection of ceramics, prints, shells, casual resortwear, swimsuits, towels, hats, pareos, sundries, books, and newspapers.

Useful Information

The *St. Vincent and the Grenadines Escape Tourist Guide*, *Discover St. Vincent & the Grenadines*, *Holiday Bequia St. Vincent & the Grenadines*, and the airline magazine *Mustique Airways* are free, informative publications to look for.

Bequia now has an airport, which makes the island more accessible, but it manages to maintain its old-time island character. Interisland transportation throughout the island by ferry is still an adventure.

There is regularly scheduled **ferry service** between Kingstown Harbor in St. Vincent to Port Elizabeth at Admiralty Bay in Bequia; (809) 458-3348 or 458-3472. The trip takes about 1½ hours. The **mail boat** *Snapper* cruises between St. Vincent to Union Island, making stops at Bequia, Canouan, and Mayreau. Call the **Tourism Department** for information: on St. Vincent, (809) 457-1502; on Bequia, (809) 458-3286; and on Union Island, (809) 458-8350.

Following are a few **car rental** possibilities in the region:

Bequia: Julie's Guest House, (809) 458-3304. Also inquire at your hotel and ask any local taxi drivers who have cars available for rent.

Mustique: Mule Stique, (809) 456-3555.

St. Vincent: Avis Rent-a-Car, (809) 456-5610; **Kim's Rentals, Ltd.**, (809) 456-1884; and **Unico Auto Rentals**, (809) 456-4744.

BEQUIA

Bequia's outstanding **beaches** are Lower Bay, Princess Margaret, Friendship Bay, and Spring, where you can view a 200-year-old working plantation. **Taxis** and **tours** are quite reasonable, and at Admiralty Bay, numbered water taxis are easily hailed with a hand wave.

Visitors are now allowed to tour **Moon Hole** on the southern side of Admiralty Bay. The compound is an incredible cave-dwelling residential community built into rock and cliffs by disenchanted Americans several decades ago. Contact the Tourist Bureau for information.

MAYREAU

Just off the island of Mayreau, and well worth seeing, are the spectacular unspoiled, uninhabited **Tobago Cays** islets surrounded by glass-clear turquoise sea.

ST. VINCENT

Don't miss a tour of the 20-acre **Botanic Gardens**. You'll be expected to hire one of the local official guides. Other interesting sights are **Fort Charlotte, La Soufrière volcano, Mesopotamia Valley**, the **petroglyphs** near the village of Layou, **Rabbaca Farms**, a vast estate producing coconuts, bananas, cola nuts, nutmeg and other spices, and the **Nature Trails** at **Buccament Valley**. Naturalists and adventurers might want to spend a day at 50-acre, beachfront **Petit Byahaut** (see hotel listing).

Bill Tewes' **Dive St. Vincent** is highly recommended for scuba diving, dive packages, certification courses, and excursions, (809) 457-4714/4928.

St. Vincent's only casino is at the **Emerald Valley Hotel and Casino**, 456-7140, in Peniston Valley. It's no Las Vegas, but roulette, blackjack, poker, and slot machines await gamblers. The resort also has a four-hole **golf course**. (More holes are being added.)

UNION ISLAND

From Union Island, the lower Grenadines, Mayreau, the Tobago Cays, Palm Island, and Petit St. Vincent, are easily reached by boat. All have stunning beaches.

Union has some good hiking trails from the Ashton area. **Chatham Bay** is a deliciously isolated, expansive white beach on the western side of the island, reached only by boat or a hike. Take a picnic and go for the day.

≈ ≈

UNITED STATES VIRGIN ISLANDS

(LITTLE ST. JAMES, ST. CROIX, ST. JOHN, ST. THOMAS)

ACCOMMODATIONS

LITTLE ST. JAMES' BEST
Little St. James

ST. CROIX'S BEST
The Buccaneer Hotel
Carambola Beach Resort
Villa Madeleine

NOTEWORTHY OPTIONS
Hibiscus Beach Hotel
Pink Fancy

ST. JOHN'S BEST
Caneel Bay ▲▲
Catered To, Inc.
East House
Gallows Point Suite Resort
Hyatt Regency St. John
Private Homes for Private Vacations
Villa Bougainvillea, Gift Hill Villa, and The Beach House

≈ ≈

≈ ≈

NOTEWORTHY OPTIONS
Estate Zootenvaal
Harmony
Maho Bay Camps and Harmony

ST. THOMAS' BEST
Grand Palazzo Hotel
Secret Harbour Beach Resort and Secret Harbourview Villas
Stouffer Renaissance Grand Beach Resort

A NOTEWORTHY OPTION
Blackbeard's Castle Hotel

RECOMMENDED RESTAURANTS

RECOMMENDED SHOPPING

PROVISIONS FOR YOUR ISLAND PANTRY

USEFUL INFORMATION

≈ ≈

≈ ≈

Accommodations

LITTLE ST. JAMES' BEST

Little St. James

Exquisite Little St. James is the Necker Island of the United States Virgin Islands. (See Necker's listing, page 122.) As at Necker, celebrities and the well-to-do stream in and out of this private island outpost, and they can elect to arrive by helicopter. Most guests, however, come to Little St. James by sea on the resort's 34-foot Sea Ray speedboat *Apostle*, which they board at Crown Bay Marina near St. Thomas' airport. Claudia Schiffer and David Copperfield spent a romantic interlude at Little St. James in early 1994, and I recently was informed that a superstar couple from Hollywood were on their way. No names, please.

Ultimate privacy and elegant accommodations in a tropical paradise can, of course, be found at Little St. James for anyone able to afford it. The only people present are Zenaida Junio, the retreat's outstanding cook, formerly at Chez Francine in St. Barts, the housekeeping staff, gardeners, the caretaker, and boat captain, who unobtrusively attend to their duties. The caretaker's quarters are on the property, but set apart. Ms. Junio's meals combine French, American, and Caribbean cuisines. Guests can request any food preferences in advance.

Owned and built as their dream house by Di and Arch Cummin, who have several other residences in the States, 72-acre Little St. James opened in 1992 as a private island retreat for up to ten people when the Cummins are away. It's located about a mile south of St. Thomas' southeastern tip, only a couple of miles west of St. John. The arid island is a wilderness of scrub bush and succulents covering undulating hillocks. From overhead its shape resembles a melting cross.

The handsome dwellings at Little St. James are in a multistructure complex sprawling over the northern ridge of the island with 360-degree sweeping sea views to St. Thomas, St. John, the British Virgin Islands, and neighbor island Great St. James, also privately owned, with a popular overnight anchorage in a well-protected harbor called Christmas Cove (spectacular snorkeling there).

Little St. James has one curved sandy beach with a dock, two other pebble/rock waterfronts, and a nature trail winding through the desertlike terrain to explore.

For the most part, though, LSJ's guests are likely to sequester themselves in the immediate vicinity of the magnificent living quarters (the sandy beach is only steps away), kidney-shaped freshwater swimming pool, and various terraces and verandas engulfed in green manicured lawns and tropical gardens. Gardens that feature four immense imported palms, bougainvillea, hibiscus, saga palms and other tropical plantings are nurtured by a water irrigation system.

The residences are assembled in a series of West Indian plantation-style one-story natural stone buildings with corrugated roofs and louvered, screenless, and glassless windows and doors, set around a central courtyard—spaced at distances at least 25 feet apart. Arched, Doric-columned entranceways lead to the Mexican coral-stone-walled great house with a 22 × 38-foot great room boasting a fireplace for the occasional chilly evening and an adjacent, well-stocked library. The bathroom in Little St. James' fabulous separate bungalow master bedroom suite contains a bidet, open shower, and Jacuzzi tub, all with gold-plated fixtures. The three other bedrooms are situated in smaller private bungalows. Paddle fans ventilate the interiors throughout when necessary, but northeasterlies keep air circulating in a steady breeze.

Everything at Little St. James has been custom-designed, from the solid mahogony doors and louvers and cabinetry to the hardwood floors in the great house and master suite.

Designer-decorated Little St. James is a showplace of shell-stone floors and walkways, antiques, reproduction plantation furniture, sleigh and four-poster beds under mosquito netting, and quality contemporary rattan pieces combined with traditional deep-cushioned white-covered sofas and chairs, sisal area rugs, Venetian mirrors, and Caribbean appointments so tastefully assembled that the island was featured in *HG* in 1993.

Little St. James' amenities include a telephone and fax machine, satellite TV, and a VCR, CD, and tape-deck stereo system. A Sunfish, ocean kayaks, windsurfers, the speedboat *Apostle,* and a 27-foot converted Maine lobster boat are at your disposal while registered at LSJ. Sister islands St. Thomas and St. John are only minutes away for tennis, golf, or shopping. But, if you're seeking solitude and relaxation, you'll very likely want to stay put at Little St. James, and like that lucky old sun, be perfectly happy to roll around this heavenly hideaway all day.

LITTLE ST. JAMES

RESERVATIONS
McLauglin Anderson Vacations, Ltd.
100 Blackbeard's Hill
St. Thomas,
United States Virgin Islands 00802
TEL: (800) 666-6246 *or*
(800) 537-6246 *or*
(809) 776-0635
FAX: (809) 777-4737

Open all year.
Rates: *Year-round daily rates—minimum stay is three nights:* Two persons, $2,500;

four persons, $3,750; six persons, $4,375; eight persons, $5,000. Nine to ten persons, add 10% to daily rates per person. Includes round-trip transportation by helicopter from St. Thomas airport or by sea from Crown Bay Marina.
Meal plan: FAP (includes all meals and beverages).
Service charge included.
Government tax: 8%.
Children welcome. With permission from owners, guests may bring pets.
Credit cards accepted.
Note: McLauglin Anderson Vacations, Ltd. (phone numbers above) also represents a select list of other villas on St. Thomas and St. John, as well as a few in the British West Indies and Grenada.

ST. CROIX'S BEST

The Buccaneer Hotel

The Buccaneer Hotel graces the rolling grounds of a 240-acre former sugar estate, and is still owned and run by members of the Armstrong family who opened the hotel in 1948. The Buccaneer is a first-class resort for sports-minded or sedentary travelers wanting a comfortable Caribbean retreat where, if so inclined, they don't have to leave the premises.

The resort has something for everyone, especially for families sharing their holidays. It's a fairly conservative, mild-mannered, almost all-American clientele.

My favorite aunt and uncle would love The Buccaneer. He's an avid golfer, and here he could get in 18 holes each day. Always ready for an adventure, he would certainly sign up for the resort's scheduled visit to Buck Island to have a look through a snorkel mask at the underwater wonderland there. Perhaps he'd even try a dive. The hotel's sports facilities include windsurfing, sailing, and special cruises. Eight LayKold tennis courts with a pro and Golf and Tennis Pro Shop, and a two-mile jogging trail are available to energetic guests.

My aunt's preferred Caribbean pastime is sunning, and she'd have two freshwater pool and three beaches to visit with her beachtowel and novel. Cutlass Cove is the main beach, and includes The Little Mermaid beach cafe. Beautiful, long (over a mile) Beauregard Beach and the adjacent freshwater pool is another option. The Grotto here serves up burgers and other simple fare. Both beaches have showers and changing areas. Whistle Beach, past the dock, has no facilities but is deliciously isolated and great for meditation or a private plunge.

After a morning in the sun, I know my aunt would enjoy a massage, facial, and further pampering or exercise in the health club, as well as shopping in the boutiques. She could even take The Buccaneer shuttle into Christiansted for duty-free shopping.

The air-conditioned Brass Parrot and outdoor breezy Terrace are the evening dining spots. Food is solid, well prepared and pleasantly served (collared dress shirts are requested). Every night of the week there's live music and dancing at the Terrace—everything from jazz to reggae.

Just where you unpack at The Buccaneer depends on personal preferences. I like the oceanfront deluxe rooms, but here are the other choices. Standard rooms are on the second (top) floor of the main building or nearby in the Strong Box. They are small and the least desirable, but also inexpensive. Superior rooms are on the second floor of the main building, too, but all have sea views. Deluxe oceanview and oceanfront rooms are spacious and most appealing. The designated "nonsmoking" accommodations are the hotel suites on the main building's ground level, handsomely furnished with four-poster beds in master bedrooms. Eight cottage suites in four two-unit buildings are strung along the driveway between the main lobby and the beach.

Ficus and Frigate suites offer the ultimate privacy at The Buccaneer. Located at Beauregard Beach, they boast two bedrooms and two baths each, with sitting rooms and outdoor terraces.

All accommodations have telephones, air-conditioning and ceiling fans, mini-refrigerators, safes, and private patios or terraces. Interiors are neat and prettily decorated.

The Buccaneer, when all is considered, is a most peaceful, desirable destination.

THE BUCCANEER HOTEL
P.O. Box 25200
Gallows Bay, St. Croix
U.S. Virgin Islands 00804-5200
TEL: (809) 773-2100
FAX: (809) 778-8215

RESERVATIONS
Ralph Locke Islands, Inc.
TEL: (800) 223-1108 *or*
    (310) 440-3225
FAX: (310) 440-4220

Open all year.
Rates: Double occupancy. *April 1 to December 20:* Standard, $160; Superior, $195; Deluxe, $215; Suites, $215 to $320. *December 21 to March 31:* Standard, $195; Superior, $265; Deluxe, $340; Suites, $305 to $500. Children under 12, $10 per child per day.
Meal plan: AP (includes full breakfast).
Service charge: None.
Government tax: 8%.
Children welcome.
Credit cards accepted.
Note: Special packages are available.

Carambola Beach Resort

St. Croix's top hideaway, Carambola Beach Resort, has had an unsteady history. It opened successfully as Rockresort in 1986, then closed for a period after damage from Hurricane Hugo in 1989, only to reopen and close its doors again in June 1991. The happy news is that Carambola celebrated its first anniversary as a Radisson hotel in June

1994. The experienced hotel group and manager Timothy Bouley seem to have set the resort on a steady course.

Located on St. Croix's unspoiled hilly northwest coast at Davis Bay, about 25 minutes by car or taxi from the airport, lovely 28-acre Carambola remains a showcase.

Architect William Cox created a modern-day Caribbean fishing village by incorporating Danish red corrugated roofs, French louvered windows, and British porches, and by using mahogany and embulla woods, a legacy from Spanish settlers. The public pavilions have West Indian touches—colorful awnings and table umbrellas, railings and tiles. A two-story bell tower, sitting at the foot of the restaurant's terraces at the center of the resort, is abstractly fashioned after old plantation windmills. At night musicians entertain at its gazebo base.

The resort's 151 rooms (including one two-bedroom suite) are housed in sprawling clusters of 27 identical two-story dwellings over a small portion of the 4,000-acre property, most of which is still undeveloped. Condominiums and homes are built on adjacent land, are well apart from the resort and don't intrude.

The best rooms are the peaked-ceiling second-floor lodgings located in the buildings that border the 750-yard, palm-fringed white sand beach at Davis Bay.

Brazilian walnut paneling and louvers and overhead fans and air-conditioning cool the insides of the charming quarters. Fanciful carved wooden headboards are attached to the walls over twin or king-size beds. Furniture is reproduction West Indian–style dressers, rocking chairs, and loveseats with cushions made out of exceptionally pretty cotton fabrics. The two-section living/bedrooms have a connecting screened porch with cushioned banquettes.

Pottery-based lamps provide good lighting throughout. Depending on the room's facing direction, interiors can be dark, but cooler. The artwork is Caribbean and new like everything else.

Large dressing-room closets have lots of hangers and come with drying racks, umbrellas, and beach towels. "Glowworm" tiny flashlights, a selection of toiletries, and an ice bucket filled daily. Rooms have mini-refrigerators, wall safes, coffeemakers, telephones, and AM/FM clock radios that provide for your wake-up call.

Carambola's bathrooms are appealing and good-sized with tiled, curtained showers, spacious twin-basin vanities, good lighting, and stacks of voluptuous towels.

Housekeeping will sew on a button or replace a split seam, collect and return laundry, supply hairdryers, irons and boards. Room service is available for continental-style breakfast only.

Carambola's facilities include four grass courts, an 18-hole Robert Trent Jones–designed golf course ($25 per round and mandatory $12.50 cart fees). Carambola's large swimming pool, with two Jacuzzis, rests off the main public areas, near to two fine side-by-side restaurants, the Saman Room and the Mahogany Room where guest alternate dining. There's also a delicatessen, open all afternoon; a fantastic two-level boutique; a library and game room with a wide-screen television showing scheduled movies; and a beachside bar.

Carambola's activities seem endless, if you can tear yourself away from the beach—you can burn off calories in the fitness room or scuba or do snorkel water aerobics.

General manager Timothy Bouley's cocktail reception is held on Mondays on the Palm Terrace. Here you'll meet and mix with other guests of all ages, almost all American. Getting back to sustenance at Carambola, well-presented dinners are served in both restaurants. The Saman Room is decorated with rattan furniture under towering ceilings. The more formal, carpeted Mahogany Room is set under timbered rafters, the walls lined with wood paneling. The changing menus at the Mahogany Room might include Caribbean black bean soup, crab cakes with lobster sauce, red snapper with a hazelnut crust and Frangelico beurre blanc sauce, or osso bucco. The Saman Room's Caribbean/ Mexican/international cuisine offers enticing selections like jerk chicken quesadillas, blackened white-tip shark with cucumber salsa, or linguine with chicken, artichoke hearts, and sun-dried tomatoes. Saman's light fare always includes monster build-your-own burgers, and croissant sandwiches. Guests can satisfy sweet cravings with mud or key lime pie, peach melba, or a variety of tropical fruit ice creams.

Pool terrace luncheon menus at the deli list seafood, pasta, and fruit salad plates, plus main selections.

Carambola is ideal for independent travelers, families, or small meetings or conventions. The 2,400-square-foot Tibet Room can accommodate over 200 people banquet style, or be divided into two separate rooms.

CARAMBOLA BEACH RESORT
A RADISSON HOTEL
P.O. Box 3031, Kingshill
St. Croix
U.S. Virgin Islands 00851
TEL: (809) 778-3800
FAX: (809) 778-1682

RESERVATIONS
TEL: (800) 333-3333

Open all year.
Rates: Double occupancy. *April 1 to December 16:* Oceanfront, $250; Ocean View, $190; Garden View, $155; *December 17 to January 2:* Oceanfront, $330; Ocean View, $260; Garden View, $235. Other rates unavailable at press time. Inquire about Radisson's special seasonal rates for Garden View rooms only.
Meal plan: EP. MAP (includes breakfast and dinner), add $60 per person per day.
Service charge: 10%
Government tax: 8%.
Children welcome.
Credit cards accepted.
Note: Dive, honeymoon, and golf packages are available.

Villa Madeleine

St. Croix's hottest luxury condominium hotel is Villa Madeleine, located on the island's east end on 6½ acres of terraced hillside above Estate Teague Bay's shorelines. Villa Madeleine, comprised of 43 separate one- and two-bedroom, West Indian–style, creamy yellow villas, each with private, 12 × 22-foot freshwater swimming pools surrounded by oversized terra-cotta-tiled patios and walled gardens, exudes understated elegance. Interiors have been harmoniously orchestrated by Carleton Varney of Dorothy Draper of New York. (The hotel has been featured on cover of *Architectural Digest.*) Quality tropical furniture, covered in a mix of pastel and bright-colored fabrics, include queen-size bamboo four-poster beds. Accommodations have cable TV, telephones, air-conditioned bedrooms, and ceiling fans throughout. Marble bathrooms are a triumph with five-foot-square marble showers. Ultra-modern, fully equipped kitchens have Corian countertops. The spacious living/dining rooms boast mahogany French doors that open wide to bring in breezes, and frame natural artwork in the form of panoramic views of St. Croix's northern and southern coastlines and beyond.

Owner/managers Greg and Marcia Roncari, originally from Connecticut, are experienced hoteliers, having managed Pavilions and Pools on St. Croix's sister island St. Thomas. The Roncaris come from a family with a long history in building, so it seemed destined, at least to them, that the couple find exactly the right property on which to create their own condominium hotel (about 80%, only two-bedroom apartments at press time, are on the rental plan). St. Croix is the lucky beneficiary. Open since the season of 1990, it now rests among thriving plantings and gardens.

One of the hotel's greatest assets is its outstanding restaurant, Café Madeleine, situated in the hotel's lovely two-storied great house. Dining is offered indoors or outside on the airy veranda and side garden area overlooking the sea. Café Madeleine, open seven nights a week for dinner only, has become one of St. Croix's most popular restaurants among discerning locals, serving Italian-inspired cuisine. The ever-changing menus might be composed of tempting dishes, such as carpaccio with fresh herbs and olive oil, lobster, ravioli, roast leg of lamb with fennel and morel sauce, bouillabaisse, and grilled swordfish with roasted eggplant sauce. Entrées are deliciously embellished with timbales of risotto and fresh vegetables; desserts include a variety of daily pastries and other sweet temptations.

There's no room service and a car is necessary for mobility. Water-sports and other sports facilities, beaches, shopping, and other restaurants are only a few minutes' drive away. Manager Yanira Melendez or one of her staff will be delighted to make recommendations or assist you.

Travelers searching for a tranquil Caribbean sanctuary possessing fashionable apartments with private pools, a friendly staff and management, and an excellent restaurant should be very content unpacking at Villa Madeleine. Who knows? — if you can afford it, you just may be tempted into buying a little piece of paradise at Villa Madeleine.

VILLA MADELEINE
P.O. Box 3109
Christiansted, St. Croix
United States Virgin Islands 00822
TEL: (800) 548-4461 *or*
(809) 773-8141
FAX: (809) 773-7518

Open all year.
Rates: *December 15 to April 14:* Two-Bedroom Villa (up to 4 persons), $425. *April 15 to December 14:* Two-Bedroom Villa (up to 4 persons), $300.
Meal plan: EP.
Service charge: None.
Government tax: 8%.
Children over 6 welcome.
Credit cards: accepted.

NOTEWORTHY OPTIONS

Hibiscus Beach Hotel

One of the nicest resorts to open in St. Croix in a long time is a 38-room charmer called Hibiscus Beach Hotel located in Estate La Grande Princesse on the north side of the island, on a wide-open palm-tree-lined beach with an excellent reef (the next door neighbor is Cormorant Beach Club). The property was formerly called Cathy's Fancy, always fun-filled but a pretty threadbare and run-down place. After Hurricane Hugo claimed Cathy's Fancy, Jerry Tobin and his partners bought the three-acre prime beach-front property, built the hotel, and opened the West Indian–style complex in May 1992.

The idea was to build a first-rate yet affordable hotel with modern-day creature comforts and amenities that travelers now require. It is all of these things. The hotel is understandably doing very well and is extremely popular with locals, always a good sign.

The 36 rooms and one two-bedroom efficiency suite at Hibiscus Beach are clustered around the grounds in six pink and white stucco buildings with white peaked corrugated roofs. Some rooms are truly beachfront and the rest have beach views, but are set back a little from the beach in a palm grove and are called beachside rooms. Frankly these beachside lodgings offer more privacy away from the action on the beach.

Accommodations have private balconies or patios, air-conditioning, and ceiling fans. The floors are white square tiles, and bathrooms are fine with stall showers. The decor features cheery new standard tropical furnishings, with mauves, pink, blue, and gold fabrics on draperies, chairs, and bedcovers. Rooms have TVs, safes, telephones, and mini-bars.

The seaside pavilion restaurant, The Hideaway, serves reasonably priced, very agree-

Hibiscus Beach Hotel on St. Croix.

able pastas, salads, and seafood. Every Wednesday there's a barbecue featuring ribs, fish, and chicken, and a live steel band. In season, there's live entertainment five nights a week; during the summer, it's reduced to four. The center of the restaurant is a congenial bar, which also provides libations for guests at the adjacent terraced freshwater swimming pool. Chaise longues surround the pool and dot the beach, and hammocks swing from the tall swaying palm trees there.

The hotel's boutique is tiny, but downtown duty-free shopping in Christiansted is only 10 minutes from the hotel.

Hibiscus Beach Hotel is an unpretentious, extremely pleasant hideaway that has a youthful "real island" quality. Manager Wendall Snider and a congenial assistant manager, Tak Walden, are directing the hotel with skill.

HIBISCUS BEACH HOTEL
4131 La Grande Princesse
Christiansted, St. Croix
U.S. Virgin Islands 00820-4441
TEL: (800) 442-0121 *or*
(809) 773-4042
FAX: (809) 773-7668

Open all year.
Rates: Double occupancy. *December 21 to March 31:* Beachfront, $190; Beachside,

$180; Two-Bedroom Efficiency Suite, $290. *April 1 to December 20:* Beachfront, $140; Beachside, $130; Two-Bedroom Efficiency Suite, $220.
Meal plan: EP.
Service charge: None.
Government tax: 8%.
Children welcome.
Credit cards accepted.
Note: Special all-inclusive Virg and other packages are available.

Pink Fancy

The movie begins: A seaplane skims through choppy aqua sea and pulls up on the cement ramp in Christiansted, on St. Croix's north shore. Humphrey Bogart disembarks and quickly walks a few blocks to a historic pink-roofed and shuttered inn called Pink Fancy. He opens the wrought-iron gate, climbs the redbrick steps to the center courtyard. Across the pink-and-white-tile-bordered freshwater swimming pool, Sidney Greenstreet is sitting on a lounge on the terra-cotta terrace under a palm tree, fanning himself. He smacks a mosquito on his neck with the palm of a hand. Unblinking, Bogart and Greenstreet exchange glances. Bogart approaches the beautiful proprietress, and, yes, she has a room for him. The camera pans around to the Limetree Bar, where Peter Lorre is making himself a drink. Bogart and Greenstreet join him to talk about the pink bird.

At Pink Fancy, the Limetree Bar is an honor serve-yourself one. With a little too much rum, sometimes the imagination soars. But, in fact, Janet Gottlieb, a Ziegfeld Follies star, bought the 1780 brick, coral, mahogany, and cedar-shingled Danish townhouse, along with three other courtyard buildings, and opened Pink Fancy in 1948. Celebrities such as Noël Coward did come to stay in the 13-room inn.

The complex was eventually renovated by R. Samuel Dillon, Jr., who carefully preserved the two-story townhouse and updated the other buildings with modern conveniences. The work was completed in early 1982.

Each room has a different configuration, and is named after old Danish plantations, such as Hard Labor and Recover Hill. Parasol is a second-story room with an attached gazebo terrace that includes a hammock, and the best room in the house. All rooms are air-conditioned, have ceiling fans, comfortable tropical furnishings, cable TVs, clock radios, kitchenettes, tub/showers, and, of course, pink fluffy towels. There are telephones and rooms are immaculately kept.

Pink Fancy is hosted by Dixie Ann Tang Yuk.

Complimentary continental breakfasts of sweet rolls, juice, and coffee or tea are set out buffet-style on the Limetree Bar counter each morning for guests to help themselves. Clientele are overwhelmingly American, with a scattering of Europeans—lots of return guests of all ages, mostly upper-middle-aged, who like the informal, friendly atmosphere and the hotel's location. Pink Fancy rests on the corner of two quiet streets, several blocks from the bustling duty-free shops in Christiansted.

Ms. Tang Yuk will guide you to sports and water facilities and suggest local restaurants. But you'll surely want to relax by the pool, have privacy, or get acquainted with the other guests. You might want to compete in Pink Fancy's Activity Scoreboard game. "Lowest score wins, no real rules, no real judges, questionable prizes, sign-up sheet somewhere." Activity Points for some of the over twenty activities are: two points for skipped the beach and napped in the room, two points for thought about Buck Island but took a nap instead, two points for slept through the news on TV, 100 points for rented a car and drove around the island, and 300 points for called the office.

Pink Fancy is a charming, in-town inn with very reasonable rates.

PINK FANCY
27 Prince Street
Christiansted, St. Croix
United States Virgin Islands 00820
TEL: (800) 524-2045 *or*
     (809) 773-8460
FAX: (809) 773-6448

Open all year.
Rates: Double occupancy. *December 22 to April 14:* Superior, $90; Deluxe, $120. Extra person, $15. *April 15 to December 21:* Superior, $75; Deluxe, $90. Extra person, $15.
Meal plan: CP (includes continental breakfast).
Service charge: $1 per room per night.
Government tax: 8%.
Children welcome.
Credit cards accepted.
Note: Special packages are available.

ST. JOHN'S BEST

Caneel Bay ◤◥

Caneel Bay is surrounded by unparalleled beauty, both on land and under water—so pristine that they've been protected as national parks. Each of our seven beaches evokes a different sense of place, whether it's a tranquil setting for reading a favorite book or discovering the colorful underwater life. We strive to provide our guests with a quality vacation in surroundings of unparalled natural beauty.

MARTIN NICHOLSON, MANAGING DIRECTOR

Friends and St. Johnians can remember visiting Caneel Bay in the fifties when the only way to reach the resort was by boat or in a donkey caravan from Cruz Bay. Before

Laurance S. Rockefeller bought the property in the early fifties, Caneel Bay was a small hotel owned by the West Indian Company and locally run—a century earlier, it was a thriving sugar plantation.

In 1956 Rockefeller purchased over 5,000 adjoining St. John acres, about two-thirds of the island, preserving forever St. John's natural environment and beauty as an extraordinary national park with hiking trails among ruins, campgrounds, and many magnificent beaches. Rockefeller donated Caneel Bay to Jackson Hole Preserve, Inc., a nonprofit family-run organization, added roads, and developed the resort into one of the finest in the Caribbean.

Rockefeller sold the majority of his resort holdings and the respected Rockresorts (the management company) in the eighties, and after two short-lived ownerships, the good news came on June 1, 1993, that Dallas-based Rosewood Hotels & Resorts had assumed operation and management control of Caneel Bay and its sister resort Little Dix Bay (see Virgin Gorda resort listing). Good news, because Rosewood has a reputation for high standards of excellence in administering such world-class hotels as The Mansion on Turtle Creek in Dallas, Hotel Bel-Air in Los Angeles, and La Samanna in French St. Martin (see resort listing).

Breathtaking 170-acre Caneel Bay peninsula, located on St. John's northwestern coastline, encompasses seven snow-white sand beaches with spectacular underwater fish and coral wonderlands. Caneel is an extravaganza of well-tended tropical grounds.

The rooms, although spacious, had become rather conventional when compared to comparable luxury-class hideaways. They needed upgrading and amenities that would satisfy the demands of new generations of nineties guests. The same held true for Little Dix. Rosewood had already proven its capabilities in the Caribbean by successfully rejuvenating the super-luxury La Samanna property in French St. Martin. Little Dix went through an impressive refurbishment during the fall of 1993. As this book goes to press, Caneel Bay is beginning the first phase of its revitalization, which should be completed by fall/winter 1995.

The major changes planned are the addition of room amenities like telephones and air-conditioning, and stylish redecoration throughout, and a redesign for some of the accommodations, restaurants, and public areas. If the idea of phones and air-conditioning aren't appreciated by diehard, conservative repeaters, who liked Caneel just the way it was, they need only disconnect the phone and let natural breezes or ceiling fans cool the rooms. Televisions are not included in the improvement effort.

Caneel's 171 rooms are judiciously spaced throughout the property in small groupings like little villages along gorgeous northern-situated Turtle, East-facing Hawksnest, and West-facing Scott and Caneel Bay beaches in one- or two-story dwellings. Tennis garden and courtside rooms are inland, but are the lowest priced and fine lodgings. The hotel's rectangular-shaped freshwater swimming pool is tucked away near the tennis courts, convenient for guests staying nearby. Cottage 7, Mr. Rockefeller's complex, has been divided into separate, double-sized spaces.

Wherever you reside at Caneel you'll be content. Open-air multiseat silent vehicles make regularly scheduled stops along the roadways leading to the rooms and facilities.

The resort offers a multitude of services and activities—massages, garden and historical walks, nature trails, aerobics, movies, a rum tasting, half-day sails, and excursions to Charlotte Amalie and Little Dix, as well as the use of windsurfers, sea kayaks, Sailfish, floats, and snorkeling gear. Scuba diving is also offered. A recent daily schedule of "Caneel Today" featured a long list of activities and events from light-tackle fishing to a scheduled movie and entertainment.

Caneel has 11 tennis courts with a Peter Burwash program, pros for instruction, and a pro shop.

The hotel's enormous two-story boutique, housed in a flower-draped, arbor-bordered, shingled pavilion, carries elegant and casual resort- and swimwear for men and women, jewelry, Caribbean and African art and crafts, gift items, and a wide assortment of Caneel T-shirts, cover-ups, and other personalized items like beach bags, hats, cosmetics, and glasswear, plus necessities. Stateside newspapers arrive late morning, although Caneel guests receive *TimesFax*es daily.

Caneel's three restaurants each have spectacular settings. The Equator, a large, round former sugar mill hilltop pavilion, was built on the ruins of the horsemill of the former Durloe Plantation. The panorama here is a picture-postcard Caribbeanscape with views across the vast palm-dotted lawns and shimmering sea to St. Thomas. In the past, we've enjoyed countless memorable lunches here. However, a few years ago lunches were canceled. Incomprehensibly, this fabulous site sits vacant throughout the day. Dinners at the Sugar Mill, reached along winding pathways lit by blazing torches, are always lovely. The menu features Asian, Middle Eastern, South American, and Mexican food.

At the Beach Terrace overlooking Caneel Bay Beach, meals are lavish cold and hot luncheon buffets as well as an à la carte menus including smoked fish platters, fresh seafood pâtés, salads, grilled swordfish, and roast leg of lamb with mango chutney. The dessert table is filled with delicious cakes, tarts, pies, and Caneel's sensational coconut meringue cookies.

Turtle Bay Estate House's terraced garden restaurant is romantically secluded; the food is consistently first-rate. (Only hotel guests are permitted here.) Live music is provided at the Equator, Beach Terrace, and Breezeway Starlight Terrace bar in the evening.

Many of Caneel's guests, understandably, never want leave the property. The clientele that lingers here is no longer as conservative as it used to be. But what attracts everyone to Caneel are the exquisite beaches, the quality of service, and the stunning natural beauty of the place. Over Christmas holidays Caneel Bay is booked almost solidly by repeat guests who make reservations a year in advance. A famous Caneel story concerns a couple who'd been coming to the resort for the holidays for many years and were in the process of getting a divorce. The only contention at the proceedings was over who would get the Caneel reservations.

Caneel Bay is gracious island living in one of the world's greatest masterpieces of nature. Manager Martin Nicholson and his friendly staff, many who are longtime employees, are welcoming and on hand to help see to it that guests enjoy their stay.

CANEEL BAY
P.O. Box 720
Cruz Bay, St. John
United States Virgin Islands 00831
TEL: (809) 776-6111
FAX: (809) 693-8280

RESERVATIONS
Rosewood Hotels & Resorts
TEL: (800) 928-8889
FAX: (214) 871-5444

Open all year.

Rates: Double occupancy. *December 20 to March 31:* Rooms from Court Side to Premium, $320 to $570; Cottage 7, $645. *April 1 to April 30* and *November 7 to December 19:* Rooms from Court Side to Premium, $220 to $440; Cottage 7, $495. *May 1 to November 6:* Rooms from Court Side to Premium, $200 to $380; Cottage 7; $440. A one-time charge of $25 per person covers the cost of airport arrival/departure and ferry transfers, plus unlimited use of Caneel Bay ferry between the resort and St. Thomas.

Meal plan: CP (includes continental breakfast). MAP (includes full breakfast and dinner), add $65 per person per day. FAP (includes three meals a day), add $85 per person per day.

Service charge: None.

Government tax: 8%.

Children welcome.

Credit cards accepted.

Note: Special plans are available.

Catered To, Inc.

Eileen Sundra represents more than two dozen privately owned homes and villas with one to four bedrooms, for two to ten people, throughout the beautiful island of St. John. All, from simple to sophisticated, provide private living with marvelous views, spacious decks, and landscaped garden grounds. The homes and villas are individually fully furnished by their owners, and decor ranges from standard to superior. Twelve of the properties have freshwater pools. Each has a fully equipped kitchen and personal amenities.

Eileen meets guests at a prearranged time at the dock in St. John as they step off the ferry. She then helps them collect their rental car (a must, so reserve well in advance), and leads them to their St. John residence.

CATERED TO, INC.

Eileen Sundra
Cruz Bay
P.O. Box 704
St. John, United States Virgin Islands 00830
TEL: (800) 424-6641 *or*
    (809) 776-6641
FAX: (809) 693-8191

Rates: *May 1 to December 14:* $700 to $3,550. *December 15 to January 4:* $1,600 to $5,500. *January 5 to March 31:* $1,200 to $4,850. Seven-night minimum in season; five-night minimum out of season (see above).
Note: For all other information contact Ms. Sundra (see above).

East House

At the entrance to exclusive Privateer Bay Estate at Long Bay near Hurricane Hole on St. John's peaceful, tropically bucolic East End is a sparkling new two-story white and pink, West Indian plantation–style villa with an adjacent guest house for rent. A one-minute walk away from the structures is a white sand beach for sunning, swimming, and water sports, or you can cruise off on your private Boston Whaler to explore St. John's many other beautiful beaches. Use of the Whaler is included in the rate.

The main house's living room is a 24 × 24-foot post-and-beam great room with a cathedral ceiling, handsomely furnished with modern amenities, including a telephone and answering machine, TV and VCR, and a stereo with CD, tape deck, and radio. The room is surrounded by a 10-foot-wide covered veranda that sweeps around the room on three sides. Views are spectacular sea vistas of Coral Bay and the hillsides.

The fully stocked kitchen comes with a Cuisinart, blender, coffeemaker, and quality china, cutlery, pots, and pans.

Two bedrooms are below on the ground level; one has a queen-size bed, the other, twins. Bathrooms are simple, but first class, with showers.

A few yards away, the guest house, a two-story miniature replica of the main villa, contains two bedrooms, one on each floor, both with covered verandas.

The immaculate East House and the cottage are brand-new and spotless. Plantings were establishing themselves when I recently inspected the property.

For guests' total convenience, an island hostess is assigned who will provision the house for you before your arrival and during your stay (her service is included, but the purchases are added to your bill).

For the rate you also have the use of a Suzuki Samurai, the aforementioned Boston Whaler, and daily maid service. Other available services, at an extra cost, are babysitters, cooks, nannies, and arrangements for special water sports like scuba diving, waterskiing, and deep-sea sport fishing, which the hostess will arrange.

East House is an exceptional property in a splendid seaside location.

EAST HOUSE
6-0-B Hansen Bay, St. John
United States Virgin Islands 00830
TEL: (809) 693-5868

RESERVATIONS
East End Property Trust
136 Bay View Avenue
Salem, MA 01970
TEL: (800) 229-USVI
FAX: (508) 745-7176

Open all year.
Rates: Weekly rates. *December 18 to January 2:* Two persons, $3,500; four persons, $4,200; extra person per week, $250. *January 3 to April 14:* Two persons, $2,750; four persons, $3,300; extra person, $175 per week. *April 15 to December 17:* Two persons, $1,900; four persons, $2,200; extra person, $175 per week. For extra days (when available), divide weekly rate by seven for cost per day. Rates include use of Suzuki Samurai, Boston Whaler, and daily cleanup service.
Meal plan: EP.
Service charge: None.
Government tax: 8%.
Children welcome.
Credit cards accepted.

Gallows Point Suite Resort

From the fifties to the early seventies, the most popular hangout on St. John was Ellington's, a rustic bar surrounded by a handful of guest houses, all perched on a four-acre bluffed peninsula called Gallows Point. Ellington's provided spectacular panoramic views across Pillsbury Sound to St. Thomas wrapping around to Cruz Bay's then-tranquil harbor and ferry dock. Ellington's was owned and run by the late Harry Fletcher Ellington, nicknamed Duke (no relation to the famous musician). Duke was a legendary island character, who'd formerly been a writer; his credits included scripts for the radio mystery show "The Shadow." Duke played the piano, and he and his wife Kay entertained guests, who spent a lot of time pitching horseshoes. Eventually they sold the place.

Today St. John is still a magnificent island paradise, but Cruz Bay, its small village, has become an active beehive. On the peninsula where Ellington's used to be rests a charming 10-year-old condominium resort/hotel called Gallows Point Suite Resort, managed by Dean Morgan. It's only a five-minute walk or two-minute drive from the hotel to Cruz Bay. Gallows Point is its own little village consisting of 60 one-bedroom apartments in 15 two-story gray wooden Caribbean-Georgian-style buildings, with arched transoms above large, jalousied windows that allow in cooling breezes. Ceiling fans take over when the wind decreases. The accommodations have oversized terra-cotta-tiled floors and enchanting, open-arm molded-front staircase entrances. Each cottage contains two garden suites with sunken living rooms and private verandas, and two peaked-roofed loft suites with outdoor balconies. The loft suites have balconied bedrooms that overlook spacious living rooms. Beds throughout are quality firm queens. Living rooms have a convertible sofa that can be made up into a queen-size bed. Furnishings are thick-cushioned, attractive modern rattan, cheerfully covered in various patterns and prints. Individual condominium owners add their own selections of artwork and appointments. Some suites come with TVs and stereo systems. All have a modern bathroom with shower, plus a fully equipped kitchen and dining area. Gallows Point supplies daily maid service, but there are no telephones here. A boutique has opened in a separate building at the entranceway.

Cottage 5 is on the point of the bluff with incredible views of the ocean and harbor, and is, of course, the hardest to reserve. Although the buildings are placed fairly close together, the architect positioned them sensibly, so that each has private views. My choice would be any of the second-floor, ocean-view suites facing St. Thomas.

Guests at Gallows Point are primarily American, the majority of whom are young to middle-aged couples and families.

Gallows Point's grounds are beautifully landscaped with magenta bougainvillea, striped and spotted croton, several types of palms, yucca, and hibiscus. The small freeform freshwater vinyl-lined swimming pool is located just above the sea in a garden with connecting two-tiered wooden-plank sun terraces. Two little gazebos provide a spot of shade and are only steps away from a small strip of sand-, coral-, and rock-lined beach excellent for snorkeling and swimming. To get to St. John's magnificent superfine stretches of beach, you'll need a car.

Gallows Point's restaurant, Ellington's, is a three-story building at the circular courtyard entrance to the hotel. Reception is on the ground floor. Up on the third floor is a penthouse bar and observation deck, offering picture-postcard Caribbean vistas, where you can relax and enjoy the sunset over hors d'oeuvres and tropical cocktails.

Gallows Point is a delightful sanctuary for self-sufficient travelers who don't want any housekeeping chores, except perhaps for a bit of cooking.

GALLOWS POINT SUITE RESORT
P.O. Box 58
Cruz Bay, St. John
United States Virgin Islands 00831
TEL: (800) 323-7229 *or*
    (809) 776-6434
FAX: (809) 776-6520

Open all year.
Rates: Double occupancy. *December 15 to March 31:* Ocean-View, $300 to $325; Harbor-View, $275 to $300. *April 1 to May 31:* Ocean-View, $225 to $250; Harbor-View, $200 to $225. *June 1 to September 30:* Ocean-View, $165 to $180; Harbor-View, $140 to $165. Third person, $30 per night; fourth person, $20 per night.

Meal plan: EP.
Service charge: None.
Government tax: 8%.
Children under 5 cannot be accommodated.
Credit cards accepted.
Note: Honeymoon, Land/Sail, Dive and Water Week packages are available.

Hyatt Regency St. John

Standing on the terrace in back of Hyatt Regency St. John's grand marbled lobby, the vision ahead is a stunning panorama. Several sloping, brick-carpeted stairways, lined with bushy-topped palms, nestled in magenta bougainvillea, lead down to the resort's extraordinary angular, 11,000-square-foot freshwater pool. The pool is dotted with little islands, waterfalls, and more palm trees, surrounded by a vast, lushly planted, chaise-lined terrace. A 1,200-foot-long strip of snow-white sand beach faces west over Great Cruz Bay Harbor and on out to wide-open sea and St. Thomas in the distance.

The sight is always particularly amazing to me, as we had a home on an adjacent hillside in the seventies, and nothing existed on Great Cruz Bay Beach except jungly scrub brush. Then it was great for shell collecting, and it's still a marvelous swimmers' beach.

The Hyatt Regency St. John is a 34-acre luxury resort with 285 accommodations ranging from gardenview, oceanview, poolside, and beachfront deluxe rooms, including two-bedroom suites and three-bedroom townhouses. The hotel is uniquely suited for conferences (it has a 10,000-square-foot conference center) and families with children. Trained counselors at Camp Paradise keep youngsters happy building sand castles, painting, going on treasure hunts, and receiving swimming instruction, among other sports activities.

Guest rooms, stylishly turned out in soft pastel colors, are elegant, sizable accommodations in two- to four-story hillside and two-story beach- or pool-front units. All nesting spots have telephones, TVs, toiletries, and stocked mini-bars.

Designed by the same architects who created Stouffer Grand Beach Resort in St. Thomas, the buildings are quite similar with high-pitched, shingled roofs, curved dormers, and arched windows. Magenta canopies and awnings accent façades throughout.

Hyatt Regency St. John has full water-sports facilities and six lighted tennis courts. A sundries shop is in a second-floor balcony space off the activities desk. In the conference building guests will find Bougainvillea Boutique, carrying men's and women's clothing; a branch of Pink Papaya (see Recommended Shopping, page 381); Bodywear jewelry; and a take-out deli minimarket.

Food at the Hyatt Regency is available in three restaurants. The Splash Bar Grill, a favorite with children, serves hamburger fare next to the beach. Menus here are printed on the sails of small ships carrying condiment cargoes. Chow Bella is a breezy beautifully appointed second-floor dining room off the main lobby, featuring Oriental/Italian cuisine. Have excellent 10-ingredient rice or scallion pancakes to begin, then farfalle with artichoke sauce, or other savory pastas. The informal main beachfront restaurant, The

Grand Café is especially remarkable for Sunday's groaning-board brunch. Meals taken here are always satisfying.

The resort offers travelers ultramodern conveniences in a meticulously tended tropical garden setting. Hyatt Regency St. John is recommended for families, lovers, weary urban travelers, and corporate executives.

HYATT REGENCY ST. JOHN
P.O. Box 8310, Cruz Bay
Great Cruz Bay, St. John,
U.S. Virgin Islands 00830
TEL: (809) 693-8000
FAX: (809) 693-8888

RESERVATIONS
Hyatt Resorts Corporation
675 Third Avenue
New York, NY 10017
TEL: (800) 233-1234 *or*
(212) 972-7000
FAX: (212) 557-5048

Open all year.

Rates: Double Occupancy. *December 20 to April 16:* Gardenview, $315; Oceanview, $380; Poolside, $425; Beachfront, $510. *April 17 to May 31* and *October 2 to December 19:* Gardenview, $235; Oceanview, $265; Poolside, $295; Beachfront, $355. *June 2 to September 30:* Rates about 40% less than *December 20 to April 16* rates.

Meal plan: EP. MAP (includes breakfast and dinner) mandatory during winter; add $60 per person per day; children 3 to 15, $29 per child per day.

Service charge: None. However, a 15% service charge is added to all food and beverages tabs.

Government tax: 8%.

Children welcome.

Credit cards accepted.

Note: Special packages are available. Information and rates on request.

Private Homes for Private Vacations

Mary-Phyllis Nogueira expertly manages 12 special St. John homes and villas from one to four bedrooms, which sleep two to eight guests. Each privately owned home is completely furnished, has a full kitchen, large deck, captivating ocean view, TV, tape deck, ceiling fan, washer and dryer, and outside barbecue grill. VCRs and microwave ovens come with all properties. Some have pools. Locations are spread around the island's southern, western, and northern shores. Due to safety precautions, there are young child restrictions on certain homes. A rental car is essential.

Guests receive the same arrival, car pick-up, and escort to residence service as listed in Catered To, Inc. (See last paragraph of its listing, page 351.)

PRIVATE HOMES FOR PRIVATE VACATIONS
Mary-Phyllis Nogueira
Mamey Peak, St. John
United States Virgin Islands 00830
TEL: (809) 776-6876
FAX: Same number. When phone is answered, press * key on phone.

Note: For rates, child restrictions, and all other specific information, contact Ms. Nogueira. Seven-night minimum is required in season; five-night minimum out of season.

Villa Bougainvillea, Gift Hill Villa, and The Beach Villa

St. John potter extraordinaire Don Schnell and his wife, Deborah, own three villas they manage as rentals. Bougainvillea and Gift Hill also have separate apartments, but the entire villas can be rented.

Three-bedroom Gift Hill Villa, located on Gift Hill five minutes from Cruz Bay, commands breathtaking views and has a freshwater pool and Jacuzzi.

The villa is a showcase for some of Don's handcrafted creations as well as for paintings and sculptures from the Schnells' private collection. Its one-bedroom apartment comes with a wraparound deck.

Villa Bougainvillea, Gift Hill's sister property and the Schnells' first residence on the island is within walking distance of Cruz Bay. The two-level home, with a two-bedroom apartment on the upper floor, is cooled throughout by ceiling fans and natural breezes. There's an outdoor deck and a patio covered by a latticework trellis. The one-bedroom apartment rests below.

The marvelous new Beach Villa sits at the water's edge on Great Cruz Bay, conveniently located a five-minute stroll along the shoreline from the Hyatt Regency's expansive beach, restaurants, shopping, and sports and water facilities.

The natural stone villa is crowned with curved-tile peaked roofs. Floors are laid with quarry tiles. The owner's ceramic creations are handsome embellishments used throughout the premises here, too, including a giant coral clay giraffe standing in the comfortable, nicely decorated living room.

The three second-story bedrooms have king-size beds and private baths. There's a fully stocked kitchen with a dishwasher, microwave, and electric coffeemaker. Cookware, dishes, and cutlery and utensils are also provided. Either elect to cool the premises naturally by opening the sliding glass doors or turning on a ceiling fan, or use the air-conditioning.

Outside is a small square-tiled swimming pool boasting a palm tree island in the center. The Beach Villa is true island living among sea grape, palms, and hibiscus, where you can relax in hammocks strung between palm trees, linger in the pool, or fall asleep on the veranda listening to a gentle sea.

Guests receive the same arrival, car pickup, and escort to residence service as described for Catered To, Inc. (see writeup, page 351).

VILLA BOUGAINVILLEA, GIFT HILL VILLA, AND THE BEACH VILLA
Deborah or Donald Schnell
P.O. Box 349
Cruz Bay, St. John
United States Virgin Islands 00831-0344
TEL: (800) 253-7107 *or*
       (809) 776-6420 (days) *or* (809) 776-6856 (evenings)
FAX: (809) 776-6920

Open all year.
Rates: Weekly rates for all Villas from Villa Apartment to Full Beach Villa. *November 14 to April 14:* two persons, $1,120 to $4,235; four persons, $1,470 to $4,235. *April 15 to November 13:* two persons, $700 to $3,185; four persons, $980 to $3,185.
Note: For all other information, contact Deborah or Donald Schnell.

NOTEWORTHY OPTIONS

Estate Zootenvaal

Located on St. John's quiet East End is an extra-special retreat, Estate Zootenvaal, a nine-mile, 30-minute winding drive from Cruz Bay. It's "we want to be alone" seaside living and housekeeping. Unless you want to hibernate here and have brought groceries, a car is necessary.

Estate Zootenvaal consists of only four small masonry houses with balconies, nicely spaced for complete privacy on a few acres of land along a small oceanside road. Three of the cottages are on the land above the road; one has two bedrooms, the others have one bedroom each. Everyone vies for the two-bedroom cottage, Beach Number 1, which is nestled just over the sea adjacent to the estate's small beach.

All cottages are prettily decorated with rattan furniture covered in quality fabrics, have fully equipped kitchens, ceiling fans, and patios. No TV, air-conditioning, or phones (there's a phone in the office that guests can use). Basic bathrooms have bathtubs and showers.

Guests' own little stretch of sand has chaises and a cabana for changing and a shower for rinsing off after swimming or snorkeling. There are no sports facilities here, but they're not hard to come by on St. John. This relatively isolated area is great for hiking or jogging.

The nearby community of Coral Bay has several good restaurants and a couple of small grocery stores. It's wiser to buy supplies in the Cruz Bay area. (See Provisions for Your Island Pantry.)

Friendly Robin Clair has managed Estate Zootenvaal for nine years. She tends the gardens daily and keeps roaming donkeys and goats at bay with closed gates on fences surrounding the property. Yearly repeaters know that Robin can be counted on for assistance of any kind—she's lived on St. John for more than 20 years.

Frills at Estate Zootenvaal amount to a limited selection of books in the office library. Apart from that you're on your own, which is just how guests prefer it.

Estate Zootenvaal is a unique find for undemanding, self-sufficient souls seeking peaceful, affordable housing in a rare primeval setting.

ESTATE ZOOTENVAAL	**U.S. RESERVATIONS**
Robin Clair	Carol Check
Hurricane Hole, St. John	TEL: (216) 861-5337
United States Virgin Islands 00830	
TEL: (809) 776-6321	

Open all year.

Rates: Double occupancy. *Year-round:* Daily rate, One-Bedroom Cottage, $175; weekly rate, $1,000; additional person $35 per person per day or $245 for a week. Daily rate, Two-Bedroom Cottage, $220; weekly rate, $1,250; additional person, $50 per person per day or $350 for a week. Children under 3, free. Full mail service available through owner's representative on an hourly or contract basis.

Meal plan: EP.

Service charge: None.

Government tax: 8%.

Children permitted by request.

Credit cards not accepted.

Harmony

Harmony is Maho Bay's sister, state-of-the-art "green" resort, which rests at the top of a hill above the camp cottages. A recent inspection of the attractive two-story four-building complex of bedroom studios and living room studio units revealed spacious lodgings, handsomely decorated, with kitchens, bathrooms, and patios or terraces, most with stunning sea views.

What is remarkable about these comfortable nests is that Stanley Selengut, a pioneer of ecotourism who conceived and developed Maho, has advanced a step further. To construct Harmony, he used some of the most sophisticated techniques in conservation available today.

The sun and wind at the resort generate the electricity. In order not to waste precious electricity, guests cannot lock their studio doors until they turn off the key-controlled power on a panel by the door, then all electricity, except for the refrigerator, goes off.

The buildings themselves are constructed from recycled materials: remelted steel transformed into nails, counter and table tops from 73% recycled glass, wallboards from paper and gypsum, entry tiles from tire rubber (they're very good looking), roof insulation from recycled milk jugs, and roof tiles from reused cardboard and cement. Floor tiles are pressed clay scraps; carpets, recycled plastic. Soft bed linens are created from unbleached cotton. Boxy white refrigerators that use 60% to 90% less energy than standard models, have thick walls and not much space inside. Showers have restricting low-flow features, so water waste is minimized. And as at Maho Bay, low-flush toilets are used. The bathrooms are first-rate.

Soon all guests will be able to monitor their energy consumption on computers in each accommodation.

Salengut's intention is to educate guests on the comforts of responsible consumption. Harmony is indeed an advance course in imaginative, miraculous ways of creative conservation. Stanley Salengut calls the rates for rooms "tuition." Staying at Harmony will afford you painless schooling in pleasing, natural shelters in St. John's wilderness. Guests at Harmony use all the facilities and beach at Maho.

For rates and facts, see the stats at the end of the Maho Bay entry, which follows.

Maho Bay

Maho Bay is one of the Caribbean's best permanent tented campgrounds. It's for nature-loving, undemanding outdoors people, who'll consider the resort's accommodations roughing it luxuriously. Maho Bay's 114 canvas-tent cottages are set among a winding network of wooden boardwalks and stairways that are spread over 17 hilly beachfront acres of tropical wilderness on the eastern end of magnificent St. John, eight miles from Cruz Bay. You must be partial to climbing to be contented at Maho.

You reach St. John by ferry from St. Thomas. Taxi shuttle service to and from the resort from Cruz Bay runs three or six times a day, but if there's going to be too long a wait, taxis are always available. You might want to rent a Jeep or car when you arrive from one of the many rental companies in Cruz Bay, since the resort's location is fantastically remote.

The trip from town to Maho takes about 25 minutes along the north coast's curving, dipping, and climbing road. St. John's small main roads are excellent, but when you reach Maho's turnoff, a dirt-and-stone, bumpy avenue leads you to the resort. While views along the way from Cruz Bay to picture-perfect Caribbean, and many of Maho's cottages do offer breathtaking ocean views, most have only partial sea views, obscured by dense growth of mahogany and kapok trees and succulents. Branches are cut back for ventilation and to prevent mildew, not to provide views. The reason for this is that Maho's founder and owner, Stanley Selengut, is a dedicated environmentalist. When he built the resort 18 years ago, nature was disturbed as little as possible; the practice continues. From the beginning no bulldozers were allowed on the property, in order to preserve the delicate ground cover, which prevents erosion of St. John's precious shallow layer of top soil. Electric cables and water pipes were attached to the underside of the walkways, so trenches wouldn't have to be dug. Water on St. John is collected in cisterns and used sparingly. Selengut installed low-flush toilets that need only two quarts of water, instead of standard ones that use up to five gallons a flush. There are watering stations along the boardwalk, but no running water in the cottages. Sinks, toilets, and showers are located in four separate bathhouses. Cold water only.

The 16 × 16-foot, three-room canvas cottages have wooden-plank decks supported by columns. Each has a sleeping area with wooden framed twin beds and camp-style mattresses (there are only a few double beds), a living room with a couch that converts into a bed, a screened cooking and dining area, and an open porch that cantilevers out over the ground. Rooms have electric lights, outlets, Igloo coolers to keep provisions cold, and multiburner propane stoves. Linens and towels and basic dishes, pots, pans, and utensils are provided. (Bring your own peppermill.) Public barbecues are scattered throughout the campground. You may also want to bring your own beach towels, flashlights, and a snap lock for your storage closet.

The camp store is stocked with frozen meat and fish, canned goods, dairy products and staples. It also sells some casual clothing, sundries, juices, sodas, and beer, but no liquor. Guests pack favorite foods from home, but supplies can be bought in Cruz Bay.

Both Maho's open-air three-tiered deck restaurant and the large, handsome peak-roofed pavilion have majestic mountain and sea views.

The food served at the restaurant, which is open for breakfast and dinner only, is sustenance/home cooking featuring health food, like grilled mahi-mahi, Caribbean chicken breast, or moussaka, served with baked potatoes, green beans, and cucumber-and-onion salad. Dessert might be banana bread. The Maho community of guests all gather at mealtime to discuss things like the temperature of the water in the showers, and how termites build their giant podlike nests. Guests are a diverse, predominately American collection of all ages: urban couples trying to get some fresh air, adventurers, families, young lovers, even newlyweds. Guests range from serious naturalists to laid-back city folk. Quiet hours begin at 10 P.M. and no radios are allowed without earphones.

Maho's calm, white-sand, west-facing private beach curves between two rocky points. It's excellent for swimming and snorkeling. Windsurfers, kayaks, and Sunfish are available, and all water sports can be easily found throughout St. John.

You're not far from the well-preserved Annaberg Sugar Mill and other ghostly plantation-day ruins. Nature trails are everywhere in the island's national park, including one down to nearby Francis Bay's fine beach where swimmers join endangered Hawksbill, green, and leatherback turtles. Manager Bobby Flanagan or Roland Kravats at the reservations desk will help you with your itinerary, or any information or arrangements you request.

You can keep constantly busy or totally unoccupied, stay completely alone or join new friends. At Maho Bay, guests rough it easy, blending right into nature with mongoose and lizards on this rare unspoiled Caribbean safari land.

MAHO BAY CAMPS AND HARMONY
Cruz Bay, St. John
U.S. Virgin Islands 00830
TEL: (809) 776-6240/6226
FAX: (809) 776-6504

RESERVATIONS
Maho Bay Camps, Inc.
17A East 73 Street
New York, NY 10021-3578
TEL: (800) 392-9004 *or*
(212) 472-9453
FAX: (212) 861-6210

Open all year.
Rates: Maho Bay. Double occupancy. *December 15 to April 30:* Cottage, $95. *May 1 to December 14:* Cottage, $60. **Harmony.** Double occupancy. *December 15 to April 30:* Bedroom Studio, $150; Living Room Studio, $170. *May 1 to December 14:* Bedroom Studio, $95; Living Room Studio, $125.
Meal plan: EP.
Service charge: None.
Government tax: 8%.
Children under 4 not recommended.
Credit cards not accepted.

ST. THOMAS' BEST

Grand Palazzo Hotel

Secluded on 15 beachfront acres at Great Bay on St. Thomas's east end is the island's most luxurious resort, the Grand Palazzo Hotel, with 148 elegant junior suites and four one-bedroom suites and a stunning replica of a Venetian Renaissance palace.

We attended the hotel's opening ceremonies on October 31, 1992, which were celebrated with a champagne and caviar reception, a dazzling display of fireworks, and dancing under a canopy of stars into the wee small hours of the morning. At long last, St. Thomas has a super-luxury resort that can compete with the best in the Caribbean.

Responsible for this beautiful resort is British entrepreneur Michael Pemberton (his other hotels are Glitter Bay and the Royal Pavilion on Barbados; see resort listings) with the help of architectural firm Wimberly Allison Tong & Goo (WAT&G) of Newport Beach, California, and design consultant Ian Morrison (Mr. Morrison designed Pemberton's other hotels). Although Michael Pemberton is no longer affiliated with Grand Palazzo (it's managed by Tishman Hotel Corporation), he and his talented team, including landscape architect Venezuela-born Fernando Tabora and then-managing director, Stephen Grant, deserve accolades for an extraordinary accomplishment. When Pemberton bought the property it was merely a desert of scrub brush.

The Grand Palazzo Hotel sprawls across a hillside facing sister island, St. John. Guests enter the resort under the Venetian palace's porte cochère. The magnificent building boasts a pinnacled campanile, arched, columned walkways, an ochre stucco exterior with red curved-tile multiple roofs, and shuttered French doors and windows. The palazzo's interior is a wealth of Portuguese marble, Venetian lanterns, hand-carved furniture, and handsome Manila consoles under immense matching framed mirrors. British artist Jacqueline Bateman was enlisted to enhance the wallways with delightful trompe l'oeil, representing the seasons.

The palazzo's dramatic central courtyard, the ground level of which rests three stories below, is open to the elements. One wall consists of three overlapping fountains featuring terra-cotta lion-head spouts. These fanciful fountain heads are spread through the property. Two beautiful rooms off the courtyard with sea views are superb venues for small business conferences or private parties.

The palazzo's main entrance top-floor lobby and hallways hold the reception and the concierge desks, a sundries shop with Grand Palazzo personalized clothing, fragrances and jewelry, and Amsterdam Sauer's fine Brazilian gemstones and jewelry shop. The lobby also houses one of the best boutiques on St. Thomas, Gaetan Benson and Ron Karr's upscale Condotti, carrying chic island resortwear from Helen Kaminski's bags and panama hats and clothing, Norma Kamali and La Perla to Moroccan imports and Caribbean and stateside jewelry, as well as an impressive men's shop. A beauty salon is tucked away on an overhead floor.

At the French-door balconies at the eastern end of the lobby of the palazzo, guests have their first glimpse of the resort—a breathtaking panorama down the fossil-stone grand staircase to the exquisite freshwater swimming pool, across the snow-white beach and the turquoise sea beyond to St. John. (See cover photograph.)

Grand Palazzo's 148 junior suites and four one-bedroom suites rest in six white-stucco red-roofed Mediterranean-style buildings cresting off the sloping grounds in a curve at various angles. All accommodations have spacious private balconies fitted with French bistro tables and chairs. Magenta bougainvillea flows out of front planters of each balcony. Views from these aeries are splendid ocean Caribbeanscapes.

Fernando Tabora created a harmonious horticultural design of rolling green lawns accented with palm trees, exotic ground covers, allamanda, croton, hibiscus, and hundreds of tropical specimens now established and thriving.

As you stand on the balcony of the Palazzo, to the left are a series of contemporary West Indian–style pink stucco structures with white corrugated peaked roofs where there are two bars and two restaurants. In back to the north are four lighted Astroturf tennis courts under the direction of Peter Burwash International. A full fitness center is on the Palazzo's ground floor.

Other sports facilities at Grand Palazzo include Sunfish, windsurfers, snorkeling, and Hobie Cats. Early morning aerobics classes are offered every day, except Sunday. The hotel's 53-foot catamaran, *Lady Lynsey*, is available for luncheons, sunset champagne sails or private excursions. Scuba diving and full certifications are also obtainable here.

Cushman vehicles carry guests to their accommodations in buildings named after flowers, alphabetically, from allamanda to freesia. Rooms have marbled entranceways, dressing areas, and bathrooms with tub/showers, double basins, baskets of natural Molton Brown toiletries, thick towels, a hair dryer, and monogrammed seersucker robes. Closets supply ample hanging and shelf space, a digital safe, and an umbrella. The only thing missing are drawers; apart from two tiny ones in the vanity table, there are none. The combined bedrooms and sitting areas (really one room) are carpeted and furnished with pretty rattan loveseats, a king-size bed (all but 14 rooms have kings), and have excellent lighting. Rooms come with armoires that have color TVs with a pay-movie channel, and a computerized fully stocked mini-refrigerator inside. Each suite has three phones—one on a writing table, one on a bed table, and even one in the water closet. Ceiling fans hang from pickled pine ceilings, and rooms are air-conditioned.

Grand Palazzo has been weak on room service. Continental breakfasts are fine and enchantingly delivered in baskets, usually on time. Other requests are slow in coming, however, if obtainable at all. A friend staying at the hotel recently was unable to get a pot of tea without walking a fair distance to the main bar. Manager Marston Winkles, I'm told, is working on correcting this.

Meantime, Grand Palazzo's two restaurants continue to please locals, like ourselves, and guests. The stunning formal Palm Terrace is a vast, columned expanse of pink marble, with towering ceilings and potted palms. Wall-to-wall glass doors and windows provide breezy sea views. Recently a new chef arrived; but before then our latest meal was a sampling of sea scallops and zucchini ravioli with lemon thyme and caramelized tomatoes and a potato risotto with Maryland crab and asparagus starters. Entrées were prawns in an onion crust with Cuban-style lentil salad and cilantro vinaigrette and an outstanding sliced roast chicken with roasted potatoes, grilled asparagus and crisp leeks. For desserts we had an ambrosial fresh berry Napoleon and a mild-flavored, creamy strawberry bombe.

Cafe Vecchio, the open-air casual restaurant with its own sweeping sea views, serves excellent food at breakfast, lunch, and dinner. Lunches are first-rate burgers, salads including grilled chicken Caesar, thin crusted crisp pizzas, and sandwiches during the day. At night the menu is based on Italian selections like osso bucco and a variety of well-prepared pastas, as well as grilled fresh seafoods. Monday's Caribbean buffet offers a wide selection of excellent island-inspired dishes, followed by a Caribbean floor show.

I've saved the best for last, and that is Grand Palazzo's lovely 125-foot freeform freshwater pool. Its undulating lipped edge creates the illusion that the pool dissolves into the sand and sea. Surrounding the pool is a graceful, chaise-lined garden terrace, and at the southern end, there's a pavilion bar and a multilevel dining area called the Reef Bar. Light meals and drinks are served here until the sun sets.

The Grand Palazzo is a beautiful sanctuary where guests can hide away in luxury on St. Thomas.

GRAND PALAZZO HOTEL
Great Bay, St. Thomas
United States Virgin Islands 00802
TEL: (809) 775-3333
FAX: (809) 775-4444

RESERVATIONS
TEL: (800) 545-0509

Open all year.

Rates: Double occupancy. *January 2 to April 2:* Double Deluxe, $415; Junior Suite, $475; One- and Two-Bedroom Suites, $865 to $1,325; extra person sharing suite, $75. *April 3 to May 31* and *November 21 to November 30:* Double Deluxe, $295; Junior Suite, $350; One- and Two-Bedroom Suites, $650 to $995; extra person sharing suite, $30. *June 1 to November 20* and *December 1 to December 19:* Rooms and Suites, $250; extra person sharing suite, $30.

Meal plan: EP. MAP (includes breakfast and dinner), add $65 per person per day year-round. MAP for children add $33.

Service charge: None.

Government tax: 8%.

Children two and over welcome.

Credit cards accepted.

Secret Harbour Beach Resort and Secret Harbourview Villas

Hidden away on St. Thomas' east end, which locals call the country, is a sentimental favorite of ours. We had an apartment here for a few years, and know and still like it a lot. It's a two-part condominium hotel with two names: Secret Harbour Beach Resort and Secret Harbourview Villas. This is a bit confusing to most, so we simply call it Secret Harbour. The resort is composed of seven three-story, contemporary, white-masonry buildings with 100 accommodations consisting of terraced studios and one- or two-bedroom apartments that are furnished by the owners in varying degrees of island trappings from standard tropical to designer superior. The combined hotels offer air-conditioning and ceiling fans, telephones, cable TV, fully equipped kitchens, maid service, five all-weather tennis courts, an fitness room, a 40 × 60-foot freshwater swimming pool, a Jacuzzi, and a beachfront restaurant serving breakfast, lunch, and dinner (no room service of any kind). There's also a boutique, car rental service, and a full water-sports facility.

Secret Harbour is first-class, neither super-luxurious nor the least bit pretentious. It's spread over eight flourishing garden acres in a residential neighborhood overlooking a peaceful harbor and palm-studded, white-sand crescent beach. This marvelous stretch of sand faces west for all-day sun and buttery-gold sunsets. Celebrities often come to Secret Harbour for sunshine, informal living, and privacy. They get it. Robert Ludlum completed one of his thrillers in a beachfront apartment at Secret Harbour, and I've seen Twiggy and Chita Rivera on the hotel's beach — all guests of the hotel. None of the many repeat guests, mostly Americans of every age, come to the hotel for chic, but rather to decompress, where they know it's always summer and the living is easy.

As you enter Secret Harbour's circular driveway, you get the impression that the one-story main building is someone's home. Indeed it once was. Arthur and Judi Witty (still island residents) bought the original house and surrounding acreage in 1960. They expanded the house and transformed the main living areas into a lounge, bar, and reception, then added two identical 18-unit buildings of accommodations, before eventually opening the hotel in 1967. By 1979 two more beachfront units had opened. The Wittys crossed the small road that separated the property and put up three more units which were completed in 1981, on the hillside. When the condominium owners took charge of the operations, by some quirk in the law, two corporations had to be formed. In this unusual arrangement, 60-unit Secret Harbour Beach Resort and 40-unit Secret Harbourview Villas each have their own management, staff, rates, and booking procedures, but amicably share all the facilities. Guests at Secret Harbourview Villas on the hillside have expansive sea views over the harbor overlooking the roofs of the lower Secret Harbour units, and have a short walk or drive down the hill to the beach and water sports, restaurant, car rental desk, and boutique at Secret Harbour Beach Resort. Two tennis courts are on a little hill adjoining Secret Harbour.

The chief differences between the two resorts are that Secret Harbour Beach Resort is beachfront and has a lobby and reception, making it the more traditional hotel. (A management team runs the hotel.) Buildings 3 and 4 have the best views, especially the second and third floors, and they are farther away from the restaurants. Building 2 has been totally rebuilt after a fire destroyed it in 1989.

Secret Harbourview Villas' units, with the exception of Building 2 on the beach at Secret Harbour, are newer, nearer to the pool, with a Jacuzzi, fitness room, and 3 tennis courts. And, Secret Harbour Villas was recently awarded a three-diamond rating by the AAA. The hotel's office is a little nook in the corner of the first unit, Building 5, which is closest to the beach and the shortest climb. If you are arriving late, the booking office must be notified in advance so that someone will remain in the office to meet you, as it closes at 9 P.M. in the winter; 7 P.M. in the summer.

So, the choice is up to you. After check-in, the two hotels appear to function as one pleasant entity.

Jody Touger's Island Odyssey Boutique in the hotel's lobby carries some better sportswear, swimsuits, coverups—plenty to cloose from—plus Caribbean art and handcrafts, costume jewelry, sundry items, soft drinks, and snacks.

At a branch of Thrifty Car Rental, also in the lobby, you can rent a car, or call in advance (776-5335) to reserve a vehicle and collect it at the airport.

Water-sports enthusiasts will be pleased to find Aqua Action, a PADI, five-star facility right on the premises at the northern end of the beach. It specializes in scuba and night dives but also offers snorkeling trips, windsurfing with private instruction, and has aqua bikes and sea kayaks. Aqua Action sells dive and snorkel-related equipment and books, as well as a small collection of swim and beachwear.

Breakfasts and lunches in the Secret Harbour Beach Café are served in the open-air gazebo room or on a delightful beachfront terrace under aqua-and-white-striped umbrellas. The food is good but standard: fritters, salads, sandwiches, and burgers with specials of the day. Lunch is also served at a little bar hut. In a curious arrangement, the wonderful long bar, facing the sea, remains closed until the end of the day.

The adjoining Tamarind By the Sea evening restaurant, in one of St. Thomas' most splendid beachfront settings, has seen better days. At press time, it needed sprucing up (dark gray plastic chairs and no tablecloths) and a talented new chef. The restaurant really should be entirely renovated. Concerned management and owners are at work on this. We're looking forward to the changes.

Guests at Secret Harbour have the advantage of being only a mile from Red Hook, a small, ever-growing district, including the handsome new American Yacht Harbour Buildings, with restaurants, markets, boutiques, a large marina, and the St. John ferry dock. If you're cooking in, Red Hook has excellent markets for stocking up on food and beverages. (See Recommended Restaurants, Provisions for Your Island Pantry, plus Useful Information in St. Thomas section for ferry information.)

Secret Harbour is a real find on St. Thomas; a peaceful, quiet sanctuary. Both hotels are highly recommended.

In comparing costs of the hotels, note that the rates at Secret Harbourview Villas on the hill are lower than Secret Harbour Beach Resort on the beach. The Villas also add no service charge to the bill.

SECRET HARBOUR BEACH RESORT
6280 Estate Nazareth, St. Thomas
United States Virgin Islands 00802
TEL: (800) 524-2250 *or*
(809) 775-6550
FAX: (809) 775-1501

Open all year.

Rates: Double occupancy. *December 19 to April 10:* Studio Suite, $265; One-Bedroom Suite, $310; Two-Bedroom Suite (4 persons), $480; extra person, $35 per person per night. Only 1994 rates were available at press time for *mid-April to December 18:* Studio Suite, $179; One-Bedroom Suite, $199; Two-Bedroom Suite (4 persons), $309; extra person, $25 per person per night. Cribs or cots, $10 daily, except in Value Season (*mid-April to mid-December*), when cribs are free.

Meal plan: EP.

Service charge: 10%.

Government tax: 8%.

Children welcome.

Credit cards accepted.

Note: Hotel dive packages in conjunction with Aqua Action and Value Season packages are available.

SECRET HARBOURVIEW VILLAS
TEL: (809) 775-6000

RESERVATIONS
Ocean Property Management,
Inc.
Box 8529, St. Thomas
United States Virgin Islands
00801
TEL: (800) 874-7897 *or*
(809) 775-2600
FAX: (809) 775-5901

Open: All year.
Rates: Double occupancy. *December 15 to April 14:* Studio, $210; One-Bedroom Suite, $280; Two-Bedroom Suite (2 to 4 persons), $360. *April 15 to December 14:* Studio, $140; One-Bedroom Suite, $170; Two-Bedroom Suite (2 to 4 persons), $250. Additional persons in room, $30 per person per night; cribs/cots, $10 per night.
Meal plan: EP.
Service charge: None.
Government tax: 8%.
Children welcome.
Credit cards accepted.
Note: Late-evening arrivals must notify office in advance. Maid service daily in season; off-season, daily except weekends and holidays.
Honeymoon and dive packages in conjunction with Aqua Action are also available.

Stouffer Renaissance Grand Beach Resort

Stouffer Renaissance Grand Beach Resort stretches across 34 acres of American paradise, over hillsides and flat land fringed by a 1,000-foot white sand beach on St. Thomas' east end. Views from the resort out to sea are a Caribbeanscape of pale blue sky merging into aqua and deep blue sea with a rich green backdrop of sister island St. John, and beyond to the British Virgins.

The hotel's 297 accommodations, a combination of guest rooms and suites, are in separate resort neighborhoods. "Bougainvillea" residents check into one of 86 lodgings housed in two-story buildings staggered around and in back of the restaurants and pool areas. These quarters are closest to the beach, and, like virtually every inch of the property, they're enveloped in dense tropical gardens. "Hibiscus" is the hillside 211-room-and-suite community, in two- to four-story buildings draped over a hillside that rises 250 feet. The views from here cannot be surpassed. Walking down to the beach is usually no problem, but in the midday tropical heat, call for shuttle transport back up.

Stouffer's architecture was created to blend into the natural environment, with cream-colored stucco structures, angled shingled roofs, arched dormer windows, and cooling marble foyers. Only the electric blue canopies that embellish buildings contradict the original intent. Inside the dwellings' rooms and public areas, colors are soothing pale greens and mauves, and other quiet pastels. Furniture is modern Deco rattan.

Special features of the carpeted accommodations include remote control cable TV, telephones, air-conditioning, fully stocked mini-bars, safes, hair dryers, and patio balconies. Guests are supplied with complimentary toiletries in bathrooms that would be agreeable to the most demanding guest—unless that person might be happier relaxing in the large whirlpool spa in the two-bedroom master suite's bathroom.

Stouffer's presents guests with an extensive list of recreational activities and excursions. The water-sports center offers windsurfing, sport fishing, and Sunfish sailing. Chris Sawyer's Dive Center operates from the hotel. Six lighted tennis courts (four hard-surface and two Omniturf courts) with a Pro Shop and USPTA certified instructor are also at guests' disposal. In addition, there's a fitness center with a six-station Nautilus, Lifecycles, and more, plus men's and women's whirlpool spas, showers, and saunas.

Stouffer's has conference facilities as well as a daily complimentary children's program called Grand Beach Club for kids from 3 to 14. Trained counselors supervise children's activities and entertainment, such as beach olympics, pool games in the designated 1.5-foot-deep children's area of the main pool, iguana hunts, and special sports training. Extra-special events, for a minimal fee, include trips to Coral World, St. John, and even special dinners and movies.

Members of the corporate set, honeymooners, and family members of all ages shop in the boutiques on the second-floor gallery of the main lobby lounge and reception building: The Grand Stand, for necessities, T-shirts, local and stateside papers; Bougainvillea, for men's and women's apparel; and Island Fancy, for tropical treasures. A hair salon is now located there too.

Just off the beach, the pyramid-shaped "Grand Pool" and terrace is, not surprisingly, the resort's most popular retreat. Bay Winds seaside restaurant serves commendable American cuisine under a sky-high ceiling. Musicians dish up nightly entertainment. At lunch, the dining room extends to an adjoining terrace. Guests nibble on salads and fresh fish under swaying coconut palms. The Palm Snack Bar, a serve-yourself set of open windows at the back of Bay Winds, cooks up tasty cheeseburgers and hot dogs, offers a grilled-chicken Caesar salad, and other quick fare.

Smugglers Restaurant and Grill, in back of Bougainvillea's accommodations, is a casual, two-level dining room overlooking Stouffer's second pool. Breakfast and Sunday brunches are tempting buffets. Suppers include grilled snapper, other seafood, chicken, steaks, and the like. A *TimesFax* and complimentary coffee are delivered with your wake-up call.

At a weekly Caribbean night, guests gather at tables set up on the beach. Festivities include live entertainment, such as mocko jumby dancers, a fire eater, and a steel band.

STOUFFER RENAISSANCE GRAND BEACH RESORT
P.O. Box 8267
Smith Bay Road, St. Thomas
United States Virgin Islands 00801
TEL: (809) 775-1510
FAX: (809) 775-2185

Open all year.
Rates: Double occupancy. *December 26 to March 29:* Rooms, $315 to $435; Suites, $595 to $895. *March 30 to May 31* and *November 1 to December 19:* Rooms, $255 to $355; Suites, $475 to $675. *June 1 to October 31:* Rooms, $215 to $315; Suites, $450 to $550.
Meal plan: EP.
Service charge: None.
Government tax: 8%.
Children welcome.
Credit cards accepted.
Note: Numerous packages available.

A NOTEWORTHY OPTION

Blackbeard's Castle Hotel

Perched just above Government Hill with a breathtaking panoramic view of the harbor and the town of Charlotte Amalie is Blackbeard's Castle Hotel, an intimate inn.

The hotel's 20 rooms, including three apartments and suites are set in several modest buildings around or near an enormous, round, natural-stone watchtower built in 1679. It is believed to be the oldest standing structure on St. Thomas.

Blackbeard's Castle is not a luxury resort on an isolated beach. It's an in-town oasis situated in a quiet, historic, mostly residential neighborhood. Sunning in chaises by the 30 × 60-foot freshwater pool on the vast terrace, sipping a "Pirate's Revenge," the fruity house rum drink, it's hard to believe that downtown's bustling waterfront is less than a mile away.

In November 1985 the owner-management team of Henrique Kozens, a transplanted Brazilian, and Bob Harrington, from St. Louis, with the aid of architect Michael Helm of Tortola, turned the former private residence into a hotel with imagination and good taste.

Each room or suite has a private entrance, cable TV, air-conditioning and ceiling fan, but no telephones.

Rooms are medium-sized with pleasant plain furnishings, comfy chairs, and solid beds. Instead of headboards, some of the rooms contain East Indian kilim rugs hanging on the wall over beds. A few of the rooms have lattice-enclosed porches surrounded by hibiscus, bougainvillea, and frangipani. Six carpeted rooms are decorated prettily with peach-colored walls and color-coordinated floral-print or striped bedcovers. The best rooms with little porches are E1 and E2. These two front rooms face the sunny south, where it's delightful to have breakfast, read, observe the activity at the pool, or simply enjoy the spectacular view over town and out to sea.

Two of the three suites are duplexes, each with a small spiral staircase leading up to the bedroom and bath. A1 is the nicest, on a southern corner. The furnishings are modest modern; nothing lavish here, but perfectly adequate. Each suite is equipped with a washer/dryer, dishwasher, range, full refrigerator, and a microwave oven.

Blackbeard's Castle displays the beautiful oil paintings of New York artist Russ Elliott throughout the hotel—still lifes or endangered species. Mr. Elliott's trompe l'oeil jungles decorate wall areas and corridors. Many of the paintings are for sale.

Blackbeard's Castle Restaurant is a favorite of locals and visitors alike, offering American nouvelle cuisine with hints of the Caribbean. Evenings at the lounge bar and outdoor terrace, a separate, reasonably priced menu of light fare is offered from 6 to 10 P.M.

Blackbeard's location is its greatest plus. The view of the harbor offers a nonstop nautical showcase of everything from cruise and tall ships and speedboats to impressive yachts.

The hotel staff will help arrange taxis or give directions to the beaches; Morningstar and Magens Bay beaches are the closest.

Blackbeard's has no shop or boutique, but Main Street shopping in town is only minutes away.

Special activities are organized at the hotel throughout the year. On Easter Sunday every year an amusing Easter-bonnet contest is held. Live music is featured throughout the year.

BLACKBEARD'S CASTLE
P.O. Box 6041
St. Thomas, United States Virgin Islands 00804
TEL: (800) 344-5771 *or*
    (809) 776-1234
FAX: (809) 776-4321

Open all year.
Rates: Single/double occupancy. *December 15 to April 30:* Standard Room, $140; Junior Suite, $170; Apartment Suite, $190. *May 1 to December 14:* Standard Room, $95; Junior Suite, $120; Apartment Suite, $145. Extra person, $15 per day.
Meal plan: CP (includes continental breakfast).
Service charge: 10%.
Government tax: 8%.
Children not recommended. It's an adult atmosphere.
Credit cards accepted.

Recommended Restaurants

ST. CROIX' FINEST*

* **The Greathouse at Villa Madeleine**, 778-7377 (Teague Bay on east end). Superb Italian/Continental cuisine served in a lovely, open-air dining room or on a veranda on the hillside overlooking the sea. (See hotel listing.) Moderate to expensive.

* **Kendrick's**, 773-9199 (Queen Cross Street near King Street, Christiansted). David and Jane Kendricks' French Provincial–style restaurant on the second floor of a restored Danish house is one of the finest dining rooms in St. Croix. The grilled rack of lamb is first-rate, as are soups, salads, homemade pastas, desserts—especially the ice creams. Good wine list. Moderate to expensive.

* **Indies**, 692-9440 (5556 Company Street, Christiansted). Gifted chef Catherine Plav Driggers has turned this small courtyard dining room into a choice dining destination. (She was formerly at Cormorant's restaurant.) From first courses and entrées to desserts, Plav Driggers consistently creates outstanding dishes with touches of Caribbean ingredients. Seafood and lobster dishes are superb. Moderate to expensive.

* **Carambola Beach Resort**, 778-3800 (Davis Bay). Whether dining in the casual Deli café, elegant Mahogany Room, or more informal Saman room, food is quite good at this luxury resort (see resort listing). Inexpensive to expensive.

* **The Brass Parrot**, 773-2100 (The Buccaneer Hotel, 10 minutes from Christiansted off East End Road). Elegant air-conditioned dining room. Mixed cuisines and grilled steaks, fish, or chops are prepared with flair (see resort listing). Expensive.

* **Top Hat**, 773-2346 (52 Company Street, Christiansted). Grilled steaks and Scandinavian specialties are cooked and presented with care here. Excellent wine list. Expensive.

* **Club Comanche Restaurant**, 773-2665 (1 Strand Street, Christiansted). Upstairs at the Comanche Hotel is the in-town place to head for for island atmosphere and to savor crunchy conch fritters, juicy burgers, and curries at lunch. At dinner, sample excellent grilled steaks, fish, or lobster. Popular with locals and visitors alike. Moderate to expensive.

* **Villa Morales**, 772-0556 (near Estate Whim House on Route 70). Delicious Spanish/Caribbean cuisine from steamed red snapper, paella, and roast pork to stewed goat served with flavorful rice and beans, plantains, and johnnycakes. Moderate.

* **Le St. Tropez**, 772-3000, (67 King Street in Limetree Court, Frederiksted). Attractive Mediterranean bistro serving up quiches, salads, seafood, and other good food with a French accent. Moderate.

OTHER DEPENDABLE CHOICES

The Galleon, 773-9949 (Green Cay Marina). Breathtaking ocean views and a first-rate menu including Caesar salad, steaks, lamb, and seafood. Moderate to expensive.
Banana Bay Club, 778-9110 (Hotel Caravelle on Christiansted waterfront). This

informal restaurant serves three meals a day—from Philadelphia cheese steak and stir-frys to pasta and steak and lobster entrées. Saturday night the feature is prime rib. Inexpensive to moderate.

On the Beach Bar & Café, 772-4242/1205 (On the Beach Resort, one mile south of Frederiksted). Chef Roger Van Sant, formerly at Café du Soleil, is in the kitchen turning out distinctive salads, seafood, and pastas in a breezy seaside location. Moderate.

Anabelle's Tea Room, 773-3990 (Quin House in Christiansted). Open for three mouth-watering Cuban/Caribbean-inspired meals throughout the day in a courtyard setting, Anabelle's features tender Cuban pork sandwiches, asopao (fragrant stew), stir-frys, and specials of the day. Locals love Anabelle's. Inexpensive to moderate.

Antoine's, 773-0263 (58A King Street, waterfront Christiansted). This island institution is located on the second floor in an open-air dining room with a view of the harbor. The large, eclectic menu features everything from conch fritters and callaloo to Wienerschnitzel and pasta to Swiss specialities. Inexpensive to moderate.

Café du Soleil, 772-5400 (625 Strand Street on the waterfront in Frederiksted.) This pleasant seaside alfresco terrace is located on the second floor and offers well-prepared pastas or seafood salads, local fish, and chicken. Fine venue for Sunday brunch. Moderate.

Dino's, 778-8005 (4C Hospital Street, Christiansted). Dine inside in an air-conditioned room or outdoors on Italian food from bruschetta and antipasto to freshly made pasta with variety of delectable sauces from tomato and basil to puttanesca. Superior veal dishes and a good wine selection. Moderate to expensive.

Luncheria, 773-4247 (Apothecary Hall in Christiansted). This popular Mexican restaurant has no table service. Order your margarita at the bar then order nachos, arroz con pollo, beef or chicken burritos, tostadas, or other savory quick foods. Just collect your food and enjoy. Inexpensive to moderate.

West End Beach Club, 772-0002 (beachside, about one mile north of Frederiksted). Spend the day at the beach certain that tasty food is available from late morning until sunset—lobster salad, fried fish, West Indian conch, burgers, and such. Sundays are a fun-filled beach barbecue. Chaise longues can be rented for the day. Inexpensive to moderate.

Sprat Hall Beach Restaurant, 772-5855 (Route 63 in Frederiksted). Another choice spot to go for a swim, then dine on appetizing fritters, burgers, salads, and other simple offerings. Inexpensive to moderate. Small fee charged for chaises.

Other good dining options are **The Hideaway** at Hisbiscus Beach Hotel, **Cormorant Beach Club**'s restaurant, **Chenay Bay Beach Resort** for casual barbecues (Tuesday night is a West Indian pig roast), **No Name Bar & Grille** at Cane Bay Reef Club, and **Sea View Restaurant** at St. Croix by the Sea. **Tommy & Susan's Taverna** in Apothecary Hall serves excellent Greek food. **Stixx** on the Christiansted waterfront at the Pan Am Pavilion and **The Cultured Pelican Cafe** (43A Queen Cross Street, Christiansted) and its sister restaurant in Coakley Bay Condos with a view of Buck Island, all dish up good seafood and promise island fun. **Amalie's Terrace** at the Hotel on the Cay, **Kim's Restaurant** on downtown King Street, **La Guitarra** at Market Square, **Gertrude's** at 114 Castle Coakley on Hess Road, **Dover's Pâté Factory** in Market Square Mall, and

Harvey's Restaurant on Company Street downtown, are the places to go for mouth-watering West Indian food.

Pizza Mare, 773-0553 (in Christiansted), or 778-5556 (at Sunny Isle Shopping Center), serves excellent pizzas, calzones, antipasto, garlic bread, and pasta dishes. Daily specials. Call ahead.

Morning Glory at the Gallows Bay Marketplace is a friendly coffee house serving freshly baked muffins, beignets, and lunches. Excellent freshly roasted coffees. **The Wreck Bar and Grill,** just east of the Fort in Christiansted, is an open-air funky eatery serving Mexican and fast foods with a lively bar, crab races, and live entertainment. **Blue Moon** on Strand Street in Frederiksted mixes good food with live jazz on Friday nights.

ST. JOHN'S FINEST*

* **Beach Terrace,** 776-6111 (Caneel Bay). Caneel's main dining room is set in an expansive two-level breezy beachside pavilion. Lavish luncheon buffets include a chilled soup, elegant salad makings, cold shrimp or crab claws, vegetables, a grilling station, and dessert table. À la carte orders are also taken. The Sunday champagne brunch is an extravaganza not to be missed. Dinners are more formal affairs, featuring fresh fish and seafood, rack of lamb, and duck, creatively sauced and artfully presented. (See resort listing.) Expensive.

* **Equator,** 776-6111 (Caneel Bay). This attractive, sizable round open-air dining pavilion sits above flora-covered sugar mill ruins overlooking Caneel's splendid grounds and beyond to the sea and St. Thomas. Nightly selections now represent flavors of Asia, Middle East, Mexico, and South America. We hope this magically situated restaurant will open again someday for lunch. Moderate to expensive.

* **Le Château de Bordeaux,** 776-6611 (Centerline Road). First-rate French/West Indian cuisine is elegantly served in this intimate dining room on a hillside with spectacular views of Coral Bay on St. John's east end. Fine wines. (The owners have opened *Asolare, 779-4747 (Caneel Road). Asian menu. Served in restaurant atop Cruz Bay.) Moderate to expensive.

* **Paradiso,** 693-8899 (Mongoose Junction). Dine at this beautiful, spacious, second-floor, air-conditioned room with a great bar; also outdoors on the balcony. It features a Northern Italian—focused menu—fried calamari, linguine al pesto, seafood put-tanesca, and fresh fish selections. The food is not as exciting as it once was, but go for a decent meal and the great atmosphere. Moderate to expensive.

* **Morgan's Mango,** 693-8141 (across street from the National Park Dock). Four energetic young and talented restaurateurs have opened a delightful, small terrace restaurant serving scrumptious "cuisine of the Caribbean," from spicy black bean soup and jerk chicken to snapper with lime. Side dishes and desserts also excel. The active bar serves no less than 25 exotic tropical cocktails, including frosty mango margaritas. It's great news that the quartet is bringing a sister **Morgan's Mango** across Pillsbury Sound to Tillett Gardens in St. Thomas for the winter of 1995. Moderate.

* **Chow Bella,** 693-8000 (Hyatt Regency St. John). You guessed it—a Chinese/

Asian/Italian menu is served in a lovely second-floor restaurant in the Hyatt Regency's main building (see resort listing). Moderate to expensive.

* Grand Café, 693-8000 (Hyatt Regency St. John). This beachside dining room offers a variety of cuisines and foods on specific nights: Monday and Friday, prime rib; Wednesday, West Indian; Mexican fare on Thursday; and lobster on Saturday night. Sunday brunches are buffets "fit for a king." Moderate to expensive.

OTHER DEPENDABLE CHOICES

Saychelles, 693-7030 (Wharfside Village). A pretty, new outdoor terrace and indoor air-conditioned waterfront café that features well-prepared tapas, including toast with Montrachet, grilled eggplant, and puréed white beans, pastas, and Mediterranean food like bouillabaise. Moderate.

Fish Trap, 693-9994 (at Raintree Inn, a short walk from ferry dock). Chef Aaron Willis turns out excellent seafood, chicken, and pasta dishes served on a covered outdoor terrace of a small inn. Very popular—sometimes service can be rushed. Moderate.

Pussers of the West Indies, 693-8489 (Wharfside Village). Second-floor terrace dining room overlooks the harbor to St. Thomas and the out islands. Hearty American/Caribbean cuisine. Good choice for children. Try the famous "Painkiller" rum cocktail. On the top floor is **Pusser's Crow's Nest**—stunning sunset views; also indoors is **Pusser's Oyster Bar**, which serves draft beer. When it rains, customers receive a discount. (New is **Pusser's Beach Bar**, 693-9080, on the first floor, offering a design-your-own pizza and nachos menu. Sports bar and take-out. Inexpensive to moderate.)

Mongoose Restaurant, Café & Bar, 693-8677 (Mongoose Junction). Here you'll find lovely open-air pavilions. The menu features good Mediterranean fare and seafood. Moderate.

Lime Inn, 776-6425/779-4299 (Lime Tree Mall). This courtyard café serves good homemade soups, salads, local seafood, and a variety of chicken and pasta dishes. Popular. Moderate.

Ellington's, 693-8490 (Gallows Point Suite Resort). Go to the wonderful third-floor Sunset Lounge for cocktails with complimentary hors d'oeuvres while viewing the sun slipping down behind distant St. Thomas. The dining room on the second floor serves up good American/Continental dishes. Moderate.

Etta's West Indian Cuisine, 693-8246 (at the Inn at Tamarind Court). Excellent seafood and West Indian dishes with johnnycakes in charming tropical courtyard. Inexpensive to moderate.

Don Carlos, 776-6866 (on the waterfront in Coral Bay). Mexican fajitas, burritos and seafood, and delicious margaritas are served in an alfresco breezy, seaside terrace room. Inexpensive to moderate.

Also consider **Cafe Roma**, 776-6524 (1½ blocks from the ferry dock) for Italian pastas, veal, and chicken dishes, plus pizzas. Downstairs is **Joe's Diner** for quick pâtés, fried chicken, and egg rolls, etc. **Vie's Snack Shop** (on the road adjacent to the calm beach at Hurricane Hole on the East End). A famous roadside stand with outside tables—here Vie fries superlative garlic chicken and johnnycakes. **The Splash Bar Grill,** 693-8000 (Hyatt Regency St. John), serves a menu of barbecued chicken, burgers, and salads. The beach and poolside terrace is a great place to take the kids, especially at Sunday's beach party with live music.

New at Mongoose Junction is **Sun Dog Cafe**, 776-6638, a little second-floor outlet offering soups, giant sandwiches, salads, and natch, hot dogs. Picnic fixings to go. **Tree Lizards Restaurant**, 776-6630 (at Cinnamon Bay), offers reasonably priced barbecue from shrimp and jerk-style chicken to ribs and fresh fish, all served in a rustic dining pavilion. Friday is West Indian Night. **Skinny Legs**, 779-4982 (at Coral Bay), is an unpretentious, fun place to go for burgers, chili, grilled chicken, and mahi-mahi. Also in Coral Bay is **Shipwreck Landing**, 693-5640, for good seafood in an informal seaside setting. **Barracuda Bistro**, 779-4944 (Wharfside Village), is a useful spot for quick breakfasts and lunches—muffins, sweet breads, soups, sandwiches, salads, and daily specials, plus take-out. Also in Cruz Bay are the new **Lumber Yard Cafe** adjacent to the Boulon Center, where Ann Sopher concocts delicious light salads like tarragon chicken and seafood salads stuffed into croissants; and **Victor's Hideout** in the courtyard at **Miss Maeda's** new shopping complex, where you'll find good West Indian food. **Garden of Luscious Licks**, across from the National Park Dock, serves imaginative vegetarian fare, including good salads, as well as frozen yogurt and ice cream.

ST. THOMAS' FINEST*

* **Old Stone Farm House**, 775-1377 (Mahogany Run Road). Not open at press time, but can count on vetran chef Pat La Corte to operate top restaurant in beautiful historical inland setting. Exquisite menu of tuna mignons, roasted snapper, fillet of beef with vidalia onion marmalade and fresh brioche. Superior confections. Fine wines. Expensive.

* **Provence**, 777-5600 (Frenchtown). Pat LaCorte's second restaurant is Mediterranean/French, offering a Provençal antipasto, soup au pistou, braised lamb shanks, or succulent roast chicken served with olive fritters. Desserts include fruit tarts and profiteroles. Moderate to expensive.

* **Hotel 1829**, 776-1829 (Government Hill). Still one of St. Thomas's most delightful dining experiences on covered terrace or in the stone-walled indoor dining room of a historic building (also a small hotel). The menu changes little, and the food isn't as inspired as it once was, so stick with the simple seafood dishes or the special warm spinach salad and the fillet of beef with green peppercorns (both prepared tableside). First-rate individual soufflés. Good wine list. Expensive to very expensive.

* **Palm Terrace**, 775-3333 (Grand Palazzo Hotel in Estate Nazareth). This is the most elegant and beautiful dining room on the island. The cuisine ranges from simple to complex. Excellent wines, but expensive. (See hotel listing.) Expensive to very expensive.

* **Cafe Vecchio**, 775-3333 (Grand Palazzo Hotel in Estate Nazareth). Here Italian food is served in a casual, lovely terrace dining room. Lunches feature excellent Ceasar

salad with grilled chicken or other light fare. Views are spectacular. Monday night stars a Caribbean buffet with entertainment. (See hotel listing.) Moderate for lunch; moderate to expensive for dinner.

* **Virgilio's**, 776-4920 (18 Dronningens Gade at Back Street). Outstanding Italian food is offered in this small air-conditioned dining room. Pasta and veal dishes are especially good. The chef likes garlic. Popular with locals. Moderate to expensive.

* **Romano's**, 775-0045 (97 Smith Bay Road, near Coral World). New Jersey–born Tony Romano's Italian offerings excel. Fresh, imaginative salads and starters, as well as tender veal, chicken, and pork dishes are offered. All pastas are recommended. This is a small air-conditioned dining room with a tiny bar. Friendly atmosphere. Locals love Romano's. Moderate to expensive.

* **Zorba's**, 776-0444 (Government Hill). One of Jim Boukas's four St. Thomas restaurants in a casual garden setting. Good food is served in generous portions— rôtisserie chicken, pastitsio (pasta and meat pie), spanakopita, Greek lamb dishes, and great seafood pizza. Excellent fresh baked breads—take a loaf home. Moderate. Also at Zorba's, in the front of the building, is **Sapago**, a cozy, attractively decorated café with a small bar. The food is light Mediterranean, plus a variety of pizzas and excellent coffees, including cappuccino. Live music Wednesday and Sunday evenings. Moderate.

* **Tavern on the Beach**, 776-8500 (Marriott's Morning Star Beach Resort). Lovely, spacious second-story seaside dining room has a new chef serving "New World" dishes like snapper over fennel and other well-executed creations, sensitively combining international ingredients and cuisines. (A great spot for breakfast—overlooking Morning Star's expansive beach.) Prices moderate for breakfast; expensive for dinner.

* **Hard Rock Cafe**, 777-5555 (on the waterfront at International Plaza). First-rate American food is served in this expansive rock 'n' roll memorabilia–decorated dining room. Always lively. First of this famous chain in the Caribbean. Rock music featured, of course. Inexpensive to moderate.

OTHER DEPENDABLE CHOICES

Bravo Cafe and **Sirocco**, 776-4466 (Gregerie East at Sugar Reef). Two more of Jim Boukas's attractive airy restaurants situated adjacent to each other in a sea-scented dockside location. Bravo features tapas from the Mediterranean. Sirocco serves seafood and sushi, and Sunday pasta suppers. (There is live music at Bravo several evenings a week.) Inexpensive to moderate.

Lemon Grass Cafe, 777-1877 (Bakery Square). An indoor air-conditioned two-level dining room and a few tables on an al fresco terrace. Try the cold Chinese noodles with scallions, grilled nut burger with sesame mayonnaise, or a host of innovative dishes. Delicious iced lemon-grass tea. Moderate.

Caesar's, 776-8500 (Marriott's Frenchman's Reef Hotel on the beach). Italian fare and terrific pizzas in this oceanside location. Moderate.

Mangrove Cafe, 777-7100 (Sugar Bay Beach Hotel). Dine in the open-air or indoor dining room. Seafood buffets on Friday nights; other nights, choose good offerings from steaks to grilled chicken. Very pleasant for lunch, served poolside. Moderate.

On Monday nights at **The Bar at Paradise Point** watch the sunset while sampling excellent **Sushi by Pattie**; live music.

Sadly, El Papagayo, Kevin Burns's dependably good, reasonably priced Mexican restaurant, has disappeared from Tillett Gardens, where it was an island institution for years. Word at press time is that the talented team from Morgan's Mango (with a Caribbean menu) in St. John is moving into a redesigned restaurant here. **Morgan's Mango St. Thomas** should be an immediate hit. Kevin was scouting for a new location for El Papagayo, so, if interested in delicious Tex/Mex and mean margaritas, look for El Papagayo's new address when you're on island.

There are too many other restaurants to list, but consider the following in Frenchtown: **Alexander's** and **Alexander's Bar and Grill, Café Normandie, Epernay** (an intimate tapas and wine bar), **Craig and Sally's**, and **Chart House**—all first-rate.

In town, try **Blackbeard's Castle** for fabulous views and consistently fine food and service (see hotel listing).

In the Red Hook area, there are finally some outstanding choices. New are **Mackenzie's** and **Tickles Pilot House** in beautiful rooms at the American Yacht Harbor. **East Coast Bar and Grill** is still going strong—reasonably priced seafood, pastas, and burgers served inside or out on the terrace (also sports bar). East Coast's new sister operation is the air-conditioned **Shark Room**, serving light food and pizzas; it has nightly live entertainment. Head for **Frigate East** for grilled steaks, chicken, and fish, plus a salad bar.

The best **West Indian Meat Pâtés** (also salt fish, conch, and shrimp) are sold in Miss Daily's white van mobile kitchen at the ferry dock at Red Hook during the day only.

For West Indian food at Smith Bay, the best is at **Eunice's Terrace**.

Other worthwhile locations around the island are **Il Cardinale, Andiamo** (also **Club Z** disco), and **Ferrari's** for Italian meals. **The Oasis** at Sapphire Village serves reasonably priced good food. Consider restaurants in other resorts and hotels, such as **Bay Winds** and **Smugglers** at Stouffer Renaissance Grand Beach, **Seagrape** at the Sapphire Beach Resort, **Windows on the Harbour** at Marriott's Frenchman's Reef, **Agave Terrace** and **Bayside Café** at Point Pleasant, **Secret Harbour Beach Cafe** at Secret Harbour Beach Resort and **The Palms** at Emerald Beach Resort, and the restaurants at Elysian, Lime Tree, and Bolongo Bay—all are oceanside. The **Manor House** in Wyndham Sugar Bay Resort is a beautiful room with stunning views of St. John across the sea. **For the Birds** at Scott's Beach at Compass Point is a funky place for family gatherings—later at night the young set moves in to swing. Tex/Mex nachos or fried zucchini or onion starters, then chicken and beef fajitas, baby-back ribs, brisket, chicken fried steak with mashed potatoes, and the like are featured. More Tex/Mex at **Bob's** en route to Cabrita Point in Red Hook area.

Recommended Shopping

ST. CROIX

Wayne James, 773-8585 (42 Queen Cross Street, Christiansted). Wayne James sells designer women's and men's fashions for day and evening, plus accessories like West Indian mahagony-handle purses and hand-painted silk scarves. He also invented and sells bottled Caribbean Calypso Spice.

Violette Boutique, 773-2148 (38 Strand Street, Christiansted). Duty-free perfumes, cosmetics, jewelry, and watches, plus designer fashions and special accessories like Fendi bags. Order toll-free, (800) 544-5912.

Quin House Galleries, 773-0404 (51 ABC Company Street at King Cross St.). Shop for antiques, fine mahogany reproduction furniture, accessories, and unique gifts. The Gallery features local artists. (Closed in summer.)

Whim Museum Gift Shop and Furniture Showroom, 722-0598 (Centerline Road near Frederiksted). Museum collection includes prints, books, ceramics, and many locally crafted items. The West Indies furniture collection contains two dozen fine reproductions that can be ordered.

Estate Mt. Washington, 772-1026 (two miles north of Frederiksted). Antiques and mahogany reproduction furniture and accessories are sold here. Open Saturday 10 A.M. to 4 P.M. Other times, call for an appointment.

Jeltrups, 773-1018 (30 King Cross Street). This is the source in St. Croix for books.

Many Hands, 773-1990 (Pan Am Pavilion). Variety of low-priced arts and crafts—jewelry, pottery, prints, cards, books, jams, and spices—all locally made.

America West India Company, 773-7325 (Strand Street). This is an interesting shop carrying products made throughout the Caribbean—art, sea island cotton, furniture, coffee and foods, and limited-production rums.

For fine jewelry, try **Little Switzerland, Colombian Emeralds, The Gold Shop, Crucian Gold, House of Vizia, Gold Dust Twins, Ay Ay Gold**, and **1870 Town House Shoppes**.

Perfumes and cosmetics are sold at **Little Switzerland, Violette Boutique, St. Croix Perfume Center, La Parfumerie**, and **The Royal Poinciana**.

The Leap (Life and Environmental Project), 772-0421 (Mahogany Road en route to Frederiksted). Artists' wood sculptures, bread boards, clocks, boxes, plaques, bookends, tables, made from thick and cross-cut pieces of mahogany trees fallen during storms or cut down legally.

St. Croix has a **Price Club** at the Oasis Commercial Center on Centerline and the West Airport Road.

There's no dearth of shops in Christiansted. Remember to visit the fine boutiques at **Carambola Beach Resort** and **The Buccaneer Hotel**. Also check out the shops at **Chandlers Wharf** at **Gallows Bay Marketplace**.

ST. JOHN

About a five-minute walk from the St. John ferry dock, talented artisans and merchants are found along a sprawling labyrinth of alleyways in the handsome natural stone buildings at **Mongoose Junction**. Glen Speer, the architect and builder and longtime St. John resident, has created a unique shopping complex; one of the most charming and environmentally natural marketplaces in the Caribbean. Even if you aren't a shopper, visit Mongoose Junction to see this beautiful work of art.

To get there, walk one block straight ahead of the ferry dock and turn left. Walk one block past the post office and turn right. Mongoose Junction is situated a hundred yards or so beyond the **National Park Headquarters**—where there is an excellent collection of island- and nature-related books and publications.

R & I Patton Goldsmithing, 776-6548. Make your first stop at Rudy and Irene Patton's beautiful custom-designed shop where artisans are at work creating original island-inspired jewelry designs in karat gold, sterling silver, exquisite gemstones, pearls, and treasure coins displayed in attractive showcase cabinets.

Donald Schnell Studio, 776-6420. Samples of Don's unique clay and Virgin Islands coral sand blend of pottery embellish luxury resorts such as Caneel Bay, Little Dix, Biras Creek, and Necker Island. Given a few days' notice, he'll create a made-to-order sign or sconce for you. The Schnells will ship items to your home, if time is a problem. Admire his vases, windchimes, dinnerware, and whimsical creatures, and glassware created by other artisans.

Bamboula Collections, 693-8699. A great shopping bazaar of ethnic folk art, both old and new, from the Caribbean and around the world. You'll find antiques, ceramics, jewelry, and men's and women's tropical clothing, furniture, and locally produced handcrafts, like coconut ice buckets here.

Caravan Gallery, 776-8677. Radha and Glen Speer's collection of ethnic jewelry and fine crafts from around the world—folk art, tribal art and masks, handmade boxes and wood carvings—is a must-see. Original jewelry designs are made on premises from unique imported beads. The Speers have traveled to India, China, Turkey, and Bali searching for ethnographic arts displayed in "museum-like setting."

Wicker, Wood and Shells, 776-6909. Aase Pedersen's shop specializes in "gifts inspired by nature" including original art, prints, jewelry, greeting cards, and books.

Fabric Mill, 776-6194. This two-story shop is stocked with designer fabrics, batik sarongs, soft sculpture, hand-painted throw rugs, cheerful tablecloths, place mats, and napkins and much more.

The Clothing Studio, 776-6585. Original hand-painted designs. Rotating local artists paint iguanas, mongooses, frogs, fish, and floral designs on women or children's bathing suits, cover-ups, dresses, lightweight cotton blouses, or visors.

MAPes MONDe, 779-4545. Fine reproductions of maps, native and Colonial artwork, prints, cards, and island books are sold in this lovely shop.

Also at Mongoose Junction is **(Bajo El Sol) Under the Sun Gallery Art Studio**, where three local artists—Aimee Trayser, Gail Vandy Bogurt, and Kat Sowa—display their drawings, paintings, ceramics, and sculpture; also **Colombian Emeralds, Parfum** de Paris, Island Galleria, Big Planet Adventure Outfitters, The Canvas Factory, and Bougainvillea Tropical Resortwear. Just a block to the right of the ferry dock is another shopping complex, **Wharfside Village**. Here you'll discover **Island Hoppers Caribbean Marketplace**, a collection of island sauces, seasonings, jams, jellies, and cakes; also batiks, pottery, metal sculpture, wood carvings, straw mats, and baskets. Also here is **Pusser's Company Store, Virgin Canvas, Let's Go Bananas**, and **The Mermaid's Garden**. **Coral Bay Folk Art Gallery**, hidden in quarters on the second floor, is where husband-and-wife team Karen Samuel and Kime Holman run a gallery that features native St. John artists, arts and crafts, and books of local interest. Kime is in charge of the business and Karen is an accomplished artist whose haunting portraits and still lifes are displayed here.

Pink Papaya, 693-8535 (in The Lime Tree Mall, one block up from Wharfside Village). Kate Campbell and artist Lisa Etre opened this special gallery and gift shop in 1986. Charming array of Etre's colorful Caribbean designs on prints, place mats, dinner and glasswear, T-shirts, aprons, frames, and many other items. Their sister shop in St. Thomas is **Guava Gallery** in the Royal Dane Mall in downtown Charlotte Amalie.

Next door to Pink Papaya is **Each Peach Boutique and Gallery**, featuring the works of Helen Eltis and Suki Dickson-Buchalter. British-born Eltis hand-paints clothing and soft furnishings. She also sculpts and paints enchanting bold and pastel watercolors reflecting the colors of the Caribbean. Originals and prints are available. She's now concentrating on furnishings, rugs, and ceramic fruit lamps. Suki designs one-of-a-kind jewelry pieces.

Another interesting gallery on St. John is **Coconut Coast Studios**, where artists Lucinda A. Schutt and Elaine E. Estern display their watercolors depicting the people, architecture, and landscape of the West Indies. Telephone them at 776-6944 or 693-5080 (Frank Bay—for directions).

Shoppers should also look in at the excellent boutiques at **Caneel Bay** and the **Hyatt Regency St. John**.

In **Sparky's** new building, at **Miss Maeda's Shopping Mall**, there are also a few interesting shops. Sparky sells liquor, gift items, newspapers, and periodicals.

ST. THOMAS

St. Thomas has the finest and widest range of duty-free shopping in the Caribbean, which includes everything from casual resortwear and designer fashions, costume and fine jewelry and watches, to cosmetics and perfumes, china, ceramics, crystal, cameras, tobacco, and liquor. The island also has excellent local and imported artwork and handcrafts, toys, and antiques. Although the streets are often crowded with cruise-ship passengers, along with other visitors and residents, walkways are easily passable, and most shops are air-conditioned, attractive, well managed, and welcoming.

Shopping is concentrated at **Havensight Mall** near the cruise-ship docks, and in the historic town of **Charlotte Amalie**, but the new **American Yacht Harbour** complex at Red Hook has several excellent shops.

As residents, we know all too well that traffic gets clogged at times, mostly at the beginning and end of each day when locals are going to work or returning home. When a number of cruise ships are in on the same day, taxis add to the congestion. The best time for travelers to shop is mid-morning and early afternoon. Since few cruise ships are scheduled on Saturdays, and the normal work force is off, this is a good day to shop in town at any time.

St. Thomas' many vendors have moved their umbrella stalls to one special open-air market called **Vendors Plaza** across from Emancipation Gardens off Main Street. It's become a favorite with tourists and locals, and the place to go where the three inexpensive Ts can be found— T-shirts, trinkets, and treasures. As this book goes to press, it looks as though the vociferous barkers will be banned from the waterfront and Main Street. Three cheers!

Certainly St. Thomas has its share of touristy souvenirs, but it is also a treasure chest of first-rate duty-free, taxfree quality merchandise. There isn't space to list the phone numbers and address of all the shops and boutiques, but some of the best, both longstanding and new, are listed below.

Remember, every visitor is allowed $1,200 worth of duty-free purchases. Locally made handcrafts, jewelry, and all original artwork doesn't count; they are tax-exempt, but be sure to save receipts as proof of purchase.

First, a few outstanding stores, then items listed by categories.

A. H. Riise Gift and Liquor Stores, located on Main Street, with perfume and liquor branches at Havensight Mall. Long established, A. H. Riise is now a gift market of boutiques which runs the entire length of an historic building from the waterfront to Main Street along Riise's Alley. (The liquor store is in a separate building a few steps away.) Shops included are Coach, Nicole Miller, Pusser's, In the Bag, Ilias Lalaounis, with a wide selection of china and crystal including special boutiques for Lalique, Rosenthal, Daum, and Baccarat. Riise has an enormous selection of jewelry and watches, cosmetics and perfumes. Look for MAPes MONDe at the **Caribbean Print Gallery**, for quality reproductions of island maps and prints, as well as postcards and books.

Little Switzerland on Tolbod Gade across from Emancipation Square and on Main Street, with branches at Havensight Mall and at the American Yacht Harbor in Red Hook, is another long-standing reliable store carrying all the top names in fine china, crystal, jewelry, and watches.

A Taste of Italy on Back Street is a wonderful, recently developed, two-story shopping complex in a restored nineteenth-century building. Here you'll find a bar and two charming restaurants, an art gallery, imported Italian ceramics, Caribbean crafts, fine jewelry, clothing, a small selection of Italian gourmet items from olive oil to sparkling prosecco, and a lot more. A most welcome addition to St. Thomas' shopping district.

Not open by press time, **Grand Hotel Court**, across from Emancipation Gardens, with galleries, boutiques, shops, and restaurants, should open soon.

Art and handcrafts: Mombasa, Caribbean Print Gallery and MAPes MONDe, Frederick Gallery, Vendors Plaza, Guava Gallery, The Kilnworks Pottery & Fine Craft Gallery, Down Island Traders, Camille Pissarro Gallery, Pampered Pirate, A Taste of Italy, Mango

Tango, Jonna White Gallery, Van Rensselaer Art Gallery, Going Caribbean, Caribbean Market Place, The Color of Joy, and Tillett Gardens.

Antiques: Carson Co. Antiques & Art, Circe, and Frederick Gallery.

Books: Dockside Bookshop, Island Print Gallery, and Island Newsstand.

Cameras and electric equipment: Boolchand's, Royal Caribbean, Radio Shack, and Quick Pic.

Ceramics and pottery: Frederick Gallery, The Kilnworks Pottery and Fine Craft Gallery, A Taste of Italy, Banana Dance, Going Caribbean, Jonna White Gallery, Color of Joy, The Cloth Horse, Pampered Pirate, and Tillett's Garden.

China and crystal: A. H. Riise, Little Switzerland, Crystal Shop, The English Shop, Rosenthal's Studio, A Taste of Italy, Pfaltzgraff Factory Store, and the Scandinavian Center.

Clothing, sportswear, and resortwear: Condotti Boutique (in the Grand Palazzo Hotel), Janines, Liz Claiborne Factory Store, Cosmopolitan, Modamare, Signatures, Gucci, A Taste of Italy, Dilly D'Alley, Pusser's, G'Day, Chico's, Caribbean Market Place, Players, Big Planet, Nicole Miller, Portofino, Local Color, Java Wrap, Polo Ralph Lauren Factory Outlet, Outrigger, BooneDocks, and Kimberly's.

Handbags and leather items: The Leather Shop (have great yearly sale in June), Little Switzerland, In the Bag (at A. H. Riise), Gucci, Ritalini, and Louis Vuitton.

Jewelry and watches: Cardow (several fine stores), Frederick Gallery, Cartier, Pierres, A. H. Riise, Circe, Little Switzerland, Little Treasures, Diamonds International, The Blue Diamond, Silver Cloud and Silver World, Blue Carib Gems, Bolero, Irmela's, Colombian Emeralds, Emerald Lady, H. Stern, Bernard K. Passman Gallery, West Indian Ice Company, Lalaounis, and Scandinavian Center.

Linen and tablecloths: The Cloth Horse, Mr. Tablecloth, Linen House, Boolchand's, and Royal Caribbean.

Perfume and cosmetics: Tropicana Perfume Shoppes, A. H. Riise, Perfume Palace, Parum de Paris, Gesine's Erno Laszlo Institute, and Sparky's.

Shoes: Stepping Out, Modamare, Ritalini, Shoe Tree, Cosmopolitan, Gucci, Liz Claiborne Factory Store, Polo Ralph Lauren Factory Outlet, Condotti, and Footsteps.

Toys: Land of Oz Toy Store, Kids Ahoy, Mini Mouse House Toys, Woolworth's, K-mart, Radio Shack, Quick Pics, and Cost-U-Less.

Among shops at the new, handsomely designed buildings at American Yacht Harbor in Red Hook are **Little Switzerland, Java Wrap** (which has a furniture shop as well as clothing), **Pusser's Candy, Shellseekers, World View Graphics, The Sunglass Mart**, and **Blazing Photos**, with one-hour processing.

You'll find many other boutiques and shops of interest at attractions like **Coral World, Mountain Top, Magens Bay,** and **Paradise Point** and in hotels and resorts such as **Grand Palazzo Hotel, Stouffer Renaissance Grand Beach, Wyndham Sugar Bay, Secret Harbour, Elysian, Saphire Beach Resort, Frenchman's Reef, Bolongo Bay,** and **Lime Tree.** Also visit the shops at **Havensight Shopping Mall, Fort Mylner, Four Winds Plaza, Tutu Park,** and **Nisky Center.**

St. John has many superb stores and boutiques now (see St. John's Recommended Shopping), so consider a trip by ferry to do some serious browsing.

Provisions for Your Island Pantry

ST. CROIX

Large, well-stocked **Pueblo** supermarkets are at Golden Rock and Ville La Reine. A **Grand Union** is at Sunny Isle Shopping Center, and a new supermarker, **Plaza Extra**, is at Sion Farm.

Gallows Bay Foods, 773-6640 (at Gallows Bay, about a quarter mile east of Christiansted). This market carries quality meats, homemade sausage, seafood, groceries, condiments, and wines, and has a bakery. Also at Gallows Bay is **The Fishnet Emporium**, 773-2135, which has a small retail service but will fill phone orders for fresh Maine lobster, grouper, and other local and stateside seafood, along with California wines. Great fish is available at **Caribbean Seafood Industries**, 773-7870, 12-A La Grande Princess next to the A to Z Paint Store.

The Royal Poinciana, 773-9892 (1104 Strand Street), for island herbs and spices.

Anything Goes, 773-2777 (Gallows Bay Marketplace), is a gourmet deli that features pastries and breads and will prepare catering trays of pâtés, smoked fish, meats, cheeses and salads.

Also at Gallows Bay is **Ice Cream Decadence**, 773-4320, for exotic ice creams and sorbets—soursop, piña colada, spiced apple, passion fruit and mango, plus ice cream pies and cakes.

The large supermarkets sell wines and liquors. **Woolworth** at Sunny Isle Center still has great bargains. Virgin Island's **Cruzan Rum** is made on St. Croix. Visit the rum factory for a tour—follow the signs to Route 64.

ST. JOHN

Marcelino's Bakery, 776-6873 (Mongoose Junction). Fresh-baked breads, pies, cookies, almond croissants, brownies, rolls, pizza, quiche, ice cream, shakes, and sodas.

The Rolling Pin, 779-4775 (on Southside Road before The Inn at Tamarind Court). Delicious fresh-baked pastries and breads, and Ben and Jerry's Ice Cream.

Marina Market, 779-4401 (South Shore Road next to Paradise Laundry). Best selection of groceries on island; also produce, frozen foods, and gourmet items. Deli cooks up barbecue and roasted chickens and ribs; also available—salads, quality cold cuts, and cheeses.

Captain John's Supermarket, 693-8100 (past Pine Peace Liquors on the way to the Hyatt Regency). Groceries, staples, and deli foods.

Nature Nook (a few steps past the Post Office en route to Mongoose Junction). Roadside stall is the best source for fresh vegetables, fruits, herbs, and spices. Also sells beverages and T-shirts.

Joe's Discount Liquor, 776-7569 (at the fringe of Cruz Bay on the South Coast Road). Selection of liquor and wines and foods. Another branch at Coral Bay.

There is also a mini-market at **Cinnamon Bay Campgrounds** on the north shore. Serious cooks may want to visit St. Thomas (see below, Provisions for Your Island Pantry in St. Thomas) to shop at the island's many excellent special food shops and supermarkets.

ST. THOMAS

Three large, well-stocked **Pueblo supermarkets** are located at Long Bay, Four Winds Plaza, and the Sub Base. A **Grand Union** is at Sugar Estate, and **Plaza Extra** at Tutu Park Mall is a huge supermarket with a deli and bakery.

Gourmet Gallery has two branches: Crown Bay Marina (776-8555) and at Yacht Haven Marina (774-5555). Each store is an excellent source of quality produce, name-brand and international imported groceries and gourmet items, meats (both fresh and frozen), and cheeses, as well as fine wines and spirits.

St. Thomas has a new warehouse facility similar to Price Club (no membership required) called **Cost-U-Less**, at Four Winds Plaza, that sells specialty-food items, at discount prices, from cheeses, cold cuts, frozen seafood and meat, and commercially prepared frozen products from guacamole and shrimp scampi to bagels and cheesecake. Many, but not all items, but many are sold in large quantities. Also sodas, beverages, wines, and liquors. A terrific place for bargains.

Red Hook Market, 775-1949, on the east end is small, but carries first-rate produce and island-grown greens like arugula and fresh herbs, plus a well-rounded supply of groceries, fresh and frozen meat and fish. If they don't have what you want, they'll try to get it for you. Excellent wine selection and liquors.

Also at Red Hook is the **Marina Market**, 779-2411, with a superb fresh meat and fish department, as well as a deli/bakery, gourmet products, and staples.

The Fruit Bowl, 774-8565, (at Wheatley Shopping Center) has an outstanding selection of fruits and vegetables. There are also many local street markets, including downtown's large **Market Square**, an open-air Saturday-morning food bazaar where vendors sell local produce, herbs, and spices. Look for the roadside markets at **Ft. Mylner Shopping Mall**, across from Al Cohen's at the foot of Raphune Hill, and in Smith Bay, for seasonal delicious mangoes, papayas, soursops, limes, bananas, pineapples, and local pumpkins, hot peppers and tubers.

Down Island Traders, 776-4641 (on the waterfront in town) is a delightful island-inspired gift shop. The owners also produce and sell tropical teas like mango and passion fruit, along with preserves, sauces, and spices. All are charmingly packaged and make wonderful gifts.

Frank's Bake Shop, 775-0611, (at the Sub Base) creates excellent pies, pastries, and breads. The seven-grain "fitness" bread is superb. Good sandwiches are made here to eat in or take out.

Bachman's Bakery, 775-2670 (at Four Winds Plaza) and 774-4143 (at Wheatley Center), produces delicious banana bread, cinnamon buns, and pastries and cakes, plus good French bread, pumpernickel, and a variety of other breads and rolls. Ask for the special rich island butter bread available on Saturdays only.

For candies go to **Pusser's West Indies Candy Company** at International Plaza; **Mama's** in the Havensight Shopping Mall; or **A Chew or Two** in Trompeter Gade in town.

Fresh fish and seafood is available at **Caribbean Seafood Industries** at 3801 Crown Bay (behind Bravo and Sirocco restaurants at Gregerie East), at **Marina Market** and **Red Hook Market**, both in Red Hook, and also at **Pueblo** and **Plaza Extra** supermarkets.

Texas Pit BBQ, at Red Hook and on the waterfront in Charlotte Amalie, is a mobile stand selling spicy barbecued chicken, ribs, and sliced brisket to go.

At Red Hook, **Wok & Roll**, 775-6246, has average Chinese take-out—you can also dine here on a small roadside terrace.

Wines and spirits are widely available throughout the island, but the best selections are at **Gourmet Gallery** markets, **Red Hook Market, A. H. Riise**, and **Pueblo** and **Plaza Extra** supermarkets. The best bargains can be found at **Cost-U-Less, Woolworth, Plaza Extra**, and (sometimes) at **Sunrise Pharmacy**—at Red Hook and Wheatley Shopping Center.

Useful Information

ST. CROIX

Pick up a complimentary pink copy of Margot Bachman's *St. Croix This Week* for all-around valuable information, including good maps, and also Friday's *Virgin Islands Daily News* for the special **Weekend** supplement with up-to-date events, restaurants, and entertainment.

St. Croix, the largest Virgin Island, 28 miles long and about 7 miles wide, has many fine beaches and historical sights to visit, so a car is necessary to get acquainted with the island. (Taxis are expensive.)

Three car rental companies on St. Croix are **Hertz**, (809) 778-1402; **Thrifty**, (809) 773-7200; and **Budget**, (809) 778-9636. All have toll-free 800 numbers.

The local guides list all the interesting places and historical sights, but don't miss **St. George Village Botanical Garden**, 772-3874 (off Queen Mary Highway, east of Frederiksted) to see the Great Hall, over 800 tropical species, a rain forest, sugar mill and rum factory ruins, and a restored blacksmith's shop; and **Estate Whim Great House Museum**, 722-0598 (Centerline Road near Fredriksted). Take a guided tour of the restored eighteenth-century sugar plantation through the fully furnished Great House (surrounded by a moat), the adjacent stone kitchen, old apothecary, sugar mill, and grounds. The museum has an excellent gift shop.

Buck Island National Park, only a short boat ride from St. Croix's east end, is an unspoiled, protected island with snow-white sandy beaches and an extraordinary underwater world of coral and sea life. There's a marked snorkeling trail. Glass-bottomed boat and diving trips are easily arranged, or simply bring a picnic and relax for the day.

Paul and Jill's Equestrian Stables, 772-2800 (Sprat Hall Route 58, north of Frederiksted). Ride horseback through the Danish ruins, rain forest, and countryside.

For a game of golf go to either **Carambola Golf Club,** 778-5638, which has an 18-hole Robert Trent Jones championship course, or the 18-hole course at **The Buccaneer Hotel,** 772-3100.

The Buccaneer Health Spa, 773-2100 (Buccaneer Shopping Arcade, 10 minutes from Christiansted on East End Road). Here you can enjoy a seaweed body wrap, sauna, Swedish massage, manicures and pedicures, facials, and foot reflexology.

One-hour photo processing is available at **Fast Foto,** 773-6727 (Queen Cross Street), and **V.I. Express,** 773-2009 (on Strand Street, corner of King Cross Street).

Consider a day or overnight trip to sister islands St. Thomas and/or St. John. Sunaire Express, (809) 778-9300, and American Eagle, (800) 443-7300, have several daily scheduled round-trip flights to St. Thomas. To reach St. John from St. Thomas, go to Red Hook and take the hourly ferry. It's a 20-minute cruise.

ST. JOHN

Visitors arriving at the tiny village of Cruz Bay now step off ferries onto the expanded new **Lorendon Lawrence Boynes Ferry Dock,** 267 feet long and 35 feet wide, which boasts an attractive terminal building. The terminal houses the dockmaster's office, the ticket booth, and an open-air waiting area with benches in the shade under the covering.

In St. John, pick up free copies of the *St. John Map,* the *St. John Guide Book, St.*

New ferry dock and terminal at Cruz Bay in St. John, U.S. Virgin Islands.

Thomas This Week, which includes a St. John section, and the islands' bimonthly newspaper, *Tradewinds*, for extremely helpful information on acclimating yourself to the island.

St. John is nine miles long and five miles wide, about two-thirds of which is blissfully unspoiled national park. The **Virgin Islands National Park's Visitor's Center** in Cruz Bay offers several interesting programs, such as cultural demonstrations at the **Annaberg Sugar Mill ruins** and adventure hikes. **Reef Bay** is a special 2.2-mile downhill trail leading to **petroglyph** rock carvings and the **Reef Bay Sugar Mill** ruins. Hikers can descend on their own or join scheduled guided tours. A map of the park's 22 trails and other maps, booklets, and information on the flora, fauna, and the surrounding underwater coral and sea life of St. John can be obtained by visiting or calling the park center at 776-6201.

There are over 30 ravishing white-sand beaches on St. John, including **Trunk Bay, Cinnamon Bay, Hawksnest, Maho Bay, Francis Bay, Saltpond Bay, Great Lameshur Bay,** and **Caneel Bay**'s seven lovely strands. To visit the beaches and explore the island independently, a car is really necessary.

St. John has over a dozen car rental companies. Here are four: **St. John Car Rental**, (809) 776-6103; **Delbert Hills Rentals**, (809) 776-6637; **O'Connor Car Rental**, (809) 776-6344, and **Budget Rent-A-Car**, (809) 693-8177.

Ferry service between Cruz Bay in St. John and Red Hook St. Thomas departs Cruz Bay from 6 A.M. until 10 P.M. every hour on the hour. The last ferry to St. Thomas leaves at 11:15 P.M. From Red Hook in St. Thomas, ferries leave at 6:30 and 7:30 A.M. and from then on, every hour on the hour until midnight. The one-way adult fare is $3; $1 for a child under 12.

From Cruz Bay, there is also regularly scheduled daily **ferry service** to and from downtown Charlotte Amalie in St. Thomas. The nearby British Virgin Islands are easily reached from Cruz Bay by ferry as well. Scheduled daily service runs to and from **West End, Tortola**. Friday, Saturday, and Sunday there is ferry service to and from **Jost Van Dyck**, and Thursday and Sunday, ferry service to and from **Virgin Gorda**. For information, call Inter-Island Boat Services at (809) 776-6597 or 776-6282. Remember that a passport or proof of citizenship is required for entry into the British Virgin Islands.

Per Dohm runs a private catamaran motorboat water taxi based in Red Hook, St. Thomas. His service is available day or night for destinations anywhere on St. Thomas, St. John, and the British Virgin Islands. For information, call (809) 775-6501.

The **Connections** office supplies all kinds of communications services: faxes, phone calls, and copying. The staff will also organize day trips or fishing charters on power boats. The office is located one block from the ferry dock in Cruz Bay; 779-4994.

If you're staying on the east end of St. John, a similar communications service in Coral Bay is **Satellite Office Services**, 779-4682.

The **Grapevine Salon** in Mongoose Junction, 693-9040, offers cutting and styling, perms and color services, facials, manicures and pedicures.

Low Key Water Sports, 693-8999 (in Wharfside Village) has parasailing, ocean kayaking, and scuba diving.

Gwen B. Beyer, in St. John since 1980, is a massage therapist whose slogan is "Give your body a vacation," 776-6080.

ST. THOMAS

St. Thomas This Week, Margot Bachman's free weekly guide for St. Thomas visitors, is the most up-to-date, accurate, and valuable of local complimentary publications. It lists taxi rates, island events, ferry schedules, restaurants, shopping, sports facilities, and more, plus good island maps. Also look for copies of the annual *Virgin Islands Playground.*

The *Virgin Islands Daily News,* the islands' local newspaper, a member of the Gannett Group and published daily except Sunday, is not only a good source for local, stateside, and international news, but also puts out a special supplement in Friday's paper called **Weekend,** a current guide to arts, entertainment, dining, and nightlife for St. Thomas, St. John, and St. Croix.

Here are four of the many car rental companies in St. Thomas. We and visiting friends and family like **Sea Breeze** best for friendly service and good, often new, Toyotas. They are not, however, at the airport, but only a short drive away, and must be notified at the time of arrival for delivery of the car. By the time you've collected your luggage, the car is usually there. **Sea Breeze,** (809) 774-7200; **Hertz,** (809) 774-1879; **Budget,** (809) 776-5774; **Avis,** (809) 774-1468.

Dockside Bookshop, 774-4937 (Havensight Mall) is *the* bookstore on St. Thomas. In addition to bestsellers, classics, children's books, reference books, and maps, it carries an extensive collection of books on the Virgin Islands and the Caribbean. Many are by local authors.

East End Secretarial Service and **Red Hook Mail Services,** 775-5262 (Red Hook Shopping Center in two offices on the second floor) provides secretarial services, telephones, a fax machine, and a private mail office with Express Mail Service. The owner, Carol King, and her right hand, Debbie Griffin, and the entire staff offer first-rate, friendly service.

Philip Sturm Hair Studio, Body & Barber Shop, 776-4353 (Royal Dane Mall at Droningens Gade 26a) is one of the best salons in St. Thomas. Everything from pedicures, facials, and waxing, to cuts, sets, and coloring is available. Also at Sturm's is **Gesine's Erno Laszlo Institute** (20% to 28% lower than stateside prices); (800) 662-1905 or (809) 774-9195. Gesine has her own line of cosmetics and a small boutique stocked with jewelry and attractive hair decorations.

One-hour film processing is available at **Blazing Photos** at the Greenhouse near Palm Passage in town, in Havensight Shopping Mall, and at Red Hook at the American Yacht Harbor.

St. Thomas is ringed with beautiful white-sand beaches. A favorite is world-famous **Magens Bay**'s long, wide, heart-shaped beach. A small fee is charged for parking. Chaises, floats, and small sailboats can be rented. There's also a boutique and a bar and restaurant. It's a great location to have breakfast (giant three-egg omelets), rent a lounge chair, and spend the day on the beach. Beach-bar service is available.

Exceptional beaches are **Sapphire, Secret Harbour, Vessup, Coqui, Bluebeard's, Pelican, Lime Tree, Frenchman's Reef, Morningstar,** and **Lindberg Bay. Hull Bay Beach**, on the north side, is the best surfing beach on St. Thomas. All sports, including golf, tennis, and water sports are easily arranged on the island.

Apart from St. Thomas' natural beauty, there's much to see, including **Coral World** undersea observatory and marine park and expansive views from many parts of the island, but especially from **Drake's Seat** and **Mountain Top**. Worth seeing, too, are historic **Government House, Fort Christian,** which includes a museum, **Seven Arches Museum,** and the **St. Thomas Synagogue**, the second oldest in the Western hemisphere, all in Charlotte Amalie.

Reichold Center for the Arts, at the College of the Virgin Islands' campus, is St. Thomas' premier cultural center. Special entertainment, events, plays, and concerts in the immense amphitheater are featured throughout the year. We attended a sensational Dave Brubeck concert last year. For information, call 774-8475.

When on St. Thomas, look for classical concerts held at **Tillett Gardens**. Tillet also holds arts and crafts festivals.

By now **Paradise Point Gondola** (St. Thomas' new tramway) should be transporting passengers on a 697-foot ride up Havensight Hill for panoramic views of Charlotte Amalie and the harbor. What's at the top? Paradise Point retail center and restaurants, of course.

Per Dohm Water Taxi Service, (809) 775-6501. The private service operates day and night, transporting passengers to St. John or anywhere in the British Virgin Islands. The boat is a catamaran motor vessel.

A trip to St. Thomas' beautiful sister island St. John, is only a 20-minute ferry ride from Red Hook, with hourly departures from each side: adults, $3, children, $1. Ferry excursions to the British Virgin Islands of Tortola, Jost Van Dyck, and Virgin Gorda depart from downtown Charlotte Amalie's docks and/or from Red Hook. For information on trips to Tortola and Virgin Gorda, call **Transportation Services** at (809) 776-6282 or 776-6597. For Jost Van Dyck, telephone **Inter-Island Boat Services** at 776-6597 or 776-6282.

The historic island of St. Croix, the largest Virgin (see St. Croix Useful Information), and only 40 miles south of St. Thomas, is an excellent day or overnight trip. There are many regularly scheduled fights daily from St. Thomas' airport on **American Eagle**, (800) 443-7300, and **Sunaire**, (809) 778-9300.

Travelers should consider coming to St. Thomas for **Carnival**, held at the end of April each year. The weeklong festival includes music contests, a carnival village with games and rides and food booths. The event also features a spectacular food day on Thursday of carnival week when the islands' best cooks compete for awards. This is a great opportunity to sample authentic island cooking. Carnival culminates with separate children's and adult's parades featuring splendid, sparkling costumes, music, and the fabulous stilt-walkers—Mocko Jumbies. On the last night of carnival, a dazzling display of fireworks set off in Charlotte Amalie's harbor lights up the sky.

Mocko jumbie dancer at St. Thomas' Carnival.

ABOUT THE AUTHOR

Michele Evans was born in Kansas, and has traveled extensively throughout the world. She has visited more than fifty islands in the Caribbean during the past twenty years and has maintained a home in the Virgin Islands for more than twelve years. She and her husband, Tully Plesser, who heads a marketing and public-opinion research firm, are residents of St. Thomas.

Also a food writer, Evans's food and travel articles have appeared in numerous publications, including *The New York Times Sunday Magazine, Food and Wine, Mademoiselle,* and *Caribbean Travel & Life.* She is also the author of 13 cookbooks.

Evans is currently writing and photographing a Caribbean cookbook and a photo journal of the islands.

She is also photographing and co-authoring a cookbook, *La Cucina Siciliana di Gangivecchio* with Wanda and Giovanna Tornabene, who live in a restored 14th-century Benedictine monastery in the Madonie Mountains in Gangivecchio, Sicily, where they have a restaurant and small hotel.

≈ ≈

AN INVITATION

Dear Caribbean Traveler:

Hotels are living things. The passage of time, management changes, and a multitude of other circumstances can alter the character and charm of any accommodation, for better or worse. I've made as many repeat visits to the hotels included in this book as possible, but deadlines must be met.

As I continue traveling throughout the Caribbean, I would like to invite you to share the personal experiences you've encountered on holiday at any of the hotels listed in *Caribbean Connoisseur*. Please give the name of the hotel and dates of your visit, along with brief, specific, positive or negative comments.

If your favorite Caribbean inn, hotel, or resort, or restaurant or shop is missing from this book, I would be delighted to hear from you.

Every letter cannot be answered, but all observations will be reviewed and seriously considered when researching, evaluating, and updating the next edition of *Caribbean Connoisseur*.

Many thanks,
MICHELE EVANS

Address correspondence to:

Michele Evans
Caribbean Connoisseur
6501 Red Hook Plaza, Suite 26
St. Thomas, United States Virgin Islands 00802

INDEX